MAY 2 7 2010

WITHDRAWN

THE NEW CAMBRIDGE COMPANION TO SHAKESPEARE

Written by a team of leading international scholars, this *Companion* is designed to illuminate Shakespeare's works through discussion of the key topics of Shakespeare studies. Twenty-one brand new essays provide lively and authoritative approaches to recent scholarship and criticism for readers keen to expand their knowledge and appreciation of Shakespeare. The book contains stimulating chapters on traditional topics such as Shakespeare's biography and the transmission of his texts. Individual readings of the plays are given in the context of genre as well as through the cultural and historical perspectives of race, sexuality and gender, and politics and religion. Essays on performance survey the latest digital media as well as stage and film. Throughout the volume, contributors discuss Shakespeare's long and constantly mutating history of reception and performance in both national and global contexts.

MARGRETA DE GRAZIA is the Sheli Z. and Burt X. Rosenberg Chair in the Humanities and Professor of English at the University of Pennsylvania. She is the author of *Shakespeare Verbatim* (1991) and *'Hamlet' without Hamlet* (2007). She has also co-edited *Subject and Object in Renaissance Culture* (1996) with Maureen Quilligan and Peter Stallybrass.

STANLEY WELLS is Chairman of the Trustees of Shakespeare's Birthplace, Emeritus Professor of Shakespeare Studies of the University of Birmingham and Honorary Emeritus Governor of the Royal Shakespeare Theatre. He was for nearly twenty years the editor of the annual *Shakespeare Survey*, is General Editor of the Oxford and Penguin editions of Shakespeare, and writes for the *New York Review of Books* and many other publications. His most recent books include *Shakespeare: For All Time* (2002); *Looking for Sex in Shakespeare* (2004); *Shakespeare and Co.* (2006); *Is It True What They Say About Shakespeare?* (2007); and *Shakespeare, Sex and Love* (2010).

A complete list of books in the series is at the back of this book

THE NEW CAMBRIDGE COMPANION TO SHAKESPEARE

EDITED BY
MARGRETA DE GRAZIA
University of Pennsylvania

STANLEY WELLS
The Shakespeare Birthplace Trust

CAMBRIDGE UNIVERSITY PRESS
Cambridge, New York, Melbourne, Madrid, Cape Town, Singapore,
São Paulo, Delhi, Dubai, Tokyo

Cambridge University Press
The Edinburgh Building, Cambridge CB2 8RU, UK

Published in the United States of America by Cambridge University Press, New York

www.cambridge.org
Information on this title: www.cambridge.org/9780521713931

© Cambridge University Press 2010

This publication is in copyright. Subject to statutory exception and to the provisions of relevant collective licensing agreements, no reproduction of any part may take place without the written permission of Cambridge University Press.

First published 2001
Second edition 2010

Printed in the United Kingdom at the University Press, Cambridge

A catalogue record for this publication is available from the British Library

Library of Congress Cataloguing in Publication data
The new Cambridge companion to Shakespeare / [edited by]
Margreta De Grazia, Stanley Wells. – 2nd ed.
p. cm. – (Cambridge companions to literature)
ISBN 978-0-521-88632-1 (hardback)
ISBN 978-0-521-71393-1 (pbk.)
1. Shakespeare, William, 1564–1616–Handbooks, manuals, etc.
I. De Grazia, Margreta. II. Wells, Stanley W., 1930–
III. Cambridge companion to Shakespeare. IV. Title. V. Series.
PR2894.C33 2010
822.3′3–dc22
2009053752

ISBN 978-0-521-88632-1 Hardback
ISBN 978-0-521-71393-1 Paperback

Cambridge University Press has no responsibility for the persistence or accuracy of URLs for external or third-party internet websites referred to in this publication, and does not guarantee that any content on such websites is, or will remain, accurate or appropriate.

CONTENTS

ILLUSTRATIONS

3 0053 00919 6026

Illustrations reproduced courtesy of: The Victoria and Albert Museum (1–4), The Shakespeare Birthplace Trust (5), The Folger Library (7b and 7c), Bernadette Swanson (8a), Cherie Daniels (8c), Remi Kiranov (8d).

CONTRIBUTORS

ANSTON BOSMAN, Amherst College

COLIN BURROW, All Souls College, Oxford

ANTHONY DAWSON, University of British Columbia

ANDREW DICKSON, *The Guardian*

JANETTE DILLON, University of Nottingham

JEFF DOLVEN, Princeton University

STEPHEN GREENBLATT, Harvard University

JONATHAN GIL HARRIS, George Washington University

TON HOENSELAARS, Utrecht University

JONATHAN HOPE, University of Strathclyde

HEATHER JAMES, University of California, Santa Cruz

SEAN KEILEN, College of William and Mary

CLAIRE MCEACHERN, University of California, Los Angeles

ANDREW MURPHY, University of St Andrews

MICHAEL NEILL, University of Auckland

STEPHEN ORGEL, Stanford University

PAUL PRESCOTT, University of Warwick

KATHERINE ROWE, Bryn Mawr College

EMMA SMITH, Hertford College, Oxford

TIFFANY STERN, New College, Oxford

STANLEY WELLS, The Shakespeare Birthplace Trust

H. R. WOUDHUYSEN, University College London

PREFACE

Shakespeare was the first author to receive a Cambridge Companion. He is also the author to have received the most Companions. This volume of twenty-one newly commissioned essays constitutes the fifth, following the Companions of 1934, 1971, 1986 and 2001.

Shakespeare may indeed be for all time, but as the times change, so also do our ways of experiencing his poems and plays. The chapters of this volume bear witness to those changes on the page, stage and screen. Written by an international group of Shakespearians (from Britain, the United States, Canada, Holland, New Zealand and South Africa), they offer a distillation of recent scholarship and criticism for readers keen to expand their knowledge and appreciation of Shakespeare.

The chapters cover the traditional categories of Shakespeare study – his life, times and work – often with an innovative twist. The facts of Shakespeare's life are provided, but with an awareness of how the biographer's imagination is needed to transform those scant facts into a smooth narrative. Shakespeare's times, his historical and cultural context, are discussed with an eye to both the continuities and differences between his past and our present. Six chapters, organized by genre, focus on the works, reflecting a turn back to literary form and value as well as a heightened sense of their embeddedness in historical discourse. Chapters on Shakespeare's reading habits and writing techniques help account for his singular genius and skill; those on the playhouse and printing house explore the practices by which his works were produced in his own lifetime.

During the four centuries since then, Shakespeare's works have retained their force and vitality, as is apparent in the chapters on the transmission of his texts, on the traditions of theatrical performance, on the critical reception of his works and on the appropriations of popular culture. The volume closes with three chapters designed to steer readers through the dynamic developments of the present: an account of Shakespeare's globalization, an overview of today's transformative new technologies and a guide through the vast welter of recent multi-faceted materials, published and online, by which interest in Shakespeare continues to be informed and stimulated.

A selective reading list appears after each chapter. Readers wishing to continue to keep abreast of current developments in Shakespearian studies may do so through the review articles in *Shakespeare Survey*, published annually by Cambridge University Press. Quotations from Shakespeare in this volume are from the Oxford *Complete Works* (1986 etc.), General Editors Stanley Wells and Gary Taylor; act, scene and line references are to the reprint of that text in the *Norton Shakespeare* (1998, etc.), General Editor Stephen Greenblatt. Quotations from the works of Shakespeare's contemporaries are normally modernized. Thanks to Sarah Stanton for her keen attention to the volume at all stages of production, to Bronwyn Wallace for her timely help with preparing the manuscript, and to Rebecca Jones and Elizabeth Davey for overseeing the final labours.

WILLIAM SHAKESPEARE: A PARTIAL CHRONOLOGY

Dates of composition below do not in all cases correspond with dates of publication given in individual chapters.

26 April 1564	baptized in Stratford-upon-Avon
28 November 1582	marriage licence issued for William Shakespeare and Anne Hathaway
26 May 1583	baptism of Susanna, their daughter
2 February 1585	baptism of Hamnet and Judith, their twin son and daughter
1592	Robert Greene refers to Shakespeare as an 'upstart crow'
1593	publication of *Venus and Adonis*
1594	publication of *The Rape of Lucrece*
15 March 1595	Shakespeare named as joint payee of the Lord Chamberlain's Men, founded in 1594
11 August 1596	burial of Hamnet Shakespeare in Stratford-upon-Avon
October 1596	draft of the grants of arms to John, Shakespeare's father
4 May 1597	Shakespeare buys New Place, Stratford-upon-Avon
1598	Shakespeare listed as one of the 'principal comedians' in Jonson's *Every Man in his Humour*
1598	mention of Shakespeare in Francis Meres' *Palladis Tamia*
1599	building of the Globe
8 September 1601	burial of John Shakespeare in Stratford-upon-Avon
2 February 1602	John Manningham notes performance of *Twelfth Night* at the Middle Temple
1 May 1602	Shakespeare pays £320 for land in Old Stratford

1603	Shakespeare named among the 'principal tragedians' in Jonson's *Sejanus*
May 1603	Shakespeare named in documents conferring the title of the King's Men on their company
24 July 1605	Shakespeare pays £440 for an interest on the tithes in Stratford
5 June 1607	Susanna Shakespeare marries John Hall
1608	the King's Men take over the indoor Blackfriars theatre
9 September 1608	burial of Mary, Shakespeare's mother, in Stratford
1609	publication of the Sonnets
1612	Shakespeare testifies in the Belott–Mountjoy case
10 March 1613	Shakespeare buys the Blackfriars Gatehouse
1613	Globe burns down during a performance of *All is True* (*Henry VIII*)
September 1614	Shakespeare involved in enclosure disputes in Stratford
10 February 1616	Judith Shakespeare marries Thomas Quiney
25 March 1616	Shakespeare's will drawn up in Stratford
25 April 1616	Shakespeare buried in Stratford (the monument records that he died on 23 April)
8 August 1623	burial of Anne Shakespeare in Stratford
1623	publication of the First Folio
16 July 1649	burial of Susanna Hall in Stratford
9 February 1662	burial of Judith Quiney in Stratford
1670	death of Shakespeare's last direct descendant, his grand-daughter Elizabeth, who married Thomas Nash in 1626 and John (later Sir John) Bernard in 1649

A CONJECTURAL CHRONOLOGY OF SHAKESPEARE'S WORKS

It is particularly difficult to establish the dates of composition and the relative chronology of the early works, up to those named by Francis Meres in his *Palladis Tamia* of 1598. The following table is based on the 'Canon and Chronology' section in *William Shakespeare: A Textual Companion*, by Stanley Wells and Gary Taylor, with John Jowett and William Montgomery (1987), where more detailed information and discussion may be found.

The Two Gentlemen of Verona	1590–1
The Taming of the Shrew	1590–1
The First Part of the Contention (2 Henry VI)	1591
Richard Duke of York (3 Henry VI)	1591
1 Henry VI	1592
Titus Andronicus	1592
Richard III	1592–3
Venus and Adonis	1592–3
The Rape of Lucrece	1593–4
The Comedy of Errors	1594
Love's Labour's Lost	1594–5
Richard II	1595
Romeo and Juliet	1595
A Midsummer Night's Dream	1595
King John	1596
The Merchant of Venice	1596–7
1 Henry IV	1596–7
The Merry Wives of Windsor	1597–8
2 Henry IV	1597–8
Much Ado About Nothing	1598
Henry V	1598–9
Julius Caesar	1599
As You Like It	1599–1600

Hamlet	1600–1
Twelfth Night	1600–1
Troilus and Cressida	1602
The Sonnets	1593–1603
Measure for Measure	1603
A Lover's Complaint	1603–4
Sir Thomas More	1603–4
Othello	1603–4
All's Well that Ends Well	1604–5
Timon of Athens	1605
King Lear	1605–6
Macbeth	1606
Antony and Cleopatra	1606
Pericles	1607
Coriolanus	1608
The Winter's Tale	1609
Cymbeline	1610
The Tempest	1611
Henry VIII (All is True)	1613
The Two Noble Kinsmen	1613–14

I

STEPHEN GREENBLATT

The traces of Shakespeare's life

What are the key surviving traces, unadorned by local colour, of Shakespeare's life? The core set of these traces, of course, consists of the printing of his name as the author of his plays and poems. During his lifetime, eighteen of the plays now attributed to Shakespeare were printed in the small-format editions called quartos. Many such editions of plays in this period were issued without the name of the author – there was no equivalent to our copyright system, and publishers were under no legal obligation to specify on their title pages who wrote the texts they printed. (See Chapter 5.) By the second decade of the seventeenth century, it had become more or less routine to include the author's name, but it remains difficult at this distance to gauge the level of contemporary interest in particular playwrights: some contemporaries compiled detailed lists of the names of those they regarded as the pre-eminent playwrights in different genres; many others, to judge from surviving texts, seem to have been no more interested in the authors of plays than audiences today are interested in the authors of television shows. (See Chapter 3.) Only occasionally were there significant exceptions, and then as now for the same principal motive: profit. By 1597 seven of Shakespeare's plays had been printed, their title pages providing details of plot and of performance but not the identity of the author. After 1598 Shakespeare's name, spelled in various ways, began to appear on the title page of quartos, and indeed several plays almost certainly not authored by him were printed with his name. His name – Shakespeare, Shake-speare, Shakspeare, Shaxberd, Shakespere, and the like – had evidently begun to sell plays. During his lifetime more published plays were attributed to Shakespeare than to any other contemporary dramatist.

Similarly, Shakespeare's name figured prominently in the editions, published in his lifetime, of his non-dramatic works: *Venus and Adonis* (1593), *The Rape of Lucrece* (1594) and the Sonnets (1609). Confirmation of Shakespeare's contemporary reputation as a love poet comes from many early sources, including those students in St John's College, Cambridge, who wrote an amateur play in which one of the characters rhapsodizes, 'I'll worship sweet Mr Shakespeare, and to honour him will lay his *Venus and Adonis* under my pillow.' Comparable praise was showered during his lifetime on Shakespeare as a dramatist. Francis Meres, who published a survey of the literary scene in 1598, wrote that 'As Plautus and Seneca are accounted the best for Comedy and Tragedy among the Latins, so Shakespeare among the English is the most excellent in both kinds for the stage.' Meres followed with a list of plays – such as *A Midsummer Night's Dream* and *Romeo and Juliet* – that seemed to him to prove his point.

But the greatest tribute to Shakespeare's genius – and the single most important trace of Shakespeare's whole life – came seven years after his death, when two of his friends and colleagues, John Heminges and Henry Condell, brought out the collected edition of his plays now known as the First Folio (1623). This edition gave the world the text of eighteen plays – including such masterpieces as *Twelfth Night*, *As You Like It*, *Macbeth*, *Measure for Measure* and *The Tempest* – that had not been published before and might well have otherwise disappeared. It included an engraved portrait of Shakespeare that, because the editors knew Shakespeare well, is probably closer to a reasonably accurate image of the author than any other that has been found. And it featured no fewer than four dedicatory poems. The poem by Ben Jonson – celebrating Shakespeare as 'Soul of the Age! / The applause!, delight! The wonder of our Stage!' – is particularly noteworthy since Jonson likens his deceased friend and theatrical rival not only to some of the greatest English writers – Chaucer, Spenser and Marlowe – but also to the greatest playwrights of antiquity – Aeschylus, Sophocles and Euripides.

This tribute is a biographical fact of great significance: a distinguished poet, playwright and classicist, notoriously competitive, defensive and combative, exalts Shakespeare – safely dead, of course – to the highest rank of literary achievement. Jonson clearly expected not to be ridiculed for the extravagance of his praise; he thought rather that it would bear witness to the justness of his judgement. We learn something important then not only about Jonson's taste but also about the esteem in which a large circle of Shakespeare's contemporaries held him a mere seven years after his death.

But literary reputation, though it was enormously important for Shakespeare and his contemporaries, is generally not regarded by modern readers as the heart of the matter. It seems to us somehow a superficial or external piece of biographical information; what we want is the details of a lived life. And it is both revealing and frustrating that the First Folio, for all the obvious care with which it was edited and presented, gives us almost nothing of what we crave. There is a single detail that Heminges and Condell bother to provide: their great friend's 'mind and hand went together', they write; 'And what he thought, he uttered with the easiness, that we have scarce received from him a blot in his papers.' If the claim is true, it helps to explain how Shakespeare managed to accomplish so much in a relatively short lifespan. But, as Margreta de Grazia has observed, the same claim was made for other writers in this period and may have had little relation to reality.[1] And indeed recent studies of the various states of Shakespeare's texts suggest that he heavily re-worked at least several of his plays.

Apart from the debatable claim that he possessed a startling authorial 'easiness', Heminges and Condell are virtually silent about Shakespeare's life. The Folio editors do not even arrange the plays in the order of their composition, so that readers could follow the evolution of the playwright's skill and vision. A major scholarly effort, over several centuries, has pored over theatrical records, allusions and internal evidence in order to establish a plausible order. Though there are still disputes over the precise years in which certain plays were first written and performed, a rough chronology of the plays is now generally accepted. Some biographers, particularly in the late nineteenth and early twentieth centuries, attempted to assign this chronology to a presumed psychological evolution that underlay it: from the mingled realism and festive laughter of the histories and comedies, to the despair and bitterness of the tragedies, to the renewed if sober hopefulness of the romances. But quite apart from certain anomalies that disrupt the comfortable flow of the psychological story – *Titus Andronicus,* for example, written uncomfortably close to *The Comedy of Errors*; *Twelfth Night* cheek by jowl with *Hamlet* – the story itself has proved difficult to coordinate coherently with the surviving biographical details of Shakespeare's life.

The Folio editors, in any case, had no interest in providing any assistance to such an attempt. Though they include the author's picture, they do not bother to include his birth and death dates, his marital status, his surviving children, his intellectual and social affiliations, his endearing or annoying quirks of character, let alone anything more psychologically revealing, such as the 'table talk' carefully recorded by followers of Martin Luther. Shakespeare may have been a very private man, but, as he was dead when the edition was produced, it is unlikely to have been his own wishes that dictated the omissions. The editors evidently assumed that the potential buyers of the book – and this was an expensive commercial venture – would not be particularly interested in what we would now regard as essential biographical details.

Such presumed indifference is, in all likelihood, chiefly a reflection of Shakespeare's modest origins. He flew below the radar of ordinary Elizabethan and Jacobean social curiosity. In the wake of the death of the poet Sir Philip Sidney, Fulke Greville wrote a fascinating biography of his friend, but Sidney was a dashing aristocrat, linked by birth and marriage to the great families of the realm, and he died tragically of a wound he received on the battlefield. Writers of a less exalted station did not excite the same interest, unless, like Ben Jonson, they were celebrated for their public persona, or, like another of Shakespeare's contemporaries, Christopher Marlowe, they ran afoul of the authorities.[2] The fact that there are no police reports, privy council orders, indictments or post-mortem inquests about Shakespeare, as there are about Marlowe, tells us something significant about Shakespeare's life – he possessed a gift for staying out of trouble – but it is not the kind of detail on which biographers thrive.

Centuries of archival labour have unearthed at least some of the basic details. William Shakespeare was baptized in Holy Trinity Church in Stratford-upon-Avon on 26 April 1564. (Since christenings usually took place within five days of a child's birth, his actual date of birth – for which there is no record – is conventionally celebrated on 23 April.) He was the first son of John and Mary Shakespeare; two daughters had already been born to them, but neither had survived infancy. Altogether they would have eight children, four daughters and four sons. William's sister Anne, born when he was 7 years old, died in 1579, just before William's fifteenth birthday. Another sister, Joan, married a hatter and survived both her husband and her celebrated brother; she is mentioned in Shakespeare's will. William and Joan were the only ones of the siblings to marry. One of Shakespeare's younger brothers, Richard, left no trace of his occupation; another, Gilbert, is said to have been a Stratford haberdasher; and the third, Edmund, became a professional actor, though evidently not a notable one. Edmund, who died at 28 in 1607, was given an expensive funeral, presumably paid for by his older brother, whose tremendous success in the theatre had by that time made him a wealthy man.

The place into which William was born was a prosperous, pleasant market town, situated on the River Avon, about 100 miles north-west of London. It was not the fiefdom of a powerful nobleman or of the church; since the mid-sixteenth century it had been an independent township, governed by an elected bailiff and a council of burgesses and aldermen. The town was graced with substantial half-timbered houses lining the three main streets running parallel to the river, a fine church with a noteworthy chapel, a bustling annual fair and – perhaps most important for our purposes – an excellent free grammar school. The origins of William's father, John, were in the countryside; his grandfather, Richard, was a tenant farmer in the nearby village of Snitterfield, where he rented a house and land from Robert Arden, a prosperous, land-owning farmer. In the mid-sixteenth century John Shakespeare moved to Stratford, where he became a glover and dresser of soft leather. He must have done reasonably well for himself, for he purchased a house and other property in Stratford and soon after married Mary Arden, the youngest daughter and favourite of his father's landlord. Mary was not one of the wealthy heiresses – Portia, Juliet, Celia, Hero and Olivia – who populate Shakespeare's plays, but, bringing both property of her own and a name of some repute, she was a prize for John Shakespeare. Continuing to prosper – in addition to making fashionable gloves, he seems to have bought and sold real estate, dealt in wool and other agricultural commodities, and lent money at high rates of interest – John steadily rose in the town's administrative hierarchy. He held a series of trusted roles culminating in 1568 – when his son William was 4 years old – in a year's term as bailiff, the equivalent of mayor. A sign of his ascent was the application he initiated for a coat of arms, which would have signalled his attaining the rank of a gentleman, someone in the upper 2 per cent of England's population.

But though a coat of arms was drawn up for him, John Shakespeare did not pursue the costly process that would have led to its actual grant. From the late 1560s onwards the course of his life became distinctly less smooth. There were repeated, unexplained failures to attend meetings; legal complaints, lawsuits and fines; the selling of family property to raise cash. When in 1592 the local authorities, attempting to ferret out Catholic sympathizers, drew up a list of those who had not been coming monthly to the Protestant church services, as the law required, John Shakespeare's name was included. Speculation that Shakespeare's father was secretly a Catholic – at a time of intense fear and persecution of Catholics suspected of conspiring to topple the regime – was furthered by the discovery, in the eighteenth century, of a document that purported to be John Shakespeare's 'spiritual last will and testament'. The original document, conspicuously Catholic in its formulations, has been lost, however, and its authenticity has been challenged. Moreover, in the list of those cited for failing to attend church, John Shakespeare's name was placed in a special category, distinct from religious recusancy: 'It was said that these last nine come not to church for fear of process for debt.' John Shakespeare never returned to public office in Stratford, though he seems to have weathered his financial difficulties and remained, until his death in September 1601, in the substantial double house in Henley Street where his celebrated son was born. Shakespeare's mother outlived her husband by seven years.

Part at least of William Shakespeare's childhood and adolescence may well have been shadowed by these family difficulties – how could it not have been? – but there is no firm evidence to prove it. Indeed, after the initial baptismal entry, there is no firm evidence of anything about his upbringing. He presumably learned his ABCs at what Elizabethans called a petty school and then presumably went on to the King's New School, a fine, free grammar school where he would have received a serious education centred on the Latin classics, but the records that might have confirmed his attendance are lost. (See Chapter 2.) There is no record, likewise, of what he did in the years immediately after he left school. His name is not listed in the well-maintained records of those who matriculated at Oxford or Cambridge University, and, if he had somehow attended anyway, we would almost certainly know it from the title pages of his plays whose authors routinely and conspicuously trumpeted such distinctions. But whether he was an apprentice to his father in the glove business or a law clerk or an unlicensed schoolteacher or a soldier – all frequently rehearsed speculations – is impossible to determine with any certainty.

The next time that William Shakespeare leaves a documentary trace of himself is in the marriage licence bond recorded on 28 November 1582 to enable him to marry Anne Hathaway of Shottery, a village near Stratford. Shakespeare was 18 years old; Anne was 26, the daughter of a modestly prosperous sheep farmer and husbandman, recently deceased. The bond, required to facilitate unusual haste in conducting the marriage, may have been linked to the fact that the bride was some three months pregnant. In May she gave birth to a daughter, christened Susanna. Before two years had passed, she gave birth to twins, a boy and a girl, whom the parents named Hamnet and Judith, after their long-term Stratford friends Hamnet and Judith Sadler. These three children, all of whom survived infancy, are the only recorded offspring of William Shakespeare. Hamnet died in 1596, at the age of 11; Susanna died in her sixty-seventh year, in 1649; and Judith reached what for the time was the ripe old age of 77, dying in 1662. Her three sons all died before she did, and Shakespeare's only grand-daughter, Elizabeth, died childless in 1670.

What role Shakespeare played in the upbringing of his three children is unknown. After the records of their births in 1583 and 1585 we have no direct evidence of his whereabouts or activities for seven years, a period that has been dubbed by frustrated biographers the 'Lost Years'. Then in 1592 a playwright, pamphleteer and fiction writer notorious for his disorderly life, Robert Greene, published a nasty attack on an 'Upstart Crow, beautified with our feathers'. 'Our feathers': Greene's attack takes the form of a warning to fellow university-educated playwrights who had been writing for the London stage. Lacking their elite educational background, the 'Upstart Crow' started off as a mere actor – one of 'those Puppets', as Greene puts it, 'that spake from our mouths, those Antics garnished in our colours' – but has now set up to be a writer as well. He has the gall to think he is 'as well able to bombast out a blank verse as the best of you'; indeed he imagines himself to be 'an absolute *Iohannes fac totum*', a Johnny-do-all. Greene does not exactly name the rival he thus characterizes as ambitious, unscrupulous and opportunistic, but he unmistakably identifies him by alluding to a line from one of Shakespeare's earliest plays, *3 Henry VI*, and informing us that its author regards himself as 'the onely Shake-scene in a country'.

It is reasonably clear then that by 1592 Shakespeare had made his way from Stratford to London, that he had become an actor and that he had established himself sufficiently as a playwright to excite the anger of an envious contemporary. Indeed Greene seems to assume that Shakespeare was well-enough known to be identified merely by a quotation and an allusion. A few months later the printer of Greene's pamphlet, Henry Chettle, published an apology. Once again, no names are directly mentioned, but referring to the person attacked as an upstart crow, Chettle testifies that he personally has 'seen his demeanour no less civil than he excellent in the quality [i.e. the occupation] he professes'. 'Besides,' he adds, 'diverse of worship' – that is, several important people – 'have reported his uprightness of dealing, which argues his honesty, and his facetious [i.e. witty] grace in writing, which approves his art.'[3] By 1592, then, Shakespeare seems to have had important friends and protectors.

The precise route by which Shakespeare entered the professional theatre – the company he may have first joined as an apprentice, the way he initially received the chance to write for the stage, the precise moment he arrived in London – has remained obscure. Theatre scholars have reconstructed with reasonable confidence his trajectory thereafter, a trajectory that led him to be an actor, playwright and shareholder in the company known first as the Lord Chamberlain's Men and then, after Queen Elizabeth's death in 1603, as the King's Men. These were the two most successful and celebrated companies of the age, and Shakespeare flourished in both reputation and wealth.

He must have worked extraordinarily hard: for the better part of two decades he wrote approximately two plays a year, plays that suggest restless and substantial background reading as well as intense compositional attention. At the same time he was somehow memorizing parts, rehearsing and performing in plays, his own and those of others. He must, at least on some occasions, have also accompanied his company when they travelled from town to town. And he was helping to manage his company's finances and his own, investing his earnings, for the most part, in country real estate in and around Stratford and perhaps lending money from time to time at a favourable rate of return. He was indeed an 'absolute *Iohannes fac totum*', and he reaped the rewards. In a profession where almost everyone else eked out a marginal existence, Shakespeare amassed a small fortune.

Combing the archives, scholars have found various documentary traces of Shakespeare's business dealings. He was twice cited for not paying his taxes on his London residence. In his Stratford house he amassed an ample supply of corn and malt, presumably for sale. He sold a load of stone to the Stratford corporation, which used it to repair a bridge. He bought an interest in a lease of 'tithes of corn, grain, blade, and hay'. A letter from one Stratford burgher to another remarks that 'Our countryman Mr. Shakespeare is willing to disburse some money upon some odd yardland or other at Shottery or near about us.'[4] Another letter, drafted but not sent, asked Shakespeare for a loan of £30; he was evidently understood, then, to dabble in money-lending. At least twice Shakespeare went to court to recover small sums of money that he claimed were owed him. None of these dealings constitutes anything out of the ordinary for a person of means in this period, but, taken together, they represent a lifelong attention to his financial resources.

If we set aside the astonishing genius of what he wrote, this set of activities and accomplishments, though considerable, might not qualify as superhuman, but it would for anyone, however gifted, have required unusual discipline, tenacity and ambition. The seventeenth-century gossip-monger John Aubrey, one of the first writers to interest himself in Shakespeare's life, is not to be trusted. But at least one of the anecdotes he collected and recorded in 1681 rings true: Shakespeare was not, Aubrey was told, 'a company keeper'. He 'wouldn't be debauched', Aubrey's informant reported, and if invited out, he would excuse himself, writing that 'he was in pain'.[5] Shakespeare must have husbanded his time extremely well: it is noteworthy that his two great narrative poems seem to have been written during a period in which the theatres were all shut down, by government order, in response to an epidemic of plague.

When this torrent of London-based activity was going on, the playwright did not live with his family: he took rented lodgings near the theatres, living at various times in St Helen's parish, Bishopsgate, in the Clink in Southwark, across the river, and on Silver Street, not far from St Paul's. How frequently Shakespeare saw his wife and children is not known; Aubrey was told that he visited them once a year. He had not, in any case, abandoned them: his wife and children remained in Stratford, living with his parents in the family house on Henley Street and then, from 1597 onwards, in New Place, the second-largest house in the town. Shakespeare's purchase of New Place is striking evidence of his prosperity, prosperity signified as well by the successful application in 1596 for a family coat of arms. His father, as we noted above, had initiated that application decades earlier, at the height of his prosperity, and then abandoned it; its renewal was almost certainly the work of his startlingly successful son. Certainly the irate York Herald, Peter Brooke, thought so: he complained that his colleague had inappropriately assigned a heraldic device to a number of base persons, including 'Shakespear ye Player'.

After the construction of the Globe theatre in 1599 Shakespeare had another source of regular income: he was in the unusual position of being part-owner of the playhouse in which his company (of which he was also part owner, as well as principal playwright) performed. After 1606 his company also took the lease on the Blackfriars theatre and thereby acquired another significant London venue. There are traces of other, more occasional remunerative activities: in 1604, along with other members of his company, Shakespeare received a cash payment and scarlet livery to attend on the visiting Spanish ambassador, and in 1613 he was paid 44 shillings for devising the *impresa*, or insignia, to be inscribed on a nobleman's tournament shield. In addition he was rumoured to have been given very substantial gifts by the fabulously wealthy Earl of Southampton to whom he dedicated *Venus and Adonis* and *The Rape of Lucrece* and who is often mentioned as one of the prime candidates for the unnamed fair young man of the Sonnets.

The Sonnets seem to promise a huge biographical payoff. They are written in the first person with exceptional intensity and reveal a passionate relationship, mingling adoration, desire and bitter reproach, with both an aristocratic young man and a dark lady. There is pain when a rival poet threatens to displace the speaker in the young man's affections, and still greater pain when the dark lady seduces the young man. In several of the sonnets the poet seems to refer specifically (and with shame) to his profession in the public theatre:

> Alas, 'tis true, I have gone here and there
> And made myself a motley to the view,
> Gored mine own thoughts, sold cheap what is most dear.
>
> (110: 1–3)

And in addressing the dark lady the poet repeatedly refers to himself by name:

> Make but my name thy love, and love that still,
> And then thou lov'st me for my name is Will.
>
> (136: 13–14)

Apart from these moments of self-identification the Sonnets do not identify the characters – despite a mountain of speculation, the identity of the young man, the dark lady and the rival poet remain in doubt – and readers have long understood that Shakespeare could have invented the whole erotic tangle. Nonetheless, the Sonnets are a distinct provocation, a tantalizing invitation to biographical speculation, even as they withhold the detailed information that would give that speculation some solid ground.

Many have accepted the invitation and constructed elaborate accounts of Shakespeare's sexual life, as revealed by the Sonnets, but Stephen Booth's wry comment in 1977 sums up some of the frustration that haunts all these accounts: 'William Shakespeare was almost certainly homosexual, bisexual, or heterosexual. The sonnets provide no evidence on the matter.'[6]

Something of the same frustration attends speculation about Shakespeare's religious beliefs or his sceptical doubts. In the late seventeenth or early eighteenth century Richard Davies, a Gloucestershire curate, jotted down that Shakespeare 'died a papist' – that is, Davies believed that on his deathbed Shakespeare received the Catholic last rites. Some have conjoined this jotting to the hints that Shakespeare's parents may have harboured faith in Roman Catholicism, and scholars, notably Sir Edmund Chambers and Ernst Honigmann, have ferreted out intriguing links between several schoolmasters in Stratford, during the young Shakespeare's years at the King's New School, and both English recusants at home (that is, those who refused to attend the Protestant Church of England religious services) and English Catholic exiles abroad.

Critics have accordingly scrutinized Shakespeare's plays and poems for signs of clandestine Catholic sympathies. The enterprise is hindered both by the complexity and ambiguity of the religious settlement in Tudor and Stuart England and by the complexity and ambiguity of Shakespeare's works. Comparable hindrances have been encountered by critics who have attempted to find in Shakespeare signs of thoroughgoing disbelief. The surviving biographical records indicate that he was baptized in a Protestant church, married in a Protestant ceremony and buried in a Protestant funeral. If he had systematically refused to attend Church of England services, he would almost certainly have been cited and fined – regular church attendance in this period was not voluntary. Since he was not so cited, he presumably met at least the minimal formal requirements for an observing Protestant. What he believed – or did not believe – in his heart remains hidden. Or, rather, here too the works are an invitation to venture forth in a speculative landscape without clear boundary markers or secure destinations.

In 1607–8, having written an astonishing succession of tragic masterpieces, Shakespeare shifted generic ground and collaborated with a freelance playwright, George Wilkins, on an episodic romance, *Pericles, Prince of Tyre*. On internal evidence it seems that Wilkins wrote most of the first two acts and Shakespeare most of the last three. This is not an obvious recipe for success, and little in Wilkins' life suggests that he was a promising candidate for a happy collaboration. (Repeatedly in trouble with the law, Wilkins was arrested in 1611 for 'kicking a woman on the belly which was then great with child', and in his later years he seems to have run a brothel.) But

Pericles was a major popular success, and in Shakespeare's career it seems to have initiated the interest in romance that dominated his last works.

Sometime in his later 40s, around 1611, Shakespeare seems to have retired from London and returned to Stratford. The reason for his retirement, at around the time he wrote *The Tempest*, is unclear. He was still busy with affairs: in 1613 he made a very substantial investment in London real estate, purchasing the Blackfriars Gatehouse, near the private playhouse in which his company performed. He busied himself in Stratford life as well, contributing to the bill to repair the highways, entertaining a visiting preacher in his home at New Place and entering into agreements to protect his personal financial interests in a dispute over the enclosure of common lands. He continued to write plays – the lost *Cardenio*, *Henry VIII* and *The Two Noble Kinsmen* – but now, it seems, from the distance of Stratford and with the collaboration of a younger colleague, John Fletcher.

Shakespeare's older daughter, Susanna, married the physician John Hall in 1607. The couple lived in Stratford and had a daughter, Elizabeth, the next year. Shakespeare's younger daughter, Judith, married Thomas Quiney of Stratford in February 1616. On that occasion, or shortly after, according to a tale recorded in a Stratford vicar's diary some fifty years later, 'Shakespeare, Drayton [that is, Michael Drayton, the poet], and Ben Jonson had a merry meeting, and it seems drank too hard, for Shakespeare died of a fever there contracted.' This tale – like the other stories that belatedly began to circulate about Shakespeare as a deer poacher, or a menial at the door of the theatre or a prompt-boy – must be taken with many grains of salt, but it is at least clear that he became seriously ill at about this time.

In the winter of 1616 Shakespeare summoned his lawyer, Francis Collins, and instructed him to draw up his last will and testament, a document he signed, with a shaky hand, on 25 March 1616. The will leaves virtually everything – the substantial house, the great bulk of its contents and the lands in and around Stratford – to Susanna, who was named executor, along with her husband. A provision was made for Judith, though the will was carefully crafted to keep Judith's husband from having access to the inheritance, and smaller sums were left for his only surviving sibling, Joan, and for several other relations and friends. A modest donation was made to the poor. To his wife of thirty-four years Shakespeare initially left nothing at all. Then, in an addition interlined on the last of the three pages, he added a new provision: 'Item, I give unto my wife my second-best bed with the furniture [i.e. bed furnishings].' Scholars have debated the significance of this addition: some have observed that Shakespeare's wife would have had certain legal rights, independent of the specific terms in the will, and have argued that the second-best bed was often the one that the couple used, the best bed being reserved for special guests. Others have found the provision, in the absence of any terms of endearment, a deliberate slight.

Shakespeare was buried in the chancel of Holy Trinity Church in Stratford. Carved on the plain slab covering his grave are four lines:

GOOD FREND FOR JESUS SAKE FORBEARE,
TO DIGG THE DUST ENCLOASED HEARE.
BLESTE BE YE MAN YT SPARES THES STONES,
AND CURST BE HE YT MOVES MY BONES.

In the north wall of the chancel above the grave a monument carved in black-and-white marble depicts Shakespeare with a quill pen in his right hand, a piece of paper under his left. Above the effigy sits the Shakespeare coat of arms, flanked by cherubs, and at the top, presiding over it all, sits a highly realistic carved skull.

In one of the dedicatory poems to the First Folio, seven years after Shakespeare's death, Leonard Digges remarks that when 'Time dissolves thy Stratford monument', here in this book 'we alive shall view thee still'. The sentiment is conventional, but anyone who has spent much time with the biographical traces of Shakespeare's life will understand Digges' point. The traces are, for the most part, frustratingly inert, and those that are not inert are frustratingly ambiguous. They provide shadowy glimpses of the questions that haunt most lives: Who am I? In what can I put my faith? Whom can I love? What should I do with my time on earth? In his works Shakespeare pursued these questions with a passionate intelligence, intensity and eloquence so remarkable that many readers instinctively desire to approach him more nearly, to penetrate the barrier that time, the negligence of his contemporaries and perhaps his own reserve erected. There is nothing amiss with this desire: it is deeply human, the consequence of Shakespeare's own great gift in seeming to speak so directly across the centuries. But its satisfaction lies in the imagination.

NOTES

1 Margreta de Grazia, *Shakespeare Verbatim: The Reproduction of Authenticity and the 1790 Apparatus* (Oxford: Clarendon Press, 1991), pp. 43–4.
2 Jonson's opinions on literature and life were recorded both by himself, in *Timber*, and by the Scottish man of letters, William Drummond of Hawthornden. On the interest the authorities took in Marlowe, see Charles Nicholl, *The Reckoning: The Murder of Christopher Marlowe* (London: Cape, 2002), and David Riggs, *The World of Christopher Marlowe* (London: Faber, 2004).
3 Chettle, in E. K. Chambers, *William Shakespeare: A Study of Facts and Problems*, 2 vols. (Oxford: Clarendon Press, 1930), vol. II, p. 189.
4 Letter of Abraham Sturley, in ibid., vol. II, p. 101.
5 Aubrey, in Chambers, ibid., vol. II, p. 252.

6 *Shakespeare's Sonnets*, ed. Stephen Booth (New Haven: Yale University Press, 1977), p. 548.

READING LIST

Chambers, E.K. *William Shakespeare: A Study of Facts and Problems*. 2 vols. Oxford: Clarendon, 1930.

Duncan-Jones, Katherine. *Ungentle Shakespeare: Scenes from His Life*. London: Arden Shakespeare, 2001.

Erne, Lukas. *Shakespeare as Literary Dramatist*. Cambridge: Cambridge University Press, 2003.

Honigmann, E.A.J. *Shakespeare: The Lost Years*. Manchester: Manchester University Press, 1985.

Greenblatt, Stephen. *Will in the World: How Shakespeare Became Shakespeare*. New York: Norton, 2004.

Honan, Park. *Shakespeare: A Life*. New York: Oxford University Press, 1998.

Nicholl, Charles. *The Lodger: Shakespeare on Silver Street*. New York: Allen Lane, 2007.

Schoenbaum, Samuel. *Shakespeare's Lives*. New edn. New York: Oxford University Press, 1991.

William Shakespeare: A Compact Documentary Life. Rev. edn. New York: Oxford University Press, 1987.

Shapiro, James. *1599: A Year in the Life of William Shakespeare*. New York: HarperCollins, 2005.

Wells, Stanley. *Shakespeare: A Life in Drama*. New York: Norton, 1995.

Shakespeare: For All Time. London: Macmillan, 2002.

2

JEFF DOLVEN AND SEAN KEILEN

Shakespeare's reading

Most of what Shakespeare wrote was played before it was read. The Sonnets are an exception, and *Venus and Adonis* and *The Rape of Lucrece*, which he probably saw through the press himself. But for the most part he committed his words to the mouths of actors, and the printers of the quartos and First Folio came later, doing their work sometimes illicitly, then posthumously. Shakespeare was a man of the theatre, not a bookworm. But then again – what performance of Shakespeare is *not* informed by reading? There is the reading that actors do as they commit scripts to memory. There is the life of reading that literate members of an audience bring to the playhouse. Finally there is what Shakespeare himself read, his sources and influences. That idiosyncratic bibliography – a compost of school text and eight-penny romance and chronicle history – has been painstakingly reconstructed by generations of scholars. But the plays also have a great deal to say about *how* he read, and what he thought about the whole business of reading. Though reading may be, after sleep, the least dramatic of activities, Shakespeare returns again and again to scenes where a character is perusing a letter or turning a page or brandishing or just talking about a book. The result is a sporadic but career-long meditation on what reading is for.

So what *is* reading for? Or what *was* it for? To ask that question of the late sixteenth century is to enter an urgent contemporary debate. London's multiplying printing presses, rising literacy and an explosion of vernacular writing put pressure on the institutions – church, school, court – once accustomed to regulating reading lives. Around 1581, a browser in the book stalls of St Paul's could find devotional manuals and recipe books alongside romances like *The Wandering Knight*, 'a work worthy of reading', as the title page protests. A good humanist might trace such boasts to Horace's *Ars Poetica* and its injunction that a poem both teach and delight. But in these new fictions nods to Horace were probably outnumbered by winks.

Such an uneasy marriage of pleasure and profit betrays a culture where reading was moving beyond the institutional contexts where its value had been secure. How did Shakespeare – schoolboy, poet, playwright, pleasure-reader – fit this changing landscape? Subsequent opinion has had it that he read everything and nothing, that he was polymath and philistine. Praising the lifelikeness of his plays, Ben Jonson, the poet's friend, let slip that Shakespeare 'had small Latin and less Greek' – the nativist Shakespeare most prized by the eighteenth and nineteenth centuries, an avid reader of Nature's book. By contrast, the new scholars' Shakespeare, the man of William Baldwin's *William Shakespere's Small Latine and Lesse Greeke*, sometimes seems to have read everything, adding to intuitive genius the achievements of scholarly expertise.

The truth must lie somewhere in between. We can say with some certainty that Shakespeare went to school, and that the classroom stayed on his mind long after he left it; also, that as an adult he did his reading in the community of actors and playwrights and hangers-on that flourished on the south bank of the Thames, the so-called 'Liberties'. Given the assault that the players endured from the keepers of civic and religious virtue, it would not be surprising if this new, popular art had turned its back on the literary culture of the schools. And yet Shakespeare thought about reading in all its forms, all his life – thought back to his own schooldays, back to ancient Rome, and across the classes and professions of his own city. The result is a portrait of reading as a culturally central but rapidly transforming practice, made from the vantage of a theatre that was changing just as fast. We will assay that variety by taking up four of Shakespeare's readers: the student Hamlet, the Stoic Brutus, the buffoon Malvolio and the scholar-magus Prospero.

Hamlet

Hamlet is first summoned to the stage only to be told he cannot return to university: 'For your intent / In going back to school in Wittenberg', his uncle says, 'It is most retrograde to our desire' (1.2.112–14). It proves easier to take the student out of school, however, than the school out of the student. Three scenes later, charged by the ghost to remember his father's murder, Hamlet falls back on the habits of the good schoolboy. They must be deeply engrained to serve him at such a moment:

Remember thee?
Yea, from the table of my memory
I'll wipe away all trivial fond records,
All saws of books, all forms, all pressures past,
That youth and observation copied there,

And thy commandment all alone shall live
Within the book and volume of my brain.
...
My tables – meet it is I set it down
That one may smile and smile and be a villain.
(1.5.97–109)

The 'table of my memory' casts Hamlet's mind as a commonplace book, one of the reading digests that schoolboys and scholars kept to organize 'saws' and other short texts for recollection and re-use. The appearance of the ghost fills Hamlet with sudden contempt for the trivia of his youth, and he vows instead to write a single, living commandment in the book of his brain. In the next breath, however, he is ready to jot down that anodyne maxim, 'one may smile, and smile, and be a villain' – as though schoolboy habit might still give him a grip on a world out of joint.

The curriculum of grammar schools like Shakespeare's at Stratford encouraged students to scan texts for such fragments of eloquence and wisdom. Records from Stratford are scant, but at the Plymouth grammar school – the best-described English school of the sixteenth century, thanks to the schoolmaster William Kempe's *The education of children in learning* (1588) – the boys began reading Latin literature in the second form, at the age of 8. Kempe describes how a passage for study (or a 'lecture') was introduced:

> The master shall first read sensibly a competent lecture, then declare the argument and scope of the author, afterward English it either word for word, or phrase for phrase ... Last of all teach ... the diverse sorts of the words, their properties and syntaxes of speech. And about three or four hours after, the scholar shall be diligently in every point examined, and tried how he can refer the examples of his lecture to the rules of art.[1]

The master read the Latin text, then declared its argument, probably by proposing a motto to summarize its parts and fix them in memory; then he translated it, then analysed the grammar. When the students were tested they had to prove that they understood the text in terms of the rules in Lily's *Grammar* – the standard in English schools and a recurring resource for foolery in Shakespeare's plays. (*The Merry Wives of Windsor* makes hay of Lily's Latin 'accidence' (4.1), while in *As You Like It* Touchstone schools the bumpkin William in a mockery of grammar, rhetoric and logic (5.1).) Memorization was paramount, both of rules and texts. That emphasis persisted as the students moved through the forms, learning to keep the commonplace books where they were trained to record – as Erasmus had it – 'any purple passage, archaism, neologism, Graecism, any obscure or verbose expression, any abrupt or confused order, any etymology, derivation, or composition worth knowing, any point of orthography, figure of speech, or rhetorical passages'.[2] It is easy to see how one might miss the forest of narrative and argument amidst those philological trees. But maxims constitute in themselves one idea of the profit of reading, embraced by Polonius when he prepares his son, Laertes, for the temptations of Paris: 'And these few precepts in thy memory / See thou character' (1.3.58–9).

The power of a choice aphorism was not lost on Stratford's most curious student. *Sententiae* round out many sonnets ('The hardest knife ill used doth lose his edge' (95)) and sound in the mouths of his aristocrats and commoners, kings and clowns. In *Hamlet*, however, they are handled with special cynicism. 'Words, words, words' (2.2.192), scoffs the prince when Polonius finds him with a book, and he goes on to disburden himself of a collection of old saws about old men. This ongoing impersonation of a bitter ex-schoolboy gives ironic point to his famous delay. The justifying end of a humanist education was praxis: boys were supposed to learn to read for action, and the commonplace book was a tool for making their reading accessible and adaptable to occasions of state. Hamlet, so desperate for a path to action, grows disgusted with books altogether, as the refuge of his own paralysis – a bitter reflection on what his training offers in an hour of need.

As Hamlet loses confidence in books, however, he begins to explore the resources of the theatre. Not only does he adopt his famous antic disposition, but at a crucial moment he dashes off new lines for an old play. Here, too, there is a debt to school. Much instruction took the form of catechism from the grammar book, so boys were reading scripts from the beginning. Older boys would participate in the more elaborated, improvised drama of *disputatio*, debating such themes as 'Should one marry?' or 'Should one go to sea?' before their classmates, exercising rhetorical techniques learned from ancient (Quintilian, Aphthonius) and modern (Susenbrotus) textbooks. Taking either side in such debates, they were trained to adopt the lawyer's pragmatical orientation towards the truth. They learned imitation, too, via techniques like double translation, casting a Latin text into English, then into Latin again. The more ambitious schoolmasters, if they followed the advice of Roger Ascham's *The Scholemaster* (1570), introduced their boys to imitations already embedded in the canon, Virgil of Homer, Ovid of Virgil.

Towards these various kinds of reading, Prince Hamlet adopts two distinctive attitudes. The first we might call *reading as refuge*. From the princes in *Love's Labour's Lost* to Prospero in his library, characters in Shakespeare's plays repeatedly retreat into study, reading to forget as much as to remember. But Hamlet also indulges in pedantic game-playing, the 'words, words, words' spouted elsewhere by overstuffed schoolmasters like Holofernes (*Love's Labour's Lost*) or Gerald (*The Two Noble Kinsmen*). We can call this *quibbling reading*: no profit, but considerable comic pleasure in its idle ingenuities. Hamlet escapes both sorts of bookishness. He may hold a codex in Act 2, but by Act 5 he holds a skull, and then a rapier, a progress of props that carries him ever further from Wittenberg. But then again, his additions to *The Mousetrap* (and the letter he writes to save his skin) display gifts of stylistic imitation that are nothing if not the fruits of a humanist education. Shakespeare may have missed no opportunity to make fun of a schoolmaster, and have seen in reading risks of abstraction, solipsism and pedantry. But like Hamlet, his debt to his education is everywhere.

Brutus

Brutus, too, is a great reader. The description of his devotion to books in Thomas North's translation of Plutarch's *Lives* caught the playwright's attention. 'Brutus, being in Pompey's camp, did nothing but study all day long, except he were with Pompey ... Furthermore, when others slept, or thought what would happen the morrow after, he fell to his book, and wrote all day long till night, writing a breviary of Polybius.'[3] A breviary is an abridgement, Polybius is the Roman historian and Brutus, in the camp of Caesar's enemy, occupies himself with a grown-up version of a schoolboy's exercise, distilling the wisdom from another man's narrative, banishing thoughts of the future that distract his inferiors. This is a kind of *reading as self-discipline*, an exercise in Stoic detachment from worldly circumstance – like Hamlet's refuge, but claiming a more vigorous, principled autonomy. Such self-centring is what Shakespeare's Brutus wants from his book the night before his battle with Antony and Octavius: 'Let me see, let me see, is not the leaf turned down / Where I left reading? Here it is, I think' (4.2.324–5). The anachronism is often noted – Romans read scrolls, not books – but the point is clear enough. Brutus, in the onrush of events, wants to go back to the page where he was before.

What is Shakespeare's Brutus reading – or what might Shakespeare have imagined him reading? Perhaps Polybius, or perhaps, anachronistically, the Roman philosophers who did most to convey Stoic doctrine to the Elizabethans, Seneca and Marcus Aurelius. The Stoic strain so evident in the Roman plays informed the curriculum from the start. The *Catonis Disticha*, or Cato's distichs, let students practise their Latin on maxims like *Plus vigila semper nec somno deditus esto; / Nam diuturna quies vitiis alimenta ministrat* ('We ought to take heed, that we lose not the greatest part of our life with sleep namely since of the same many vices be engendered'). Aesop's ubiquitous *Fables* feature a maxim at the end, as in the story of the wolf and the lamb: *satis peccavit, qui resistere non potuit* ('he sinned enough who was not able to refrain').[4] A more generically various diet awaited students in later forms, but still with a generous helping of Roman virtue. At the Plymouth school, it was Johannes Sturm's school edition of Cicero, leavened by Terence's comedies, prized as models of conversational Latin. By the sixth form, Virgil, Ovid and Horace. History, too: the older boys at Canterbury read 'the best poets and historians', the latter probably including Sallust, Livy, Justin, Valerius Maximus or Julius Caesar himself.

The humanists who prescribed this canon – men like Erasmus, Sturm, Sir Thomas Elyot (*The Boke Named the Governour*, 1531) and Ascham (*The Scholemaster*, 1570) – advocated reading these books personally, in a double sense. First, *reading for the style*. In his *Ciceronianus* (1528) Erasmus asserts that 'it is stupid to try to write in another man's humour and endeavour to have [his] mind breathing in what you write'. Better, he says, to digest reading such that your speech will be 'redolent of your personality, your sensitivities, your feelings'.[5] Imitation is a balance between respecting the strangeness of another mind (or another time) and finding and fashioning yourself in the words that affect you. In contemplating this ideal we are a long way from Hamlet's estranged 'Words, words, words'. Shakespeare could hardly have escaped contact with such high humanistic ambitions, articles of faith for his friend Ben Jonson and much bandied about, if not always piously, by so-called university wits like Robert Greene and Thomas Nashe.

The charisma of exemplary lives also asks readers to take the past personally: imitation was practical as well as stylistic, proposing the deeds of historical and sometimes fictional figures as patterns for action. Here is another sort of humanist profit in reading, *reading for exempla*. Early in *Julius Caesar*, Cassius flatters himself with an analogy to Aeneas (1.2.114–17), and Brutus in turn compares himself to another legendary ancestor – Junius Brutus, who liberated Rome from monarchy. 'There was a Brutus once that would have brooked / Th'eternal devil to keep his state in Rome / As easily as a king' (1.2.160–2). The preface to North's Plutarch, translated from Jacques Amyot's French, is full of incitement to such reading. By the contemplation of the self in the past's mirror, Amyot argued, the reader of history may proceed to glorious action all his own. Indeed, 'not to feel the sparks of desire of honour is an infallible sign of a base, vile, and cloyish nature'.[6] In the world of *Julius Caesar*, however, such imitative desire is an ambivalent business. How can a Stoic tell the difference between finding a model of conduct in the deeds of the past and projecting into history his present desires for wealth or power? Between principle and appetite? Shakespeare's Cicero observes sceptically that 'men may construe things after their fashion, / Clean from the purpose of the things themselves' (1.3.34–5), and the play appears to wonder whether, were it not for the candle of the reader's desire, history's page could be read at all.

Such is Brutus' Stoic dilemma. But perhaps it should be said – tacking back again from character to author – that Shakespeare hardly seems to have been troubled by such scruples. The Plutarch he used for *Julius Caesar* was no school text and is only one of a host of history books he must have read on his own, not only classical historians, but also the English chroniclers, Edward Hall and Richard Grafton and above all Raphael Holinshed, whose *Chronicles* were in their second edition in 1587. Shakespeare's relation to Holinshed is typical, at least in its freedom. As with his ancient sources, he was liberal in his adaptation of the facts, reconstructing even the genealogies to suit his narrative needs. Moreover he quarried all these histories for some version of the same plot. His plays repeatedly enact a transition from some idealized and long-standing order to a new world of *Realpolitik*. The lurch from republic to monarchy described in *Julius Caesar* and *Antony and Cleopatra* covers this ground, as do Bolingbroke's irregular succession in *Richard II*, Prince Hal's transformation into Henry V, even the murder of Duncan in *Macbeth*. We can only speculate what it was about his own moment – the always-about-to-end reign of Elizabeth and the succession of James – that made this story so urgent and appealing. But this was the plot that Shakespeare read for, and his skill in adapting his narrative sources went quite beyond the training his school would have provided.

But back to Brutus – who himself never gets back to the place in his book he marked so deliberately. Once Cassius recognizes that his friend's desire to mirror great deeds makes him vulnerable to self-deception, Brutus' fate is sealed: 'Well, Brutus, thou art noble; yet I see / Thy honourable mettle may be wrought / From that it is disposed' (1.2.302–4). Brutus is slow to catch fire and, having been lit, he is reluctant to burn, but it is not long before even he perceives Caesar as tyrant and himself as Rome's best hope for liberty. He is prompted by letters that Cassius has thrown through his window, supposedly written by Roman citizens exhorting him to imitate his ancestor. When letters are projectiles, it seems inevitable that reading will be projection: 'O Rome, I make thee promise, / If the redress will follow, thou receivest / Thy full petition at the hand of Brutus' (2.1.56–8). We are inducted into another problem of Shakespearian reading – *reading what you will*, no matter what is written. When he turns to his book on the eve of battle, Brutus tries to contain himself, all too aware that he has become like the man he killed. It is then that Caesar's ghost appears, as though to tell him how futile it is to seek in the pages of history a reprieve from events that he himself has set in motion.

Malvolio

In *Twelfth Night* the ambitions behind Malvolio's reading take the problem of interpretative desire to its limit, but this time the limit is comic. The puritanical steward's great scene of reading comes when he stumbles upon a counterfeit letter left in his path by Maria, his fellow servant in the household of the countess Olivia. Malvolio fantasizes that their mistress harbours a secret passion for him, and the letter, written in an imitation of Olivia's hand, plays upon that hope – most ingeniously in its last line, 'M. O. A. I. doth sway my life' (2.5.97). Throughout all the plays there is great traffic in letters, between lovers or soldiers or senators, and they are always read by someone, like Brutus, who wants something from them. When Malvolio reads this one aloud, he makes no attempt to disguise from himself what he hopes for: 'And the end: what should that alphabetical position portend? If I could make that resemble something in me. ... to crush this a little, it would bow to me' (106–8, 123). Here is another case of reading what you will, seasoned with a modest gift for quibbling – reading not as self-discipline, now, but as wish-fulfilment.

Shakespeare himself seems to have taken what he wanted from the sources of *Twelfth Night* even more freely than from the histories – a business not so much of crushing as dismantling them and absconding with whatever was useful. The deep lineage of these plays of confused identity and relentless reversal runs to Roman New Comedy, and like most of his fellow comic playwrights Shakespeare was a student, in school and after, of Terence and Plautus. Sometimes those borrowings are direct, as in *The Comedy of Errors*, based closely on Plautus' *Menaechmi*. In *Twelfth Night* the influence is more mediated, and the main plot – Olivia and Orsino and the nearly identical twins Viola and Sebastian – is adapted from the Barnabe Rich tale 'Of Apolonius and Silla'. Rich tells the story of Silla, who disguises herself as a boy and runs away from home to serve the duke she loves, only to find herself wooing his intended Julina on his behalf. The characters' affections are somewhat purified by Shakespeare – there is, in Rich's version, a scandalous pregnancy, and Silla's brother is considerably more cavalier in his amorous conduct than *Twelfth Night*'s Sebastian – but the lineaments of the plot are retained.

The volume that gathers these tales – 'for the only delight of the courteous gentlewoman', as Rich puts it on his title page – is called *Riche His Farewell to Militarie Profession* (1581), and its composition describes in little the growing market for vernacular fictions in Shakespeare's era. Three of the stories are versions of *novelle* from Giraldi Cinthio's *Gli Hecatommithi* (1565), prime examples of the Italian tales that the schoolmaster Ascham thought were 'commended by honest titles the sooner to corrupt honest manners'.[7] Five others draw more freely upon a wide range of sources, from Giovanni Straparola's *Le piacevoli notti* (1550–5) to George Pettie's *A Petite Pallace of Pettie His Pleasure* (1576). All of these collections were themselves translations and adaptations, and with each step towards their origins we move further away from any great certainty, or great concern, about particular authorship. In borrowing from Rich, therefore, Shakespeare could be said to have borrowed from most, if not from all, of these stories, at least as far back as Plautus, just as he borrowed from many romance writers, low and high, closer to home: from Thomas Lodge's *Rosalynd* (1590) for *As You Like It* (1600), from Philip Sidney's *Arcadia* (1593) for *King Lear* (1608), from Greene's *Pandosto* (1588) for *The Winter's Tale* (1611).

The sea-traffic in these romances amounts to another sphere of prodigious imitation in a culture of imitation – though perhaps not *imitatio*, or at least, not the discipline that was taught at school. For what circulate among the Painters and Petties are stories, characters and notable properties, the names and details of which change freely with each new printed or performed occasion. Because such borrowings usually go unacknowledged, the only clues for source-hunting scholars are the resemblances discovered by wide reading. Wide reading was likewise the only way to learn the craft of making such plots. Schoolmasters may have cultivated stylistic and argumentative virtuosity in their pupils, but the wholesale imitation of a narrative had no place in the typical curriculum. Just like a Rich or a Lodge, Shakespeare would have had to pick up his tricks as he read through the unbound quartos for sale in the bookstalls of St Paul's. We have seen how he borrowed narrative from histories, and how he was drawn to moments of transition to a new order. As he read these fictions, it seems to have been disguise, cross-dressing and other species of confused identity that attracted his attention – perhaps because, on a stage where boys played at being women, such stories already had something theatrical about them. Call this *reading for the plot*: from Plautus to Rich, Shakespeare the comedian had an eye for a tale that he could keep roiling in delightful confusion until a final anagnorisis (or discovery), followed by marriage, put everyone in place.

What can we say that Shakespeare learned from this extra-curricular reading in romance? He seems to have been free to discover and invent uses for these texts that the syllabus of classical authors could not countenance, prescribe or imagine. Presumably the only virtue of these stories was that they were *good*, and in giving pleasure they reinforced the idea that what counts in narrative is a pragmatic facility in changing the pitch and direction of a familiar plot, or mixing plots together in order to generate surprising results. For Shakespeare, this way of using texts was evidently linked to flexibility of perception and resourcefulness in finding multiple meanings in language. 'A sentence is but a cheveril glove to a good wit', says Feste to Viola. 'How quickly the wrong side may be turned outward!' (3.1.10–12). This is quibbling reading, again, or maybe *reading as foolery*, if not as folly: agile, uninhibited, sceptical and, perhaps most importantly, clever. Its pleasure is immediate; its profit, keeping just beyond the reach of authority's whip.

Prospero

These problems of liberty and authority, generosity and constraint, bring us to Prospero, the character in whom tradition has been most tempted to see Shakespeare himself. Cast out of Milan, what survives of the library beloved above his dukedom? The isle that he comes to govern is certainly full of reading. As for its master, there is no one in Shakespeare's corpus, with the possible exceptions of Aaron, Titus and Lavinia, whose fortunes are more directly bound to books. At the end of a line that includes Hamlet, Brutus and Malvolio, Prospero bears a certain resemblance to all these readers. Like Hamlet, he takes refuge in books. Like Brutus, he finds there the promise both of self-control and of controlling others. And perhaps he shares with Malvolio a tendency to read wilfully – though there is in Prospero's library one book (it is always singular) that gives him a power that Olivia's steward never dreamed on. With this book he can crush the wills of the island's natives and nonce-citizens and make them bow, and much of the moral drama of the play turns on whether he can relinquish his book-given power and the volume that gives it.

Along the way, the play traffics with many other books, of more traditional composition. In Milan, he tells Miranda, 'the liberal arts' were 'all my study' (1.2.73). He means the *trivium* of the grammar school (grammar, logic and rhetoric) and the *quadrivium* (arithmetic, geometry, music and astronomy). His pupils, Miranda and Caliban, testify that his lessons reached from one end of this curriculum to the other, from parts of speech to the bigger and lesser lights in the sky. Somewhere in the middle are the poets, and *The Tempest* is as closely engaged with the classical tradition – especially Virgil and Ovid – as anything that Shakespeare wrote. The recollections of Virgil range from indisputable local echoes to elusive narrative symmetries. On the one hand, there is Ferdinand's astonished 'Most sure the goddess' (1.2.425) when he first sees Miranda, a phrase that translates Aeneas' exclamation to his disguised mother, Venus, O *dea certe*. On the other, there is Prospero's exile and Aeneas' flight, *fato profugus*; or the arrival of Ferdinand on the island to woo its heir apparent, and Aeneas' suit to Dido. The most explicit and extended allusion – tediously, calculatedly extended – is the banter about Dido in Act 2. Gonzalo's passing reference to 'widow Dido' sparks twenty lines of debate with Sebastian and Adrian about her marital history, sustained by a misunderstanding: Gonzalo properly remembers that Dido's husband, Sychaeus, was murdered, while the others, forgetting this, are hung up on the question of her dubious marriage to Aeneas ('What if he had said "widower Aeneas" too?' (2.1.78)). Generations of scholars have worried about the significance of this allusion, but it may just as well be said to stand for the obliquity of the play's relation to the epic, and perhaps to remind us how dependent allusion is upon imperfect audiences. Does all this Virgil point us to a kind of counter-epic, contrasting the forgiveness that Prospero extends to his enemies with the slaughter of Turnus, Aeneas' rival, at the conclusion of Virgil's poem? Is Prospero's return home to Milan a kind of heroic backsliding? The *Aeneid* lends the play weight, but it has been hard to agree in which direction its ballast lists.

If we try to bring Shakespeare into focus as a reader of his poetic predecessors, not just as an opportunistic borrower, what then of Ovid? The most conspicuous use of the *Metamorphoses* in *The Tempest* is the speech where Prospero abjures his magic. 'Ye elves of hills' (5.1.33), he begins, borrowing from Arthur Golding's rendering of Medea's incantation over the body of old Aeson: 'Ye airs and winds: ye elves of hills, of brooks, of woods alone, / Of standing lakes, and of the night, approach ye everyone' (7.265–6).[8] There are other scraps from Golding as the speech continues, as well as echoes of Ovid's Latin – whether from memory, or from a book open on his writing table. (He would not be the first imperfect Latinist to make such use of a crib.) But the allusion matters because of the story it recalls. Medea is a magician, a commonplace in Renaissance treatments of witchcraft, and the spell that she casts in Ovid's poem rejuvenates Jason's father. When Prospero invokes her words, he is preparing to revive the conspirators he has charmed into compliance; perhaps he is thinking about his own age too. But most importantly, the witch is a revenger, who will turn on Jason and slaughter their children when he betrays her. Shakespeare knows his source, and maybe Prospero does too, and yet he does not seem bound to reach the same conclusion. Yes, he makes use of the resurrection trope that Ovid gives him (he has been preoccupied with making men new throughout the play), but in choosing to drown his book, he forswears new youth and revenge. Every third thought, he later remarks, will be his *own* death.

It is worth contrasting the way Shakespeare handles Virgil and Ovid in *The Tempest* with the early play that brings them most conspicuously together, *Titus Andronicus*. There, Tamora suggests that she and Aaron play at being Dido and Aeneas in the forest, only to be convinced by Aaron that they should make the rape of Philomela the model for their imitation – an Ovidian plot manifested both as a series of increasingly gruesome borrowings and also as a material book, Ovid's *Metamorphoses*. In its pages, Titus recognizes himself as a character in a revenge story that has but one ending: 'For worse than Philomel you used my daughter, / And worse than Progne I will be revenged' (5.2.193–4). In *The Tempest*, by contrast, allusions to Virgil and Ovid tend to be implicit and except, perhaps, for Prospero it is rarely clear that characters who allude to their stories know they are doing so. Unable to hold Virgil and Ovid in the same frame of reference, *Titus Andronicus* gives ample evidence that Shakespeare could talk about these poets the way that his contemporaries did, at opposite ends of a spectrum of ideas about civility and barbarism. But in *The Tempest*, Virgilian and Ovidian texts float more freely through a range of meanings, with respect to each other and to the events unfolding in the play.

The difference from *Titus* to *Tempest* suggests something about Shakespeare's own development as a reader, and one more of his sources may help us to see where that development leads. Among his debts to authors from his own time, one stands out: Michel de Montaigne, whose *Essays* appeared in John Florio's English translation in 1603. The most prominent borrowing from this book is the vision of a utopian commonwealth that Gonzalo fashions from the description of New World societies in 'Of Cannibals'. More recently, scholars have queried this passage for evidence of Shakespeare's views of European colonialism in North America and the English conquest of Ireland. Here, in free speculation that is reminiscent of the foolery of Shakespeare's most knowing clowns, Gonzalo's adaptation of Montaigne models a kind of reading that seems typical of *The Tempest*'s relation to all its sources. Gonzalo's textual wit, with its lightness of touch, tolerance of internal contradiction, and readiness to sympathize with its raw materials and its audience, suggests that there is something more at stake in reading than a literal or exhaustive application of text to context, book to life.

The Tempest's allusions to Virgil and Ovid do not oblige its plot to end in blood, and Montaigne is a humanizing influence in the story. Nevertheless, Prospero's book must be drowned. For there is still a shadow that falls on this magician's reading – doubly dark with self-absorption and discipline – and perhaps that shadow darkens all reading in Shakespeare's plays, where there are no beneficent schoolmasters to be found, and not much happy leafing under trees. And yet there is also ample evidence in *The Tempest* that Shakespeare himself was a different kind of reader from Prospero. For one thing, the range of Shakespeare's books wildly exceeds the catalogue of Prospero's library. There is Virgil and Ovid, of whom Prospero may not be entirely innocent; but there is also Hakluyt, Strachey and any number of other examples of travel writing that walk a fine line between fact and fantasy. The walls of the Milanese library in which Prospero devoted himself to 'liberal studies' were presumably lined with books written in classical languages, drawn from the range of Renaissance disciplines, but Shakespeare's reading extends itself into popular and vernacular writing and, as we have seen, includes imitations of contemporary romance plots, English translations of Latin poetry and the adaptive mediations of Stoic philosophy that are characteristic of Montaigne's essays.

And this is only the first distinction that we might draw between Prospero and Shakespeare as readers. If, from the stuff of Virgil and Ovid, Prospero makes a pageant of forgiveness that embraces every other character in the play, not everyone plays his part willingly. *The Tempest* reaches its conclusion without staging the massacre that announced Odysseus' long-awaited homecoming, or launched Aeneas on his way to Rome, or made Medea a horror to the Greeks, but in the final scene Antonio's silence – like Ariel's pleas to be released from bondage – reminds us that Prospero's mercy and generosity are coercive. In contrast, Shakespeare's extraordinarily wide reading brings him to a point from which he appears to be free in a way that Prospero is not: free not to judge, among the many different perspectives to which the plays gives voice, which is right and which is wrong. The success of Prospero's forgiveness is qualified by his insistence that there is only one way to interpret his story correctly, or even that there is only one story to tell. How different Shakespeare's reading is: how disinclined to struggle with the texts from which it borrows; how apt to entertain the possibilities that arise from them; and how unencumbered by the idea that to read, or to write, well is to arrive at a point beyond all contradiction.

Shakespeare?

Reading as refuge. Reading what you will. Reading for style and for plot. Reading as quibbling; as foolery; reading as self-discipline, and as a tool for disciplining others. Reading for profit, reading for pleasure. It is something of a commonplace among historians of this polyglot practice that, in the sixteenth century, reading was a more communal business, more likely to be done out loud and with others. Certainly Shakespeare's London harboured no class of cloistered novel readers, any more than it harboured novels. And yet, whatever route we take through Shakespeare's career-long meditation on books and their uses, we encounter the idea that reading is somehow a private activity. More than anything else it was the propensity for solace, solipsism and self-delusion that attracted his attention. Whether it is Hamlet pondering his tables or Brutus brooding in his tent, Malvolio strolling in the garden or Prospero deep in study, reading in his plays is perforce on display, there to be scrutinized and interpreted by other characters and by the audience – but on display by accident, under protest or as a performance of power. In making reading so much the subject of his dramatic work, Shakespeare sought to understand a potentially reclusive activity with the resources of a profoundly social genre, exploring what it means to read and asking whether one ought to read otherwise, or even not at all.

Having read his works, could we then – as a speculative exercise – write the scene of Shakespeare reading? We know so little about the physical particulars. Did he read with a pen in hand, filling the margins with comment, as many of his contemporaries did? None of his books survives to tell us. Did he own the books he read, or did he borrow them from other men, or women? Did he keep a library? Did he read at night, by candlelight? On the job, between the acts; reclining in bed? Reading itself is such an inscrutable activity, and to watch someone read is to be forcefully reminded of everything we cannot know about another mind. Shakespeare, whose mind has always seemed so unknowable, recedes from us yet again as we try to picture him in study, recedes towards the very literate privacy that his plays relentlessly pry open. About that privacy – which lies at the heart of even the most public exhibition of reading – he seems to have had his doubts. Shakespeare loved books, and made much of them, for pleasure and profit, but he was always suspicious of reading.

NOTES

1 Robert D. Pepper (ed.), *Four Tudor Books on Education* (Gainesville, FL: Scholars' Facsimiles & Reprints, 1966), p. 227.
2 Erasmus, *Collected Works* (Toronto: University of Toronto Press, 1974–), vol. XXIV, ed. Craig R. Thompson, pp. 682–3.
3 Plutarch, *Shakespeare's Plutarch*, ed. Walter W. Skeat (London: Macmillan, 1875), p. 129.
4 *Catonis Disticha* (London: 1562), A7r–v; *Aesopi Fabulae* (London: 1568), B1r.
5 Erasmus, *Collected Works*, vol. VI, p. 402.
6 Plutarch, *The Liues of the Noble Grecians and Romanes* (1579), *iiiir.
7 Roger Ascham, *The Schoolmaster (1570)*, ed. Lawrence V. Ryan (Ithaca, NY: Cornell University Press, 1967), p. 67.
8 *Shakespeare's Ovid, Being Arthur Golding's Translation of 'The Metamorphoses'*, ed. W. H. D. Rouse (New York: Norton & Company, 1961), p. 142.

READING LIST

Baldwin, T. W. *William Shakespere's Small Latine and Lesse Greeke*. Urbana: University of Illinois Press, 1994.

Barkan, Leonard. 'What Did Shakespeare Read?', in *The Cambridge Companion to Shakespeare*, Margreta de Grazia and Stanley Wells (eds.). Cambridge: Cambridge University Press, 2001, pp. 31–47.

Bate, Jonathan. *Shakespeare and Ovid*. Oxford: Clarendon Press, 1993.

Bullough, Geoffrey. *Narrative and Dramatic Sources of Shakespeare*, 8 vols. London: Routledge and Kegan Paul, 1957–75.

Burrow, Colin. 'Shakespeare and Humanistic Culture', in *Shakespeare and the Classics*, Charles Martindale and A.B. Taylor (eds.). Cambridge: Cambridge University Press, 2004, pp.9–27.

Charlton, Kenneth. *Education in Renaissance England*. London: Routledge and Kegan Paul, 1965.

Gillespie, Stuart, ed. *Shakespeare's Books: A Dictionary of Shakespeare's Sources*. London: Continuum, 2004.

Grafton, Anthony and Lisa Jardine. *From Humanism to the Humanities*. Cambridge: Cambridge University Press, 1986.

Hampton, Timothy. *Writing from History: The Rhetoric of Exemplarity in Renaissance Literature*. Ithaca, NY: Cornell University Press, 1990.

Kraye, Jill, ed. *The Cambridge Companion to Renaissance Humanism*. Cambridge: Cambridge University Press, 1996.

Mack, Peter. *Renaissance Rhetoric: Theory and Practice*. Cambridge: Cambridge University Press, 2002.

Miola, Robert. *Shakespeare's Reading*. Oxford: Oxford University Press, 2000.

Muir, Kenneth. *The Sources of Shakespeare's Plays*. New Haven: Yale University Press, 1978.

Whitaker, Virgil K. *Shakespeare's Use of Learning: An Inquiry into the Growth of His Mind and Art*. San Marino: Huntington Library, 1953.

Zwicker, Steven N. 'Habits of Reading and Early Modern Literary Culture', in *The Cambridge History of Early Modern English Literature*, David Loewenstein and Janel Mueller (eds.). Cambridge: Cambridge University Press, 2006, pp. 170–98.

3

H. R. WOUDHUYSEN

Shakespeare's writing: from manuscript to print

Most contemporary audiences know that films need stars and money; directors, producers and script writers also play some sort of a part. But how many audiences actually know or care what the 'best boy' does or even how long it takes to make a film? In late sixteenth-century and early seventeenth-century England, general or popular knowledge of how plays reached the stage may well have been just as limited. It is probably a mistake to suppose that audiences or readers had a strong sense of the processes by which plays came into existence, were licensed and realized on the stage, and under what circumstances they were transmitted to the page: these may have been matters of relative or of complete indifference to them.

Like any mass-market commercial enterprise, the pre-Civil War theatre was not static: it sprang to life in the later 1580s and continued developing and changing right up to the closing of the theatres in 1642. This makes generalizing about writing and theatrical and publishing practices particularly difficult: what happened in the 1590s, say, may well have borne no relation to what went on in the 1630s and vice versa. Similarly, the surviving evidence is very limited, and it is dangerous to draw firm conclusions about one part of it from another. For example, the entrepreneur Philip Henslowe's 'diary', an enormously important and valuable set of accounts for 1592–1603 that survives with a mass of associated documentary material at Dulwich College in south London, reveals a great deal about what went on in his theatrical empire at the Rose theatre and elsewhere. But Henslowe's record of his activity changed during the course of the period for which the accounts survive: he stopped listing daily receipts for plays and instead left details of advances for buying plays, properties and costumes, and of payments for licensing plays and to the players. Furthermore, in many ways Henslowe's interest in the entertainment business was exceptional – he was also employed at court – and it is unsafe to extrapolate from his surviving records to what went on in the rest of the profession during the whole period of its greatest activity.

The history of the study of the other extant theatrical documents of the period shows a similar sort of wish to generalize on the basis of scanty and very partial evidence. Although most of the individual surviving manuscripts of plays from the period have been catalogued, described and edited, what they actually represent has been much debated. Broad categories for these manuscripts – authorial 'foul papers', scribal 'prompt books', non-theatrical scribal copies – have been established, but they have also been questioned. Notoriously, those manuscripts are especially hard to date, their authorship may well be uncertain and the companies for which they were produced may not be definitely identifiable. The example of the manuscript of *Sir Thomas More*, three pages of which are thought to be in Shakespeare's hand, springs to mind as posing many problems of this kind: it is a rich source of information about all sorts of contemporary practices of commissioning, collaborative composition, revision, licensing and censorship, but it is also in the end almost by definition an exceptional case, and generalizing on the basis of its uncertain and much-disputed evidence is hazardous.

To a great extent the same goes for the surviving printed texts. At least these can usually be dated fairly securely, but what they represent may still be uncertain. Again, the desire to establish neat categories for dramatic printed texts has advanced general understanding of the subject: there are 'good' and 'bad' quartos; like plays in Shakespeare's First Folio (1623), the 'good' may derive from 'foul paper' or from 'prompt book' manuscripts. (See Chapter 5.) But what exactly the 'bad' quartos represent or even how the texts of the 'good' quartos may relate to what was performed on the stage is disputed. There is no simple model that can describe the relations between different authors or theatre companies and printers or publishers: each case needs to be looked at individually. In a comparable way, different printers found the mechanical tasks of setting and printing plays more or less easy. Although there are limits to our knowledge and the dangers of generalization are always present, it is nevertheless possible to provide a usable picture of theatrical activity by concentrating on what is known about how Shakespeare worked, while recognizing that he too was exceptional in what he wrote and how it reached different audiences.

Authorship and playwriting as a profession

During the sixteenth century, contesting senses began to emerge of what a 'profession' meant. The older idea that a profession was a vocation or calling with a body of knowledge that could be gained only after long training and with a formal qualification was supplemented by the idea that it was what people did to gain their living. In that second sense, Shakespeare was clearly a professional playwright: whether he had an apprenticeship as such, whether he felt the theatre was a vocation or not are matters for argument. But he was more than a playwright: he had other careers – as a poet, an actor, a sharer in his theatre company, and as a man of business and of property – all of them successful and financially rewarding. Authors' earnings during this period are hard to estimate, not least because the actual rewards of patronage are unknown: his relations with the Earl of Southampton (to whom the narrative poems were dedicated) and the Earls of Pembroke (to whom the First Folio was dedicated) remain matters for speculation. It is, however, fairly clear that to make any sort of decent living from the pen alone required hard work. When Thomas Heywood in *The English Traveller* (1633) claimed to have had 'either an entire hand or at the least a main finger' in 220 plays, he may have been exaggerating, but the careers of other writers of the period suggest that a degree of hyperactivity was essential to survive as a professional writer. Heywood's fifty years as a writer compare well with Shakespeare's twenty-five, during which he was involved in the writing of around forty plays and in the production of three substantial volumes of poems. Equally, the collected works of Jonson, Middleton, Greene, Dekker, Ford, Massinger, and Beaumont and Fletcher suggest how busy authors had to be to make any sort of living, but they also indicate that other playwrights – Peele, Kyd, Webster – may not have lived entirely by their pens, although the question of lost works hovers over this subject.

The need to earn a decent living undoubtedly spurred an author's productivity. Yet a concern with authorship, exemplified by Shakespeare's standing as the paradigm of the individual author, may have passed the notice of contemporary playgoers. Since original advertisements for the performance of plays have not survived, it is impossible to judge how much prominence was given to naming authors as part of a play's marketing. Early theatregoers rarely mention who wrote the plays they saw, and the full extent of the collaborative nature of authorship for the popular theatre was probably as unknown then as the correct writer credits were in Hollywood's golden age. Somewhere between a half and two-thirds of vernacular plays written for the popular theatre between 1590 and 1642 appear to have been produced by two or more men in collaboration; figures for the academic drama and for the children's companies point to a far greater reliance on solitary authorship.[1] By its nature, it has been argued, the theatre is a site for collaboration, yet it is remarkable how many marks of individual genius still survive in the texts that have come down to us.

Collaboration was not a fixed and always formal arrangement: it might take many different forms, and a single model for the process by which jointly written plays came into being is not adequate. The original division of a play between two authors, such as that Shakespeare and Fletcher appear to have undertaken with *King Henry VIII*, *The Two Noble Kinsmen* and *Cardenio*, might be supplemented by interventions to complete unfinished plays or to make them actable, to supply the initial plot, additional scenes, dialogue or other material, and to incorporate revisions resulting from the experience of performance. It is quite likely that pairs or teams of writers revised each other's work; they may have been expected to follow a style favoured by the company or the entrepreneur that employed them. Equally, a play might need to be revised for new circumstances as a result of changes to personnel, to meet the wishes of the theatre company for which it was being written, or to adapt it for production in a new location or for a special occasion. On the other hand, common sense suggests that most players and audiences would have wanted plays that were internally coherent and made sense: creaking joints between parts written by different authors, muddled plots and stylistic incongruities make for poor theatre. In the same way, modern teams of writers, film-makers and drama producers strive to create 'artistic' wholes which will satisfy their audiences.

The growing scholarly consensus around Shakespeare's collaborating hand in some early works (*Edward III*, *1 Henry VI*, *Titus Andronicus* and *Sir Thomas More*) with a variety of authors (Peele, Kyd and Nashe in the two histories and the tragedy, and Munday, Heywood, Chettle and Dekker in *More*) has been complemented by arguments about Middleton's original contribution to *Timon of Athens* and about his possible revisions to *Macbeth* and *Measure for Measure*, as well as by speculation about the nature of Shakespeare's links with the unsavoury George Wilkins that gave rise to *Pericles*.[2]

Actors may have had the glamour and been the subject of the salacious stories that went with the theatrical profession, but on the title pages of early play texts names counted – or perhaps some names counted, or at the very least Shakespeare's name counted. Unusually, he must have had the experience of seeing work (poetical as well as theatrical) attributed to him that he knew he had not written: as early as 1594 the anonymous tragedy of *Locrine* was said to have been 'Newly set forth, overseen and corrected by W. S.'

Composition

Henslowe's diary suggests that his writers took between four and six weeks (sometimes fewer) to finish plays, and that preparations before their initial performance took about two weeks. The speed at which plays were written resulted from the need to feed the ravenous appetite for popular entertainment: teams of writers, it is supposed, could write more quickly than individual authors.

One obvious form of collaboration entailed an author supplying the original plot or outline for a play which another author or authors then wrote up. It is probably in this sense that Francis Meres described Anthony Munday in 1598 as 'our best plotter'. Devising plots, like pitching scenarios in the modern cinema, might well have been a separate activity from writing the resulting play. One way of dividing the work of writing might have been to allocate the source book (Holinshed's chronicles or North's Plutarch, for example) from which the plot was taken to one author, while the other worked on material he devised for himself or took from another source. The theatre company or a theatrical entrepreneur may have owned copies of several such source books from which plots could be extracted and lent them out to authors, so that Shakespeare need not have bought or owned copies of the books from which he adapted material.

In writing plays, whether singly or collaboratively, the unit of composition in which dramatists worked might have been the single line, the speech, the role for the character or, quite simply, the comic or tragic element. The most obvious unit might have been the scene, or part of a scene, or the act. The issue should be easy to determine, but this is not quite the case, for it is complicated by arguments about act and scene divisions. Although intervals between acts had been used in private performances, as well as at court, at the Inns of Court and by the children's companies, and in plays written by University Wits, in the popular theatre they seem not to have come into general use until 1607 or later. Acts themselves were not inherent elements in the popular theatre before about 1607.[3]

Yet perhaps scenes and acts were only elements in the story during the composition of plays. One solid piece of evidence survives of an author's defining his hand in a play. Dekker deposed that his part of *Keep the Widow Waking* consisted of 'two sheets of paper containing the first act' along with 'a speech in the last scene of the last act of the Boy who had killed his mother'.[4] In this case, the unit for composition seems not necessarily to have been a discretely identifiable part of a play, such as an act or a scene, so much as the sheet of paper, each sheet consisting when initially folded once of two leaves or four pages. The importance of the sheet is clear from a variety of sources, including Henslowe's diary and the licences of the Masters of the Revels (the official in charge of entertainments at court). This is not to say that the practice of composing plays by the sheet was invariable. In this respect, as in so many others, the so-called Melbourne Manuscript – a folded sheet of an autograph play attributed to James Shirley, discovered in 1985 among the Coke family papers at Melbourne Hall in Derbyshire – provides ambiguous evidence.[5] The writing on the sheet begins in what is clearly the middle of a scene, and it is not entirely certain that the scene ends with the fourth and final page. As the scribe reached the last page he wanted to get as much material in as possible, with the result that the page looks distinctly crowded: presumably the scribe did not want to start a new sheet. The Melbourne Manuscript suggests that the sheet as a unit played some part in the play's evolution.

The manuscript

Whether working alone or collaborating, at some stage the playwright had to put pen to paper. It is possible that the company or the entrepreneur supplied the playwrights with paper, which would have been relatively expensive, in loose sheets. Authors might fold the sheets to produce inner and outer margins for their writing: mistakes often found in the form and position of speech prefixes and some stage directions may have occurred because dramatists tended to add them outside the folded margins after the main dialogue had been written. The common handwriting of the period was the secretary hand which had its own distinctive forms, abbreviations (especially the tilde [~] for omitted *m* and *n*) and easily confused letters (such as *p* and *x*, *r* and *v*, and so on). Stage directions, speech prefixes and names of people and of places were generally written in an italic hand which would usually have required a pen cut differently from the one used for secretary hand. Writing with a handcut pen with handmade ink on handmade paper of varying quality and smoothness was not an easy business. A sloping desk with a cloth cover was considered the ideal place for writing, but it could be carried out more or less anywhere with a solid surface such as a table or, with a penner (a portable pen-and-ink set) and a writing box, wherever was convenient; the private study might give way to much more public places, such as the theatre or the tavern.

In addition to their source books, dramatists may well have written with note- or table- or commonplace books beside them.[6] These might contain anything from odd words to striking images or sayings, to whole speeches: Webster's use of second-hand ideas and quotations has been explored in depth.[7] The initial process of composition might be relatively slow or quite rapid, needing much, heavy revision or very little. 'His mind and hand went together', John Heminges and Henry Condell wrote of Shakespeare in the First Folio, 'And what he thought, he uttered with that easiness, that we have scarce received from him a blot in his papers' – to which Ben Jonson replied, 'Would he had blotted a thousand.' Heminges and Condell might not have realized that the manuscripts from which they worked were not Shakespeare's first drafts, but his (or someone else's) fair copies of them. Yet there is evidence from the quartos of some of his plays (*Love's Labour's Lost*, *Romeo and Juliet*, *Henry V*, among others) that Shakespeare wrote and rewrote passages, sometimes neglecting to signal clearly which version was to be cancelled.

Authorial drafts were called foul papers or foul copy to distinguish them from the recopied fair version. 'I promised to bring you the last scene', Robert Daborne wrote to Henslowe in November 1613, 'which that you may see finished I send you the foul sheet and the fair I was writing.' Surviving manuscripts showing an author at work on a literary composition of any kind are extremely rare, and the existence of examples of theatrical foul papers as opposed to fair copies revised in the process of transcription or later has been disputed.[8] Theatrical foul papers might contain deletions and revisions (first and subsequent ideas), changes in the forms of speech prefixes (including the naming of actors expected to play the part) and stage directions which were not detailed and specific; even exits and entrances might not be fully articulated. These are some of the indications said to be characteristic of foul papers; the traditional outline of manuscript production suggests that these irregularities were ironed out when the papers were copied for the production of the prompt book, the company's official record of the play. In this model, Shakespeare's foul papers were generally sent to be printed in the early quartos, while the prompt book was kept carefully by the company and was eventually used in the production of the texts for the First Folio. Again, this two-manuscript model for dramatic works has been challenged and closely interrogated.[9]

How foul were foul papers? If they were too foul, too chaotic and difficult to read, they would scarcely supply adequate evidence for a company or an entrepreneur that a play in fact existed in an actable form. They would also prove a hindrance for licensing by the Master of the Revels, who was expected to read and approve them (or not) for performance. Similarly, the foulest of foul papers might prove too illegible to be copied for the prompt book. There was therefore some incentive for dramatists not to send their first drafts to the company they hoped would buy the book of the play, or that had commissioned it. Instead, they might be expected to send fairer copies which the dramatist had tidied up and corrected from his drafts. A busy playwright or a company in need of a workable script might well turn to a professional scribe to make a fair copy of the foul papers before or in addition to the preparation of the prompt book.

Yet if the foul papers were reasonably tidy in themselves, there seems to have been no reason to suppose that they could not have served as the prompt book. Its function and status are just as warmly disputed as such other 'technical' terms as 'foul papers', 'bad quartos' and so on. Shakespeare's theatre recognized the role a prompter played in a play's performance, and it would seem sensible that the prompter would have a copy of the text from which he could follow its action. Yet what are taken to be surviving examples of prompt books differ widely in their evident purpose: they are by no means consistent in their marking of stage directions, especially entrances and exits, or the use of props. Furthermore, if the prompt book represents a set of instructions for the recreation of a performance of a play, its often great length and the presence of extraneous elements, such as non-authorial comic material, remains puzzling.

The prompt book was without doubt a valuable property and was apparently prepared with some care from material that ultimately derived from the author's foul papers. In turning the foul papers into the prompt book, theatrical companies might well have used an in-house professional such as Edward Knight, book-keeper to the King's Men. It might also have been the book-keeper's task to prepare two other items connected with the play's production. All or some of the actors, especially those playing the principal characters, would have been supplied with their parts or their roles in what may have actually been a roll – only one example of such a role survives from the popular theatre of Shakespeare's time – which may have contained cue prompts. (See Chapter 5.) The second item is better attested, but its precise function remains disputed. The 'plot' of the play was written on a sheet of paper, mounted on pasteboard and apparently hung up on a peg: its scene-by-scene account of the play's dramatic action was copied in two columns and included actors' names as well as their roles. Although these 'plots' – of which seven survive from the 1590s and early 1600s – supply valuable evidence concerning the theatre of the period, their significance remains unclear.[10]

Nevertheless, these two kinds of document bear additional witness to the theatre as a site for the production of manuscripts related to its work. Were manuscripts prepared for circulation outside the theatre? Greg argued that it was not until 1624 and the scandal of Middleton's *A Game at Chess* that private transcripts of public plays began to be produced.[11] Yet the professional copying of literary works in manuscript was well established by the 1590s, and, even if plays might not have qualified as 'literary works' in the eyes of some contemporaries, it is reasonable to assume that private individuals sought out copies of plays they had seen acted; so, too, theatre companies or their individual members saw that supplying manuscript copies provided a way of supplementing their income. The career of the poet and professional scribe or scrivener Ralph Crane, who was extensively involved in the preparation of private transcripts for sale on behalf of authors and, apparently, on commission for himself, supplies some evidence for the form this sort of activity might have taken. Crane had been working for authors in the theatre from as early as 1618, when he prepared a copy of Jonson's masque *Pleasure Reconciled to Virtue*, and went on to supply the printer's copy that lies behind various dramatic texts, including five or six of Shakespeare's plays for the First Folio, as well as Webster's *The Duchess of Malfi*. A great deal has been found out about Crane's activities and about his distinctive scribal practices (parentheses, elisions, 'massed entry' stage directions and so on), but there is no reason to think that the sorts of copying service that Crane supplied could not have been undertaken twenty or even thirty years before he came on the scene.[12]

Revision

If theatrical manuscripts had a commercial value, it is possible that they would proliferate by hand in the same way that poems, letters, tracts and other documents did. London audiences demanded a high turnover of new plays supplemented by frequent revivals – a well-organized system of copying and storing manuscripts would have been an essential feature of the theatre companies' business. Furthermore, when companies, for whatever reason, went on tour outside London or in Europe, they might well have needed to take with them copies of the plays they were to perform. All this argues against a simple two-manuscript model for theatrical production. In the same way, authors almost certainly kept manuscript copies of their own plays – they might not have been the cleanest or fairest of copies, but they were probably usable for the purposes of revision.

No subject has attracted more attention in the last twenty or so years than the question of the authorial revision of plays of this period. There are at least three reasons for this. First, if Shakespeare did revise some of his plays and poems, it undermines his image as a spontaneous genius. If revision shows authorial rethinking, then it usually does so in the light of theatrical experience: therefore it is the result of collaboration of one kind or another. Second, a theory of revision chimes with ideas about textual instability and indeterminacy. If, for example, quarto and Folio *King Lear* definitely are different plays, it becomes impossible to say which is the 'real' one, indeed which is to be read first. The certainty of a single conflated *King Lear* can be replaced by two or more texts, offering the reader distinctive works in the process of becoming, rather than a single finished and evolved masterpiece. In this uncertain textual world, readers can play a significant part in the selection and even creation of the work(s). Facsimile and hypertext editions allow them to choose their own texts and eliminate – so it is argued – the allegedly intrusive role of the editor.

The third reason for interest in revision relates to a desire to understand more about Shakespeare's creative process. In the past, Shakespeare was thought to have been indifferent to the publishing of his plays. For one thing, since the play texts belonged to the theatre company, he had no financial stake in selling them, except as a sharer of that company. In addition, he was believed to have intended his plays exclusively for the theatre, where they were subject to continual change, as a result of suggestions from the actors, for example, or a change of performance venue. But the revision theory allows for the possibility that these changes might represent Shakespeare's second or even third thoughts. Thus texts once thought to reveal nothing more than the vagaries of the playhouse and printing office are now being subjected to minute bibliographical and critical analysis in the expectation that they will provide insights to the process of Shakespeare's writing.

What were play texts?

Shakespeare's plays were published (made public) by being performed, but around half of them were also published during his lifetime in print – the other half appearing in the First Folio after his death. The editions of his plays and of his poems that he might have seen were produced mainly in quarto, with a few in octavo: in a quarto book, the sheet of paper on which the text is printed is folded twice to produce a square-shaped book, in an octavo it is folded four times to produce a smaller, pocket-sized volume. Quartos of the plays, such as *Othello* in 1622, went on being produced after Shakespeare's death and after the First Folio's publication. Although there seems little doubt that the texts of the narrative poems *Venus and Adonis* (1593) and *The Rape of Lucrece* (1594), with their signed dedications to the Earl of Southampton and the use of inscriptional capitals (large and small) for proper names in the later poem, were published on Shakespeare's behalf and with his approval, the status of his other poems, notably the Sonnets (1609) and of the plays is disputed. In the case of the Sonnets, which have several unresolved textual cruces of a kind not found in the narrative poems, the argument revolves around whether their publication was authorized by Shakespeare or whether the volume was in effect pirated by Thomas Thorpe, who is usually identified with the 'T. T.' of the book's enigmatic dedication. There are strong arguments for and against Shakespeare's hand in the book's publication, arguments that have also involved doubts about his authorship of the poem *A Lover's Complaint* that accompanied the Sonnets.[13]

The status of the play quartos (and octavos) is equally still a matter of dispute. When Heminges and Condell told 'the great variety of readers' of the First Folio that 'where (before) you were abused with divers stolen, and surreptitious copies, maimed, and deformed by the frauds and stealths of injurious impostors, that exposed them: even those, are now offered to your view cured, and perfect of their limbs', did they intend to condemn the texts of all the quartos or just some of them? During the course of the last century, scholarly opinion moved from thinking that all quartos were stolen and surreptitious to defining a particular group as being 'bad quartos': they were short, mangled parts of the text (when compared against 'good quartos' or the Folio), sometimes included material from other literary works or just obvious comic banter and rarely seemed performable. Such 'bad quartos' could be found among Shakespeare's plays (*Romeo and Juliet* in 1597, *Henry V* in 1600, *The Merry Wives of Windsor* in 1602 and *Hamlet* in 1603) and elsewhere. How these 'bad quartos' came into being remains uncertain: various theories have been put forward, including the use of shorthand and the idea that they are, in effect, Shakespeare's first drafts (rather blotted) of his plays.[14] Most scholars tend to accept that they were in fact memorial reconstructions by one or more members of the theatre company that put them on – this would explain why some scenes in which those characters appear seem better remembered (when compared against 'good quartos' or the Folio) than others. Yet why it was thought worthwhile to try to reconstruct the plays from memory to sell to a stationer with all the attendant risk of accusations of piracy and of exposure is still by no means clear. Nor has anyone managed to explain convincingly the circumstances under which the plays were reconstructed, although it has often been said that these were versions produced for the provinces in time of plague when companies toured the country, forced to leave London without their prompt books.

The badness of the 'bad quartos' has been challenged, so that they are often now known as 'abbreviated' or 'suspect' texts. Although their dialogue and speeches are generally thought to be unreliable witnesses to what Shakespeare wrote, some scholars have argued that their stage directions ('*Enter the Ghost in his night-gown*') reveal something about contemporary performance practices. This calls into question what contemporary readers thought they were getting when they read one of those quartos. If it approximated in some distant way to what they saw on the stage – a corrupt version of a play, but one that could be performed within a few hours – then what do the texts of the 'good quartos' and of the Folio represent? A dozen or so of those 'good' texts are, by most modern standards, too long to be acted within the performance times that scholars generally attribute to the contemporary stage. Yet the contemporary appetite for lengthy sermons might suggest that some audiences had a highly developed ability to concentrate for long stretches of time; fully performed texts of plays lasting several hours may have caused them few problems.

One answer that has been put forward to the problem of the widely differing length of plays in different versions is that several of the 'good quartos' and of the plays in the Folio represent some sort of 'reading' texts for those who enjoyed the shorter versions actually put on the stage.[15] In this account, the status and function of those quartos is called further into question. To many editors and scholars even the 'good quartos' appear to be poorly printed, cheap and ephemeral items, books of low status and (comparatively) little merit or importance, sent by the company to the printers when the play's peak of commercial, performing worth had passed. The alternative view holds that the quartos were published as part of a coherent marketing strategy in relatively expensive formats and that their typography often shows a real concern to present the text in as careful and attractive a form as possible.[16] A test case for some of these arguments might be the 1608 quarto of *King Lear*. Originally thought to be a 'bad quarto' because its text appeared so garbled and so poorly printed, the intensive investigation of its printing history has shown the lengths to which Nicholas Okes' compositors went to try to get the text right and to do a decent job of setting and printing their first ever play. Equally, the publishing history of the early Shakespeare quartos shows that there was a considerable market for them. Shakespeare's may not have been the most popular plays of the period in print, but his full name was attached to the work of others, such as *A Yorkshire Tragedy* in 1608, 'Written by W. Shakespeare', to make it more saleable. After his death, in 1619 William Jaggard (already a guilty party in the publication of *The Passionate Pilgrim* in 1599) and Thomas Pavier put together a collection of quartos featuring plays by or associated with Shakespeare, supplying several of them with false dates, such as *King Lear* '1608'.

Conclusion

If the certainties that hedged in the investigation of Shakespeare's writing during much of the last century seem largely to have disappeared, it could be argued that there has been some compensation for their loss by a new willingness to think afresh about what texts – manuscript and printed – represent. A growing sense that the production of theatrical texts needs to be looked at within the broader context of the entertainment industry of the time has been complemented by a deeper understanding of the ways in which the physical forms texts take determine and articulate their meanings. The evidence of the narrative poems shows that Shakespeare took some interest in the appearance of his writings in print; the challenge for future scholars will be to understand the relationship between the printed versions of the plays, versions which their author must have seen and perhaps owned, and his own dramatic productions.

NOTES

1 Gerald Eades Bentley, *The Profession of Dramatist in Shakespeare's Time* (Princeton, NJ: Princeton University Press, 1971), p. 199.
2 Brian Vickers, *Shakespeare, Co-Author: A Historical Study of Five Collaborative Plays* (Oxford: Oxford University Press, 2004).
3 Gary Taylor, 'The Structure of Performance: Act-Intervals in the London Theatres, 1576–1642', in Taylor and John Jowett, *Shakespeare Reshaped 1606–1623* (Oxford: Clarendon Press, 1993), pp. 3–50.
4 C. J. Sisson, *Lost Plays of Shakespeare's Age* (Cambridge: Cambridge University Press, 1936), p. 110.
5 British Library, Loan MS 98.
6 Peter Stallybrass, Roger Chartier, J. Franklin Mowery and Heather Wolfe, 'Hamlet's Tables and the Technologies of Writing in Renaissance England', *Shakespeare Quarterly*, 55 (2004), 379–419.
7 R. W. Dent, *John Webster's Borrowing* (Berkeley, Los Angeles: University of California Press, 1960).
8 Grace Ioppolo, *Dramatists and Their Manuscripts in the Age of Shakespeare, Jonson, Middleton and Heywood* (London: Routledge, 2006), esp. pp. 75–99.
9 W. W. Greg, *The Shakespeare First Folio: Its Bibliographical and Textual History* (Oxford: Clarendon Press, 1955), pp. 106–37, 141–2; Paul Werstine, 'Narratives about Printed Shakespeare Texts: "Foul Papers" and "Bad" Quartos', *Shakespeare Quarterly*, 41 (1990), 65–86.
10 Simon Palfrey and Tiffany Stern, *Shakespeare in Parts* (Oxford: Oxford University Press, 2007); David Bradley, *From Text to Performance in the Elizabethan Theatre: Preparing the Play for the Stage* (Cambridge: Cambridge University Press, 1992).
11 W. W. Greg, *The Shakespeare First Folio* (Oxford: Oxford University Press, pp. 85–6).
12 Ibid., pp. 189–95.
13 *Shakespeare's Sonnets*, ed. Katherine Duncan-Jones (London: Arden Shakespeare, 1997); Brian Vickers, *Shakespeare, 'A Lover's Complaint', and John Davies of Hereford* (Cambridge: Cambridge University Press, 2007).
14 Laurie Maguire, *Shakespearean 'Suspect' Texts: The 'Bad' Quartos and their Contexts* (Cambridge: Cambridge University Press, 1996).
15 Lukas Erne, *Shakespeare as Literary Dramatist* (Cambridge: Cambridge University Press, 2003).
16 Cf. H. R. Woudhuysen, 'The Foundations of Shakespeare's Text', *Proceedings of the British Academy*, 125 (2004), 69–100.

READING LIST

Bawcutt, N. W., ed. *The Control and Censorship of Caroline Drama: The Records of Sir Henry Herbert, Master of the Revels 1623–73*. Oxford: Clarendon Press, 1996.

Blayney, Peter W. M. *The Texts of 'King Lear' and Their Origins*, vol. I: *Nicholas Okes and the First Quarto*. Cambridge: Cambridge University Press, 1982.

Carson, Neil. *A Companion to Henslowe's Diary*. Cambridge: Cambridge University Press, 1988.

Dawson, Giles E. and Laetitia Kennedy-Skipton. *Elizabethan Handwriting 1500–1650: A Guide to the Reading of Documents and Manuscripts*. London: Faber and Faber, 1968; Shopwyke Hall, Chichester, Sussex: Phillimore &Co., 1981.

Finlay, Michael. *Western Writing Implements in the Age of the Quill Pen*. Wetherall, Carlisle, Cumbria: Plains Books, 1990.

Foakes, R. A., and R. T. Rickert, eds. *Henslowe's Diary*. Cambridge: Cambridge University Press, 1961.

Greg, W.W. *A Bibliography of the English Printed Drama to the Restoration*, 4 vols. London: The Bibliographical Society, 1939–59.

Dramatic Documents from the Elizabethan Playhouses, 2 vols. Oxford: Clarendon Press, 1931.

English Literary Autographs, 1550–1650, 3 parts. Oxford: Oxford University Press, 1925–32.

Greg, W.W., ed. *Henslowe Papers*. London: A. H. Bullen, 1907.

Howard-Hill, T. H., ed. *Shakespeare and 'Sir Thomas More': Essays on the Play and Its Shakespearian Interest*. Cambridge: Cambridge University Press, 1989.

Jowett, John. *Shakespeare and Text*. Oxford: Oxford University Press, 2007.

Lesser, Zachary. *Renaissance Drama and the Politics of Publication: Readings in the English Book Trade*. Cambridge: Cambridge University Press, 2004.

Masten, Jeffrey. *Textual Intercourse: Collaboration, Authorship, and Sexualities in Renaissance Drama*. New York: Cambridge University Press, 1997.

Osley, A.S., ed. *Scribes and Sources: Handbook of the Chancery Hand in the Sixteenth Century*. London and Boston, MA: Faber and Faber, 1980.

Wells, Stanley and Gary Taylor. *William Shakespeare: A Textual Companion*. Oxford, Oxford University Press, 1987.

4

TIFFANY STERN

The theatre of Shakespeare's London

Actors

Hamlet, excited at having just successfully extemporized a verse, turns to his friend Horatio, asking 'Would not this ... get me a fellowship in a cry of players, sir?' Horatio is less impressed. He thinks it would win Hamlet only 'half a share', but Hamlet is adamant: 'A whole one, I' (3.2.253–7). The exchange works on a number of levels. Hamlet is delighted that he has the improvisational skill of an actor; the irony is, of course, that Hamlet is actually able to 'act' only in this performative sense, while in reality, as he recognizes elsewhere, he can merely 'unpack my heart with words' (2.2.563). But the conversation also references the structure of an early modern acting company. 'Cries' or troupes were set up by 'sharers' who contributed to them two separate but equally important qualities: acting talent and money. Thus Hamlet thinks his skills alone should earn him a 'share' in a company, while Horatio thinks they merit only half that right.

Shakespeare himself was a full 'sharer' in a company known first as the Lord Chamberlain's Men (1594–6; 1597–1603) and later as the King's Men (1603–1642). This meant that Shakespeare was bound to be performance-focused, for it was at the end of a day's playing that the money taken at the doors of entrance was 'parcel'd out upon the sharing-board' – placed upon a table and distributed among the sharers.[1] And, as theatrical income was specifically linked to performance, then if plague closed the theatre, or fire destroyed it, Shakespeare would make no money, and nor would anyone else. So there was seldom any 'spare' money in the theatre – which explains why no performers were provided who did not act (there were no understudies), no conceptualizers were acquired who did not organize performances (there were no directors, only prompters) and few theatrical activities took place for which there was no financial return (there seems to have been very little in the way of group rehearsal).

Sharers sometimes kept and trained apprentices: young boy players to whom they taught the art of acting. As 'playing' was not a formalized profession, an actor who wanted apprentices had to acquire and maintain membership of a professional guild as, for example, a grocer, goldsmith or carpenter; he would then technically take on apprentices in his trade, though he would in fact teach them to act. So John Heminges, one of the actors responsible for the publication of Shakespeare's First Folio, took on a number of apprentice 'grocers' during his acting career.[2] These apprentices performed not just the roles of boys like Mote in *Love's Labour's Lost* and Arthur in *King John*, but also those of women, a fact that leads to a certain amount of metatheatrical jesting on Shakespeare's part. When Cleopatra imagines how she will one day be represented on stage, she fears to 'see / Some squeaking Cleopatra boy my greatness / I'th' posture of a whore' (5.2.215–18), a line that derives its humour and ironic poignancy from the fact that it will indeed be spoken by a boy.

Though 'hirelings' – players paid by the week – were sometimes acquired, scenes were, when possible, simply swollen with non-speaking characters ('mutes') performed by people already working for the troupe: 'gatherers', who collected entrance money from the audience, and 'tiremen', who helped dress the actors backstage. Hamlet views the silent onlookers of his tragedy as 'but mutes or audience to this act' (5.2.277); earlier in the play 'genuine' mutes have been requested by a stage direction which asks '*The poisoner, with some two or three mutes*' to '[*come*] *in again*' (3.2.122 SD). It is sometimes suggested that Shakespeare's habit of increasing the number and complexity of his crowd scenes towards the latter half of his plays reveals the fact that more 'mute' actors are available when the gatherers have completed their job.[3]

As Shakespeare wrote largely for a group of actors whom he knew well, he shaped his characterizations to the skills of his colleagues. For this reason, he regularly repeats character types. The fool with a beautiful singing voice, for instance, is to be found in several of his plays – he is Touchstone in *As You Like It*, Feste in *Twelfth Night* and the wise Fool in *King Lear*, because Shakespeare is writing for Robert Armin (c. 1563–1615), an actor, lute-player, singer and professional fool, who joined the company in 1600. A new verse for Armin's 'clown' song sung at the end of *Twelfth Night*, with its chorus of 'the rain it raineth every day' (5.1.376–95), is provided for the Fool to sing in *King Lear* (3.2.72–5), suggesting that Shakespeare makes a positive effort to link both roles. One play, that is to say, gains resonance from its gesture towards another: *Lear* and *Twelfth Night* share a moment of tragic vision with each other and with the knowing spectators in ways that confound distinctions between comedy and tragedy. Other roles that he wrote are also clearly shaped to the skills of a single actor, and, again, the connections between such roles erode the separation between one play and another. A talkative and gullible old man who thinks he is smarter than he is can be seen in Polonius (*Hamlet*), Brabanzio (*Othello*), Duncan (*Macbeth*) and Menenius (*Coriolanus*); an attractive, wily, charismatic villain appears as Iago (*Othello*), Edmund (*King Lear*) and Iachimo (*Cymbeline*). As soon as an actor with a known range of roles stepped onto the stage, then, he brought with him elements from the other characters he had played that Shakespeare could manipulate and complicate.

Though the term 'typecasting' was not to come into use until the twentieth century, the repeated characters written for a regular group of performers with individually identifiable skills suggests the very way Shakespeare conceived of a theatrical company. When Hamlet meets a group of players, he knows from experience what part each will play, though he has not seen them perform for a year: one is 'He that plays the King' (2.2.308); another is 'the adventurous Knight' (2.2.309). He identifies the type of each member of the group in front of him, joshing 'the lady' that 'she' has grown taller over the last year (2.2.408–10); he even guesses at the stories that will attend on the players:

> the Lover shall not sigh gratis, the Humorous Man shall end his part in peace, the Clown shall make those laugh whose lungs are tickled o'th' sear, and the Lady shall say her mind freely. (2.2.310–13)

Hardly surprisingly, when Shakespeare created roles it was with a limited number of character types in mind, representative of the acting skills of his company. His texts in the form in which they were first printed often alternate, in speech prefixes and stage directions, between using a generic name (like 'Queen') and a character name (like 'Gertrude'), suggesting that Shakespeare probably wrote for 'types' found in his troupe and individualized them only later. Instances of 'types' in more than one play include 'braggart' (referred to in the 1603 *Hamlet* as an alternative title for 'Osric' and in *Love's Labour's Lost* as an alternative title for Don Adriano) and 'Old man' (the title for Leonato's brother in *Much Ado About Nothing* and for the person who accompanies the newly blinded Gloucester in *King Lear*). Sometimes only the type is ever supplied, explaining 'names' such as 'Nurse' in *Romeo and Juliet* and 'Fool' in *Lear*.[4]

Different plays were put on every day in the early modern theatre: hence the commotion when Middleton's politically provocative *A Game at Chess* was performed for an unprecedented nine days in a row. As a result, actors needed to have a method for putting on up to forty plays (some old, several new) in a season, with minimal preparation. Sharers in a company would hear a reading of a new play given by its author, partly to decide whether or not to accept the text, and partly to learn the tale it told; so they – but not other actors – did at least know the story in which they were to feature and the staging issues it raised. After that, they would each be given texts known as 'parts' or 'rolls' containing the speeches they were to speak, each speech preceded by a 'cue' of one to three words. No actor received a full copy of the play, because paper and scribes were prohibitively expensive. These 'parts' of plays would then be learnt by heart, a process known as 'study' or sometimes, when a helper was involved, 'instruction'. This is fictionalized by Shakespeare, whose mechanicals in *A Midsummer Night's Dream* prepare their play in ways remarkably similar to those described in account books of the period. Just as in York the actors would 'haue ther part*es* fair wryt-ten & delyu*er*ed theym [in tyme] soo that they may haue leysure to ku*n*ne [learn] euery one his part', so in *A Midsummer Night's Dream* actors are given their parts ('here are your parts') but are issued with strict instructions to 'con them by tomorrow night' before they meet to rehearse (1.2.82); after this they have only one brief and unfinished collective rehearsal before they put on the performance itself.[5]

As a result, the part was a very important unit of a play, for it was the text that actors knew best; their characterizations were created by working outward from their individual lines and cues rather than from the narrative. In 'study' and 'instruction' alike, actors would read their parts looking to identify their 'passions' and to isolate the particular transitional moment when one 'passion' yielded to another. So important were the passions to playing that the poet and divine Samuel Nicholson asks an actor, 'Tell me whose person did you passionate?' Acting at the time was even sometimes called 'passionating', and when Hamlet wants to have 'a taste' of a player's 'quality', it is 'a passionate speech' (2.2.414) that he demands.[6] So one reason Shakespeare's speeches involve such abrupt switches of emotion – Macbeth's 'Is this a dagger?' speech shifts over a few lines from confused mental torment to purposeful resolution, 'I go, and it is done' (2.1.62) – is to allow the players to illustrate their skills at transitioning from one passion to another.

Once isolated, the passions also needed to be manifested in themselves, as did other more technical features of the writing: the verse and the prose, the rhetorical tropes, the pauses. For all of this, actors needed to decide which words in their text to choose and emphasize (in the language of the time, to determine their 'pronunciation') and which telling gestures to use to accompany them (in the language of the time, to determine their 'action'). When Polonius (*Hamlet*) says that the player's text has been 'well spoken, with good accent and good discretion' (2.2.446–7), he is praising the actor's choice of verbal and gestural emphasis; when Titus (*Titus Andronicus*) laments, 'How can I grace my talk, / Wanting a hand to give it action', he is bemoaning the fact that, having cut off one of his hands, he is incapable of illustrating his lamentation with the proper gestures (5.2.17–18).

Though technicalities of production were rehearsed *en masse*, generally under the auspices of the prompter – who was in charge of the practical side of performance – there is no indication that sharers were concerned with the narrative arc of a play; hirelings, unlikely to have attended 'readings', certainly were not.[7] But in many ways this was positive, for actors became focused on their characters as created by the words they spoke rather than by context. A potentially tragic character, like Ford in *The Merry Wives of Windsor*, might not be conscious of the fact – and so would not play the fact – that the story around him is a comedy, allowing for a broader range of interpretation within a single play than is often found today. This also goes some way towards explaining Shakespeare's ability to create individual characters with their own habits of rhetoric: Hamlet's confusion of 'soul' and 'mind' is a particular character note, speaking of his over-rationalized, yet religiously murky world – 'Since my dear Soule was mistress of her choice' (3.2.56); 'it offends me to the soul' (3.2.7–8). For Shakespeare, separate parts would have constituted a vital way of conceiving of a text in the first place: he was an actor who wrote in the knowledge that his plays, like all plays, would be disseminated in part-form; he constructed his texts accordingly.

Theatres

London was a small, walled city and could not, until the late sixteenth century, supply enough theatre-loving people to make up a daily audience for a permanent playhouse. Only in 1567 was a fixed theatre, the Red Lion, constructed, and it did not last long. But everything changed in 1576 when an enormous round theatre, called 'the Theatre', was built in Shoreditch (just outside the city walls) by the ex-actor and entrepreneur James Burbage. The Theatre, with its shape and name gesturing towards a classicism that the wood and thatch of the structure scarcely merited, was to stand for over twenty years; it was so successful that copies of it sprang up around the city.

One of several reasons for the popularity of the Theatre was James Burbage's talented family. His son Cuthbert was an excellent manager and theatre-keeper; his son Richard was a superb actor. Shakespeare, who started writing for the Theatre in about 1594, originally penned many of his star roles for the 'delightful Proteus' (the god of shape-shifting) Richard Burbage, who was famous for his spectacular acting range; these were played so masterfully that when Richard died it was assumed that the plays written for him had died too. As an elegy lamented, 'young Hamlet, old Hieronimo / kind Lear, the greivèd Moor, and more beside, / that lived in him have now for ever died'.[8]

Much of London was in the hands of puritans, so all playhouses, the Theatre included, were constructed in areas known as 'the Liberties' which were outside the jurisdiction of the lord mayor and not bound by London laws. Some Liberties were sites of former monasteries within the city, but most were outside the London walls or opposite them on the south side of the Thames. Indeed, the Lord Chamberlain's Men found themselves moving from the northern Liberty that housed the Theatre to the Liberty of Southwark on the south bank of the Thames in 1599.[9] This was because their entire playhouse had to be relocated. The Theatre had been built on a rented field; so when the owner of the field decided not to let his property any longer, the company found themselves without legal access to the site of their stage. The moment seared itself in Shakespeare's memory, for in *The Merry Wives of Windsor* he has Ford describe misplaced love as 'a fair house built on another man's ground, so that I have lost my edifice by mistaking the place where I erected it' (2.2.193–4). The company's solution, as legal records attest, was forcibly to enter the field they no longer owned and to pull down their theatre: they conveyed it over the Thames for re-use on the other side.[10] During the next year, the Globe playhouse was built from the Theatre's remains – perhaps re-using the slatted sides that made it up, or perhaps simply plundering its wood.

While waiting for the Globe to be completed, the Lord Chamberlain's Men moved to another round theatre, the Curtain, which had been constructed some years earlier in the Theatre's environs. Perhaps *Henry V*, with its stress on the smallness and meanness of the stage – 'Can this cock-pit hold / The vasty fields of France?' (Prologue 11–12) – was first performed here as the company waited with increasing urgency for the completion of their glamorous new playhouse.

The attraction of Southwark, attested to by the fact that other public theatres, the Rose and the Swan, had already been built there, was that the area had a well-established reputation for light-hearted entertainment. Once a year Southwark Fair was held there, so that for centuries the Bankside had housed temporary booths for puppet shows, performing animals, rope-dancers and, of course, plays. But the Liberty, opposite London, yet visible from it, and easily accessible by boat or London Bridge, had over time become known for hosting more dubious pleasures. It was to this place that a Londoner would resort for a day's drinking – the area abounded in alehouses – or bear-baiting, or paid sex. Thus playhouses settling in Southwark chose a context that simultaneously enhanced and threatened their livelihood: Globe plays often refer to bear-baiting (Olivia in *Twelfth Night* says that Viola/Cesario has 'set mine honour at the stake / And baited it with all th'unmuzzled thoughts / That tyrannous heart can think' (3.1.110–12)) and whores and bawdy-houses (in *Measure for Measure* Pompey is 'a Bawd, a wicked bawd' (2.1.274)) because they are rivalling, by subsuming, some of the other surrounding entertainments. It was sensible, too, for playhouses themselves to offer as many of the pleasures of Southwark as possible, which would have provided ironic context to the dramas that critiqued them. Both bottled ale and women seem to have been readily available at most playhouses. A nervous playwright 'when he hears his play hissed ... would rather think bottle-ale is opening', writes John Stephens; the puritanical William Prynne holds that 'our common strumpets and adulteresses after our stage-plays ended, are oft-times prostituted near our play-houses, if not in them'.[11]

The movement from Theatre to Globe as one playhouse mutates into the other works its way into Shakespeare's plays too. In *As You Like It*, which is often thought to have been Shakespeare's first Globe play, the Duke describes life as being like a (or the) Theatre: 'This wide and universal theatre / Presents more woeful pageants than the scene / Wherein we play in' (2.7.136–8) ('scene', here, means both 'stage' and the action performed on that stage). Jaques continues the analogy but repositions the statement: 'All the world's a stage, / And all the men and women merely players...' (2.7.138–9) – which is to say, more particularly, that the Theatre is now the Globe.

Round theatres of the period had a structure that, itself, became part of the plays performed inside them. They contained stages that 'thrust' into the middle of the building, around which was space for a standing audience. Thus the audience nearest the stage were also the people who paid least – standing cost just a penny; they are regularly insulted in the plays of the period, being known as 'penny stinkards', 'groundlings' (because they stood on the ground) or 'understanders' (because they stood lower than the raised stage). Shakespeare directly taunts the standing audience in moments when his characters refer to crowds with crowd mentalities: 'What's the matter, you dissentious rogues, / That, rubbing the poor itch of your opinion, / Make yourselves scabs' (*Coriolanus*, 1.1.153–5); he also rouses them when he wants an external mass of people like the army in *Henry V* ('Cry, "God for Harry! England and Saint George!"' (3.1.34).

Over the stage was an internal roof that protected the clothes of the actors and aided with the amplification of their voices. Known as 'Heaven', it seems to have been decorated with signs of the night sky. Hamlet refers to the actual heavens, but simultaneously to this space, when he speaks of 'brave o'erhanging, this majestical roof fretted with golden fire' (*Hamlet*, 2.2.291–2). Under the stage was an area known as 'Hell'; so when actors used the trap door to go up to or down from the stage, the audience would be acutely conscious of the fact that characters were entering or exiting a demonic region. Thus when Hamlet questions whether the ghost he has seen has really been his dead father or is actually an evil spirit, a 'goblin damned' (1.4.21), the audience will have had an answer. The ghost, having exited, repeatedly cries out from what Hamlet describes as 'the cellarage' (1.5.153) under the stage; he is called 'old mole' (1.5.164), reminding the observers that he burrows under the surface on which Hamlet stands. Every effort is made, that is to say, to remind the audience that the ghost is situated under the stage in 'Hell'. Hence the disposition of the stage could be used to give indications to the audience of which the characters in the fiction of the story are unaware.

A couple of pillars supported the weight of the Heavens, attaching the area to the stage. They existed for practical reasons, but naturally made their way into the drama too. They were probably used as the trees in *As You Like It* on which poems to 'Rosalind' are hung; they would also have provided convenient onstage 'hiding places' that allowed characters to be 'invisible' from other players but visible to the audience. Beatrice in *Much Ado About Nothing* is likely to have sheltered here where the audience could watch her face as her friends 'discuss' Benedick's love for her. But the pillars could also be used as stage-dividers: there were two of them, just as there were two doors to the left and right of the stage for entrances (between them was an aperture for 'discoveries') which collectively split the stage into separate areas. In *Antony and Cleopatra*, for instance, Egypt and Rome are staged in close succession, but a combination of doors and pillars will have allowed one side of the stage to 'become' the one, and the other side of the stage to 'become' the other.

On top of all round theatres was a flagpole on which, in advance of performance, colourful ensigns were hung. These signified that a play was soon to begin; they were visible from a great distance and were embellished with signs directly related to the theatre they represented. The flag of the Rose showed a star-like rose (hence an early map that calls the Rose 'the starre'), the flag of the Swan showed a swan, as de Witt's contemporary drawing illustrates (see Figure 1), while the flag for the Globe seems to have depicted Atlas or Hercules holding the globe on his shoulders. This means that any reference to Hercules, Atlas or the Globe in a play written for performance in that theatre becomes metatheatrical too. When Antony's god, Hercules, 'now leaves him' (*Antony and Cleopatra*, 4.3.13–14), the very stage has given up on its hero; more literally, when the players in *Hamlet* say that 'an eyrie of children' (2.2.326) are winning audiences over 'Hercules and his load' (2.2.345), they are addressing a current problem that was besetting the King's Men: performances by boy actors were more popular than performances by the adult players at the Globe.

1 The Swan playhouse, Aernout van Buchel, copy of drawing by Jan de Witt, 1596.

In addition to the round (or sometimes square) large public theatres were the smaller, more intimate and pricier private theatres. They were often in Liberties within the city walls, like Blackfriars or Whitefriars; they were more acceptable than public theatres.[12] For a long time, for instance, choirboys and talented schoolboys performed in private theatres using the claim that they were not lowly professional actors, but scholars putting on productions (for which an audience had to pay) as part of their education. Private theatres had a number of advantages over public ones: they were enclosed rather than open to the elements; they were well lit by candles (so performances did not have to happen only in daylight hours); and they were comfortable (seats were provided for everyone) and well heated. As a result, private theatres could charge considerably higher prices for entrance than public theatres. This meant that they attracted a slightly different kind of audience: one that was richer and more educated, with higher expectations for their entertainment. The preoccupations of such an audience tended to be taken up in the plays written for them.

Given that Shakespeare changed the nature of his playwriting around 1608 – the time when his company was finally granted the right to perform in a private theatre, the Blackfriars – the physical playhouse, its stage and audience seem to have affected his style. Certainly he started writing plays in a five-act structure from roughly this time onwards (before that he had written plays in a series of scenes rather than acts), which may relate to the indoor theatre's need for regular breaks so that the candles could be trimmed. He also started adding courtly entertainments into his dramas, perhaps to appeal to an audience who wished to replicate court habits. There are masques in *Henry VIII*, *The Tempest* and *The Winter's Tale* that are cut-down versions of the court masques of their day. The slightly magical properties of Shakespeare's late plays, too, can be traced to qualities supplied by the indoor theatre: yellow candlelight, perfumed air (smells, which lingered in an enclosed space, were used as part of performance – in *Pericles*, Thaisa's coffin 'smells / Most sweetly' (12.58–9); Innogen's breath 'perfumes the chamber' in *Cymbeline* (2.2.19)), cloying smoke from wicks and tobacco, and a bejewelled, highly visible audience (one poet writes of a suit that 'glistered at the torchy [Black]Friars').[13]

Playgoers

Playgoers of the early modern period could come from any class and walk of life if they could scrape together the money to pay for entrance. John Taylor the Waterpoet writes of the beggar who, at the Bankside, is able 'with his many / [to] Come in at a play-house, all in for one penny': public playhouses attracted a wide social range – though as their performances started at two o'clock in the afternoon, working men could only attend if they had time off, or if it were a holiday.[14] Private theatres, which charged considerably more – the cheapest seats cost sixpence – attracted a better-educated audience; court performances were in front of royalty and members of the nobility; touring productions were, like public theatre plays, performed in front of anyone prepared to pay to see them. So Shakespeare had to write for all sorts of people, and his immense literary range, from slapstick to deep tragedy, may well stem from the fact that he is targeting specific groups with different forms of writing.

Whatever walk of life they came from, with no numbered seating in any kind of theatre and no way of securing advance ownership of a particular space, spectators needed to turn up well in advance of performance to 'save' good places for themselves. To occupy the time, it was usual to arrive at the theatre with portable entertainments, particularly books. Dekker instructs a 'gull' to carry *The Guls Hornbook* to the playhouse; there he is to 'draw forth this book, read aloud [and] laugh aloud'.[15] Books were even sold at theatres. Blade in Cowley's *The Guardian* (4.3) tells Dogrel that if he is not careful his job will be to 'make and sell small pamphlets i'the playhouse'; Parrot begs the book-seller that his *The Mastive* be not 'at play-houses, 'mongst pippins sold'.[16] So the theatre was a place where the audience met literature first in book and then in performance form, suggesting that they may have perceived a close relationship between the two. Audiences also learnt of plays in print before they saw them in performance (all playbills were printed); the close connection between performance and publication, often questioned now, was visible then and situated directly around and inside the playhouses themselves.

Literate members of the theatre audience also responded to plays in a bookish fashion. Spectators would take writing equipment to the playhouse to note down the passages they liked. 'I am one that hath seen this play often', Webster makes Sly say; 'I have most of the jests here in my table-book'.[17] When Hamlet says, 'My tables – meet it is I set it down, / That one may smile and smile and be a villain', he means that 'one may smile and smile and be a villain' is worth recording in his erasable notebook ('tables') (1.5.108–9); he jests darkly at the audience members who are doing just that.[18] Shakespeare would also be pleased that audiences captured and circulated his lines, for that would act as a form of advertisement for him, his plays and his theatre. He made an effort to give spectators 'extractable' passages for their tables, 'sententiae', as well as plenty of new words that they could take home as gifts (the theatre was famous as 'the mint that daily coins new words').[19] Over 500 coinages are attributed to Shakespeare in the *Oxford English Dictionary*, and when he pokes fun at word-gatherers, it is with a cruel consciousness that they are some of his greatest admirers. 'Remuneration', he has Costard the clown say in *Love's Labour's Lost*, having misunderstood the meaning of the term, 'I will never buy and sell out of this word' (3.1.125, 129–30).

Spectators who attended first performances, however, were different in make-up from any subsequent set of spectators. They were monied and judgemental, for they paid double the normal entrance charge in order to be able to evaluate the play. They would clap the passages they liked and hiss those they didn't; at the end of a performance they would be collectively asked whether the text could be performed again. Their cries of 'ay' (yes) and 'no' supplied the answer.[20] Some of Shakespeare's prologues and epilogues anticipate this terrifying moment of judgement for their playwright, and are obviously relevant for first performances only. The epilogue for 2 *Henry IV* is haunted because 'I was lately here in the end of a displeasing play, to pray your patience for it, and to promise you a better'; the trouble is that he does not yet know whether *this* play will be seen as an improvement: 'if like an ill venture it come unluckily home, I break; [...] here I commit my body to your mercies' (Epilogue 8–13). Hardly surprisingly, given the connection between prologues and epilogues and first (rather than repeated) performance, Shakespeare plays that survive in more than one form often differ as to the presence or absence of stage orations. *Henry V*, *Romeo and Juliet* and *Troilus and Cressida* all survive in two or more textual forms, at least one of which contains a prologue and at least one of which does not.

Court versus playhouse

Court approval, as well as audience approval, was another separate but worrying moment for a playwright, and additional special prologues and epilogues were written for royal productions. One freestanding epilogue survives that is thought by some to be by Shakespeare; starting 'As the dial hand tells o'er', it is a special one-off oration for a play in front of Queen Elizabeth.[21] It, and/or others like it, must have worked, for Shakespeare's dramas were put on at court year after year. Indeed, the entire company for which he wrote gained ever-increasing royal approval. When King James gave the troupe the title 'the King's Men' in 1603, he elevated its sharers, Shakespeare included, to the position of 'grooms of the chamber'; they were allowed to wear scarlet livery and march in state processions. As time went on, then, Shakespeare would have spent more festival and celebratory occasions in royal palaces; the contents of royal libraries may have provided some of his sources.

Court performance was a boon for any company both in terms of money – about £10 would be paid for a royal production (£6.13s.4d if the monarch were absent) – and in terms of reputation and prestige.[22] More important still, court performance offered troupes protection. There was a heavily puritanical faction in London who were keen to stop all plays and pull the theatres down, but theatre companies, using the argument that public performances were 'rehearsals' for performance at court, insisted that putting on productions was a royal duty. The Master of the Revels, in charge of entertaining the king, concurred, taking the best or most favoured of the new plays mounted each year for court performance over Christmas.

Naturally, sections were specifically inserted into plays for the court's delectation. In some Shakespeare texts traces of this habit can be guessed at. So in *The Tempest* the masque prepared for does not seem to be the one presented: Prospero asks Ariel to return with dancers 'in a twink' (4.1.43) – Ariel then returns with one goddess; Prospero tells Ariel to come again with 'a corollary' (4.1.57) – Ariel then does not return at all, and Iris enters. The 'marriage' masque actually performed inside *The Tempest* appears to replace a different and more relevant masque, having perhaps been added into the text for performance at the court celebrations of the wedding of Princess Elizabeth and the Elector Palatine.[23] Similarly, the single extant version of *Macbeth* contains a moment when Macbeth is shown the line of kings who will descend from Banquo: he sees '*A show of eight kings, [the] last with a glass in his hand, and Banquo*' (4.1.127 SD). The '[looking] glass', it has been suggested, would only make absolute sense if James I were supposed to look into it; a descendant of Banquo, he would then see the line of kings stretching out to – himself.[24]

Shakespeare's writing, then, may have been (re)shaped – not necessarily by him – to match court preoccupations. Nevertheless, Shakespeare's works were, in the first instance, designed for repeated performance on the public stage in front of a public audience. Leonard Digges, in his 'Upon Master William Shakespeare', even claimed that 'the Globe ... prospered' only because of Shakespeare, detailing what happened 'when Caesar would appear, / And on the stage at half-sword parley were, / Brutus and Cassius'. Then, he wrote, 'the audience / Were ravished'.[25] They were 'ravished', as he makes clear, by the 'parley', the words, but as he also indicates, they were moved too by the vigorous staging, the swords, the powerful presence of the actors. Shakespeare's popularity – and full complexity – was reliant on the stage(s) that nurtured him; this chapter has attempted to show why and how.

NOTES

1 Richard Brome, *The English Moor*, in *Five New Playes* (1659), p. 86.

2 For more on apprentices, see David Kathman, 'Grocers, Goldsmiths, and Drapers: Freemen and Apprentices in the Elizabethan Theater', *Shakespeare Quarterly*, 55 (2004), 1–49.

3 W. J. Lawrence, *Old Theatre Days and Ways* (London: G. G. Harrap & Co., 1935), p. 178.

4 'Types' and acting range are considered in detail in Simon Palfrey and Tiffany Stern, *Shakespeare in Parts* (Oxford: Oxford University Press, 2007), pp. 43–56.

5 *REED York*, 2 vols., ed. Alexandra F. Johnston and Margaret Rogerson (Toronto and Buffalo, NY: University of Toronto Press, 1979), vol. I. p. 353. The *Midsummer Night's Dream* rehearsal and its relationship to other rehearsals is explored in Tiffany Stern, *Rehearsal from Shakespeare to Sheridan* (Oxford: Clarendon Press, 2000), chapters 2 and 3. For an in-depth look at Shakespeare's plays divided into actors' parts, see Palfrey and Stern, *Shakespeare in Parts*.

6 Samuel Nicholson, *Acolastus* (1600), sig. G3v.

7 For an exploration of how little narrative actors sometimes knew, and how reliant they were on cues, see Palfrey and Stern, *Shakespeare in Parts*, pp. 83–8.

8 Richard Flecknoe, *Love's Kingdom* (1664), sig. G7a–b; 'On Mr Richard Burbidg an Excellent both Player, and Painter', Folger MS, v.a.97. For typecasting versus acting range, see Palfrey and Stern, *Shakespeare in Parts*, pp. 43–5.

9 For more on the London Liberties, see Steven Mullaney, *The Place of the Stage: License, Play, and Power in Renaissance England* (Chicago: University of Chicago Press, 1988).

10 The legal records are reproduced in C. W. Wallace, *Shakespeare and his London Associates* (Nebraska: University Studies, 1910). For a dramatic description of what this moment may have been like, see James Shapiro, *1599: A Year in the Life of William Shakespeare* (London: Faber and Faber, 2005), chapter 1.

11 John Stephens, *New Essays and Characters* (1631), p. 292; William Prynne, *Histriomastix* (1633), sig. 3D3v.

12 For the 'private theatre' Liberties situated within the London walls, see Mary Bly, 'Playing the Tourist in Early Modern London: Selling the Liberties Onstage', *PMLA*, 122 (2007), 61–71.

13 Francis Lenton, *The young Gallants Whirligigg* (1629), p. 16. For smells in the early modern theatre, see Jonathan Gil Harris, 'The Smell of Macbeth', *Shakespeare Quarterly*, 58 (2007), 465–86, and Tiffany Stern, '"Taking Part": Actors and Audience on the Blackfriars Stage', in Paul Menzer (ed.), *Inside Shakespeare: Essays on the Blackfriars Stage* (Selinsgrove: Susquehanna University Press, 2006), pp. 35–53.

14 John Taylor, *The Praise, Antiquity, and Commodity, of Beggery* (1621), sig. C3v. For the kind of person who attended the playhouses more generally, see Andrew Gurr, *Playgoing in Shakespeare's London* (3rd edn. Cambridge: Cambridge University Press, 2004).

15 Thomas Dekker, *The Guls Hornbook*, in Alexander B. Grosart (ed.), *The Non-Dramatic Works*, 5 vols. (1884; New York: Russell and Russell, 1963), vol. II, p. 203.

16 Abraham Cowley, *The Guardian* (1650), sig. D3r; Henry Parrot, *The Mastive* (1615), sig. A4b. For the reading and writing audience, see Tiffany Stern, 'Watching as Reading: The Audience and Written Text in the Early Modern Playhouse', in Laurie Maguire (ed.), *How to Do Things with Shakespeare* (Oxford: Blackwell, 2008), pp. 136–59.

17 John Webster's additions to John Marston's *The Malecontent* (1604), sig. A3r.

18 For more on table-books, see Peter Stallybrass, Roger Chartier, J. Franklin Mowery and Heather Wolfe, 'Hamlet's Tables and the Technologies of Writing in Renaissance England', *Shakespeare Quarterly*, 55 (2004), 379–419.

19 Richard Flecknoe, *Miscellania* (1653), pp. 103–4.
20 Tiffany Stern, '"A Small-Beer Health to His Second Day": Playwrights, Prologues, and First Performances in the Early Modern Theatre', *Studies in Philology*, 101 (2004), 172–99 (175–6).
21 Tiffany Stern, *Making Shakespeare* (London and New York: Routledge, 2004), p. 119.
22 Though it is unclear what takings were made at public performance, sharers would attract between £100 and £150 a year from collected productions; they would make more if they had additional 'house-keeper' roles. Thus money for royal performance was a boon but not essential. See E. K. Chambers, *The Elizabethan Stage*, 4 vols. (Oxford: Clarendon Press, 1923), vol. I, p. 370.
23 Irwin Smith, 'Ariel and the Masque in *The Tempest*', *Shakespeare Quarterly*, 21 (1970), 213–22.
24 Stern, *Making Shakespeare*, pp. 32–3.
25 Leonard Digges, in William Shakespeare, *Poems* (1640), sigs. *3v–*4r.

READING LIST

Chambers, E.K. *Elizabethan Stage*, 4 vols. Oxford: Clarendon Press, 1923.
Cox, John D. and David Scott Kastan, eds. *A New History of Early English Drama*. New York: Columbia University Press, 1997.
Gurr, Andrew. *Playgoing in Shakespeare's London*. 3rd edn. Cambridge: Cambridge University Press, 2004.
The Shakespearian Stage, 1574–1642. Cambridge: Cambridge University Press, 1992.
Kastan, David Scott, ed. *A Companion to Shakespeare*. Oxford: Blackwell, 1999.
Kastan, David Scott and Peter Stallybrass, eds. *Staging the Renaissance*. London and New York: Routledge, 1991.
Kinney, Arthur F. *Shakespeare by Stages: An Historical Introduction*. Oxford: Blackwell, 2003.
Menzer, Paul ed. *Inside Shakespeare: Essays on the Blackfriars Stage*. Selinsgrove: Susquehanna University Press, 2006.
Mullaney, Steven. *The Place of the Stage: License, Play, and Power in Renaissance England*. Chicago: Chicago University Press, 1988.
Palfrey, Simon and Tiffany Stern. *Shakespeare in Parts*. Oxford: Oxford University Press, 2007.
Shapiro, James. *1599: A Year in the Life of William Shakespeare*. London: Faber and Faber, 2005.
Stern, Tiffany. *Documents of Performance in Early Modern England*. Cambridge: Cambridge University Press, 2009.
Making Shakespeare. London and New York: Routledge, 2004.
Rehearsal from Shakespeare to Sheridan. Oxford: Clarendon Press, 2000.
'Watching as Reading: The Audience and Written Text in the Early Modern Playhouse', in *How to Do Things with Shakespeare*, Laurie Maguire (ed.). Oxford: Blackwell, 2008, pp. 136–59.
Thomson, Peter. *Shakespeare's Theatre*. London and New York: Routledge, 1992.

5

ANDREW MURPHY

The transmission of Shakespeare's texts

A theatre-goer who had seen *1 Henry IV* when it first appeared on the stage in London might subsequently have ventured to the area around St Paul's Churchyard – at the time the centre of the English book trade – in search of a copy of the play. The printed text on offer there would have been strikingly different from its modern counterpart. For one thing, the title would not have been our compact *1 Henry IV* but rather the more elaborated *The History of Henry the Fourth; With the battle at Shrewsbury, between the King and Lord Henry Percy, surnamed Henry Hotspur of the North. With the humorous conceits of Sir John Falstaff*. This title serves not just to identify the play, but also acts as a kind of 'teaser', flagging up the exciting content of the book. An even more striking aspect of the original edition of the play, from a modern perspective, would be the fact that nowhere in the book is Shakespeare identified as the author. Like many other plays published in the closing years of the sixteenth century, *1 Henry IV* appeared without any indication of who had written it.

The title page of the first edition of *1 Henry IV* alerts us to the fact that the Renaissance was a period of cultural transition in England. The London theatre scene was an adventurous innovation, and it was not entirely clear whether the products of this new commercial venture should even be considered worthy of being preserved in print, a medium which had hitherto in large measure been used to disseminate works of a devotional or practical nature. To begin with, playwrights were little regarded within the cultural hierarchy of the time, and it was for this reason that their names were not included on the title pages of printed plays: this was not considered to be information likely to boost sales. It was much more common, in the early years of the theatre, to foreground the name of the acting company which had performed a given play. Thus, for example, the first edition of *Titus Andronicus* (1594) informs us that it 'was plaide by the right honourable the Earle of Darbie, Earle of Pembrooke, and Earle of Sussex their seruants', but not that it was written by Shakespeare. Eventually, Shakespeare's work became sufficiently popular that his name did become a selling-point. By the time we get to the 1608 edition of *King Lear*, for example, 'M. WILLIAM SHAK-SPEARE' appears at the very top of the title page, in bold capitals.

The texts of Shakespeare's plays themselves also reflected the complexities of the evolving world from which they emerged. A number of the plays (most notably *Romeo and Juliet*, *Hamlet*, *The Merry Wives of Windsor*, *Henry V*, 2 and *3 Henry VI*, *King Lear*, *Richard III* and *The Taming of the Shrew*) were published in multiple variant forms, some of them appearing in both a shorter and a more expansive version. The mechanisms which occasioned these variations have never been satisfactorily accounted for, though it seems likely that they were in some way connected to shifting demands within the theatre of the time. One scholar (Lukas Erne) has speculated that Shakespeare may have been a 'dual-mode' writer, producing extended texts with an eye towards publication, while expecting that these scripts would be cut down for production in the theatre. Erne has proposed that the shorter versions of the plays may give us some insight into what these abridged theatrical versions may have looked like.[1]

By 1623, seven years after Shakespeare's death, both the theatre and theatrical publishing had begun to find their settled forms. In that year, Shakespeare's colleagues from the King's Men brought to print a folio volume of his collected plays – the folio being the largest-sized printed book in this period (the individual play editions had mostly been published as quartos – half the size of a folio). In doing so, they followed the example of Ben Jonson who, in 1616, had issued his own collected works, also in folio format. What distinguished the Shakespeare collection was that it was the first such volume dedicated exclusively to play texts. The folio added to the canon eighteen plays that had not previously appeared in print: *The Tempest*, *The Two Gentlemen of Verona*, *Measure for Measure*, *The Comedy of Errors*, *As You Like It*, *The Taming of the Shrew*, *All's Well that Ends Well*, *Twelfth Night*, *The Winter's Tale*, *King John*, *1 Henry VI*, *Henry VIII*, *Coriolanus*, *Timon of Athens*, *Julius Caesar*, *Macbeth*, *Antony and Cleopatra* and *Cymbeline*. It seems clear that those responsible for the volume went to considerable trouble to seek out what they considered to be the best available texts of the plays. They made a point of noting in their address to the volume's anticipated 'great Variety of Readers' that they had reproduced none of the previously published attenuated versions, and, in some cases, they seem also to have sought out playhouse alternatives even for plays that had previously been published in full-scale texts.

With the publication of the folio volume, Shakespeare had achieved the kind of status as an author that is most readily intelligible to us in modern terms. The volume is firmly anchored in his personal identity, with the iconic Droeshout engraving of his image appearing on the title page. On the contents page, the plays assume their familiar designations, so that, for example, *The first part of the contention betwixt the two famous houses of Yorke and Lancaster, with the death of the good Duke Humphrey: and the banishment and death of the Duke of Suffolke* ... (to quote part of the title of the 1594 quarto edition) becomes simply: *The second part of King Hen. the Sixt.* The plays are sorted into the categories of Comedies, Histories and Tragedies, 'history' here referring specifically to *English* history – *Macbeth*, for instance, is classed as a tragedy. The Folio had a relatively modest print run – probably something in the region of 750 copies were issued.[2] It was successful enough to require a second edition in 1632, a further edition being issued in 1663. In the following year, this third edition was re-issued, seven new plays being added to those originally published. Of these only one – *Pericles* – has been accepted into the canon. A fourth folio in 1685 rounds off the history of collected editions published in the seventeenth century.

The printhouse workers who prepared the 1632, 1663/4 and 1685 folios for the press corrected and regularized the text in various ways, often with an acute eye for the errors of their predecessors (though the folios also, inevitably, introduced errors of their own into the text). These correctors were entirely anonymous printhouse functionaries, but just as the playwright emerged from the shadows of anonymity at the beginning of the seventeenth century, so too was the editor brought forward into the light of public recognition at the beginning of the eighteenth. By that point, the majority rights in Shakespeare had been acquired by the publisher Jacob Tonson I (his business subsequently passed to his nephew, Jacob II, and then to Jacob II's son, Jacob III). Shakespeare was now an old property, in need of some kind of new marketing strategy to recharge its commercial potential. Tonson hit on the idea of having the text prepared for the press by a celebrated contemporary writer, and he chose Nicholas Rowe, the poet and playwright, as his editor, Rowe's edition appearing under the Tonson imprint in 1709. Rowe thus became the first publicly identified editor of Shakespeare, and he was also the first person to map out his editorial strategy in the preliminaries to his edition. Working with the Fourth Folio as his base text, Rowe compared it with a (relatively narrow) selection of earlier editions, and he noted several significant discrepancies. For example, the Folio text of *Hamlet* lacks a scene (4.2, where Fortinbras appears with his army) that is present in the quarto line of texts, from the second quarto edition forwards. Rowe added this scene to his own edition. He also continued the process of regularizing the text, providing *dramatis personae* lists for all of the plays, adding locations for most scenes and standardizing the names of many of the characters (it is Rowe, for instance, who regularised 'Puck' as the proper name of the character more frequently known as 'Robin Goodfellow' in *A Midsummer Night's Dream*).[3] Rowe's edition was illustrated, and it set something of a trend for expensive first-run editions which would serve as ornamental additions to gentlemen's libraries.

Rowe's Shakespeare was a commercial success, reaching its third edition by 1714. Tonson was thus prompted to replay his marketing strategy for a second time. In 1725 he issued a wholly new text, edited this time by the foremost poet of the day, Alexander Pope. Pope continued the process of regularizing the text, in particular smoothing out the verse and adding more consistent act and scene breaks. Like Rowe, he referred back to a selection of the earliest editions, from which he cherry-picked particular readings that appealed to him. Pope's editorial mindset was generally pessimistic: he felt that the published texts had been greatly corrupted by, among other things, actorly interference, and he granted himself considerable freedom to intervene in the text to reverse perceived errors. Material that Pope particularly disliked was 'degraded' to the bottom of the page, to signal the fact that he felt it could not possibly have been part of Shakespeare's own original text. Pope also identified passages he considered to be particularly fine by adding asterisks in the margin of the text.

Pope's edition prompted an unexpected (and, from Pope's perspective, an unwelcome) response. In 1726 Lewis Theobald attacked Pope's text in a short volume entitled *Shakespeare Restor'd: or, A Specimen of the Many Errors as well Committed, or Unamended, by Mr. Pope in his Late Edition of this Poet*. Theobald was a small-time writer whose literary achievements fell very far short of Pope's. But he was a lawyer by training, and he brought to textual studies a mind well acquainted with the business of sifting evidence and tracing materials to their source. He also took a lively interest in developments in biblical and classical scholarship, and was deeply influenced by the editorial work of Richard Bentley on ancient Greek and Latin texts. At the heart of Pope's editorial strategy was a desire to bring the text into line with eighteenth-century aesthetic standards. Theobald, by contrast, sought to engage with the text within its own historical moment. Thus, to take one simple example, where Pope complained of the early texts that 'every page is ... scandalously false spelled',[4] Theobald – being far more widely read in the literature of Shakespeare's time – understood that spelling conventions, together with grammar and usage, change over time and therefore what may have appeared incorrect to eighteenth-century eyes might well have been wholly acceptable to Shakespeare and his contemporaries. The dispute between Pope and Theobald prompted Tonson to invite Theobald to produce his own edition of Shakespeare, which was published in 1733.

One of Theobald's editorial innovations was the use of a 'parallel passages' approach, whereby difficulties in a particular text are explained by reference to analogous moments elsewhere in the plays.

The first edition of Shakespeare to be published outside London was issued by the university press at Oxford in 1743–4. It was sponsored and edited by Sir Thomas Hanmer, who had served as Speaker of the House of Commons. Hanmer had little experience as an editor, but his text was beautifully printed and illustrated. The Tonsons regarded the edition as a piracy, but they appear to have been reluctant to enter into a legal dispute with the university. Ultimately, the London firm appropriated the text for use in a number of cheap, downsized editions.

Theobald was succeeded as a Tonson editor by the Reverend William Warburton, whose text appeared in 1747, three years after Theobald's death. The clergyman launched a mean-spirited attack on his predecessor in the preliminaries to his edition, and he strongly aligned himself with Pope, allowing himself great freedom in emending the text and frequently changing passages that were in fact perfectly intelligible in the original. Just as Pope's edition prompted Theobald to write *Shakespeare Restor'd*, so Warburton's text provided the occasion for Thomas Edwards to publish *A Supplement to Mr. Warburton's Edition* (1748), subsequently known as the *Canons of Criticism*. Edwards humorously punctured Warburton's absurdities by outlining a set of editorial principles which he presented, tongue in cheek, as a distillation of Warburton's thinking. The first 'canon' he offered is: 'A Professed critic has a right to declare, that his Author wrote whatever he thinks he should have written, with as much positiveness as if he had been at his elbow.'[5]

Edwards' parody indicates that, by the mid-point of the century, unfounded interference in the text was ceasing to be acceptable. Most subsequent editors would effectively align themselves with Theobald's broad editorial principles (though they did not always give him the credit he deserved). Samuel Johnson, for example, whose first edition appeared in 1765, thought it better always 'to save a citizen, than to kill an enemy', and he therefore avoided changing the text if the original could be made in some way to yield sense. 'It has been my settled principle', he writes, 'that the reading of the ancient books is probably true, and therefore is not to be disturbed for the sake of elegance, perspicuity, or mere improvement of the sense.' Johnson also tentatively mapped out a principle that would become increasingly important in Shakespeare editing. Writing of the four folios, he observed that 'the first is equivalent to all others, and that the rest only deviate from it by the printer's negligence'.[6] The point that Johnson is making here has to do with precedence and authority. The First Folio is closer to the original manuscripts than any of the other folio editions; the other folios essentially reproduce the First Folio, speculatively correcting some of its errors, but also adding errors of their own. Therefore, in the folio sequence, the 1623 text should be regarded as having an authority and a status wholly different from that of its three successors.

Johnson himself did not fully register the implications of this textual principle. Pope, Theobald and Warburton had followed Rowe's practice of sending to the printers a marked-up copy of the edition of their immediate predecessor. Johnson did much the same: he began by marking up a copy of Warburton's edition and then, part-way through, he switched to a copy of the fourth edition of Theobald's text. Logically, then, these editors were simply adding to the line of texts which began with the sequence First Folio–Second Folio–Third Folio–Fourth Folio. In doing so, they were perpetuating the errors and miscorrections (and, of course, legitimate speculative corrections) introduced into the text by all of their predecessors. The first person to see this problem with any degree of clarity was Edward Capell, who published an edition with the Tonson firm in 1768. Capell created his text from the ground up, returning directly to the earliest quartos and the First Folio. What he gave the printer was not an annotated printed text, but a handwritten manuscript independently compiled directly from the earliest printed source texts. In the process, Capell cleared away a very large number of errors that had been accumulating in the text, edition by edition, over many decades. Capell also attempted, as best he could, to make sense of the relationships among the earliest quarto texts and their First Folio equivalents. His work in tracing these relationships and in collating the differences among the earliest texts was carried forward by Edmond Malone, whose edition of 1790 can be seen as representing both the culmination of eighteenth-century Shakespeare textual scholarship and also as laying the foundation for editorial work in the nineteenth century. Malone included the poems as part of his edition. A second edition of his text was issued posthumously in 1821, under the stewardship of James Boswell the younger. This edition (together with a final incarnation of Johnson's text, re-edited by George Steevens and Isaac Reed, and published in 1803) served as standard for much of the first half of the nineteenth century.

If the seventeenth century saw the emergence of the playwright as author and the eighteenth century witnessed the public foregrounding of the editor, then we can say that the next century marked the emergence of the reader as a significant figure in the history of the transmission of Shakespeare's texts. Of course Shakespeare always had readers – from the 'private friends' who Francis Meres, in *Palladis Tamia* (1598), tells us enjoyed his 'sugred sonnets' in manuscript before they appeared in print, to the subscribers who paid in advance for copies of editions such as Pope's and Johnson's. But these readers were always limited to a rather select band, largely because of the high price of editions. A copy of the first edition of Pope's text, for example, would have run to about £7, when the cost of binding is taken into account. Up through the eighteenth century the price of books was kept artificially high by a system of copyright which granted legal ownership to publishers in perpetuity. Publishers traded ownership rights (and even fractions of such rights) at auction, and they also bequeathed these rights to their families and associates. In 1774, this situation altered radically when the House of Lords was asked to rule on the precise meaning of the terms of a piece of copyright legislation that had been passed in 1709, the exact provisions of the act having always been in dispute. Against the expectations of the principal London publishers, the Lords ruled that copyright was actually of limited duration only. The ruling had the effect of creating a 'public domain' of older canonical texts, which were freely available to any publisher who wished to produce a competitively priced edition.

One of the first publishers to capitalize on the House of Lords ruling was John Bell, who began issuing canonical texts, including editions of Shakespeare, at reduced prices. Bell had particularly high hopes for an edition he published in 1785–8, of which he observed that it was 'intended to supersede the necessity for any other Edition whatever, as it will be calculated to gratify every class of reader'.[7] Of course, the Shakespeare publishing (and editing) trade did not come to a halt simply because this edition appeared in the bookshops. But, in time, Bell's idea of gratifying 'every class of reader' became a potent ideal for other publishers. One obstacle blocking the path towards the realization of this ambition was the high rate of illiteracy in Britain in the closing decades of the eighteenth century. This problem was eventually tackled from the beginning of the following century by church societies anxious to inculcate working-class children in establishment values (particularly in the context of the French Revolution and its aftermath). Illiteracy rates declined progressively over the course of the nineteenth century and, by the early 1900s, more than 90 per cent of the adult population could read and write.

As the reading public grew in Britain, so publishers gradually began to think through the logistics of selling their Shakespearian wares into an expanding market. Multi-volume – and even single-volume – edition prices declined relatively slowly over the course of the first half of the century, but by the 1830s some firms were beginning to use publishing by parts as a way of selling into the bottom end of the market. In 1839, Robert Tyas commenced issuing what he styled a 'SHAKSPERE FOR THE PEOPLE' in weekly numbers at just twopence each, with complete plays running to a total of between four and six numbers. In advertising the edition, Tyas asserted that 'Books are no longer the exclusive luxuries of the rich – they are become the necessary food of the poor.'[8] J. C. Moore followed Tyas into the part-publishing market, and he began issuing a penny-a-number edition in 1845, the whole series being projected at sixty numbers. One working-class reader, W. E. Adams (1832–1906), commented on the impact the penny series had on him as he encountered it while working as a messenger boy: 'Well do I remember this cheap treasure. It was my first introduction to the great bard. Gracious! how I devoured play after play as they came out!'[9]

As the tercentenary of the playwright's birth approached in 1864, the London publisher John Dicks offered what he styled 'an edition of Shakspere for the millions', which sold at the rate of two plays for a penny. These texts were then gathered into a two-shilling clothbound collected volume and Dicks subsequently reissued the edition in paper covers at just one shilling – less than 1 per cent of the full cost of Pope's 1725 edition. The reduction of prices to this level was achieved, in part, by technological advances in printing and papermaking – the cost of raw materials and production having both declined very considerably over the course of the century. Responding to an enquiry from the *Bookseller* in 1868, Dicks claimed that total sales for his edition in its various forms amounted to almost 1,000,000 copies.[10] If this number is accurate, then it is possible that Dicks may have put more copies of the complete works into circulation than just about all of his predecessors combined. The success of the Dicks edition was not universally welcomed. The London-based publisher Alexander Macmillan could not understand how his rival had managed to reduce his price by so much and still make a profit. Macmillan was particularly vexed by the 'Shilling Shakespeare's' success because he had himself, in 1864, issued a clothbound single-volume edition at a price of 3s 6d, expecting thereby to gain a substantial share of the popular market. This was the 'Globe Shakespeare', and, while it failed to match the success of Dicks' edition, it was nevertheless a steady seller, remaining in print in one form or another long into the twentieth century, helped by the fact that its line-numbering system became the standard for scholars when referring to the plays. The edition was also widely distributed internationally, becoming the preferred Shakespeare of the expanding British Empire.

The Globe was based on a multi-volume edition which Macmillan had published in 1863–6. This edition was known as the 'Cambridge Shakespeare', in part because Macmillan published it in collaboration with Cambridge University Press, but also because the bulk of the editorial work was undertaken by a pair of Cambridge University scholars, William George Clark and William Aldis Wright (drawing in large part on the collection of early Shakespeare texts that had been bequeathed to Trinity College, Cambridge by Edward Capell). This development represented an important shift in the history of Shakespeare editing. All of the eighteenth-century editors had been gentleman-amateurs, enjoying an income either from their professions or from family investments. This editorial tradition carried on into the nineteenth century, important new editorial work being carried out by Alexander Dyce (an Anglican clergyman with an inherited income), John Payne Collier (a journalist), Charles Knight (a publisher) and James Orchard Halliwell-Phillipps (whose wife had an inherited income). Clark and Wright, by contrast, were university professionals, and while they were not based in English literature departments (English was only beginning to emerge as a university subject at this point), it is nevertheless the case that, from the closing decades of the nineteenth century forwards, most major editions would be produced by scholars based at such departments. Thus, when the Arden Shakespeare was launched in 1899, the original general editor for the series was Edward Dowden, the first professor of English to be appointed at Trinity College, Dublin.

In the twentieth century, the professionalization of Shakespeare editing, and of Shakespeare studies more generally, intensified as university English departments proliferated. It is rather striking, in this context, that while most of the actual editing of texts at this time was carried out by academics, much of the theorizing which informed editorial practice was formulated and driven forwards primarily by a remarkable trio of scholars whose connections with the professional academic world were somewhat peripheral. W. W. Greg had been destined to become editor of the *Economist* (which was founded by his grandfather), but instead he served for a spell as librarian of Trinity College, Cambridge before eventually resigning to live off his private income. R. B. McKerrow trained as an engineer in order to enter the family business, but he abandoned the profession on coming into his inheritance. A. W. Pollard was Keeper of Printed Books at the British Museum and served as editor of the Bibliographical Society's journal, the *Library*. The work of these three scholars, who, together with their followers, became known as the 'New Bibliographers', cast a long shadow over editing and textual studies during the course of the twentieth century.

Greg sought to define bibliography as 'the study of books as material objects', and the New Bibliographers certainly paid closer attention to the book as a physical entity than any previous scholars had done.[11] A nice example of the kind of breakthrough that this approach made possible is Greg's own work on a problematic group of quarto texts which, while they were variously dated on their title pages, nevertheless puzzlingly shared certain characteristics in common. By a thorough examination of the watermarks and other physical aspects of these editions, Greg was able to demonstrate that they had all, in fact, been published in the same year (1619) by Thomas Pavier, who had sought to pass some of the texts off as earlier editions.[12] This kind of precise, almost forensic, investigation laid the foundation for other work of this kind, most notably Charlton Hinman's extraordinary study of the First Folio, published in two volumes in 1963.[13] By attending to such details as the repeated appearance of damaged pieces of type, patterns of spelling variations and the manner in which type was distributed on the page, Hinman was able to provide an astonishingly detailed account of how the volume had proceeded through the press, even projecting the likely number of compositors who had worked on the book and identifying which sections of the text each compositor was likely to have set.

Examining the physical evidence on the page was not an end in itself for the New Bibliographers. They essentially saw this forensic work as being preliminary to something much more important. Their ultimate aim was to strip away the external accretions in the inherited printed text in order to work back towards the original authorial manuscript. As the editor John Dover Wilson put it, in a slightly unsettling image, the objective of the approach was to 'creep into the compositor's skin and catch glimpses of the manuscript through his eyes'.[14] Evidence such as details of broken type and watermarks could only provide a limited amount of assistance in reaching this goal, and the New Bibliographers ventured into more speculative territory in an attempt to identify the source text underlying the printed editions. For example, they proposed that most plays were based on one of two types of manuscript: either authorial 'foul papers' or theatrical 'prompt books'. McKerrow suggested some simple ways in which it would be possible to distinguish between the two.[15] An authorial manuscript was, he proposed, likely to be rather vague on specifics, whereas a prompt book – which would be used to govern the text in performance – would need to be far more precise. Thus, where, for example, in a play such as *Romeo and Juliet*, Shakespeare may have conceived of a character's identity differently depending on the particular local context – identifying the character variously in speech prefixes as Wife, Mother, Lady, Old Lady – the Renaissance equivalent of a stage manager would need a singular, coherent identity, such as 'Lady Capulet'.

Drawing on McKerrow's suggestion, editors in the New Bibliographic mode felt that in certain printed texts they could virtually see the trace of Shakespeare's hand beneath the marks on the printed page. This sense was strengthened by the proposal that the 'Hand D' pages of the manuscript play *Sir Thomas More* may have been written by Shakespeare, thus giving clues to the peculiarities of his handwriting and, more particularly, the kinds of characteristic error that it may have given rise to when misread by a compositor.[16] By advancing these and other theories, the New Bibliographers offered editors a set of tools which appeared to allow them to uncover, with a high degree of certainty, Shakespeare's original authorial text. In the best-case scenario, they might conclude that the printed text was based on authorial foul papers and so needed to be cleansed of compositorial errors and sophistications. A more complicated scenario might involve stripping away both compositorial interventions and changes introduced into the text by a scribe who had turned authorial papers into a working playhouse script. These two kinds of base text are not exhaustive, but they represented two common scenarios which the New Bibliographers felt were likely to be faced by editors of Shakespeare.

The New Bibliography brought a high degree of stability to Shakespeare editing for most of the twentieth century. Editions proliferated, but – with occasional eccentric exceptions, such as John Dover Wilson's fascinating, but often wayward, Cambridge New Shakespeare – they all provided very similar texts. In the closing decades of the century, however, the textual scene began to shift. The New Bibliographic approach can be said to have been wholly focused on the author and on the business of recovering the author's intended text. In *A Critique of Modern Textual Criticism*, published in 1983, however, Jerome J. McGann (building, in part, on the work of D. F. McKenzie) began to stress the importance of the 'social text', noting that 'literary works are not produced without arrangements of some sort'.[17] This insight is, of course, particularly relevant to works of drama, since the fullest incarnation of a play is never the sole product of an author working in isolation. Something of the impact of McGann's work could be seen in an edition produced by Stanley Wells and Gary Taylor (with John Jowett and William Montgomery) published by Oxford University Press in 1986. Wells and his colleagues departed from the New Bibliographic orthodoxy by seeking to recover not the text closest to Shakespeare's authorial original, but rather the text closest to each play's Renaissance theatrical incarnation.

Wells and Taylor offered one further significant departure from New Bibliographic orthodoxy. The New Bibliographic enterprise was focused on the business of uncovering the singular true text which embodied Shakespeare's authorial intentions. But, as we noted at the beginning of this chapter, a number of the plays existed in variant versions. The New Bibliographers dealt with the most attenuated of the variant texts by identifying them as 'bad quartos' and suggesting that they were piracies based on 'memorial reconstructions' assembled by bit-part actors. But what of those plays, such as *King Lear*, which existed in two extended versions, both of them appearing to have their own integrity? Wells and Taylor proposed that these texts represented discrete, coherent versions of the plays in question. They raised the possibility that Shakespeare himself may have reconceived aspects of these plays over time and that the two incarnations represented an original and a revised version of the text. For this reason, Wells and Taylor offered two versions of *King Lear* in their edition – *The History of King Lear*, based on the first quarto, and *The Tragedy of King Lear*, based on the First Folio.

Wells and Taylor challenged the orthodoxies of the New Bibliography by refusing to accede to the notion of the uniform, singular text. As the century drew to a close, many of the most fundamental building-blocks of the New Bibliographic approach also began to be undermined. Scholars such as William B. Long and Paul Werstine questioned the notion that the texts underlying the early printed editions could so easily be divided into 'foul papers' and 'prompt books'; indeed, they questioned the very validity of these categories.[18] Werstine also cast doubt on whether 'Hand D' really could be securely identified as Shakespeare's (though some scholars, such as MacDonald P. Jackson, still maintain that the balance of evidence is in favour of the attribution).[19] Laurie E. Maguire and others have convincingly challenged the concepts of 'bad quartos' and 'memorial reconstruction'.[20] Piece by piece, the sure structure built by the New Bibliographers began to crumble, and editing became a much less certain affair.

The demise of the New Bibliography roughly coincided with the rise of post-structuralist literary theory. A number of scholars (most notably Margreta de Grazia, Peter Stallybrass, Jonathan Goldberg and Stephen Orgel) compellingly drew upon the insights of theorists such as Michel Foucault and Jacques Derrida, and combined them with a detailed understanding of editorial issues to map out a more complex view of Renaissance textuality, seeking thereby to break away from the author-centred orthodoxies of the New Bibliographers.[21] While the impact of contemporary theory was certainly a significant element in reconfiguring conceptions of the text at the turn of the century, it should be noted that the advent of the electronic text has also played an important part in remapping textual paradigms. As we have seen, the goal of the New Bibliographers was to produce a singular text coincident with the author's own intentions. But the rise of the personal computer can be said to have naturalized the idea that texts often exist in multiple versions and that the authority of any particular incarnation of a text is often purely provisional. At the same time, the computer made possible the preservation and dissemination of texts in multiple versions. The print era, for logistical and economic reasons, always tended to favour the singular, compacted text. The computer, by contrast, favours multiplicity. Wells and Taylor's decision to include two complete texts of *King Lear* in the Oxford Shakespeare doubled the production costs for the play, and the printing costs of every single copy of the volume were also necessarily increased. Multiplying texts electronically does not have quite the same financial implications.

In the wake of both the 'New Textualism' prompted by post-structuralist theory and the expansion of textual possibilities facilitated by the electronic text, the signature characteristic of Shakespeare publishing in the twenty-first century has been multiplicity. In the realm of print, the most recent Arden edition of *Hamlet* has been published in two volumes offering three separate texts. Electronic editions have offered even more choice: the web-based Internet Shakespeare Edition of *Romeo and Juliet* provides a modernized edited text; a transcription of the First Folio version of the play; transcriptions of the first and second quarto texts; and access to electronic facsimiles of the play in two different copies of the First Folio, plus copies of the Second, Third and Fourth Folios and the first and second quartos. To some extent these developments can be said to have taken us back full circle. Shakespeare himself lived in a time when the playwright was not necessarily foregrounded as a source of textual authority, and his plays often appeared in multiple variant forms. The editorial tradition sought to reduce the inherited complexity of the Renaissance text to a single coherent incarnation, validated by a direct link back to the author himself. In our own time, the text has fractured again, as competing incarnations of the text are recognized as having their own authority. Four centuries after Shakespeare's death we live in a world that would be unrecognizable to the playwright, yet we privilege textual values that would, in some respects at least, have been intelligible to his contemporaries. Having said all of this, we should also note that Shakespeare editions always reflect the culture of the era in which they are produced. Alexander Pope fundamentally wanted to fashion a Shakespeare who was intelligible within the context of the aesthetic criteria of the early eighteenth century. We too have refashioned Shakespeare's text in our own image. Doubtless, our successors will do just the same, and our current investment in textual multiplicity may well look quaintly anachronistic to future generations of editors and scholars.

NOTES

1 See Lukas Erne, *Shakespeare as Literary Dramatist* (Cambridge: Cambridge University Press, 2003).

2 See Peter W. M. Blayney, *The First Folio of Shakespeare* (Washington, DC: Folger, 1991), p. 2.

3 See Barbara A. Mowat, 'Nicholas Rowe and the Twentieth-Century Shakespeare Text', in Tetsuo Kishi, Roger Pringle and Stanley Wells (eds.), *Shakespeare and Cultural Traditions* (Newark: University of Delaware Press, 1994), pp. 314–22, (p. 317).

4 Alexander Pope (ed.), *The Works of Shakspear*, 6 vols. (London: Jacob Tonson, 1725), vol. I, p. xv.

5 Thomas Edwards, *A Supplement to Mr. Warburton's Edition of Shakespear. Being the Canons of Criticism, and Glossary, Collected from the Notes in that Celebrated Work and Proper to be Bound up with it* (London: M. Cooper, 1748), p. 16.

6 Samuel Johnson (ed.), *The Plays of William Shakespeare*, 8 vols. (London: J. & R. Tonson, *et al.*, 1765), vol. I, sigs. E1r, D8v, D1v.

7 John Bell (publisher), *Dramatick Writings of Will. Shakspere*, 76 parts forming 20 vols. (London: J. Bell, 1785–8), pasted in preliminary matter.

8 Advertisement in the *Publishers' Circular*, 2:33 1 (February 1839), 72.

9 W. E. Adams, *Memoirs of a Social Atom*, 2 vols. (London: Hutchinson, 1903), vol. I, p. 102.

10 See the *Bookseller* (1 July 1868), 451.

11 W. W. Greg, 'Bibliography – an Apologia', in J. C. Maxwell (ed.), *Collected Papers* (Oxford: Clarendon Press, 1966), p. 241.

12 See W.W. Greg, 'On Certain False Dates in Shakespearian Quartos', *Library*, 2nd series, 9 (1908), 113–31 and 381–409.

13 See Charlton Hinman, *The Printing and Proof-Reading of the First Folio of Shakespeare*, 2 vols. (Oxford: Clarendon Press, 1963).

14 John Dover Wilson, 'Introduction' to Arthur Quiller-Couch and John Dover Wilson (eds.), *The Tempest* (Cambridge: Cambridge University Press, 1921), p. xxx.

15 See R. B. McKerrow, 'A Suggestion Regarding Shakespeare's Manuscripts', *Review of English Studies*, 11 (1935), 459–65.

16 See Edward Maunde Thompson, *Shakespeare's Hand* (Oxford: Clarendon Press, 1916; A. W. Pollard (ed.), *Shakespeare's Hand in the Play of Sir Thomas More* (Cambridge: Cambridge University Press, 1923).

17 Jerome J. McGann, *A Critique of Modern Textual Criticism* (Charlottesville: University of Virginia Press, 1992; originally published Chicago: University of Chicago Press, 1983), p. 48.

18 See William B. Long, ' "Precious Few": English Manuscript Playbooks', in David Scott Kastan (ed.), *A Companion to Shakespeare* (Oxford: Blackwell, 1999), pp. 414–33; Paul Werstine, 'Narratives about Printed Shakespeare Texts: "Foul Papers" and "Bad" Quartos', *Shakespeare Quarterly*, 41 (1990), 65–86.

19 See MacDonald P. Jackson, 'Is "Hand D" of *Sir Thomas More* Shakespeare's? Thomas Bayes and the Elliott–Valenza Authorship Tests', *Early Modern Literary Studies: A Journal of Sixteenth- and Seventeenth-Century English Literature*, 12:3 (January 2007). Online article, accessible at http://extrashu.ac.ul/enls/12–3/jackbaye.htm

20 See Laurie E. Maguire, *Shakespearean Suspect Texts: The 'Bad' Quartos and their Contexts* (Cambridge: Cambridge University Press, 1996).

21 See Margreta de Grazia and Peter Stallybrass, 'The Materiality of the Shakespearean Text', *Shakespeare Quarterly*, 44 (1993), 255–83; Jonathan Goldberg, 'Textual Properties', *Shakespeare Quarterly*, 37 (1986), 213–17; Stephen Orgel, 'What is a Text'?, in David Scott Kastan and Peter Stallybrass (eds.), *Staging the Renaissance: Representations of Elizabethan and Jacobean Drama* (London: Routledge, 1991), pp. 83–7; originally published in *Research Opportunities in Renaissance Drama*, 26 (1981), 3–6.

READING LIST

Black, N.W. and Matthias Shaaber. *Shakespeare's Seventeenth-Century Editors, 1632–1685*. New York: MLA, 1937.

de Grazia, Margreta. *Shakespeare Verbatim: The Reproduction of Authenticity and the 1790 Apparatus*. Oxford: Clarendon Press, 1991.

Franklin, Colin. *Shakespeare Domesticated: The Eighteenth-Century Editions*. Aldershot: Scolar Press, 1991.

Geduld, Harry M. *Prince of Publishers: A Study of the Work and Career of Jacob Tonson*. Bloomington, IN: Indiana University Press, 1969.

Greetham, D.C. *Textual Scholarship: An Introduction*. New York: Garland, 1994.

Ioppolo, Grace. *Revising Shakespeare*. Cambridge, MA: Harvard University Press, 1991.

Kastan, David Scott. *Shakespeare and the Book*. Cambridge: Cambridge University Press, 2001.

Lynch, Kathleen M. *Jacob Tonson, Kit-Kat Publisher*. Knoxville: University of Tennessee Press, 1971.

McKerrow, R.B. *The Treatment of Shakespeare's Text by his Earliest Editors, 1709–1786*. British Academy Annual Lecture, 1933. London: British Academy, 1933.

Martin, Peter. *Edmond Malone, Shakespearian Scholar: A Literary Biography*. Cambridge: Cambridge University Press, 1995.

Massai, Sonia. *Shakespeare and the Rise of the Editor*. Cambridge: Cambridge University Press, 2007.

Peters, Julie Stone. *Theatre of the Book 1480–1880: Print, Text, and Performance in Europe*. Oxford: Oxford University Press, 2000.

Seary, Peter. *Lewis Theobald and the Editing of Shakespeare*. Oxford: Clarendon Press, 1990.

Taylor, Gary. *Reinventing Shakespeare: A Cultural History from the Restoration to the Present*. 1989; repr. Oxford: Oxford University Press, 1991.

Taylor, Gary and Michael Warren, eds. *The Division of the Kingdom: Shakespeare's Two Versions of 'King Lear'*. Oxford: Clarendon Press, 1983.

Walsh, Marcus. *Shakespeare, Milton and Eighteenth-Century Literary Editing: The Beginnings of Interpretive Scholarship*. Cambridge: Cambridge University Press, 1997.

Wells, Stanley. *Re-Editing Shakespeare for the Modern Reader*. Oxford: Clarendon Press, 1984.

West, Anthony James. *The Shakespeare First Folio: The History of the Book*, vol. I: *An Account of the First Folio Based on its Sales and Prices, 1623–2000*. Oxford: Oxford University Press, 2001.

6

JONATHAN HOPE

Shakespeare and language

When Shakespeare and his contemporaries thought about language, they thought of speech: breathy, ephemeral sounds cast into the air. This very ethereality was taken as a proof of one of the key Renaissance ideas about language: inasmuch as it allowed humans to make evident their ability to reason, it was a divine gift, distinguishing humanity from, and elevating it above, the rest of creation. The gift of language could raise the monstrous to the level of the human, as it does Caliban, and the voluntary abandonment of language suggested a descent: as when the arrogant Ajax, swollen with pride at the prospect of single combat with Hector, loses his ability to distinguish social rank, along with his humanity, to a mumbling silence:

> THERSITES The man's undone for ever, for if Hector break not his neck i'th'combat he'll break't himself in vainglory. He knows not me. I said, 'Good morrow, Ajax', and he replies, 'Thanks, Agamemnon'. What think you of this man that takes me for the General? He's grown a very land-fish, languageless, a monster... he'll answer nobody. He professes not answering. Speaking is for beggars ... He wears his tongue in's arms.
>
> (*Troilus and Cressida*, 3.3.249–60)

Language is social in the Renaissance in a formal, public sense we no longer quite appreciate: there is a clear link here between Ajax's loss of language and his mistaking the lowly Thersites for the highest of the Greek generals. His loss of language is not complete: Ajax can still manage a dismissive 'Thanks, Agamemnon', and he can proudly declare that speaking is for beggars – but he has lost his reason, and therefore his membership of society. He is instead its laughing-stock.

In *Romeo and Juliet*, we see the reverse journey. The play begins with Romeo, conventionally moping, in love with Rosaline, while Mercutio seeks him out, mocking the halting language of the stereotypical lover:

> Romeo! Humours! Madman! Passion! Lover!
> Appear thou in the likeness of a sigh.

Speak but one rhyme and I am satisfied.
Cry but 'Aye me!' Pronounce but 'love' and 'dove'.
Speak to my gossip Venus one fair word.

(2.1.7–11)

Romeo avoids his friend, lurking silently offstage, coming forward only when Mercutio departs – and the next time they meet, Romeo has fallen for Juliet, and the authenticity of this love recharges his social and linguistic energy:

MERCUTIO You gave us the counterfeit fairly last night.
ROMEO Good morrow to you both. What counterfeit did I give you?
MERCUTIO The slip, sir, the slip. Can you not conceive?
ROMEO Pardon, good Mercutio. My business was great, and in such a case as mine a man may strain courtesy.

(2.3.40–5)

Here, the two indulge in a passage of wordplay: Mercutio begins, proleptically substituting 'counterfeit' for 'slip', a term for a counterfeit coin. Romeo is slow to pick up on this at first, hence Mercutio's explanation, but he neatly plays on Mercutio's 'conceive' with his 'great' business ('great' being a synonym for 'pregnant'), and there is also an obscene meaning of 'case', which could refer to the vagina. So on the surface, Romeo says, 'Sorry, Mercutio, but my business was important, and in those circumstances it is allowable to be impolite' – but a possible second meaning is, 'You should have seen the woman I was with last night!'

This quick interplay of polysemy is typical of much discourse in Shakespeare and has, as we shall see, sometimes irritated Shakespeare's later critics, but it is important we recognize (however obscure or laboured we now find the humour) that wordplay like this was a sign of intelligence and social engagement in the Renaissance – as Mercutio goes on to say.

Why, is not this better now than groaning for love? Now art thou sociable, now art thou Romeo, now art thou what thou art by art as well as by nature, for this drivelling love is like a great natural.

(2.3.76–9)

Romeo has regained his language and has become 'sociable' again – fit for society – and he does this by demonstrating 'art' (the artificial control of language) through a series of puns we now find excruciating (for example, 'O single-soled jest, solely singular for the singleness!' (2.3.58)). Mercutio's values are (for us) unexpected: 'nature' is associated with simplicity (a 'drivelling... natural', or simpleton). The Renaissance inherited from the classical rhetorical tradition a radically different approach to creativity from our own: as Mercutio implies, 'art' (or craft) is what distinguishes the educated, rational being from the 'natural' accident. Language should be consciously manipulated: creativity is to be controlled by learned rhetorical practice.[1] To the Renaissance, creativity without years of studied craft, learning tropes and figures, consciously channelling the products of imagination by art, was literally nothing – it produced the empty nonsense of the moping Romeo. Similarly, in *Hamlet*, Ophelia's madness produces an outpouring of unconstrained language:

> She speaks much of her father, says she hears
> There's tricks i'th' world, and hems, and beats her heart,
> Spurns enviously at straws, speaks things in doubt
> That carry but half sense. Her speech is nothing,
> Yet the unshapèd use of it doth move
> The hearers to collection. They aim at it,
> And botch the words up fit to their own thoughts,
> Which, as her winks and nods and gestures yield them,
> Indeed would make one think there might be thought,
> Though nothing sure, yet much unhappily.
>
> (4.5.4–13)

Ophelia talks of her murdered father, Polonius, suggests there are plots ('tricks') afoot, stumbles over her words ('hems'), makes the gestures associated with grief and distraction, is suspicious of harmless things ('Spurns... at straws'), says things which cannot be understood or which have no clear sense ('things in doubt / ...carry but half sense'). The absence of conjunctions in this report ('She speaks ... says ... Spurns ... speaks ...') mimics the confused, 'unshaped' nature of her speech; 'unshaped' carries a particular force here and in the Renaissance generally, where the craft of oral performance was the focus of almost the entire educational system. Ophelia's madness causes her to lose control of language – to lose the ability to structure discourse under the control of reason. While for the Romantics such a loss of constraint might have been seen as liberating, offering the possibility of insight beyond the everyday, for the Renaissance it represented the potential triumph of the forces of chaos over the order imposed by man's rational intellect. As the report goes on to suggest, unregulated expression is a dangerous force, liable to introduce error and confusion into the world. Ophelia's 'unshaped' language makes those who hear it attempt to reconstruct its lost meaning ('botch the words up'), but their conjectures are uncertain ('nothing sure') and dark.

This prizing of artifice in language, the stress on display of craft and formal learning, is almost entirely alien to us and results in many of our difficulties with Shakespeare's texts (especially his wordplay) – indeed, it is a far greater block to understanding Shakespeare's language than the relatively minor changes in semantics and grammar that have occurred since the seventeenth century. Complaints about Shakespeare's puns enter the critical tradition in the eighteenth century – Samuel Johnson complained that 'a quibble, poor and barren as it is, gave [Shakespeare] such delight, that he was content to purchase it, by the sacrifice of reason, propriety and truth'. Subsequent critics, even as late as the twentieth century, have been made uneasy by the apparently arbitrary nature of puns.[2] Such hostility to wordplay is, however, relatively rare before the eighteenth century. Miriam Joseph traces the history of critical valuations:

> [T]o play upon the various meanings of a word represented an intellectual exercise, a witty analysis commended and relished by Aristotle, practiced by Plato and by the great dramatists of Greece, esteemed and used by Cicero, employed by medieval and Renaissance preachers in their sermons, regarded as a rhetorical ornament by the Elizabethans, but frequently despised as false or degenerate wit from the eighteenth century to the present day.

Only a small number of other critics have followed Joseph in arguing for a serious approach to wordplay.[3] Joseph's account lays out the complexity of classical approaches to wordplay and gives a sense of the range of effects Shakespeare and his characters could generate:[4]

> *Antanaclasis* – a figure which, in repeating a word, shifts from one of its meanings to another:
>
> To England will I steal, and there I'll steal
>
> (*Henry V*, 5.1.78)
>
> *Syllepsis* – a figure also involving one word with more than one meaning, distinguished from antanaclasis by the fact that the word appears only once, with both meanings brought simultaneously into play:
>
> hang no more about me, I am no gibbet for you
>
> (*Merry Wives of Windsor*, 2.2.16–17)
>
> *Paronomasia* – like antanaclasis, this involves two iterations, but, crucially, in paronomasia the words are not pure homophones:
>
> Out, sword, and to a sore purpose!
>
> (*Cymbeline*, 4.1.19)
>
> *Asteismus* – a deliberate shifting of sense by a second speaker:
>
> CLOTEN Would he had been one of my rank!
> SECOND LORD[*aside*] To have smelled like a fool.
>
> (*Cymbeline*, 2.1.13–15)

This four-fold analysis of wordplay is rather more complex than the definition of a pun offered by Addison in the early eighteenth century[5] – 'Having pursued the History of a Punn... I shall here define it to be a Conceit arising from the use of two Words that agree in Sound but differ in Sense' – and this goes some way to explaining post-seventeenth-century hostility to wordplay. Enlightenment critics saw puns as involving two words brought together by a trivial and arbitrary resemblance of form (hence Addison's 'two Words that agree in Sound but differ in sense') – but, as Margreta de Grazia has argued, before dictionaries established fixed spellings and associated particular meanings with particular spellings of words, it is possible that speakers of a language would not have identified the 'words' associated with each meaning as being distinct entities.[6] Addison's model of a 'word' presupposes the ideal of one sense to one form. He clearly assumes that, where there are two senses, but apparently one form, we must be dealing with a case of two superficially identical, but actually different, words. This ideal, of one form to one sense, is what dictionaries bring to the language: the spellings dye/die are separated into two stable, distinct forms only by orthographic standardization. The 'two' words are created and maintained by orthographic standardization – before dictionaries were available, there was no stable basis on which to identify variant spellings like dye/die or corse/coarse/ course/ cours/cors as anything other than multiple possible realizations of a single 'word', which has a range of possible meanings.

Puns thus have value for Renaissance users of language because their production and recognition involve the active use of the linguistic system, and demonstrate a facility with it prized in the rhetorical tradition. To recognize wordplay, a speaker has to bring into play two or more possible meanings associated with one word, producing an aesthetic effect of complexity. The Renaissance audience is involved in actively maintaining the double play of meaning, but the post-Enlightenment audience is a passive observer of what appear to be merely facile and arbitrary similarities of form. This allows us to begin to appreciate what Shakespeare might have perceived in these apparently 'barren' interplays of wit.

As we have seen, language was central to the notion of the human in the Renaissance. But this did not mean that all languages were equally regarded. The prestige of classical rhetorical culture and continental European learning meant that for some commentators English was a 'base', undeveloped language. Scholars such as Richard Mulcaster advocated the deliberate expansion of English through the borrowing of words which would enable its users to talk, and write, on more sophisticated topics. There was much contemporary comment on such borrowings: on the one hand, new words were held to enrich the language by expanding its resources and stylistic potential; on the other, the often Latinate terms were sometimes felt to be overly scholarly ('Inkhorn', as contemporary writers had it), because such words were obscure to most speakers of English. Those who had a classical education could be expected to understand and be impressed by words borrowed from Latin, as Shallow is when he works out what Bardolph means by the newly coined 'accommodated' in 2 *Henry IV*:

> 'Better accommodated' – it is good; yea, indeed is it. Good phrases are surely, and ever were, very commendable. 'Accommodated' – it comes of '*accommodo*'. Very good, a good phrase. (3.2.64–6)

Bardolph's response to Shallow's praise is surprisingly defensive, however:

> Pardon, sir, I have heard the word – 'phrase' call you it? – By this day, I know not the phrase; but I will maintain the word with my sword to be a soldier-like word, and a word of exceeding good command, by heaven. (3.2.67–70)

His defence of 'accommodated' as a 'soldier-like' word suggests that he suspects that Shallow is accusing him of linguistic pretension in using Latinate words. Although there is no reason to doubt the genuine nature of Shallow's praise, the source of Bardolph's linguistic insecurity becomes clear when he attempts to give his own definition of 'accommodated'. He has no idea of what this fashionable word means and can only offer a confused and circular definition:

> 'Accommodated'; that is, when a man is, as they say, accommodated; or when a man is being whereby a may be thought to be accommodated; which is an excellent thing. (3.2.70–3)

If aspirational speakers were sometimes caught out over-reaching, 'ordinary' speakers could also offer wry comment on the stylistic pretensions of Latinate English. In *Love's Labour's Lost*, the knight Armado pays Costard to deliver a letter for him, saying, as he hands over the money, 'There is remuneration' (3.1.120). Left alone on stage, Costard tallies his fee: 'Now will I look to his remuneration. Remuneration – O, that's the Latin word for three-farthings' (3.1.125–6). Faced with an audience which would have included the equivalents of Shallow, capable of identifying the Latin root of newly borrowed words, and a large group of Costards, able to spot a Latin word but dependent on hearing it in context to derive a meaning, Shakespeare developed a self-glossing style, deftly mixing borrowed and native English terms:

> for *cogitation*
> Resides not in that man that does not *think*
> (*The Winter's Tale*, 1.2.273–4)

> O, matter and *impertinency* mixed!
> Reason in *madness*!
> (*King Lear* 4.6.168–9)

> By all your vows of love, and that great vow
> Which did *incorporate* and *make us one*.
> (*Julius Caesar*, 2.1.271–2)

As Bardolph's example shows, Shakespeare was well aware of the dangers of borrowing – and, perhaps contrary to the popular notion of Shakespeare as the supreme coiner of words, the plays are full of characters who are satirized either for the outright misuse of the new Latinate vocabulary (Dogberry in *Much Ado About Nothing*, Quickly in the *Henry IV* plays, *Henry V* and *Merry Wives*, Dull in *Love's Labour's Lost*) or for putting on more general, often courtly, linguistic airs (Osric in *Hamlet*, Oswald in *King Lear*, Armado and Holofernes in *Love's Labour's Lost*). Statistical studies show that Shakespeare employs less Latinate vocabulary than do his contemporaries, and, as Daniell points out in his Arden edition of *Julius Caesar*, Shakespeare gives the suspect Cassius a vocabulary of new words and the noble Brutus one of old ones – Iago too is keen on 'fire new' words.[7]

While Renaissance authors consciously expanded English vocabulary by borrowing from Latin and other languages, such borrowings were numerically less important than derivation, or the creation of new words from existing resources. Shakespeare makes particular use of the processes of affixation (changing the role or meaning of a word by adding morphemes to the start or end) and conversion (shifting the grammatical role of a word without any necessary change in the morphology). For example, Lear takes the fashionable borrowing 'accommodated', used, as we have seen, satirically in 2 *Henry IV*, and turns it into a serious element of his discourse on the fragility of humanity by adding the English prefix 'un-': 'unaccommodated man is no more but such a poor, bare, forked animal as thou art' (*King Lear*, 3.4.98–100). Shakespeare seems particularly drawn to 'un-' as a way of negating concepts, perhaps because it suggests an active process of undoing something, rather than simple absence. It crops up in the linguistically self-conscious display of Holofernes: 'his undressed, unpolished, uneducated, unpruned, untrained, or rather unlettered, or ratherest unconfirmed, fashion' (*Love's Labour's Lost*, 4.2.15–17). Even when not motivated by character, one use can often set up a string of further uses:

> Haply that name of chaste unhapp'ly set
> This bateless edge on his keen appetite,
> When Collatine unwisely did not let
> To praise the clear unmatchèd red and white
> (*The Rape of Lucrece*, 8–11)

This passage is then followed quickly by 'unlocked' (16); 'unknown' (34); 'untimely' (43).

Shakespeare's attraction to linguistic forms that express activity can also be seen in his fondness for the agentive '-er' suffix. In contrast to 'un-', this suffix is not found throughout his work, but its use is marked in *Antony and*

Cleopatra, where ' -er' is frequently added to verbs to produce a noun with the meaning 'one who does [verb]'. When the defeated Antony returns from battle to find Cleopatra allowing Caesar's messenger to kiss her hand, he first rails at her for deigning to look on 'feeders' (3.13.109), and when she tries to justify her actions, he persists: 'You have been a boggler ever' (3.13.111). Here 'feeder' means a servant, one who is fed (by his master), and 'boggler' means one who starts with fright ('You boggle shrewdly; every feather starts you' *All's Well That Ends Well*, 5.3.235) and/or quibbles with words. Either sense (or both) could work here, since Antony's defeat is prompted by Cleopatra's flight from the battle, while her entertaining Caesar's messenger could be interpreted as equivocation. 'Feeder' is relatively common in this sense in the early modern period, but 'boggler' appears to be unique. Later in the same scene, there is another rare '-er' formation, as Antony calls Cleopatra's hand a 'plighter' (3.13.127). The play employs several relatively established '-er' forms, such as 'surfeiter' (2.1.33), 'wearer' (2.2.7), 'reporter' (2.2.194) and 'master-leaver' (4.10.21), which occur elsewhere in Renaissance literature, but, as with 'boggler' and 'plighter', there are others which are unique, or for which Shakespeare himself is the only repeat user in the period: 'strangler' (2.6.119), 'breather' (3.3.21) and 'sworder' (3.13.30).

While *Antony and Cleopatra* is marked out by the frequency of '-er' forms it contains, they also cluster around descriptions of Antony in *Julius Caesar*:

CASSIUS A peevish schoolboy, worthless of such honour,
Joined with a masquer and a reveller!
ANTONY Old Cassius still.

(5.1.61–3)

Shakespeare's grammar (or more correctly, morphosyntax – the system of grammatical relations between words and the inflections that mark them) does not differ greatly from our own. The most significant difference is contextual, in that he wrote at a time when written English was in the process of being standardized. This meant that Shakespeare had a wider range of morphosyntactic options open to him than we do today. Whenever he wrote a question or a negative, for example, Shakespeare might have followed the now standard pattern and used the auxiliary verb 'do': 'What do these fellows mean? Don't they know Achilles?' Alternatively, as he actually did in this case, he could use a much older system, slowly disappearing from the language, which reversed the subject and verb: 'What mean these fellows? Know they not Achilles?' (*Troilus and Cressida*, 3.3.64). The system without 'do' was increasingly sounding old-fashioned to those younger than Shakespeare and can sometimes be seen to pattern stylistically with formal contexts. Shakespeare's fondness for it, compared with that of younger writers like Fletcher and Middleton, may be one of the reasons the Restoration found Shakespeare somewhat dated; it may also have licensed adaptation of his plays, rather than straight revival. Other areas of choice included the formation of relative clauses, where the constraints governing the use of the relative pronouns were not so restrictive as they now are in standard English: 'Here is a sick man that would speak with you' (*Julius Caesar*, 2.1.309). Most writers now would avoid the use of 'that' with a human antecedent, as here. Conversely, early modern English allowed the use of 'who' with non-humans: 'Against the Capitol I met a lion / Who glazed upon me' (*Julius Caesar*, 1.3.20–1). Shakespeare could also use zero pronouns in subject position, something confined to speech today: 'Let him that will a screech-owl aye be called / Go into Troy and say their Hector's dead. / There is a word will Priam turn to stone' (*Troilus and Cressida*, 5.11.16–18). That is, 'There is a word *which will* turn Priam to stone.'

Because these choices were disappearing from standard written English – along with others, such as the '-eth' ending on third person singular present tense verbs ('goeth'), the use of 'thou' and subjunctives – they quickly become associated with older speakers and formal situations. Shakespeare was born just early enough in the sixteenth century, and far enough away from the centre of linguistic innovation in the southeast, that he retained a more ready access to these disappearing linguistic features than did most of his contemporaries, and all of the generation of writers who followed him.

While the choices available to Shakespeare at the level of morphosyntax rarely cause problems for us in reading his texts, one feature that does make it difficult for many people initially is his often highly unusual word order. The normal order for elements in English clauses is Subject – Verb – X (where X stands for a variety of possible entities, most frequently object, complement or adverbial), as in these three consecutive clauses from Claudius: 'O, my offence is rank! It smells to heaven. / It hath the primal eldest curse upon't' (*Hamlet*, 3.3.36–7). But Shakespeare frequently inverts or disrupts the expected order of elements in a clause, sometimes in order to bring the most salient word to the front, as happens in the very next clause in Claudius' speech: 'Pray can I not' (*Hamlet*, 3.3.38), that is, 'I cannot pray.' Clauses are similarly inverted in the parallel syntax of this exchange from *Troilus and Cressida*:

ACHILLES *Of this my privacy*
I have strong reasons.
ULYSSES But *'gainst your privacy*
The reasons are more potent and heroical.
(3.3.184–6)

Here, in each case a final adverbial is brought to the front of the clause. Disruption can also involve movement within the clause, as in, 'Let him that will *a screech-owl* aye be call'd / Go into Troy and say their Hector's dead', where the complement ('screech-owl') is moved in front of the main verb. Often these disruptions are for emphasis, but they can also function to shift words around in the line so that the metrical template is met. Compare this line and a half as it appears in *Antony and Cleopatra* with the more 'normal' word order: 'With news the time's in labour, and throws forth / Each minute some' (3.7.80–1), as opposed to, 'The time's in labour with news and each minute throws some forth.' The 'normal' version has the content noun 'news' in an unstressed position and has an extra unstressed syllable at the end of the first line – not fatally unmetrical, given Shakespeare's practice elsewhere, but perhaps clumsy enough when combined with the flatness of the 'normal' version to prompt a rewrite to the less expected one. Here we see perhaps the real key to Shakespeare's variation on word order: an unexpected order can freshen otherwise mundane language, forcing the hearer to work harder and producing a pleasing aesthetic effect of complexity.

This brings us naturally on to Shakespeare's use of verse forms. He writes most often in blank verse – unrhymed iambic pentameter – but he also makes extensive use of the sonnet form (fourteen lines of rhymed iambic pentameter), and on occasion other stanzaic forms, all still employing iambic pentameter (six-line stanzas rhyming ababcc for *Venus and Adonis*; seven-line stanzas rhyming ababbcc for *Lucrece*). He breaks with iambic pentameter for songs and for the enigmatic lyric 'The Phoenix and the Turtle', which uses a trochaic form (initially, seven-syllable, four-stressed lines, in stanzas of four lines rhyming abba, shifting to three-line stanzas rhyming aaa).

The most detailed and subtle account of Shakespeare's iambic pentameter is George Wright's *Shakespeare's Metrical Art*, though beginners may at first find confusing the fact that most of his discussion is of Shakespeare's complex variations on the basic iambic pattern.[8] That basic pattern consists of a metrical template which controls the number of syllables allowed in a line (ten) and the positions in the line where stressed syllables are allowed to appear (only in even-numbered slots):

1	2	3	4	5	6	7	8	9	10
	[stress]		[stress]		[stress]		[stress]		[stress]

A key to avoiding confusion is the fact that the metre does not demand that *every* even position in any particular line has to have a stressed syllable: unstressed syllables can appear in even positions. The metre simply requires that, when a lexically stressed syllable is used, it must appear in an even position.

What is a lexically stressed syllable? Stress on English words is produced in two ways, depending on the nature of the word. If the word is polysyllabic, then the stress is fixed and will always be the same, whenever the word is used (*Shake*speare, for example, is always stressed on the first syllable, and attempting to stress it on the second will generally produce humorous effects). This is lexical stress. If a word is a monosyllable, however, stress is unfixed and will depend on the context in which the word is used, and the whim of the speaker. It is perfectly possible to imagine several different ways of stressing monosyllabic clauses depending on the intended meaning:

I gave it to *him*.
I gave it *to* him.
I gave *it* to him.
I *gave* it to him.
I gave it to him.

This optionality of stress on monosyllables in performance, coupled with the fact that iambic metre only seeks to determine the position of lexically stressed syllables, means that there is huge potential variation in the construction and performance of iambic lines. For example, when Ulysses says of Cressida, 'There's language in her eye, her cheek, her lip' (*Troilus and Cressida*, 4.6.56), there is only one polysyllabic word in the line – 'language' – which has two syllables, the first of which always carries stress ('*lan*guage'). So the first syllable has to be placed in an even numbered position in the line – which it is:

1	2	3	4	5	6	7	8	9	10
There's	lan-	guage	in	her	eye	her	cheek	her	lip

The rest of the words are monosyllables, so the metre is not explicitly concerned with them: whether or not they carry stress will depend on the meaning and the sense that an actor wishes to convey, but note the way that the nouns 'eye', 'cheek' and 'lip' all appear in even positions: these content nouns are more likely to attract stress in performance than the pronoun 'her'. The most likely performance of this line would have an obligatory stress on 'lan-', then further optional stresses on 'eye', 'cheek' and 'lip'. Note too that although 'in' is placed in an even position, it is very unlikely to be given stress in performance – so there is a slight tension between the metrical form (which might lead us to expect a stress here) and natural speech (which would very rarely have a stress on a preposition like 'in'). This tension between the norms of speech and the demands of the metrical form is the key to the sophistication of Shakespeare's iambic metre. Were he to follow the metrical template too closely by filling all the potentially stressed slots with stressed syllables, the verse would be mechanistic and tedious. Become too loose, however, and the tension between form and expression that raises poetry above prose would be lost.[9]

Theories of meaning (semantics) were much discussed in the Renaissance (particularly in regard to legal and theological matters), and the main positions were inherited from classical debates. Vivian Salmon cites as a typical summary of Renaissance theories of meaning the work of Juan Huarte, whose *Examen de Ingenios* (1575) was translated into English (from an Italian version) as *The Examination of Men's Wits* (1594).[10] The principal question was, 'From where do words derive their meaning?' Huarte identifies two competing positions on this, which he associates respectively with Plato and Aristotle (he calls the debate 'a question much hammered between Plato & Aristotle' (p. 117)).

The 'Platonic' position, voiced by the characters of Cratylus and Socrates in Plato's *Cratylus*, is that there is, or should be, a 'natural' relationship between a word and its referent – that words derive their meaning from a non-arbitrary connection to the thing named. The 'true' name for something is thus mystically linked to, and expresses, the essence of the thing named – as Huarte has it, 'there are proper names, which by their nature carry signification of things, and ... much wit is requisite to devise them' (p. 118). That is, names are 'proper' in the sense of being naturally linked to the thing they refer to, and 'much wit' is required to devise such names, since the namer must understand the nature of things in order to be able to name them correctly. The standard Renaissance example of such a process was Adam's naming of the animals:

> And this opinion is favoured by the divine scripture, which affirmeth that Adam gave every of those things which God set before him, the proper name that best was fitting for them. (p. 118)

Hence this is sometimes referred to as the 'Adamic' theory of meaning.

The alternative position, best known from Aristotle's *On Interpretation*, stressed the conventional nature of meaning: words have meaning because of the way they are used ('custom', as many writers have it) and through their relationships with each other. Under this theory, names are arbitrary, and Huarte claims that this can be shown by cross-linguistic comparison:

> Aristotle will not grant that in any tongue there can be found any name, or manner of speech, which can signify aught of it own nature, for that all names are devised and shaped after the conceit of men. Whence we see by experience, that wine hath above 60 names, and bread as many, in every language his, and of none we can avouch that the same is natural and agreeable thereunto, for then in all the world would use but that. (p. 118)

If the Platonic theory were correct, Huarte argues, the terms for such staples as 'wine' and 'bread' would be the same in all languages – since the nature of these things does not change between languages. The fact that names change between languages shows that they are conventional and arbitrary, rather than linked to the essential nature of the thing to which they refer.

'Custom' is recognized by many Renaissance writers as the governing force in meaning, and the best guide to usage: Juliet, when she muses on Romeo's name and notes that 'That which we call a rose / By any other word would smell as sweet' (2.1.85–6), reveals herself to be an Aristotelian. But the strange links that could be established by wordplay, indeed even by Shakespeare's punning on his own name and 'will' in the Sonnets (135, 136), remind us that the occult attraction of the Adamic theory ran deep, even as Renaissance writers attempted to explain language rationally.

NOTES

1 See Brian Vickers, *Classical Rhetoric in English Poetry* (London: Macmillan, 1970).

2 Samuel Johnson, 'Preface to Shakespeare', from *The Plays of William Shakespeare* (1765). For Coleridge, see T. M. Raysor (ed.), *S. T. Coleridge: Shakespearean Criticism* (London: Dent, 1960), vol. I, p. 86; the discussion in Keir Elam, *Shakespeare's Universe of Discourse: Language Games in the Comedies* (Cambridge: Cambridge University Press, 1984), pp. 1–6. For Stephen Booth, see Booth, 'Exit, Pursued by a Gentleman Born', in Wendell M. Aycock (ed.), *Shakespeare's Art from a Comparative Perspective*, Proceedings of the Comparative Literature Symposium (Lubbock, TX: Texas Technical University, 1981), vol. XII, pp. 51–66; and Booth, 'Shakespeare's Language and the Language of Shakespeare's Time', *Shakespeare Survey*, 50 (1997), 1–17.

3 Miriam Joseph, *Shakespeare's Use of the Arts of Language* (New York: Columbia University Press, 1947), esp. pp. 165–71. For further favourable assessments of Shakespeare's wordplay, see Molly Mahood, *Shakespeare's Wordplay* (London: Methuen, 1957); 'M. M. Mahood, *Shakespeare's Wordplay* – Some Reappraisals', in *Connotations*, 6:1 (1996–7), 1–45; Patricia Parker, *Shakespeare from the Margins: Language, Culture, Context* (Chicago: University of Chicago Press, 1996); Russ MacDonald, *The Bedford Companion to Shakespeare* (New York: Bedford/St Martin's, 2001), p. 44; MacDonald, *Shakespeare and the Arts of Language* (Oxford: Oxford University Press, 2001), chapter 7. Two general approaches to puns and wordplay are: Walter Redfern, *Puns* (Oxford: Blackwell, 1984) and Jonathan Culler (ed.), *On Puns: The Foundation of Letters* (Oxford: Blackwell, 1988).

4 Joseph, *Shakespeare's Use*, p. 165.

5 Quoted here from the *OED*, 'pun'.

6 Margreta de Grazia, 'Homonyms before and after Lexical Standardisation', *Deutsche Shakespeare-Gesellschaft West Jahrbuch* (1990), 143–56.

7 David Daniell (ed.), *Julius Caesar* (London: Arden Shakespeare, 1998), pp. 60–2.

8 George T. Wright, *Shakespeare's Metrical Art* (Berkeley: University of California Press, 1998).

9 Wright carries these arguments much further – see ibid., pp. 259ff. Note that for the sake of clarity I have omitted mention of two common irregularities in Shakespeare's iambic metre: 1) the first position in a line can sometimes hold a stressed syllable (trochaic inversion): '*Speak*ing in deeds and deedless in his tongue' (*Troilus and Cressida*, 4.6.101); 2) an unstressed eleventh syllable is sometimes allowed (this becomes more frequent over Shakespeare's career and has been used to date the plays): 'Yet gives he not till judgement guide his boun*ty*' (*Troilus and Cressida*, 4.6.105).

10 Vivian Salmon, 'Views on Meaning in Sixteenth-Century England', in *Language and Society in Early Modern England: Selected Essays* (Amsterdam: John Benjamins, 1990), pp. 55–75.

READING LIST

Adamson, Sylvia *et al. Reading Shakespeare's Dramatic Language*. London: Arden Shakespeare, 2001.

Alexander, Catherine, ed. *Shakespeare and Language*. Cambridge: Cambridge University Press, 2004.

Barber, Charles. *Early Modern English*. Edinburgh: Edinburgh University Press, 1996.

Blake, Norman. *A Grammar of Shakespeare's Language*. Basingstoke: Palgrave, 2002.

Blank, Paula. *Broken English: Dialects and the Politics of Language in Renaissance Writings*. London: Routledge, 1996.

Crystal, David. *Pronouncing Shakespeare*. Cambridge: Cambridge University Press, 2005.

'Think on my Words': Exploring Shakespeare's Language. Cambridge: Cambridge University Press, 2008.

Dobson, E. J. *English Pronunciation 1500–1700*, 2 vols. Oxford: Clarendon Press, 1968, 2nd edn.

Elam, Keir. *Shakespeare's Universe of Discourse: Language-Games in the Comedies*. Cambridge: Cambridge University Press, 1984.

Freedman, Penelope. *Power and Passion in Shakespeare's Pronouns: Interrogating 'You' and 'Thou'*. Aldershot: Ashgate, 2007.

Hope, Jonathan. *Shakespeare's Grammar*. London: Arden Shakespeare, 2003.

Houston, John Porter. *Shakespearian Sentences: A Study in Style and Syntax*. Baton Rouge: Louisiana State University Press, 1988.

Lass, Roger, ed. *The Cambridge History of the English Language*, vol. III: *1476–1776*. Cambridge: Cambridge University Press, 1999.

Magnusson, Lynne. *Shakespeare and Social Dialogue: Dramatic Language and Elizabethan Letters*. Cambridge: Cambridge University Press, 1999.

Nevalainen, Terttu. *An Introduction to Early Modern English*. Edinburgh: Edinburgh University Press, 2006.

Salmon, Vivian and Edwina Burness, eds. *Reader in the Language of Shakespearian Drama*. Amsterdam: John Benjamins, 1987.

Vickers, Brian. *The Artistry of Shakespeare's Prose*. London: Methuen, 1968.

Wright, George T. *Shakespeare's Metrical Art*. Berkeley: University of California Press, 1988.

7

COLIN BURROW

Shakespeare the poet

Everyone would agree that Shakespeare was a poet. We all know 'a bank where the wild thyme blows' and 'what light from yonder window breaks' and umpteen other set-piece descriptions and poetical rhapsodies from the plays. Compilers of anthologies of verse in Shakespeare's lifetime clearly regarded him as one of the finest poets of his generation. Readers of Robert Allot's *England's Parnassus, or the Choicest Flowers of our Modern Poets* (1600) could find passages from *Richard III* and *Richard II*, all duly ascribed to 'W. Shakespeare', set beside similar passages from Spenser, Marlowe, Jonson and Sir Philip Sidney. But Shakespeare was not just known as a poetical playwright at the close of the sixteenth century. At that date he was regarded more as a poet to be read on the page than as a writer of plays. In *England's Parnassus* quotations from the plays were outnumbered around two to one by extracts taken from his early narrative poems, *Venus and Adonis* and *Lucrece*.

It was of these poems that Francis Meres was thinking when in 1598 he described Shakespeare as 'honey-tongued'. Meres was also keen to show he knew that Shakespeare was at work producing sonnets: 'As the soul of Euphorbus was thought to live in Pythagoras, so the sweet, witty soul of Ovid lives in mellifluous and honey-tongued Shakespeare, witness his *Venus and Adonis*, his *Lucrece*, his sugared sonnets among his private friends, etc.'[1] At the end of the sixteenth century the name 'Shakespeare' meant 'ultra-fashionable poet', and by 1599 demand for Shakespeare's poems outstripped supply so much that the entrepreneurial printer William Jaggard set about printing a slim volume which purported to contain lyrics by Shakespeare. This volume, called *The Passionate Pilgrim*, included three of the courtiers' poems from *Love's Labour's Lost* and two early (or perhaps corrupt) versions of sonnets by Shakespeare. These were padded out by a selection of sonnets and lyrics by Richard Barnfield, Christopher Marlowe and Bartholomew Griffin, as well as other nameless authors, all of which were implicitly ascribed to Shakespeare. In 1600 Shakespeare was not simply a poet: he was close to being *the* poet, one so important that if printers could not get hold of poems by him they had to pretend they had done so.

It may be that the relatively small number of plays which had appeared with Shakespeare's name attached to them before 1600 distorts the picture a little,[2] but the association of his name at that date with poetry was chiefly the result of the extraordinary success of the first publication ascribed to him, *Venus and Adonis*, which appeared in 1593 with a dedication to the Earl of Southampton signed by Shakespeare. This erotic poem about the love of Venus for the ephoebic young Adonis was printed by Richard Field, who had probably been educated at the same school in Stratford-upon-Avon as Shakespeare. Field had a monopoly of printing texts of the classical author Ovid, who is the largest single influence on Shakespeare's poem, and had in the years before 1593 printed several books which had played a key part in raising the status of English poets and poetry to something equivalent to that of their classical predecessors. Shakespeare's first published poem joined Sir John Harington's 1591 translation of *Orlando Furioso* (one of the most lavish books of verse printed in England by that date) and George Puttenham's *Arte of English Poesie* from 1589 (the most systematic piece of literary criticism printed in the sixteenth century) on Field's bookstall some time in the summer of 1593. It was an instant hit, read by lunatics, lovers, poets, women, and young men with strong libidos and too much time on their hands.[3]

The poem contributes to a genre which modern critics tend to call either 'erotic narrative verse' or the 'epyllion' (short or minor epic). Neither term is Elizabethan, and readers from that period would probably have thought of *Venus and Adonis* simply as a 'pamphlet'. But it was a pamphlet of a recognizably racy kind. Thomas Lodge's *Scylla's Metamorphosis* (1589) had established a vogue for erotic poems about classical figures, while Christopher Marlowe had left at his death in May 1593 the unfinished *Hero and Leander*. The market for Elizabethan poetry was ready for *Venus and Adonis*, and by 1600 the poem had gone through six editions (over a similar period *Hamlet* would go through five). By that year it was familiar enough for the author of the Cambridge University *Parnassus* plays to poke fun at young men who borrowed Shakespeare's luscious rhetoric to seduce their mistresses. And seductive is probably the right word for it:

> 'Thrice fairer than my self,' thus she began,
> 'The fields' chief flower, sweet above compare,
> Stain to all nymphs, more lovely than a man,
> More white and red than doves or roses are –
> Nature that made thee with her self at strife
> Saith that the world hath ending with thy life.
> (7–12)

Venus is one of the most rhetorically sophisticated lovers in early modern literature. Indeed her eloquence is sometimes a barrier for modern readers. This is partly because we might be told by the edition we are reading that *Venus and Adonis* is a 'narrative' poem. That rather unfortunate label suggests that its main focus should be on telling a story. Read with that expectation the poem is extremely frustrating. Events are consistently hurried over so that Shakespeare can move on to the elaborately ornamented descriptions and rhetorically embellished speeches which are where his real interest lay. Actions are rattled through in seconds. When Adonis decides to leave Venus he simply 'hasteth to his horse' (258); when Venus sprints towards the sounds that alert her to Adonis' death she takes two bare lines to arrive where her lover lies dead: 'As falcons to the lure, away she flies. / The grass stoops not, she treads on it so light' (1027–8). The 'narrative' poems are actually poems which briefly sketch narrative scenarios and then use them as a pretext for descriptions and speeches. It's easy to explain why this is so. *Venus and Adonis* and *Lucrece* are the products of years spent in the classroom learning rhetorical figures and acquiring what was known in the period as 'copia', an endless copiousness of vocabulary, a complete mastery of figures and tropes of style, combined with a store of examples and phrases from classical literature, all of which could enable early modern schoolboys to speak persuasively on any topic anyone cared to mention. At length. And then, if you asked them, to speak on the other side of the case, too. Also at length.[4]

It was the art of rhetorical ornamentation – not simply layered on with a trowel, but carefully and ironically manipulated in relation to the events that provide its pretext – which made *Venus and Adonis* so popular. The story as Shakespeare found it in Ovid's *Metamorphoses* was very short – a mere seventy-two lines if you remove the long inset tale which Venus tells her lover in order to keep him with her. Shakespeare made one brilliant decision in adapting Ovid: to make Venus argue as well as narrate. As a result she became the embodiment of the rhetorical skills which his (mostly but not exclusively male) readers had acquired at school and which some of them went on to perfect at university. And she uses those arts not to persuade a mistress to succumb, but to seduce a young boy:

> Torches are made to light, jewels to wear,
> Dainties to taste, fresh beauty for the use,
> Herbs for their smell, and sappy plants to bear.
> Things growing to themselves are growth's abuse.
> Seeds spring from seeds, and beauty breedeth beauty:
> Thou wast begot; to get it is thy duty.
>
> (163–8)

Shakespeare's England by the 1590s was flooded with young men skilled in the arts of rhetoric. There were indeed too many such men for all of them to obtain the kinds of employment they wanted.[5] Shakespeare's poems presented these grammar school and university educated men with a fantasy that was not quite wish-fulfilment. He gave them an endlessly eloquent goddess of love, deliciously, sensuously ornamented in her speech and goddesslike in bulk and sexual appetite, and he made her speak like them: with apparently endless eloquence but almost zero practical effect. Whatever Venus says, Adonis will not yield. As a result Shakespeare probably made many of his readers feel their own eloquence, vainly directed towards professional goals that were unattainable (and perhaps also towards unattainable erotic goals, since marriage followed money in this period), becoming divine – and also, since Venus is attempting to seduce a boy, slightly queer. Many people would fork out sixpence in 1593 in order to experience those delights.

The poem is particularly focused on imaginary pleasures, as befits a piece which simultaneously mocks and fulfils the wishes of its audience. When Venus finally pulls Adonis down on top of her she is 'in the very lists of love' (595), and Shakespeare seems to promise his readers a full representation of carnal delight; but Adonis' body will not oblige: 'All is imaginary she doth prove' (597). The poem represents two people (and two genders) who inhabit contiguous but autonomous imaginary realms. That is, Venus and Adonis occupy almost the same space, but what each of them sees and feels is quite different from what the other sees and feels. This concentration on what these two characters see or do not see is reinforced by the extraordinary density of the vocabulary of looking within the poem: similes are introduced by 'Look how' (67, 79, 815, 925); repeatedly we are urged to 'see'. But the poem's interest in perception goes well beyond a concern with the visual and the illusionistic. When his stallion bolts in pursuit of a passing mare, Adonis sees it as an annoying barrier to his hunting: 'My day's delight is past; my horse is gone' (380). Venus sees it as a clear moral (or immoral) lesson in how all males should welcome 'the warm approach of sweet desire' (386). The poem explores the boundaries between different people's perceptions and the ways in which even the most sumptuous rhetoric cannot overcome the irreducible distinctness of different viewpoints. Sometimes this is little more than an excuse for irony on the part of the narrator or characters within the poem, as when Venus says with mock incredulity when Adonis finally answers her, ' "What, canst thou talk?" quoth she, "Hast thou a tongue?"' (427). But when Venus finally sees the body of her lover gored by the boar, the poem widens its gaze beyond the visual and ironical and imagines the kinds of illusion which make lovers fail to see what is in front of their eyes, or hate their own perceptions:

Upon his hurt she looks so steadfastly
That her sight, dazzling, makes the wound seem three;
And then she reprehends her mangling eye,
That makes more gashes where no breach should be.
His face seems twain; each several limb is doubled;
For oft the eye mistakes, the brain being troubled.
(1063–8)

Venus' eyes dazzle with grief. That moment stands near the start of what was to be for Shakespeare a career-long interest in the imaginary hurts which love can create, and those which it can receive from those who do not feel it. *Venus and Adonis* marks the beginning of Shakespeare's career as a perspectival artist, for whom what each person sees may differ from what everyone else sees, and in whose work speeches of persuasion and exhortation might ornament but not alter these differences of perspective.

After the extreme success of *Venus and Adonis*, Shakespeare turned to the 'graver labour' which he had promised to the Earl of Southampton in its dedicatory epistle. The result was the publication in 1594 of *Lucrece* (as it is called on its title page), or *The Rape of Lucrece*, as its raunchier running-titles have it. The double title may well have been the result of a wish not to blazon the word 'rape' on a title page but to keep it in the picture (that word in the sixteenth century was not quite so unequivocally related to sexual violation as it is today, since it could refer to abduction as well). *Lucrece* was dedicated to the Earl of Southampton in notably warmer terms than its predecessor ('What I have done is yours; what I have to do is yours, being part in all I have, devoted yours') and may indicate a growing relationship of patronage between the Earl and the poet. Its ambience is profoundly different from that of *Venus and Adonis*. It describes a historical event about which early modern readers would have known and which they would have believed to have been of immense historical significance. The rape of the chaste Roman wife Lucretia by Sextus Tarquinius, son of one of the early rulers of Rome, was believed to have precipitated the banishment of kings and the introduction of republican government to Rome.[6] The poem's repertoire of images – cities under siege, houses under threat – continually keeps the larger historical consequences of Lucrece's rape in the periphery of a reader's vision, and the poem creates a milieu – internal, tense, enclosed – which is notably different from the unpopulated outdoor summerscape of *Venus and Adonis*. *Lucrece*'s sources lie in Roman history, in Ovid's calendrical poem called the *Fasti* and in Virgil's epic *Aeneid*, the ultimate origin of the lengthy description of the picture of the sack of Troy onto which Lucrece projects her grief (1366–1568). All of these features mark it as indeed a 'graver labour' than its predecessor, and its seriousness of tone and the gravity of its repertoire of allusions might suggest that Shakespeare was constructing a career for himself as a poet, which moved away from the erotic tingles of *Venus and Adonis* towards quasi-epic gravity.[7]

Lucrece is, however, clearly designed as a companion-piece for *Venus and Adonis*. Its interior landscape, its focus on sexual desire and even its political themes seem to grow almost naturally from the virtuoso final sequence of the earlier poem. Venus' eyes flee from the sight of the dead Adonis into the 'deep dark cabins of her head' (1038), which anticipate the dark interiors and dark psychological spaces of *Lucrece*. When Venus sees her dead lover her body goes into revolt and her heart is 'like a king perplexèd in his throne' (1043), as though a psychological version of a political rebellion has occurred. Like the earlier poem, *Lucrece* repeatedly conjoins rapidly sketched actions (Tarquin shoots from Ardea to Collatium in the first four lines) with speeches which seem unstoppable. But perhaps the greatest difference between the two poems is that in *Lucrece* gender roles are almost oppressively conventional: a feminine eloquence that cannot move a male will is pitted against an appetite that simply sees and seeks to take what it wants. Lucrece's copious style, despite its sententious learning, is entirely unable to prevent Tarquin's rape:

> 'The cedar stoops not to the base shrub's foot,
> But low shrubs wither at the cedar's root.
> So let thy thoughts, low vassals to thy state – '
> 'No more,' quoth he, 'by heaven, I will not hear thee.'
> (664–7)

Lucrece is full of paradoxes and does not simply succumb to orthodoxy in its representations of gender relationships: Tarquin becomes a 'captive victor that hath lost in gain' (730) as a result of the rape and is rendered passive by his enslavement to passion. Meanwhile, although Lucrece's eloquence (she speaks more than one-third of the poem's 1,855 lines) has no practical effect, she acquires a curious form of agency through passivity, since the display of her body in Rome leads (as the prose argument prefixed to the poem informs us) to a political transformation in the city.

Lucrece was popular, although less so than its sunnier predecessor, going through four editions within a decade of its publication. Readers may have been less eager for it than for its predecessor because the pleasures it offers are almost relentlessly anticlimactic. Tarquin is not satisfied by his rape, and Lucrece's rhetoric does not directly cause the constitutional transformation of Rome that results from her violation – and indeed that political transformation is not even directly represented in the poem, which ends with Tarquin's personal punishment ('everlasting banishment', 1855) rather than an explicit change in the government of Rome. The power of the poem lies in its capacity to frustrate: it seems to take its readers outside time, into an unchanging landscape of trauma, in which temporal flow hastens to allow the rapid fulfilment of desire, and then slows to take full and anguished account of pain. It dwells on the murky and uncertain relationships between desire and action, and on the boundaries between acting and being acted upon. The failure of the heroine's endlessly multiplying apostrophes and exclamations to make her, as she claims to be, 'mistress of my fate' (1069) suggests that the poem pushes the vain eloquence of *Venus and Adonis* one step further, to explore a rhetoric of despair.

The almost superabundant rhetoric of Lucrece's complaints might also suggest that Shakespeare found it difficult to follow *Venus and Adonis*. How could he write about sexual and rhetorical frustration again, only more so and in a 'graver' key? That question leads to a more general point. Being a printed poet of longer poems in the late Elizabethan period brought with it constraints. There were expectations in this period – not fully formed or rigid, but expectations nonetheless – that poets would work their oeuvre into some kind of career pattern.[8] The literary marketplace, which encompassed the tastes of patrons and readers of printed books as well as the desires of booksellers to have marketable commodities to sell, also exerted pressures on those who wrote for it. These forces encouraged writers to develop a style and a persona which would mark works that carried their name as a particular kind of commodity. Some of the features of *Lucrece* which are less attractive than *Venus and Adonis* may be the consequences of these pressures: Shakespeare the poet knew that he had become famous for speeches which stood in ostentatiously excessive relation to their occasions. When Lucrece complains against Night, Opportunity, Time and Tarquin in a speech of nearly 300 lines it almost seems as though Shakespeare's public stylistic identity is forcing him to produce more and yet more lengthy displays of copious complaint. It is often suggested that Shakespeare returned to writing plays after the end of the serious plague which had closed the London playhouses from the summer of 1592 to the middle of 1594, and that the 'narrative' poems were composed only to earn a crust during what must have been a particularly dark period for a newly established playwright. Others have argued that after the mid-1590s Shakespeare was regarding his plays as poems, which were printed for a learned readership.[9] It is also possible that Shakespeare was forced away from the sweet, witty idiom of Ovid by pressures that came from being a printed poet, and which were not fully congenial to him – he was forced, as it were, to rewrite *Venus and Adonis* in ever more serious keys, and after 1594 felt the need to turn in a different direction. Whatever the reasons for it, Shakespeare is known to have published only one work apart from plays for fifteen years after *Lucrece*, and the single work with which he broke his silence, 'Let the bird of loudest lay' (generally called since the nineteenth century 'The Phoenix and the Turtle'), is so short and enigmatic – dense and beautiful too – that it is difficult to relate to any larger poetic project.

We do not know the exact chronology of Shakespeare's poetic activity after the early 1590s, but it is almost certain that he began to compose sonnets in and after that period. Sonnets, and short lyric poems more generally, were sometimes printed in long sequences, but sometimes they were circulated in manuscript in smaller groups. Some were copied, often anonymously, into notebooks and commonplace books for private enjoyment. Sonnets could therefore offer something of a release from the constraints of a career in print: they could be casual, occasional, aimed at pleasing a small group rather than selling in bulk. It was also possible to experiment in sonnets with relationships between rhetoric and occasion without having to engage in the potentially open-ended flow of copious eloquence which marks, and sometimes mars, narrative verse in the period, since sonnet sequences could sketch out a story without having to ornament or describe its every moment. Shakespeare frequently embeds songs in his plays and was particularly prone to do so after 1599 when his company recruited the professional fool Robert Armin (who had a fine voice). But he also wrote short poems which were not designed to be set to music from at least the middle of the 1590s, and furthermore in that period he was thinking carefully about what it meant to write such poems. *Love's Labour's Lost* (c. 1594) explores the pleasures and pressures which could arise from composing shorter lyric pieces and circulating them in manuscript rather than in print. In that play the king and his courtiers set about wooing their mistresses by composing lyrics, despite the fact that they have all sworn to give up the company of women. In 4.3 they rehearse their 'sonnets' in private – or so they think: actually they are overheard by their fellow courtiers and are caught in breach of their oaths of celibacy, with their poems in their hands and in their own handwriting. The whole scene is an exemplary representation of the social deployment of short love poems in this period, and the dangers and embarrassment of having your name directly linked to them. Poems of this kind might be meant as a secret address to a particular addressee from an author who wished to keep his identity unknown to other readers, and who might even not want his inamorata to be sure of its authorship (as the anonymous circulation of verse on Valentine's Day shows, there is nothing more sexy than suspicion without certainty). But once such poems entered the public domain, other readers might connect them to their authors and notice awkward relationships between what the poems say and the public identity of the author – their oaths, or their marital status, or their promises to other women. *Love's Labour's Lost* was the first printed play to which Shakespeare's name was attached, and uneasy reflections about what it is to be identified as the author of lyric poems shape its actions. It is therefore ironic that three of the four lyrics by the courtiers in *Love's Labour's Lost* were printed under Shakespeare's name in 1599 as part of the miscellany called *The Passionate Pilgrim*. The printer of this volume, William Jaggard, wanted Shakespeare the brand name, even during a period when Shakespeare himself may have been circulating in private poems which sought to escape from the printed poetic identity that had built up around *Venus and Adonis*. The courtiers' poems become in Jaggard's collection Shakespeare's poems – poems which might record his own voice rather than those of his characters.

We don't know with absolute certainty when Shakespeare circulated his sonnets 'among his private friends', as Meres describes them in 1598 (and Meres' preposition is significant: it refers to circulation 'among' rather than address 'to' his 'private friends'), or when he wrote them.[10] Jaggard had obtained two of them for *The Passionate Pilgrim*, but the complete collection of 154 Sonnets, followed by their enigmatic end-piece *A Lover's Complaint*, were not printed until 1609 when the bookseller Thomas Thorpe published them under the title *Shake-speares Sonnets*. It used to be generally believed that this was a 'pirated' publication, and that Thorpe had got hold of a manuscript which he had scrambled into print without Shakespeare's consent. More recent scholars tend to believe that Shakespeare authorized the publication.[11] Whatever its origins, the 1609 volume *looks* unauthorized. Most authorized sonnet collections of the 1590s included dedications by the author, and most also printed whole sonnets on a single page. Thorpe's 1609 volume instead opens with an address by the printer to the 'only begetter of these ensuing sonnets', a 'Mr W. H.', and it spreads poems messily across pages, in a text which contains some notable gaps and irregularities. We shall never know whether Shakespeare authorized the publication. That means we cannot be certain that Shakespeare put the sonnets in the order in which they appear in 1609. We also cannot know how the poems and their dedication relate to Shakespeare's life and sexuality, although those questions have been endlessly, sometimes tiresomely, debated.[12]

Sonnets belong in a peculiar social and intellectual space in early modern England. They might be addresses to particular individuals, and they might, like Biron's 'sonnet' in *Love's Labour's Lost*, be caught up in narratives about fidelity and authorship. They might raise questions about the author and his or her gender and identity, and about the occasions on which they were written, and about whether their mode of address is directly epistolary, meditative, private or public. But they are not confessional narratives. It is the questions the Sonnets raise, rather than the answers to those questions, which make them important works. They stand after Shakespeare's name on the title page to the 1609 edition ('SHAKE-SPEARES SONNETS'); but are they testaments to Shakespeare's thoughts, or are they lyric experiments? (See Chapter 1.) Are they signs that he wished to resume his career as a printed poet after a gap of fifteen years, or are they works conceived for private circulation and smuggled into print?

The possibilities are endless. Shakespeare might have written the first group of seventeen 'procreation' sonnets, which urge a young man to get a son, to William Herbert (W. H.), Earl of Pembroke, at his seventeenth birthday. Or when he punningly alludes to the young man's penis in 'But since she [Nature] pricked thee out for women's pleasure, / Mine be thy love and thy love's use their treasure' (20.13–14), he may (who knows?) have been remembering a night of homoerotic passion with the Earl of Southampton – who as Henry Wriothesley does at least have a 'W' and an 'H' in his name. (See Chapter 15.) On the other hand, he may just have thought that it would be marvellously perverse to write a group of poems which versified an exemplary speech by Desiderius Erasmus urging a young man to marry and to charge the voice of the great humanistic educator with homoerotic energies of a kind which are decidedly unorthodox in a sonnet sequence. We simply cannot know. The important thing in reading the Sonnets is not to let our inability to determine their precise origins or their earliest rhetorical purposes become imaginatively stifling. Truth, life and autobiography are not what they do or deliver. The point of these poems is that they only tell you half at best of the story or stories and relationship or relationships into which they may or may not fit. They leave their readers trying to reconstruct a possible story and a possible set of sexual adventures around the poems, and they challenge their readers to see what riches the teeming plurality of their language will throw up in response to that story, and to wonder about how 'the living record' (55.8) of a changing, mobile and sexually ambiguous love affair might endure for all time. (See Chapter 15.) This makes the Sonnets a sort of para-narrative, a lyric form which seems to derive from a story which they themselves seem simultaneously to be creating and concealing. In the plays Shakespeare very often allows under- and cross-currents to emerge from a passage of dialogue as a result of what we know about the characters involved and their relationship to each other. The Sonnets are the product of the same artist, but their effect is more radical and unsettling than anything in the plays because they take away from their readers the reassuring framework of interpersonal address. In ordinary conversation (and in plays) we know roughly what words are attempting to do because we can read a variety of social and gestural signs which anchor an utterance within a pragmatic framework. With Shakespeare's Sonnets we are left to imagine that framework. And that makes those poems dramas of language and imagination. There are times in reading them (and anyone who has attempted to edit the poems and explain their language will have felt) when they appear to let words do more than it is possible for them to do:

They that have power to hurt and will do none,
That do not do the thing they most do show,
Who moving others are themselves as stone,
Unmovèd, cold, and to temptation slow –
They rightly do inherit heaven's graces,
And husband nature's riches from expense.

(94.1–6)

Is this praise of a nobleman? Is it criticism of someone who is unable to reciprocate passion? How far is its statement of a general truth ('They that...') intended to relate to a single person? The Sonnets ought to liberate their readers from those concerns. They give us a form of erotic desire embodied in language that refuses to limit itself to particular objects and individuals, where judgements about tone of voice affect how you imagine the persons involved in the exchange, and where imaginings about the people involved, in an unsteadily reciprocal way, influence judgements about tone. They are poems in which you can lose yourself because you begin to wonder how much of them, their circumambient stories and their linguistic undertones, you are inventing.

One of the more self-contained mysteries about the 1609 volume is the presence at its end of a 300-line poem called *A Lover's Complaint*, which describes the experiences and adopts the voice of a woman who has been abandoned by a lovely young man. Since Samuel Daniel's *Delia* (1592), Elizabethan sonnet sequences had sometimes concluded with a longer poem in a different genre, which might explore the perplexities of love from the perspective of a woman rather than a man. During the period in which it was believed that Thorpe had pirated Shakespeare's Sonnets it was often assumed that *A Lover's Complaint* was not by Shakespeare and that the unscrupulous bookseller had simply tacked a poem by another hand onto the end of the volume. There was then a period in which *A Lover's Complaint* was welcomed into the canon as a strikingly intelligent contribution to the tradition of female complaint which also made the themes of the Sonnets – betrayal, ambiguous genders, the unreliability of speaking voices – reverberate with the voice of the 'fickle maid full pale' (5) whose own voice echoes in the hollow in which she complains.[13] Those arguments, like all of those inspired by the volume called *Shakespeare's Sonnets*, will not finally close: recent stylometric tests have associated the poem with the style of John Davies of Hereford, and those stylometric tests have themselves been tested and found wanting.[14] It is almost too tempting to bundle these uncertainties over authorship into a general delight about the systemic uncertainties generated by the 1609 volume as to who is speaking and to whom, and to see *A Lover's Complaint* as a work in which the questions raised by the Sonnets about who is speaking how to whom expand to include questions about who even wrote the poem.

How does the Sonnets volume, including its enigmatic coda, relate to Shakespeare's earlier work as a poet? In many ways it is the extreme endpoint of the project which began with *Venus and Adonis*. That poem swaps gender roles and asks questions about the relationship between rhetoric and its occasions, about the relationship between rhetoric and desire, and about the compatibility or otherwise of different agents' ways of seeing the world. The Sonnets and *A Lover's Complaint* take all those experiments several steps further: they lack the copious sweetness of the earlier narrative poems, and they deliberately eschew their freshness and quotability in favour of a style that is tangled even when it seems epigrammatic. But they are obsessively concerned with the relationship between how people feel and how they see the world around them – how a woman who is 'black' can be counted 'fair', or how a specious and beautiful youth can be an object of devotion and mistrust at the same time. They are also about the ways in which speeches of persuasion and praise may (or may not) relate to their objects and occasions.

Perhaps the larger question which readers of this volume will want to ask is how do the Sonnets relate to Shakespeare's work as a dramatist? They do resonate with a wide range of tonalities from the plays in ways which may reflect their (probably) extended genesis: the final sequence of poems from 127–54, with their hard-edged paradoxes of a 'black' woman being considered 'fair', has suggestive connections with Shakespeare's work from the earlier 1590s; other poems to the young man have flavours of the lordly and reserved Hal from the mid-to-late 1590s; others on the entangling energies of sexual desire seem to belong to the same landscape as *Measure for Measure* and *Troilus and Cressida*, while Othello's world-transforming jealousy never seems far away from those sonnets which seem to be about a mistress. But the really deep relationship between Shakespeare's careers as playwright and poet goes far beyond either verbal parallels or connections of theme and mood: in the Sonnets it seems as though Shakespeare wanted to go beyond his own dramatic practice, to turn away from directly represented scene and relationship into imagined scene and relationship, and as a result to allow words to come as close as possible to bearing an unrelieved and total burden of social meaning – where every theoretically possible sense for every word seems also to be a practical possibility. The Sonnets were not widely read in their own period, and this is usually put down to the fact that they appeared after the main vogue for the sonnet sequence had died down (except, curiously, in Scotland). This may be why they had to wait more than thirty years to be reprinted, while *Venus and Adonis* had to wait only twelve months. The Sonnets may have looked like throwbacks in 1609, by which date Shakespeare's name on a title page was more likely to indicate that the work to which it was attached was a play than a poem. But the way in which they make their readers work to imagine Shakespeare's 'private friends' and their private interchanges, the ways in which they persistently thwart attempts to deduce the narrative pretexts from which their rhetorical performances derive, may well have meant that early readers found them too difficult. Their difficulty is, however, the most intellectually energizing kind of difficulty found anywhere in world literature. They are the capstone of Shakespeare's career as a poet. His early narrative poems explored how voices and emotions might extend far beyond the lightly sketched occasions which gave rise to them. His sonnets are dramatic monologues which require their readers continually to invent and reinvent their dramatic occasions. They are words which simultaneously construct and dissolve their occasions, where a whole world of relationships could depend on the interpretation of a single word.

NOTES

1 Francis Meres, *Palladis Tamia* (1598), fols. 281v–282r.
2 By 1599 only four plays had been printed with indications of Shakespeare's authorship: *Love's Labour's Lost*, *Richard II*, *Richard III* and *1 Henry IV*. In 1600 that number doubled to include *2 Henry IV*, *Much Ado About Nothing*, *A Midsummer Night's Dream* and *The Merchant of Venice*. See Lukas Erne, *Shakespeare as Literary Dramatist* (Cambridge: Cambridge University Press, 2003), pp. 248–9.
3 See Sasha Roberts, *Reading Shakespeare's Poems in Early Modern England* (Basingstoke: Macmillan, 2003); for the lunatic, see Katherine Duncan-Jones, ' "Much ado with red and white": The Earliest Readers of Shakespeare's *Venus and Adonis* (1593)', *Review of English Studies*, 44 (1993), 479–501.
4 On this tradition, see Terence Cave, *The Cornucopian Text: Problems of Writing in the French Renaissance* (Oxford: Oxford University Press, 1979); Joel B. Altman, *The Tudor Play of Mind: Rhetorical Inquiry and the Development of Elizabethan Drama* (Berkeley and London: University of California Press, 1978); Marion Trousdale, *Shakespeare and the Rhetoricians* (London: Scolar Press, 1982); Peter Mack, *Elizabethan Rhetoric: Theory and Practice* (Cambridge: Cambridge University Press, 2002); Colin Burrow, 'Shakespeare and Humanistic Culture', in Charles Martindale and A. B. Taylor (eds.), *Shakespeare and the Classics* (Cambridge: Cambridge University Press, 2004), pp. 9–27.
5 See Muriel Bradbrook, 'No Room at the Top: Spenser's Pursuit of Fame', in John Russell Brown (ed.), *Elizabethan Poetry* (London: Arnold, 1960), pp. 91–110.
6 On the political dimension of the poem, see Andrew Hadfield, *Shakespeare and Republicanism* (Cambridge: Cambridge University Press, 2005), pp. 130–53.

7 On Shakespeare's career as a poet-playwright, see Patrick Cheney, *Shakespeare, National Poet-Playwright* (Cambridge: Cambridge University Press, 2004).
8 Richard Helgerson, *Self-Crowned Laureates: Spenser, Jonson, Milton and the Literary System* (Berkeley: University of California Press, 1983; Patrick Cheney and Frederick De Armas (eds.), *European Literary Careers: The Author from Antiquity to the Renaissance* (Toronto: University of Toronto Press, 2002).
9 See Patrick Cheney (ed.), *The Cambridge Companion to Shakespeare's Poetry* (Cambridge: Cambridge University Press, 2007), p. 66.
10 On dating, see A. Kent Hieatt, Charles W. Hieatt and Anne Lake Prescott, 'When did Shakespeare Write Sonnets 1609?', *Studies in Philology*, 88 (1991), 69–109.
11 Katherine Duncan-Jones, 'Was the 1609 Shake-speares Sonnets Really Unauthorized?', *Review of English Studies*, 34 (1983), 151–71.
12 See Colin Burrow, 'Life and Work in Shakespeare's Poems', *Proceedings of the British Academy*, 97 (1997), 15–50.
13 MacDonald P. Jackson, *Shakespeare's A Lover's Complaint*: *Its Date and Authenticity* (Auckland: University of Auckland Press, 1965); John Kerrigan, *Motives of Woe: Shakespeare and 'Female Complaint', A Critical Anthology* (Oxford: Oxford University Press, 1991).
14 The findings of Brian Vickers, *Shakespeare, A Lover's Complaint, and John Davies of Hereford* (Cambridge: Cambridge University Press, 2007) have been challenged by MacDonald P. Jackson, 'Brian Vickers, *Shakespeare, 'A Lover's Complaint', and John Davies of Hereford*', *Review of English Studies*, 58 (2007), 723–5.

READING LIST

Booth, Stephen. *An Essay on Shakespeare's Sonnets*. New Haven: Yale University Press, 1969.

Burrow, Colin, ed. *Complete Sonnets and Poems*. Oxford: Oxford University Press, 2002.

Cheney, Patrick, ed. *The Cambridge Companion to Shakespeare's Poetry*. Cambridge: Cambridge University Press, 2007.

Dubrow, Heather. *Captive Victors: Shakespeare's Narrative Poems and Sonnets*. Ithaca, NY: Cornell University Press, 1987.

Edmondson, Paul and Stanley Wells, eds. *Shakespeare's Sonnets*. Oxford: Oxford University Press, 2004.

Hyland, Peter. *An Introduction to Shakespeare's Poems*. Basingstoke: Palgrave Macmillan, 2003.

Kolin, Philip C., ed. '*Venus and Adonis*': *Critical Essays*. New York: Garland, 1997.

Mortimer, Anthony. *Variable Passions: A Reading of Shakespeare's 'Venus and Adonis'*. New York: AMS Press, 2000.

Orgel, Stephen and Sean Keilen, eds. *Shakespeare's Poems*. New York: Garland, 1999.

Schalkwyk, David. *Speech and Performance in Shakespeare's Sonnets and Plays*. Cambridge: Cambridge University Press, 2002.

Schoenfeldt, Michael, ed. *A Companion to Shakespeare's Sonnets*. Oxford: Blackwell, 2007.

Sharon-Zisser, Shirley, ed. *Critical Essays on Shakespeare's A Lover's Complaint: Suffering Ecstasy*. Aldershot: Ashgate, 2006.

8

STANLEY WELLS

Shakespeare's comedies

When the compilers of the First Folio, published in 1623, came to decide on the order in which they would print the plays, they divided them into Comedies, Histories and Tragedies. It was a bad idea. Comedy and tragedy refer to the forms of plays, history to their content. One of Shakespeare's history plays, *Henry V*, which sees obstacles overcome and ends with the promise of the marriage of its main character, approximates to comedy in its form. Others, such as *Richard II* and *Richard III*, are tragic in form and effect. Most of the histories make extensive use of invented material: the two parts of *Henry IV* include some of Shakespeare's greatest comic scenes, especially those featuring the unhistorical Sir John Falstaff. Moreover both British and Roman history lie behind some of the plays classed as tragedies, such as *King Lear* and *Macbeth*, *Julius Caesar* and *Coriolanus*.

Shakespeare's was an eclectic genius which refused to stay within the limits of traditional forms. He was a professional, writing for a popular theatre which welcomed variety of effect within plays. None of his tragedies, even *King Lear*, is without comedy; none of his comedies, even *The Comedy of Errors* or *The Taming of the Shrew*, lacks serious elements. And as the principal resident dramatist of the Lord Chamberlain's, later King's, Men from their founding in 1594 to the end of his career in 1613, he acknowledged a duty – which was also an invaluable stimulus to invention – to ring the changes in the nature of the plays that he contributed to the repertoire, constantly experimenting in content and form, never producing a steady, consecutively written sequence of plays in a single genre.

The result of the Folio editors' decision has been that posterity, in the attempt to categorize the plays, has found a need to create a proliferation of subdivisions, especially of those classed in the Folio as comedies, distinguishing some as early comedies, others as Romantic comedies, problem plays, problem comedies, tragicomedies or romances; and even these subdivisions have had fluid boundaries, so that some critics have called *Hamlet* a problem play, *Cymbeline*, classed as a tragedy in the Folio and based on both British and Roman history and also, probably, on pre-existing plays, has been called a romance and a tragicomedy, and no one, including the compilers of the Folio itself, has ever known quite where to place *Troilus and Cressida*.

There is, then, a degree of arbitrariness about the categories adopted for this volume. We have not straightforwardly adopted the Folio divisions, and we might, for example, have placed *Measure for Measure* and *The Two Noble Kinsmen* not among the comedies but among the tragicomedies. And, as Janette Dillon writes in Chapter 12, 'Tragedy seems narrowly avoided … in *The Merchant of Venice* (1596–7) and *Much Ado About Nothing* (1598).' The result is that this chapter will survey a wide range of plays under the overall category of comedy, attempting to show how each of them has its own identity and integrity within the generic boundaries.

When Shakespeare started to write plays, around or slightly before 1590, there was no great body of theoretical writing on which he could draw as a guide. Sir Philip Sidney's *Apology for Poetry*, written around 1581 – when the great period of English drama had only just started – was not printed until 1595, by which time Shakespeare had written several of his comedies; but it probably circulated in manuscript, and Shakespeare may have read it. Sidney had written eloquently that 'the whole tract of a comedy should be full of delight' while also insisting that 'our comedians [writers of comedies] think there is no delight without laughter, which is very wrong, for though laughter may come with delight, yet cometh it not of delight, as though delight should be the cause of laughter … Delight hath a joy in it, either permanent or present; laughter hath only a scornful tickling.'[1] Certainly Shakespeare intended to delight his audiences, as Peter Quince means to say when he introduces one of the most hilarious episodes in all the plays – 'Our true intent is. All for your delight / We are not here.' (*A Midsummer Night's Dream*, 5.1.114–15). But the comic error that Quince is led into by his nervous over-riding of punctuation reminds us that Shakespeare sought also to raise laughter; there is a danger that in attempting to persuade us how important and serious the comedies really are, critics may neglect to mention their funniness.

In his pragmatic way, Shakespeare was more indebted to previous practice than to theory. At school he probably studied, and may have performed in, comedies by the Roman dramatists Plautus and Terence. In Stratford's guild hall he could have learned from performances by travelling companies of players which may have starred the brilliant and versatile comic actor Richard Tarlton (d. 1588), who engaged closely with his audiences in comic byplay. Shakespeare may himself have taken part in amateur dramatic performances, such as the 'pastime at Whitsuntide' which the Stratford town council subsidized in 1583 – the year after he married – and which was organized by Davy Jones, whose wife, like Shakespeare's, was a Hathaway. (It is even conceivable that Shakespeare wrote it.) In *The Two Gentlemen of Verona*, almost certainly his earliest play, Julia describes how, disguised as a young man, she took part in such an amateur entertainment:

> At Pentecost [Whitsuntide],
> When all our pageants of delight were played,
> Our youth got me to play the woman's part
> ... Which I so lively acted with my tears
> That my poor mistress, movèd therewithal,
> Wept bitterly.
>
> (4.4.155–68)

Clearly, though this entertainment offered 'delight', it was pathetic, too, mingling serious with comic elements. In his youth Shakespeare may have seen performances of biblical dramas, which often included robustly comic episodes, and of secular interludes. During his young manhood, and especially after the opening of London's professional playhouses (effectively from 1576 onwards) English drama greatly expanded its boundaries. As the number of available actors grew, and as audiences came to expect longer and more ambitious entertainments, plays became more complex in structure, often running separate plots alongside each other.

This was also a time at which, more than at any other period in English history, writers for the popular theatre were self-consciously literary artists, many of them, such as John Lyly (c. 1554–1606), Robert Greene (1559–92) and Ben Jonson (1572–1637), also practising other literary forms, and vying in ambition with mainly non-dramatic poets such as Edmund Spenser (1552–99) and Sir Philip Sidney (1554–86). Plays were written largely, sometimes wholly, in verse; blank verse became the staple medium of their more serious plots, and prose too, used often in counterpoint to them, was inflected by the rhetorical training offered by grammar schools and universities. Shakespeare was ambitious for literary as well as theatrical fame, as we see in his poems *Venus and Adonis* (1593) and *The Rape of Lucrece* (1594), and in his comedies he draws on the conventions of non-dramatic lyric, the sonnet and epic verse. He incorporates too elements of popular entertainment such as songs, dances, pageant-like episodes and plays-within-plays, along with comic wordplay, often – especially in the earlier plays – bawdy, and anecdote. The content of his plays was determined partly by the conventions in which he worked: a theatre in which boys played women's parts naturally lends itself to the disguise of young women as youths.

Arrived in London, Shakespeare could have seen some of Lyly's early courtly comedies, written mostly in prose, notable for their learning, their wit and their linguistic elegance, and the more poetically romantic comedies of Robert Greene such as *Friar Bacon and Friar Bungay* (c. 1589) and *James IV* (1591 – not a history play, in spite of its title). His imagination was fed by prose romances, many of them deriving from Italian writers such as Bandello and Boccaccio. Real life must also have played its part: shrewd observation went into the creation of comic characters such as the labourers in *A Midsummer Night's Dream* and Constable Dogberry in *Much Ado About Nothing*. But by and large Shakespeare's comedies owe more to literature than to the life of the period. None is set firmly in his own time, and all except *The Merry Wives of Windsor* and the Induction of *The Taming of the Shrew* have foreign, mostly Italian, settings.

Diverse though they are in content and in effect, these are essentially romantic plays. They concern themselves, by and large, with love and marriage. They show characters passing through a series of obstacles to a more or less happy resolution of their problems. They are not primarily satirical, and they have none of the claims to social realism to be found in the citizen comedies of, for example, Ben Jonson and Thomas Middleton (1580–1627), which began to appear well after Shakespeare's career got under way and which had little influence over him.

Although all Shakespeare's comedies seek to delight, to entertain and to raise laughter, they do so in varying degrees, and the uses to which he put the form and conventions of comedy deepened in seriousness as his career advanced. This is not to say that moral earnestness should be equated with artistic success, or that his earliest comedies can be written off as apprentice works. Even his first surviving plays are the work of an already highly accomplished writer of verse and prose; only *The Two Gentlemen of Verona* (c. 1590?) falters in dramatic craftsmanship. In my view *The Comedy of Errors* (1594) is no less technically assured in construction than *The Tempest* (1611), and *A Midsummer Night's Dream* (1595) is as profound – and certainly as funny – in its exploration of the processes of the artistic imagination as any other work in English literature.

Nevertheless, Shakespeare's five earliest comedies are the lightest in tone, while also demonstrating the range of his ambition in the variety of traditions on which they draw. *The Two Gentlemen of Verona*, relatively slight in itself though full of delights, is a seedbed of motifs that Shakespeare was to develop in later plays. Based partly on a romance tale written in Spanish, *Diana* (published in 1559) by Jorge de Montemayor (the English translation by Bartholomew Yonge was not published till 1598, but may have been available to Shakespeare in manuscript), it takes as its central theme the common Renaissance debating topic of the relative claims of friendship and love. The comradeship of the two young men, Valentine and Proteus, is put under pressure when Proteus falls for Silvia, to whom Valentine is engaged, and builds to a melodramatic and underwritten climax, difficult to believe on the page and to carry off in the theatre, in which Proteus threatens to rape Silvia, after which Valentine quixotically displays the depth of his friendship by offering to hand Silvia over to him: 'All that is mine in Silvia I give thee' (5.4.83). All is rapidly resolved, and the play ends with the promise of a double marriage.

In the meantime Shakespeare has incorporated devices that will recur in later comedies. The heroine, Julia, and her maid Lucetta joke about suitors (1.2), as will Portia and Nerissa in *The Merchant of Venice*. Julia disguises herself as a boy in order to follow the man she loves, as will Rosalind in *As You Like It* and Viola in *Twelfth Night*; Proteus displays guilt over the conflict between his duty to his friend and his desire for Silvia which anticipates so serious a situation as the self-excoriation of Angelo in *Measure for Measure* when he discovers his lust for Isabella (2.2.168–82). Lance is the first in the great, developing line of Shakespeare's clowns, anticipating Lancelot Gobbo, Dogberry, Touchstone and even Falstaff (though Shakespeare would not repeat the experiment of giving a significant role to a dog). The echo in the relationship between Lance and Crab of that between Proteus and Julia in the main plot, though sketchy, looks forward to the more fully developed interlocking multiple plots of later comedies. Similarly the comedy of situation underlying the episode (3.1) in which Valentine fails to conceal from Silvia's father the rope ladder with which he is planning to elope with her anticipates great scenes of situation comedy in, for example, *Love's Labour's Lost* and *Twelfth Night*.

The Two Gentlemen of Verona is Italianate in style and predominantly lyrical in its verse. *The Taming of the Shrew* is also nominally set mostly in Italy and portrays character types – the romantic lovers Lucentio and Bianca, the old man Gremio, the comic servants Grumio and Biondello – that link with those of the Italian *commedia dell'arte*, but it draws more closely on the robust traditions of English farce, as in the playlets of John Heywood (c. 1497–c.1578). Shakespeare's originality reveals itself in the contrast between the love plots: the relationship between Lucentio and Bianca is shown to be emptily conventional, whereas there is far more emotional reality in the developing relationship between the tamer, Petruccio, and the eventually tamed Katherine, whose scenes crackle with wit and show a development in self-awareness on the part of both characters. Some of the liveliest writing comes in the prose speeches of comic characters such as Biondello, in his account of Petruccio on the way to his marriage (3.2.42–69), and Grumio, in his description of Katherine's journey to Petruccio's house (3.3.64–75). Although the Christopher Sly framework includes some of the play's finest verse, it is omitted in some productions, reducing the play's complexity and diminishing its stature.

We should be clearer about Shakespeare's intentions if we knew whether the rounding-off of the Sly scenes found in the related, probably derivative play known as *The Taming of A Shrew* (anonymously printed in 1594) formed part of Shakespeare's own conception of the action. Modern interpreters have been embarrassed by the reformed shrew's apparent capitulation to patriarchal ideas in her climactic speech of submission to Petruccio, but the sting is taken out of it if, as in *A Shrew*, at the end of which Sly says 'I know now how to tame a shrew', it is seen as his wish-fulfilment of his own turbulent relationship with his wife.

The shortest of Shakespeare's comedies – and of all his plays – is also the one that is most clearly indebted to classical sources. *The Comedy of Errors*, apparently written for private performance at one of the Inns of Court in 1594, and – perhaps as a result – the only one of his plays to include no cues for music, is based principally on Plautus' *Menaechmi*, with some debt to his *Amphitruo*. It conforms to the classical unities of place and time – all the action happens in Ephesus within a single day. But Shakespeare brilliantly complicates the action of his source play by giving each of its twin brothers, Antipholus of Syracuse and Antipholus of Ephesus, a twin servant named Dromio, thus exponentially increasing the possibilities of mistaken identity which form the play's main source of laughter. He also relaxes the potentially relentless, mechanical nature of the action by incorporating a number of set-pieces, notably the comic catechism (3.2.71–152) in which Dromio of Syracuse describes to his master the fat kitchen wench who has designs upon him.

This play is too often directed for knock-about as if it were no more than a farce – paradoxically, since it is Shakespeare's only play with Comedy in its title – whereas in fact Shakespeare has deepened the emotional complexity of the Latin original by setting the action within a serious framework derived from the Greek romance of Apollonius of Tyre which he was later to use in *Pericles*. Many years ago old Egeon, a Syracusan father of twins both carelessly named Antipholus, had been separated from his wife, his elder son and that son's servant Dromio in a shipwreck. Now he has arrived in the enemy city of Ephesus in search of his (slightly) younger son, who five years previously, along with his servant also no less carelessly named Dromio, had set off in search of their long-lost relatives. The Duke of Ephesus condemns Egeon to die unless he can raise a ransom of 1,000 marks. The wholly serious emotional climax of the play's action comes when Egeon believes that the son who appears to have been miraculously restored to him has rejected him (5.1.296–331). This plot line provides a ground bass to the comic action which is finally resolved only when both sons come on stage at once, at a priory of which, by happy chance, the Abbess is Egeon's long-lost wife. The joy of the family reunions of the play's ending links it with *Twelfth Night* and with Shakespeare's final tragicomedies.

The influence of Lyly's comedies of wit is most apparent in *Love's Labour's Lost* (1594–5), the first of Shakespeare's plays to have a plot which is entirely of his own invention. This highly patterned play has a clearly intellectual basis to its structure. At its centre are the King of Navarre and his three courtiers who have banded together in a pact to abjure worldly pleasures, including love of women, in the search for 'fame' which will 'live registered upon our brazen tombs' (1.1.1–2). Their resolve is to be tested, and broken, by a visiting party of four ladies, headed by the Princess of France. The sterility of the path the men might have trodden is polarized in the arid intellectualities of the pedantic schoolmaster Holofernes and the curate Sir Nathaniel. The dangers that lie in the other direction are pointed by the amoral antics of the clown Costard, a cheerful sinner, the wench Jaquenetta and the affected courtier Don Adriano de Armado, with both of whom she has an affair; she is revealed to be pregnant by Armado in the closing scene. Much fun springs from the lords' embarrassed attempts to hide from one another that each of them is falling in love with one of the women, and from the ladies' practical joke in exchanging identities when the men, disguised as Russians, come to entertain and to woo them. The brilliantly funny scene in which one by one the men reveal their apostasy is climaxed by Biron's eloquent paean to love, 'Have at you now, affection's men at arms' (4.3.288–341), in which he acknowledges that they can find themselves only by breaking their oaths:

> It is religion to be thus forsworn,
> For charity itself fulfils the law,
> And who can sever love from charity?

The play's coruscating wit extends to some of the bawdiest wordplay in the whole of Shakespeare (notably 4.1.107–35 – a conversation between three of the women, their attendant lord Boyet and Costard: 'Fie, fie, you talk greasily, your lips grow foul', says Maria, not without justice). But it is also flecked from the beginning with intimations of mortality – Cupid, we learn, had killed Catherine's sister (5.2.13) – which break surface in the final scene with one of Shakespeare's most daring strokes of theatre. The mirth has reached a delirious climax when it is abruptly interrupted by the entrance of a new character, Mercadé, inevitably dressed in black. The most important communication in this immensely wordy play is made without words: the messenger's very appearance is enough to tell the Princess that her father is dead. 'The scene', as Biron says in an image from the playhouse, 'begins to cloud.' This comedy of wooing will not end, 'like an old play' (5.2.851), with marriage. Thrown suddenly into mourning, the ladies impose on their suitors penitential tasks which will extend for 'A twelvemonth and a day' (5.2.813). In the play's closing minutes the lords and ladies seek painfully to readjust themselves to the new situation; finally all the characters come together in new-found courtesy and humility to listen to the songs of the owl and the cuckoo.

As with *Love's Labour's Lost*, the plot of *A Midsummer Night's Dream*, written probably around 1595, is of Shakespeare's devising, though it draws on diverse elements of literature – including Chaucer's *Knight's Tale* – drama, legend and folklore, and Shakespeare's favourite Latin poet, Ovid. It unites in complex counterpoint four strands of action: the approaching marriage of Theseus and Hippolyta; the wooing against parental opposition of Lysander and Hermia, complicated by the fact that Demetrius also loves her while Helena loves him; the marital dissension and eventual reconciliation of the Fairy King and Queen, Oberon and Titania; and the efforts of a group of labourers, headed by Bottom the Weaver, to rehearse a play for performance at Theseus' wedding. The linkman spanning the worlds of the play is Robin Goodfellow, a mischievous puck (or pixie) serving Oberon, who delights in the confusion wrought by his master's attempts to seek revenge on Titania for her refusal to allow him the services of 'a little changeling boy' whose mother, a mortal, died when he was born. The fantasy of the comedy, the brilliant lyricism of its portrayal of the fairy world, its virtuosic deployment of a wide range of poetic forms, the humanity of its depiction of the efforts of the labourers to please their rulers and the sheer parodic fun of the entertainment that they put on have conspired to make this one of Shakespeare's most popular plays, especially among the young. (Is it entirely by chance that his own children would have been aged about 12 and 10 when he wrote it?) Yet along with *The Tempest* – whose plot is also of Shakespeare's devising – this is the play in which Shakespeare is most clearly, however playfully, concerned with his own art, with the powers of the imagination (the subject of an extended passage, 5.1.1–27), the creative capacity of the artist and the imaginary interplay between the dramatist, his actors and his audience. Most of Shakespeare's comedies end not, as is often said, with marriage but with marriage expected or deferred; this one ends in celebration not of one but of three marriages, and with a benediction on all of them.

All the principal characters share in the more or less harmonious endings of Shakespeare's first five comedies. The five that followed, sometimes distinguished as the Romantic Comedies, introduce an antagonist who must be expelled before the action can reach a happy conclusion for the comic protagonists. Shakespeare based the love plot of *The Merchant of Venice* (c. 1596–7) on an Italian story attributed to Ser Giovanni of Florence written in the late fourteenth century which remained unpublished until 1558; as no English translation is known Shakespeare must be supposed to have read it in Italian. Characteristically he transforms a rather sordid tale of a widow who challenges suitors to seduce her on pain of losing their wealth, and who thwarts them by drugging their wine, into the more romantic plot of the wealthy maiden, Portia, obliged by her father's will to accept only the suitor who makes the right choice among caskets of gold, silver and lead. Beautiful Belmont, where Portia lives, is set against the commercial world of Venice, where her preferred suitor, Bassanio, needs to borrow money from his friend Antonio to cover his expenses. Again Shakespeare takes up the theme of the conflict between friendship and love when Antonio enters into a 'merry bond' with the Jewish money-lender Shylock by which he will forfeit a pound of his flesh if he cannot repay the debt he enters into on Bassanio's behalf. Shakespeare builds excitement to a high pitch in the trial scene (4.1) in which, against expectation, Antonio is required to fulfil the bond and is saved only by a last-minute intervention by Portia disguised as a (male) lawyer.

The intensity of Antonio's affection for Bassanio – 'I think he loves the world only for him' (2.8.50) – is such that in modern times the relationship has understandably been interpreted as sexual in its orientation. But the central interpretative crux of the play lies in Shakespeare's portrayal of Shylock. Vindictive though he is, Shakespeare complicates the moral issues by making him true to his own code of conduct and by giving him powerful speeches of self-defence ('Hath not a Jew eyes ...?' (3.1.54)); – and by making the Christians also susceptible to criticism ('You have among you many a purchased slave ...' (4.1.89)) Shylock accuses them. In some interpretations this role has taken on tragic dimensions, and the play has often been condemned as anti-Semitic. Forcibly converted to Christianity, and stripped of his wealth, Shylock leaves the courtroom a broken man; the play's last act modulates from romantic lyricism to high comedy while sustaining its concern with true and false values.

The Merry Wives of Windsor (1597?) is an offshoot of the *Henry IV* plays in that it features their central comic character, Sir John Falstaff, as a butt in his simultaneous, mercenary wooing of two married women, Mistresses Page and Ford. Passages in the final scene often omitted in performance which allude directly to the ceremonies of Britain's highest order of chivalry, the Order of the Garter, give substance to the suggestion that the play was written for a specific occasion, perhaps the ceremony in 1597 at which Lord Hunsdon, patron of Shakespeare's company, was installed at Windsor as a member of the Order. Critics often complain that the Falstaff of this play is less richly characterized than the man of the same name of the histories; the comedy might have had a better press if Shakespeare had given him a different name.

Of all Shakespeare's plays this is the one that uses the highest proportion of prose – and excellent prose it is, racy, characterful and actable. The play deploys comedy of situation with great skill in episodes such as that in which the wives read to each other the love letter that Falstaff has sent to each of them simultaneously, and that involving a laundry basket in which he conceals himself, and the later one in which he turns out not to be in the basket after all. Master Ford's unjustified jealousy is a source of farcical comedy, but after the complex midnight scene in which Falstaff, who plays the role of antagonist in this play, is frightened out of his lechery all ends romantically in forgiveness and love.

The antagonist of *Much Ado About Nothing*, Don John, is a two-dimensional villain. But the real enemy of the young Claudio, whom Don John, in Shakespeare's re-working of a familiar story, easily misleads into believing that his fiancée, Hero, is untrue to him and consequently repudiating her at the altar, is his own immature caddishness. As in *The Taming of the Shrew*, this superficially romantic pair of lovers contrasts with a professedly unromantic relationship, that of Benedick and Beatrice, conducted mainly in prose, whose friends trick them into falling in love with each other in cleverly devised scenes of situation comedy. Their eventual recognition and reluctant admission of their love, at the end of the scene in which Claudio casts aside his bride, touches deeper chords of emotion than anything in what is technically the main plot. Hero's apparent death, anticipating that of Hermione in *The Winter's Tale*, brings the play close to the genre of tragicomedy. Though the action – like that of part of *The Winter's Tale* – is set in Sicily, Don John's machinations are finally brought to light through the bumbling but well-intentioned incompetence of the very English Constable Dogberry, a role specifically written for Will Kemp, the leading comic actor of the Lord Chamberlain's Men, and his fellows of the watch.

The somewhat sketchy forest scenes of *The Two Gentlemen of Verona* link it with the traditions of pastoral literature, but Shakespeare's first full-blown pastoral is *As You Like It* (c. 1600), which adapts one of the best and most popular of Elizabethan prose romances, Thomas Lodge's *Rosalynde*, first printed in 1590. This play has two antagonists: the tyrannical usurper Duke Frederick, in whose court the action opens, and Oliver, elder brother of its hero, who however undergoes a sudden conversion to goodness when he experiences the beneficial influence of the forest. Shakespeare repeats but subtilizes the patterning of *Love's Labour's Lost*, placing Silvius, whose idealized love for the apparently unattainable Phoebe reflects the conventions of Petrarchan literature, on one side of the romantic hero and heroine, Orlando and Rosalind, and on the other side the jester Touchstone and his woman Audrey, with whom his 'loving voyage / Is but for two months victualled' (5.4.189–90). Shakespeare also adds as commentator the wryly acerbic Jaques. Once Rosalind and her friend Celia have fled to the forest, Shakespeare virtually suspends plot in favour of a series of scintillating, often lyrically poetic conversations which nevertheless are written mainly in prose.

Like Julia in *The Two Gentlemen of Verona*, the heroine, Rosalind – Shakespeare's longest female role – spends most of the play disguised as a boy. Her name, Ganymede, is that of Jupiter's favoured cupbearer, often used in Shakespeare's time for a boy-lover. Inevitably Orlando's wooing of the 'boy' and their mock-marriage raise homoerotic overtones. Shakespeare skilfully incorporates into his lightly plotted script many elements of popular entertainment: songs, dances, comic set-pieces and, anticipating the final romances, his first theophany – the appearance at the play's resolution of the god of marriage, Hymen, in a climactic masque-like episode. As the comedy ends the good Duke promises to 'begin these rites / As we do trust they'll end, in true delights' – which would have pleased Sir Philip Sidney.

As with *The Comedy of Errors*, the plot of *Twelfth Night, or What You Will*, centres on twins – and we cannot but remember that Shakespeare had fathered a twin boy and girl, though the boy, Hamnet, had died by the time his father came to write this play. The plot revolves around courtship – that of Duke Orsino, Sir Andrew Aguecheek and even Malvolio, for the Countess Olivia, and that of Olivia for the girl Viola disguised as the boy Cesario, and later, when the disguise is penetrated, for Viola's twin brother, Sebastian. Clearly there is room for much gender confusion, and the scene between Viola and Orsino (2.3) in which, disguised as a boy, she comes close to revealing her love for him has the same kind of potential for homoerotic interpretation as the mock-marriage of Orlando and Rosalind in *As You Like It*. And in the subplot, the maid Maria eventually marries Sir Toby.

But *Twelfth Night* is concerned too with other sorts of love and friendship: the sea-captain Antonio's affection, amounting to 'desire' (3.3.4), for the boy Sebastian, the love of brother and sister in Viola and Sebastian which results in the great antiphon of reunion (5.5.1.224–56) when each discovers that the other has not, after all, died in a shipwreck, and on other levels, Malvolio's self-love – 'O, you are sick of self-love, Malvolio', says Olivia (1.5.86) – and the mercenary relationship between Sir Toby and Sir Andrew. The comic antagonist of this play is also (like Falstaff in *The Merry Wives of Windsor*) its butt, Malvolio, provoker of much of the play's mirth in the trick played on him to make him suppose that his mistress is in love with him, but (like Shylock) a victim who can arouse sympathy even though he expels himself from the play's happy ending with the threat 'I'll be revenged on the whole pack of you' (5.1.374). And constantly mediating between the audience and the world of the play is the melancholy clown Feste, with his songs, his jests and his air of subtly knowing everyone better than they can know themselves.

With *Twelfth Night*, written probably soon after *Hamlet*, the great line of Shakespeare's romantic comedies stops. He continues to work in comic form but puts it to very different ends, first in the two plays sometimes distinguished as problem comedies, then in the tragicomedies that form the topic of Chapter 12.

The very title, *Measure for Measure* (c. 1604), with its allusion to Christ's Sermon on the Mount – 'with what measure ye mete, it shall be measured to you again' – signals a play with a greater degree of moral seriousness than the comedies that had gone before it. The maxim implied by the title is explored rather than asserted. Like *The Merchant of Venice* this play is much concerned with issues of justice and mercy, which it examines through the uses and abuses of power. Angelo, deputed by the Duke of Vienna to reinforce the laws of a state that has become morally lax, finds himself tempted to seduce the novice Isabella even as she pleads with him to show mercy to her brother Claudio, condemned to death for fornication – a severe judgment since he and his Juliet had been contracted in marriage, lacking only the formality of a church service. The scenes between Angelo and Isabella as he tries to bribe her with a pardon for her brother are tense with excitement which reaches a climax in the prison where the condemned Claudio, having received consolation from the Duke disguised as a friar, breaks down in terror at the prospect of death: 'Ay, but to die, and go we know not where' (3.1.118). Up to this point the play might be going to conclude in tragedy, but the Duke averts disaster by thinking up the bed-trick by which Angelo is deceived into sleeping, not with Isabella, but with Mariana, whom he had previously jilted. The play's main vehicle of expression turns from verse to prose, and its emotional temperature goes down as Shakespeare and the Duke between them manipulate it to a morally dubious ending with the restoration to his sister of the supposedly dead Claudio, two forced marriages – that of Angelo to Mariana, and the go-between Lucio to a whore – and an unanswered proposal of marriage from the Duke to Isabella.

The title of *All's Well That Ends Well* (c. 1604–5), like that of *Measure for Measure*, represents a concept that the play interrogates rather than asserts. Whereas the latter play is about a woman who is desperate to preserve her virginity, and who uses the bed-trick to do so, *All's Well That Ends Well* is about one who yearns to lose hers, and succeeds by the same means. But her success is deeply qualified and, in the end, highly conditional. The play is based upon Boccaccio's tale of how a dead physician's daughter, Helen, sought to heal a sick king and demanded as a reward the hand in marriage of a handsome, rich, but reluctant young nobleman, Bertram. It might have turned out as a fairy tale, but although Helen cures the King, who uses his power to make Bertram marry her, he cannot make the young man love her. Bertram's refusal to consummate the marriage because Helen is only 'a poor physician's daughter' turns this from a play of ideas to a psychologically probing study in embarrassment, mirrored in the bitterly comic subplot, invented by Shakespeare, of the braggart soldier Paroles whose exposure as a coward reflects upon Bertram's behaviour. Finally the action, like that of *Measure for Measure*, can be resolved only by a resurrection. Bertram believes Helen to have died, but as a consequence of the bed-trick she is now pregnant by him. His sudden claim to repentance and plea for forgiveness leave much to the actor. He is likely to kneel as Isabella does as she asks pardon for Angelo. But though the moment can be impressive and moving, it is unlikely to make us feel that heaven has effected through Helen a moral cure of Bertram equivalent to her physical cure of the King, whose last, conditional words both to those on stage and to the audience belie the assurance of the play's title. To the first he says:

> All yet seems well; and if it end so meet,
> The bitter past, more welcome is the sweet.

And to us:

> All is well ended if this suit be won:
> That you express content ...

'*Seems* well' indeed.

After writing these two conditional comedies (a new category!), Shakespeare modified comic form still further in the tragicomedies, or romances, discussed in Chapter 12, interspersing them with some of his greatest tragedies, *King Lear*, *Macbeth*, *Timon of Athens*, *Coriolanus* and *Antony and Cleopatra*. At the very end of his career he returned to the story of Chaucer's *Knight's Tale*, which had provided him with a framework for *A Midsummer Night's Dream*. He returned as well to the theme of his first play, also about two gentlemen, with the conflicting claims of love and friendship. The opening of *The Two Noble Kinsmen* (1613), which he wrote in collaboration with a junior partner, John Fletcher (1579–1625), shows the marriage of Theseus and Hippolyta with which the earlier play had ended. It continues with the tragicomic tale of the cousins Palamon and

Arcite, who, like Valentine and Proteus before them, both fall in love with the same woman, Emilia. It is generally agreed that Shakespeare wrote the first and last acts of the play, and perhaps a few other scenes; his style here, intricate, involuted, differs strongly from that of Fletcher, who contributed the less psychologically plausible but more theatrically effective, and highly entertaining, scenes involving the Jailer's Daughter (she has no personal name). The play comes to a firmly tragicomic conclusion with the death of Arcite following a combat in which the friends vie for Emilia's hand; she duly marries Palamon.

Varied though Shakespeare's achievements in comic form are, other playwrights of his time played different variations upon it. Lyly's comedies are no less delicate in wit and fancy. Dekker learned from Shakespeare in the portrayal of rich-hearted human ordinariness. Ben Jonson made more sharply intellectual use of the conventions of classical drama and, like Thomas Middleton, brought a satirist's sharp eye to the depiction of the society of his time. But Shakespeare's body of work in the genre is unequalled in lyricism, in enjoyment of the spirit of laughter, in warmth of humour as well as sharpness of wit, in clear-sighted perception, understanding and, ultimately, forgiveness of the waywardness of human behaviour. Throughout his career, but especially in his later comedies, he explores moral issues in relation to friendship and to love. These plays represent a continuing struggle to comprehend the limits of human folly and, above all, the importance of what Keats was to call 'the holiness of the heart's affections'.

NOTES

1 Sir Philip Sidney, *An Apology for Poetry*, ed. G. Shepherd, rev. R. Maslen (Manchester: Manchester University Press, 2002), p. 112.

READING LIST

Much invaluable information and criticism is to be found in Introductions to the major editions of the plays, such as the Arden, the New Cambridge, the Oxford, and the Penguin. There are also many worth-while critical and scholarly studies of individual plays on the page and in performance.

Barber, C. L. *Shakespeare's Festive Comedy: A Study of Dramatic Form and its Relation to Social Context*. Princeton, NJ: Princeton University Press, 1959.

Barton, Anne. *Essays, Mainly Shakespearean*. Cambridge: Cambridge University Press, 1994.

Bullough, Geoffrey, ed. *Shakespeare's Narrative and Dramatic Sources*, 8 vols. London: Routledge, 1957–73.

Carroll, William. *The Metamorphoses of Shakespearian Comedy*. Princeton NJ: Princeton University Press, 1985.

Evans, Bertrand. *Shakespeare's Comedies*. Oxford: Clarendon Press, 1960.

Maslen, Robert. *Shakespeare and Comedy*. London: Arden Shakespeare, 2004.

Salingar, Leo. *Shakespeare and the Traditions of Comedy*. London: Cambridge University Press, 1974.

Tillyard, E. M. W. *Shakespeare's Early Comedies*. London: Chatto and Windus, 1965.

Vickers, Brian. *The Artistry of Shakespeare's Prose*. London: Methuen, 1968, rev. edn published by Routledge, 1979, 2005.

Wells, Stanley. *Shakespeare: The Poet and His Plays*. London: Methuen, 1997, etc.; originally published as *Shakespeare: A Dramatic Life*, London: Sinclair-Stevenson, 1994.

Wiles, David. *Shakespeare's Clown: Actor and Text in the Elizabethan Theatre*. Cambridge: Cambridge University Press, 1987.

9

MICHAEL NEILL

Shakespeare's tragedies

'There is no such thing as Shakespearian tragedy,' a distinguished critic has declared, 'only Shakespearian tragedies.'[1] One reason for the remarkably various character of the plays customarily assigned to this genre is that Shakespeare and his contemporaries had no very clear prescription for the kind of work a tragedy ought to be, beyond the simple working assumption that it would be concerned with death and the downfall of the mighty. The term itself was derived from Greek and Roman practice, but like so much else in the European Renaissance, most tragedies of the period were less recoveries of ancient forms than radical reinventions cloaked in classical authority. In this they resembled the playhouses for which they were written. When the entrepreneur James Burbage erected London's first purpose-built playhouse in 1576, he dignified it with a grandly Latinate name whose pretensions were reflected in the 'gorgeous' architectural ornament that reminded contemporaries of 'Roman work'.[2] Looking now at the strange architectural amalgam in Johannes de Witt's sketch of the Swan (see Figure 1), we may be struck less by the classical pretensions of the two great columns that support the 'heavens' over its platform stage than by the vernacular form of an auditorium that strongly resembled the wooden animal-baiting arenas that preceded the playhouses on the Bankside in Tudor London. But, associated as they were in the official mind with such riff-raff as 'Fencers Bearwardes ... Mynstrels Juglers Pedlers [and] Tynkers',[3] the players sought to advertise the prestigious ancestry of their craft in every way they could.

Thus when John Heminges and Henry Condell put together the first collected edition of *Mr William Shakespeare's Comedies, Histories, and Tragedies* (1623), they divided its contents according to Graeco-Roman dramatic genres. By assigning the greater part of the canon to the classically sanctioned genres of tragedy and comedy, the editors sought to inform readers that here was a writer whose work (as Ben Jonson's encomiastic verses declared) invited comparison with 'all that insolent Greece or haughty Rome / Sent forth, or since did from their ashes come'.[4] The extraordinary cultural authority of the First Folio has served to endow its arrangement with something of the power of natural taxonomy, disguising the extent to which it was a construction after the fact, and one that – despite the addition of the novel genus 'Histories' – did not easily accommodate the mixed forms with which Shakespeare repeatedly experimented. There is no distinct place here for the uncomfortably 'dark' comedies or tragical satires of his middle period, nor for the tragicomic romances of his last phase: thus *Pericles*, *The Winter's Tale* and *The Tempest*, like *Measure for Measure* and *All's Well that Ends Well*, are listed among the comedies; *Cymbeline* (rather bafflingly) appears, alongside *Troilus and Cressida* and *Timon of Athens*, among the tragedies;[5] while both *Richard III* and *Richard II*, previously published as tragedies, are assigned, along with the collaborative *Henry VIII*, to a group of plays united principally by their interest in the politics of national history.

The reclamation of 'tragedy' and 'comedy' as specifically dramatic terms was itself a Renaissance phenomenon. For medieval writers these terms had merely defined certain kinds of narrative: Dante's *Divine Comedy* had nothing to do with the theatre, while Chaucer thought of tragedy as something that belonged between the covers of 'olde bookes' rather than upon a stage; it was simply, in the Monk's words, 'a certeyn storie...Of him that stood in greet prosperitee / And is y-fallen out of heigh degree / Into miserie, and endeth wrecchedly' (*Canterbury Tales*, ll. 3163–7). By contrast, Elizabethan and Jacobean writers were familiar with at least the broad outlines of Aristotle's foundational account of dramatic form in his *Poetics* – albeit mainly through later Latin commentaries and the work of contemporary critics like Sir Philip Sidney. From the Aristotelian tradition came the idea of tragedy as the loftiest of theatrical kinds, whose style should match the grandeur of its characters, and whose action (in contrast to the fanciful fictions of comedy) should be founded upon 'truth'. In addition to these general precepts, Shakespeare clearly had some first-hand knowledge of ancient drama – notably the Latin tragedies of Seneca. Widely read in grammar schools and universities, Seneca's plays had been further popularized by the translations in Thomas Newton's collection of *Tenne Tragedies* (1581). Their influence is particularly marked in Shakespeare's early work – not merely in stylistic homages, but also in the 'aesthetics of excess'[6] that characterize *Titus Andronicus*, as well as in the revenge machinery and vindictive ghosts of *Richard III* which (together with their successors in *Hamlet* and *Macbeth*) look back through Thomas Kyd's *Spanish Tragedy* (c. 1589) to the work of the Roman tragedian.

However, the stiffly rhetorical character of Seneca's plays – which in fact may never have been intended for the stage[7] – limited their value as models of dramatic construction for a popular theatre, and very little was known of the cultural contexts and the performance traditions that had given Greek and Roman theatre its original life. The result was that, while classicizing dramatists like Ben Jonson might labour to adapt ancient tragic forms to stages and audiences for which they were not designed, more practically minded playwrights, like Shakespeare, indulged in stylistic experimentation, drawing impartially from a variety of other traditions, including medieval religious theatre, folk drama, street pageantry and even fairground entertainment. Shakespeare's own awareness of the hybrid tradition in which he worked is nicely foregounded in the closing scenes of *Macbeth* (c. 1606). As his enemies close in upon Dunsinane, Macbeth imagines himself as one of those hapless creatures regularly torn to pieces in theatres like the adjacent Hope, which doubled as an animal-baiting house: 'They have tied me to a stake. I cannot fly, / But bear-like I must fight the course' (5.7.1–2). A few lines later, however, he will imagine his predicament very differently, measuring himself against the most famous of heroic suicides from the classical past: 'Why should I play the Roman fool, and die / On mine own sword?' (5.10.1–2). Tormented bear and noble Roman – set together they might serve as icons for the opposing genealogies of the drama that emerged in late sixteenth-century London under the rubric of 'tragedy'.

If the ancients provided no fully satisfactory models of tragic construction, they nevertheless exercised a powerful grip on the imagination of dramatists, serving as an inexhaustible mine of ornament and didactic analogy and helping to endow tragedy with the dignity suitable to its elevated status. In *Romeo and Juliet*, for example, the height of the heroine's erotic rapture is signalled by self-conscious imitation of a Latin original: longing for the consummation of her passion, she inverts one of Ovid's most famous love-lyrics – *lente currite noctis equi* ('Run slowly, horses of the night'):[8] 'Gallop apace, you fiery-footed steeds, / Towards Phoebus' lodging' (3.2.1–2). Even in *Hamlet* (1600–1), a drama with a plot that ultimately derives from Viking legend, it is the classical past that supplies the paradigms of tragic action – whether in the insistent recollections of Julius Caesar's assassination (3.2.93–4; 5.1.195–6) or in Hamlet's use of the tale of 'Priam's slaughter' (2.2.428) to figure forth his own apocalyptic fantasies of revenge.

More importantly, classical history, myth and legend provided playwrights with their richest single source of plot material. In the case of Shakespeare, it was the 'matter of Rome' that most consistently informed his tragic vision, from his earliest attempt at formal tragedy, *Titus Andronicus* – whose title recalls the name of the first Roman tragedian, Livius Andronicus (c. 284–c.204 BC) – to the sequence of 'mature tragedies' bracketed by *Julius Caesar* (1599), and *Coriolanus* (1607/8). Despite their very considerable differences in style and structure, these are linked by the dramatist's recurrent fascination with Roman history as a key to understanding the nature of what would later come to be called 'civilization'. The words 'Rome' and 'Roman' sound repeatedly through each play, drawing attention to the complex relationship between the protagonist's individual destiny and the social order of the city to which he belongs.

Set in the late empire, *Titus Andronicus* (c. 1591–3) is structured around the archetypal opposition between Rome – 'The imperial seat, to virtue consecrate' (1.1.14) – and the chaotic violence of invading barbarism; it pitches 'Rome's best champion', Titus (1.1.65), against the Goth Tamora and her Moorish lover, Aaron, just as it opposes the city itself against the 'ruthless' wilderness (2.1.129) beyond its walls. This pattern of symbolic oppositions has its formal equivalent in the tension between the ceremonious stiffness of the play's Ovidian rhetoric and the blood-boltered extravagance of its action. *Titus*' disturbing power, however, comes from the way in which this insistent binarism is systematically undermined, to the point where its moral extremes seem to collapse into one another. 'Thou art a Roman,' Titus is admonished in the opening scene, 'be not barbarous' (1.1.375). But, even as the 'barbarous' Tamora and Aaron become 'incorporate in Rome' (1.1.459), so the man hailed as 'Patron of virtue' (1.1.65) reveals his own savagery, and the idealized city is reduced to 'a wilderness of tigers' (3.1.53). The hero dies stained with the blood of his only daughter, his filicide matching the cruelty of the Gothic queen, whom he has made to feast upon 'the flesh that she herself hath bred' (5.3.61) (cf. Chapter 11). The spectacle mirrors the self-destructiveness of a Rome that has become 'bane unto herself' (5.3.72) in a grotesque re-enactment of the tragic fable from which Virgil had traced the city's origins: 'Tell us ... who hath brought the fatal engine in / That gives our Troy, our Rome, the civil wound' (5.3.84–6).

The theme of civil wounds, as Shakespeare's English histories remind us, spoke with peculiar force to a country racked by religious dispute and dreading return to the internecine chaos of the Wars of the Roses (see Chapter 10); and it is one to which each of his Roman tragedies returns, as though he were haunted by the fear that the very virtues of classical civilization might be bound up with its destruction. Thus if *Titus* looks forward to the collapse of the empire, *Julius Caesar* (1599) and its belated sequel, *Antony and Cleopatra* (1606–7), focus on the internecine strife that brought down republican Rome, while *Coriolanus* (1607–8) looks back to an earlier struggle between aristocratic and popular factions for control of the republic. In each case the conflicts that threaten to destroy the Roman state are reflected in the internal contradictions of the central characters. Torn between republican principle and love for Caesar, Brutus is 'with himself at war' (*Julius Caesar*, 1.2.48). In this tragedy, whose rival factions repeatedly define their cause in terms of what it means to be a 'true Roman' (2.1.222), it is precisely Brutus' notion of himself as the quintessential 'son of Rome' (1.2.174) that licenses him to conspire against his own patron – from whose corpse 'great Rome' will supposedly 'suck / Reviving blood' (2.2.87–8). Yet the ironic outcome of Brutus' idealism is the undoing of his cause; if the rivalrous Antony can pronounce him 'the noblest Roman of them all' (5.5.67), it is only because, like Titus, he has 'overcome himself' by falling on his own sword.

Simultaneously admired and deplored in the Renaissance, as both a demonstration of antique heroism and a pagan act of self-murder, suicide is once again a touchstone of Roman identity in *Antony and Cleopatra*. When Pompey looks back nostalgically to the 'all-honoured ... Roman Brutus' and his 'courtiers of beauteous freedom' (2.6.16–17), he celebrates not merely the ideals of republican liberty, but also the Stoic autonomy of their deaths; for Antony, suicide is the one act that can restore the integral selfhood that has seemed to melt away from him: 'not Caesar's valour / Hath o'erthrown Antony, but Antony's / Hath triumphed on itself' (4.16.14–16). This triumph in turn prompts Cleopatra's vow to Romanize herself in death: 'what's brave, what's noble, / Let's do it after the high Roman fashion' (4.16.88–9). Yet here too, where 'valour preys on reason' (3.13.201) and 'honour ... violate[s] itself' (3.10.22–3), the very qualities that define the hero's stature bring about his downfall. Nor is the tragedy's self-undoing logic embodied only in Antony's self-cancelling virtues – or even in Cleopatra's mysterious charms that 'what they undid did' (2.2.211). It is equally evident in the conflict between rational self-interest and emotional loyalty that drives the play's satirical chorus-figure, Enobarbus, to suicide. And if the ending invites us to contemplate a 'dull world' rendered so poignantly empty by the lovers' passing that 'there is nothing left remarkable / Beneath the visiting moon' (4.16.63–70), then even the victorious Caesar, bringer of 'universal peace' (4.6.4) may appear an 'ass / Unpolicied' (5.2.298–9), undone by his very success.

Shakespeare's last tragedy also deals with a Rome divided against itself and with a hero whose peculiar style of Romanness leaves him 'a man by his own alms impoisoned, / And with his charity slain' (*Coriolanus*, 5.6.10–11). Coriolanus' extreme idea of aristocratic virtue and entitlement collides with the populist politics of the tribunes, who proclaim that 'The people are the city' (3.1.200). For Coriolanus, on the other hand, the masses do not belong within her walls at all: 'I would they were barbarians, as they are, / Though in Rome littered; not Romans, as they are not, / Though calved i'th' porch o'th' Capitol' (3.1.237–9). Despising the 'many', he constructs his self-image through a fantasy of godlike singularity, 'As if a man were author of himself / And knew no other kin' (5.3.36–7), and ultimately turns against the ungrateful city that has made him. His claim to self-sufficiency is confounded by the revelation of his dependence on others – on his domineering mother, Volumnia, and on Aufidius, the Volscian enemy whom he chooses as the mirror for his own martial identity. It is the mother who fatally unmans her son by deflecting his vengeance upon Rome; it is the rival who orchestrates his unheroic death, ensuring that he falls not in the glory of single combat but overwhelmed by a crowd of nameless conspirators, their blows accompanied by the howling of a mob – 'Tear him to pieces! ... Kill, kill, kill, kill, kill him!' (5.6.121–30).

Second only to the classics as shaping influences on Shakespearian tragedy were a set of medieval traditions both narrative and dramatic – prominent among them the collections of stories that exemplified Chaucer's notion of tragedy as a didactic 'storye' of fallen greatness. Originating in Boccaccio's widely read *De Casibus Virorum Illustrium* (1374) and carried into English via Lydgate's adaptation *The Fall of Princes* (1439), this tradition achieved its most influential form in *The Mirror for Magistrates* (1559). When Sir Philip Sidney lauded tragedy as a genre that 'maketh kings fear to be tyrants and showeth upon how weak foundations gilden roofs are builded',[9] it was to this model that he appealed; and it clearly underlies Richard II's prophetic moralization of his own end:

> For God's sake let us sit upon the ground,
> And tell sad stories of the death of kings –
> How some have been deposed, some slain in war,
> Some haunted by the ghosts they have deposed,
> Some poisoned by their wives, some sleeping killed,
> All murdered.
>
> (*Richard II*, 3.2.151–6)

The sentiments are conventional, of course, but what is immediately striking about this litany is that Shakespeare uses it for dramatic purposes rather than as an explanatory template: it reveals more about the speaker's state of mind and his sense of histrionic occasion than about the playwright's 'philosophy'. This points us towards one of the great innovations of Renaissance drama, and of Shakespearian tragedy in particular: its interest in exploring the tormented inner life of its subjects. The same psychological focus is evident in the deposition scene, where Richard's conviction of the sacred nature of kingship leads him to see his degradation and suffering as a re-enactment of Christ's sacrifice:

> Nay, all of you that stand and look upon ...
> Though some of you, with Pilate, wash your hands,
> Showing an outward pity, yet you Pilates

> Have here delivered me to my sour cross,
> And water cannot wash away your sin.
>
> (4.1.227–32)

Behind this outburst lies a different medieval model – that of the great mystery-play cycles which rehearsed the history of humankind from the Creation to the Last Judgement. In a fashion reminiscent of those emotionally charged moments when the lookers-on at Christ's passion were lifted out of time to became participants in the eternal drama of sacred history, the King appeals to an audience that includes not merely Bolingbroke's parliament, but also the whole crowd of playgoers assembled in the pit and galleries of Shakespeare's theatre. Here, however, the audience, aware of Richard's habit of manipulative self-dramatization, are placed at an ironic distance from his metatheatrical appeal.

Medieval religious drama in its various forms – including miracle plays dramatizing the lives of saints and martyrs, and allegorized 'moralities' staging the tribulations of the human soul on its path to salvation – survived until Elizabeth's reign, when Protestant reformers were successful in suppressing what they regarded as relics of popish idolatry. When Othello imagines the wife he has murdered as a martyred saint whose very look will 'hurl [his] soul from heaven' on Judgement Day (5.2.280–2), the last act of his tragedy begins to resemble a miracle drama – just as when the Porter in *Macbeth* drunkenly imagines himself as the 'porter of Hell Gate', his lord's fortress is transformed into the hell-castle that formed part of 'The great doom's image' in plays of the Last Judgement (2.3.1–2, 75). Other traces of medieval convention survived in quasi-allegorical plays like Marlowe's tragedy of damnation, *Doctor Faustus*. Shakespeare's tragedies offer no exact equivalents for *Faustus*' Good and Bad Angels, for the devil Mephistophilis, or for his pageant of the Seven Deadly Sins, but when Richard III compares himself to 'the formal Vice, Iniquity' (3.1.82), he locates himself within a morality convention that also helped to shape such self-consciously diabolical figures as Aaron the Moor in *Titus Andronicus* and Iago in *Othello*. From the Vice derived the villain's habit of wooing the audience's sympathy in speeches that really amount to lengthy asides, but that formed the dramaturgical basis for the device through which Shakespeare developed his most penetrating psychological insights – the internalized soliloquy, most famously exemplified in Hamlet's agonized self-inquisition.

Perhaps the most important legacy of the medieval theatre, however, was a generic one. Shaped as it was by the Christian *mythos* of salvation, this was a theatre whose scriptural, hagiographical and allegorical narratives, for all their deep seriousness, presupposed a redemptive outcome that was comic rather than tragic. The result was a powerful bias towards tragicomic forms,[10] a tendency enhanced by an 'eldritch' tradition that sought to disarm the terror of evil through caricature,[11] reducing the machinations of Satan to the crowd-pleasing antics of merry devils and ebullient vices. As a result, early modern dramatists inherited habits of composition that, in their tendency towards generic mixture, ran counter to the 'rules' of tragic composition as classicizing writers understood them. In a famous passage from his *Apology for Poetry* (1581), Sir Philip Sidney complained of a woeful disregard for the decorum appropriate to 'the high and excellent tragedy' – a genre that sat alongside epic at the summit of the poetic hierarchy. Citing their wanton propensity 'to match hornpipes and funerals', he found the playwrights of his day capable only of a 'mongrel tragi-comedy', whose indecorous yoking of tears with laughter flouted the practice of the ancients by 'mingling kings and clowns, not because the matter so carrieth it, but thrust in clowns by head and shoulders, to play a part in majestical matters, with neither decency nor discretion'.[12] Echoing Aristotle's prescription for a *katharsis* or purging of 'pity and terror', Sidney declared that such generic monsters could never arouse the 'admiration and commiseration' proper to true tragedy. Whilst Sidney's shafts were directed at the shortcomings of a slightly earlier generation, there is little reason to think that he would have felt more sympathetic to the work of Shakespeare and his contemporaries. What was different about their practice, however, was a new kind of artistic self-consciousness that made the disruption of generic boundaries less a function of habit than of deliberate choice – something out of which dramatic capital could be made.

Nowhere is such transgression more apparent than in the tragedies written by the rival of Shakespeare's youth, Christopher Marlowe, most notably in *The Jew of Malta* (1590), whose nominally tragic action is reduced to satiric grotesquerie, turning the protagonist's serial murders into a sequence of grisly practical jokes. Although the scabrous wit of *Troilus and Cressida* comes closest to it, Shakespeare never wrote a whole tragedy in the rumbustiously cynical humour of *The Jew*. The sardonic villainy of Barabas is, however, echoed in the gleeful legerdemain of Aaron in *Titus Andronicus*, when he tricks the hero into the amputation of his own hand or parodies the shrieks of the Nurse as he cuts her throat (' "Wheak, wheak" – so cries a pig preparèd to the spit' *Titus*, 4.2.145). Shakespeare's penchant for self-delighting hypocrisy is developed with increasing sophistication through a succession of trickster villains for whom the lofty emotions of the tragic stage serve only as a form of guise, to be relished for their histrionics. 'Why, I can smile, and murder whiles I smile ... And wet my cheeks with artificial tears, / And frame my face to all occasions', declares Richard of Gloucester in *3 Henry VI* (3.2.182–5); 'Tut,' echoes his partner Buckingham in *Richard III*, 'I can counterfeit the deep tragedian, / Tremble and start at wagging of a straw, / Speak, and look back, and pry on every side ... ghastly looks / Are at my service, like enforcèd smiles' (3.5.5–9); their descendant, Iago, revelling in the 'heavenly shows' with which 'devils' like himself can distract attention from their 'blackest sins', boasts his mastery of an 'outward action' that triumphantly conceals 'The native act and figure of my heart' (*Othello*, 2.3.325–6, 1.1.61–2).

Of course, the comic spirit of subversion is not always embodied in Vice-like trickster figures of this sort. More often it finds a voice through a character whose commentary, like some sardonic travesty of the Greek chorus, functions merely to mock the pretensions and self-deceit of the main characters. The extreme example of such a figure is the bitter jester Thersites, whose brutally reductive account of the Trojan war ('All the argument is a whore and a cuckold' *Troilus and Cressida*, 2.3.65) turns the epic 'matter of Troy' into burlesque absurdity. Similarly, the cynic philosopher Apemantus, the self-proclaimed 'dog' of *Timon of Athens*, with his contemptuous conviction that 'The strain of man's bred out / Into baboon and monkey' (*Timon*, 1.1.251–2), provides the model for Timon's own transformation into '*Misanthropos*' (4.3.53), an alienated creature of the wilderness. Yet the same spirit of sardonic deflation can be heard in Lear's Fool ('there's not a nose among twenty but can smell him that's stinking', *King Lear*, 2.4.65–6), or in Antony's hard-bitten deputy, Enobarbus ('the tears live in an onion that should water this sorrow', *Antony and Cleopatra*, 1.2.154). More fleetingly, it surfaces in the sexual puns with which the Clown mocks the frustrated love-making of Othello and Desdemona ('Thereby hangs a tail', *Othello*, 3.1.8), or in the debauched quibbling of *Macbeth*'s Porter, which implicitly reduces the hero's tormented indecision to the sexual 'equivocation' of a lecher overcome by drink ('it makes him and it mars him; it sets him on and it takes him off; it persuades him and disheartens him, makes him stand to and not stand to', 2.3.29–31).

The effect of such parodic deflation is more unsettling, more complex and much closer to the heart of Shakespeare's tragic vision than the shopworn explanation of 'comic relief' would imply. A better way of understanding how comic elements function within the tragic design is suggested by the framing material attached to two popular plays, *Mucedorus* (c. 1588–98) and *A Warning for Fair Women* (c. 1598–9), the first a tragicomedy and the second a tragedy. Their anonymous authors seem to have thought of a genre as determined not by the application of mutually exclusive sets of rules and conventions, but as the outcome of a dialectical struggle between competing emotional impulses and different ways of understanding human experience. Each opens with an elaborate dramatized prologue (or 'induction') in which the representatives of different dramatic kinds wrangle for control of the action. The tragicomic *Mucedorus* opens with the female figure of

Comedie (*'joyfull with a garland of baies on her head'*) vying for possession of the stage with the hypermasculine Envie (*'his armes naked and besmeared with blood'*). An obvious surrogate for tragedy, Envie promises to 'mixe your musicke with a tragic end ... Turning thy mirth into a deadly dole: / Whirling thy pleasures with a peale of death, / And drench[ing] thy methods in a sea of bloud' (10, 57–9). Comedie is outraged by this indecorous threat: 'Mixe not death amongst pleasing comedies', she replies – but then goes on to promise a tragicomic resolution to their contest: 'Ile grace it so, thy selfe shall it confesse; / From tragick stuffe to be a pleasant comedie' (50, 69–70). Thus the audience are invited to construe the ensuing play as embodying a struggle between two genres for control of the characters' fates and to take satisfaction in a conclusion that forces the temporary submission of the tragic spirit to his benevolent adversary: '*Comedie* thou hast overunne me now. / And forst me stoope unto a womans sway' (Epilogue, 1364–5).

Something like the contest figured here can be discerned in the structure of *Romeo and Juliet* and *Othello*, tragedies whose preoccupation with love itself creates a generic instability, since love, as Francis Bacon observed, was typically regarded as the 'matter of comedies'.[13] Accordingly Shakespeare bases the action of these two plays upon familiar comic plots involving the impediments to marriage and (in the case of *Othello*) the groundless frenzies of jealous husbands, which he then turns to tragic ends.[14] In *Romeo and Juliet* even the protagonists' death scene is teasingly prefaced by the standard comic device of a feigned death and a mock funeral, resulting in a violent reversal of expectation that, in retrospect, gives a peculiar poignancy to Old Capulet's lament as he gazes down upon his supposedly dead daughter: 'All things that we ordainèd festival / Turn from their office to black funeral' (4.4.111–12). By confounding comic norms in this way the play contrives to increase the audience's sense of shock and distress at the lovers' suicides. Romeo's suicide under the misapprehension that Juliet is dead leaves him in the same condition of tragic absurdity he recognized after killing Tybalt: 'O, I am fortune's fool!' (3.1.131). Moreover the *grand guignol* of the tomb scene, with its 'grubs and eyeless skulls' (5.3.126), itself lurches towards grotesque humour, as Romeo himself uneasily recognizes: 'How oft, when men are at the point of death, / Have they been merry' (3.1.88–9). This grotesquerie is especially apparent in the extravagant conceits with which (ignorantly supposing the still-living Juliet to be a corpse) he dresses the scene:

> Shall I believe
> That unsubstantial death is amorous,
> And that the lean abhorrèd monster keeps
> Thee here in dark to be his paramour?
> (3.1.102–5)

For Biron in *Love's Labour's Lost*, 'To move wild laughter in the throat of death' defines a rank impossibility (5.2.832–3); yet in the tragedies, death is often associated with such fearful hilarity. This 'wild' laughter marks death's symbolic relation to the disordered wilderness and its threat to the fragile constructs of human society. In the closing scenes of *Macbeth*, where Malcolm's ingenious sleight makes it appear that the wilderness itself, in the form of Birnam Wood, is about to engulf the royal castle of Dunsinane, Macbeth's end comes upon him like a monstrous practical joke, engineered by the darkly witty equivocation of 'juggling fiends ... That palter with us in a double sense' (5.10.19–20). No wonder that to him life seems no better than 'a tale / Told by an idiot', an absurd succession of temporal fragments whose only function is to usher 'fools / The way to dusty death' (5.5.25–6, 21–2). Against this absurdist vision of life stripped of all coherent meaning, the victorious and self-satisfied Malcolm, looking forward to his own coronation, vainly promises a restoration of 'measure, time, and place' to his disjointed kingdom (5.11.39). Macbeth is forced to learn in good earnest the ironic lesson that Duke Vincentio tries to teach Claudio in *Measure for Measure*: 'merely thou art death's fool, / For him thou labour'st by thy flight to shun, / And yet runn'st toward him still' (3.1.11–13).

The last irony of this terrifying confrontation, of course, is that Death himself is familiarly imagined in the cap and bells of a fool or jester: so to be Death's fool is to be faced by one's own macabre *doppelgänger* – the sardonic 'antic' imagined by Richard II as 'Scoffing [at the king's] state and grinning at his pomp', a parodically royal figure who keeps his court within the compass of a 'hollow crown' that is at once golden diadem and empty skull (*Richard II*, 3.2.156–9). The origins of this figure lie in the Dance of Death paintings and engravings of late medieval and Renaissance iconography, where a mocking skeleton, dressed in jester's motley, is perhaps the most terrible of all the bony summoners by whom the representatives of humankind are compelled to face their doom.[15] This is the creature who is most conspicuously remembered in the final act of *Hamlet*, whose penultimate scene is ushered in by 'two clowns', a pair of clownish sextons, one of whom uncannily began his work on 'that very day that young Hamlet was born' (5.1.136). The gravediggers' irreverent jesting over the bones of previous clients climaxes in the First Clown's gleeful introduction of the wittiest fool of all: throwing up one last 'grinning' skull from Ophelia's newly dug grave, he informs Hamlet that 'This same skull...was Yorick's skull, the King's jester' (5.1.166–7). As the Prince cradles Yorick's grinning remains, his imagination transforms the skull into Ophelia's derisive summoner: 'Now get you to my lady's chamber and tell her, let her paint an inch thick, to this favour she must come. Make her laugh at that' (5.1.178–80).

In the bloody chaos of the play's final moments, where Hamlet finds himself in the grip of the 'fell sergeant, Death' (5.2.278) who is his own strict summoner, Horatio longs to put a form of order on the confusion by mimicking the heroic end of some 'antique Roman' (5.2.283); but the imaginative power of his classical fantasy has been undermined in advance by the sour jingles of the graveyard:

> Why may not imagination trace the noble dust of Alexander till a find it stopping a bung-hole? …
> Imperial Caesar, dead and turned to clay,
> Might stop a hole to keep the wind away.
> O, that that earth which kept the world in awe
> Should patch a wall t'expel the winter's flaw!
>
> (5.1.187–99)

Instead of being allowed to follow Brutus' stoic example, Horatio is forced into the role of Hamlet's chronicler – the man whose job it is to 'Report me and my cause aright / To the unsatisfied' (5.2.281–2). All he seems able to offer, however, is a confused catalogue 'Of accidental judgments, casual slaughters … And … purposes mistook / Fall'n on th'inventors' heads' (5.2.326–9). It is left to Fortinbras to dignify the hero's ending with a parade of ceremony:

> Let four captains
> Bear Hamlet like a soldier to the stage,
> …and for his passage,
> The soldier's music and the rites of war
> Speak loudly for him.
>
> (5.2.339–44)

It must, at the very least, be an open question whether the strong-armed military adventurer who is about to profit from this spectacle of mayhem is the right person to orchestrate such a rite – let alone whether his martial instruments are really tuned to speak for Hamlet in the way the prince envisaged when he begged that Horatio remain alive 'To tell my story' (5.2.291). Nevertheless, Fortinbras' stately rhetoric and the ensuing funeral procession are designed to create an impression of formal closure that was clearly felt to be an important part of the tragic effect, for it is a device we see repeated in play after play. Thus *Titus Andronicus*, *Antony and Cleopatra* and *Coriolanus* all conclude with similar instructions for funeral obsequies. In *Coriolanus*, Aufidius' promise that the hero 'shall have a noble memory' (5.6.154) – like the fathers' vow in *Romeo and Juliet* to raise their children's statues 'in pure gold' (5.3.298) – acts as a reminder that funeral is, among other things, a memorial rite. Fortinbras' instructions thus serve to identify the tragic drama itself as a vehicle of heroic remembrance. It is precisely the tragic dramatist's power to confound the anarchic power of death by conferring a kind of immortality that Octavius is made to signal when, gesturing at a stage that has *become* Cleopatra's monument, he declares that 'No grave upon the earth shall clip in it / A pair so famous' (*Antony and Cleopatra*, 5.2.349–50). At such moments the stage gives visible life to the classically derived conceit that animates Shakespeare's great sequence of sonnets on time and mortality: 'Not marble nor the gilded monuments / Of princes shall outlive this powerful rhyme' (Sonnet 55,1–2).

The monumentalizing impulse that governs the endings of early modern tragedies can be seen as responding to the same crisis of faith that produced the extraordinary elaboration of heraldic obsequies and of funeral monuments in post-Reformation England.[16] Not only had the Protestant abolition of purgatory removed any possibility of intercession for the dead, leaving them suddenly beyond the reach of the living, but the Anglican Church, under Elizabeth and James, promoted an essentially Calvinist theology in which eternal bliss was available only to a small band of 'elect'. If one effect of these changes was to make the assaults of death seem more terrible than ever, another was to generate an acute longing for remembrance and for that form of secular immortality known as fame.[17] It is in this context that we need to understand the acute anxieties about death's 'undiscovered country' by which a tragedy such as *Hamlet* is haunted – a haunting that takes the literal form of a ghost's unappeasable longing for remembrance, but that is equally evident in the protagonist's own tormented soliloquizing on 'the dread of something after death' (3.1.80–1).

As early as *Richard II*, Shakespeare had created a king who brooded Hamlet-like on the vulnerable humanity that underlies the theatre of royal self-presentation. Looking at the soliloquy that immediately precedes Richard's murder – 'Nor I, nor any man that but man is, / With nothing shall be pleased till he be eased / With being nothing' (5.5.39–41) – we can begin to see the extent to which the development of interior monologue grew out of Shakespeare's ongoing preoccupation with the fearful enigma of unbeing and with death's undoing of the differences by which humans make sense of their world. The 'rest' that Hamlet urges on his father's 'perturbèd spirit' (1.5.183) is the same that he himself, in an echo of Richard's 'nothing', will claim with his dying words, 'the rest is silence' (5.2.300). The willing self-surrender of that exhausted silence stands at the greatest possible distance from Fortinbras' attempt to make the brass and cannon of military obsequies 'speak loudly' for the dead prince, and the gap between the two draws attention to Shakespeare's unease with the formulaic confidence of monumental conclusions. It is surely significant that in the two most painful of his tragedies, he should have deliberately turned his back on this convention, producing endings so bleak that Dr Johnson found them unbearable.

At the end of *Othello*, there is no order to 'take up those bodies', no attempt at ceremony, no consoling promise of remembrance. Gazing at the spectacle of slaughter that makes up 'the tragic loading of this bed', Lodovico simply demands its effacement: 'The object poisons sight. / Let it be hid' (5.2.373–5). For all the magnificent eloquence of Othello's suicidal farewell, it is as if the only possible response to his tragedy and Desdemona's is one of unbearable shame. In the case of *King Lear*, a tragedy whose overwhelming preoccupation is with shame itself, with the shamefulness of mere flesh, and with the extreme shamefulness of mortification and death, the ending is still more bare of consolation. 'All's cheerless, dark, and deadly', declares Kent (5.3.289), even before Lear, gazing at the body of Cordelia, makes his unanswerable demand, 'Why should a dog, a horse, a rat, have life, / And thou no breath at all?' (5.3.305–6). The play's concluding speech is notable for the conscious rhetorical inadequacy with which its speaker[18] abandons all attempt at funeral decorum: 'Speak what we feel, not what we ought to say' (5.3.323). The Folio version of the scene allows the actors to *Exeunt with a dead march*, but the quarto, more sensitive perhaps to a play that marks the bleak extreme of Shakespeare's tragic scepticism, denies them even that minimal proclamation of resistance to death's absolute authority.

NOTES

1 Kenneth Muir, *Shakespeare's Tragic Sequence* (London: Hutchinson, 1972), p. 12.

2 Cited from Andrew Gurr, *The Shakespearean Stage, 1574–1652* (Cambridge: Cambridge University Press, 1970), p. 89.

3 'Acte for the punishment of Vacabondes' (1572), cited in Gurr, *The Shakespearean Stage*, p. 19.

4 Verses prefacing the First Folio, 'To the memory of my beloved, the author, Mr William Shakespeare, and what he hath left us', ll. 38–40.

5 *Troilus and Cressida* provides a particularly striking example of generic instability in this period: variously identified in its early publication as a 'history', a 'tragedy' and a 'comedy', it appears in the Folio at the beginning of the section devoted to Tragedies; but since it was a late addition to the collection, we cannot be certain that its placing was the product of a principled generic decision, rather than simple ad hoc convenience.

6 Alessandro Schiesaro, 'Roman Tragedy', in Rebecca Bushnell (ed.), *A Companion to Tragedy* (Oxford: Blackwell, 2005), p. 277.

7 Ibid., pp. 278–80.

8 *Amores* I, xiii, 40, in Ovid, *Heroides and Amores*, with an English translation by Grant Showerman, rev. G. P. Gould (Cambridge, MA: Harvard University Press, 1977), 2nd edn, pp. 370–1.

9 Sir Philip Sidney, *An Apology for Poetry*, in Edmund D. Jones, ed., *English Critical Essays: Sixteenth, Seventeenth, and Eighteenth Centuries* (London: Oxford University Press, 1994), p. 26.

10 See Glynne Wickham, *Early English Stages 1300–1660*, 4 vols. (London: Routledge, 1959–2002), vol. II, *Plays and their Makers to 1576* (1981), pp. 220–7.
11 See Muriel C. Bradbrook, 'Marlowe's *Dr Faustus* and the Eldritch Tradition', in Richard Hosley (ed.), *Essays on Shakespeare and Elizabethan Drama in Honor of Hardin Craig* (Columbia: University of Missouri Press, 1962), pp. 83–90.
12 Sidney, *Apology*, p. 46.
13 Francis Bacon, 'Of Love', in Oliphant Smeaton (ed.), *Essays* (London: Dent, 1962), p. 29.
14 For a rich account of the ways in which Shakespeare adapted elements of comic plotting to his tragic designs, see Susan Snyder, *The Comic Matrix of Shakespeare's Tragedies* (Princeton NJ: Princeton University Press, 1979).
15 See e.g. Michael Neill, *Issues of Death: Mortality and Identity in English Renaissance Tragedy* (Oxford: Clarendon Press, 1997), pp. 4–22, 51–101.
16 See e.g. ibid., pp. 38–48, 265–374.
17 See e.g. Stephen Greenblatt, *Hamlet in Purgatory* (Princeton NJ: Princeton University Press, 2001) and Neill, *Issues of Death*, pp. 38–40, 244–7.
18 In the quarto text given to Albany, in the Folio to Edgar.

READING LIST

Aristotle. *Poetics*, ed. and trans. Stephen Halliwell. Cambridge, MA: Harvard University Press, 1995.

Bamber, Linda. *Comic Women, Tragic Men*. Stanford: Stanford University Press, 1982.

Bayley, John. *Shakespeare and Tragedy*. London: Routledge, 1981.

Bradley, A. C. *Shakespearean Tragedy*. London: Macmillan, 1961.

Bratchell, D. F., ed. *Shakespearean Tragedy*. London: Routledge, 1990.

Bushnell, Rebecca, ed. *A Companion to Tragedy*. Oxford: Blackwell, 2005.

Cavell, Stanley. *Disowning Knowledge in Seven Plays of Shakespeare*. Cambridge: Cambridge University Press, 2003.

Dollimore, Jonathan. *Radical Tragedy: Religion, Ideology and Power in the Drama of Shakespeare and his Contemporaries*. Basingstoke: Palgrave Macmillan, 2003, 3rd edn.

Dutton, Richard and Jean E. Howard, eds. *A Companion to Shakespeare's Works*, vol. I: *The Tragedies*. Oxford: Blackwell, 2003.

Drakakis, John and Naomi Conn Liebler, eds. *Tragedy*. London: Longman, 1998.

Miola, Robert S. *Shakespeare and Classical Tragedy: The Influence of Seneca*. Oxford: Clarendon Press, 1992.

Muir, Kenneth. *Shakespeare's Tragic Sequence*. London: Hutchinson, 1972.

Neill, Michael. *Issues of Death: Mortality and Identity in English Renaissance Tragedy*. Oxford: Clarendon Press, 1997.

Poole, Adrian. *Tragedy: A Very Short Introduction*. Oxford: Oxford University Press, 2005.

Sidney, Sir Philip. *An Apology for Poetry*, in *English Critical Essays: Sixteenth, Seventeenth, and Eighteenth Centuries*, Edmund D. Jones (ed.). London: Oxford University Press, 1994.

Snyder, Susan. *The Comic Matrix of Shakespeare's Tragedies*. Princeton NJ: Princeton University Press, 1979.

Zimmerman, Susan, ed. *Shakespeare's Tragedies*. New York: St Martin's Press, 1998.

10

TON HOENSELAARS

Shakespeare's English history plays

Shakespeare's English history plays were originally grouped together in the First Folio of 1623, where they are termed Histories both on the title page and in the table of contents. They appear there as a distinct dramatic genre, along with Comedies and Tragedies. Under this heading, the Folio offers ten plays structured around key moments in the monarchical history of England, from the reign of King John (1199–1216) to that of Henry VIII (1509–47).[1] They are organized by historical chronology, here in modernized spelling, as follows:

1195–1216	*The Life and Death of King John*
1367–1400	*The Life and Death of Richard the Second*
1400–1403	*The First Part of King Henry the Fourth*
1403–1413	*The Second Part of King Henry the Fourth*
1415–1420	*The Life of King Henry the Fifth*
1422–1451	*The First Part of King Henry the Sixth*
1445–1455	*The Second Part of King Henry the Sixth*
1455–1471	*The Third Part of King Henry the Sixth*
1476–1485	*The Life and Death of Richard the Third*
1520–1533	*The Life of King Henry the Eighth*

In terms of names and numbers, this play list has a pleasing regularity, but it is not Shakespeare's doing. Shakespeare wrote some but not all of these plays in the chronological Folio order. For this reason, when we see, read or study the English history plays, we ought to be aware not only of their place in the long line of English history, but also of their individual place in the dramatist's writing career, which – using the more or less standard titles that publishers worldwide adopt today – would look as follows:

2 Henry VI (1591)
3 Henry VI (1591)
1 Henry VI (1592)
Richard III (1592–3)
Richard II (1595)

King John (1596)
1 Henry IV (1596–7)
2 Henry IV (1597–1598)
Henry V (1598–9)
Henry VIII (1613)

As we gather from the surviving quarto texts of a number of the plays published during Shakespeare's lifetime, some of them had other, often descriptive, titles of their own. For reasons of succinctness and clarity, it would appear, the Folio editors regularized these titles, and most editors since have followed their practice. Once we ignore the Folio editors' cosmetic intervention, we lose something of the focus of the plays' early readers. There is a vital difference between the Folio's *Second Part of King Henry the Sixth* and the title under which it first appeared in quarto in 1594, which eliminated the monarch and emphasized the rivalry between two royal houses – *The First Part of the Contention betwixt the Two Famous Houses of York and Lancaster*. Also, *1 Henry IV* mentally prepares us for a different history than does the title page of the second quarto edition (1599): *The History of Henry the Fourth; With the battle at Shrewsbury, between the King and Lord Henry Percy, surnamed Henry Hotspur of the North. With the humorous conceits of Sir John Falstaff.* Naturally, with a title of such length, one understands why Heminges and Condell considered it necessary to apply the editorial hatchet and opt for a degree of homogenization.

In his *Poetics*, Aristotle offered generations of dramatists and critics a useful classical frame of reference for considering tragedy and comedy as stage genres. Aristotle, however, did not write about the history play, as the genre was only a sixteenth-century development. Critics have therefore tried to see the histories as a fusion of Aristotle's tragedy with the genre of epic, which focuses on the birth and rise of nations and empires. Accepting this, we should not lose sight of the multiple native traditions that also manifest themselves in the new genre, like that of the saints' lives or of the Vice character in the medieval morality plays. Given the relative novelty of the genre, we continue to be largely dependent on contemporary materials, including the plays themselves. Here, new complications arise. Heminges and Condell introduced the term 'Histories' in the Folio, but the editions of Shakespeare's plays published during his lifetime tend to carry different genre markers: the 1597 quarto of *Richard III*, for example, refers to the play as a tragedy. We may understand the categorization as tragedy in this particular instance, but how do we make sense of a contemporary critic like Francis Meres, who in his *Palladis Tamia* (1598) also lists *Henry IV* as a tragedy? Do we not recognize the Falstaff sequences in both parts of *Henry IV* as some of the finest comic material in the canon? And does not the royal marriage which happily concludes *Henry V* also align that play with the tradition of comedy? All of Shakespeare's plays tend to be notoriously amphibious in terms of genre, and none more so than the histories.

Shakespeare's histories are distinguished from his other plays (as well as those by his contemporaries) by their primary interest in the late medieval English past, as they depict successive monarchs in their attempts to secure their position and protect the nation's integrity. More often than not, the action involves war, including the Hundred Years' War with France, and the dynastic and domestic Wars of the Roses between the Houses of Lancaster and York (whose badges displayed a red and a white rose respectively). Characteristic, too, is the delineation of personal and political identities throughout, as well as the complex interaction between more or less traditional Christian perceptions of kingship on the one hand and, on the other, the pragmatic views of statecraft as formulated by Niccolò Machiavelli and others in the course of the sixteenth century.

Besides a handful of plays of unknown authorship – including *The Famous Victories of Henry V*, *The True Tragedie of Richard III* and *The Troublesome Reign of King John* – the main sources that Shakespeare used for the histories were Thomas More's *History of King Richard the Third* (c. 1513), Edward Halle's *Union of the Two Noble and Illustre Families of Yorke and Lancastre* (c. 1548), Raphael Holinshed's *Chronicles of England, Scotland, and Ireland* (1587), the highly popular anthology of verse biographies about the rise and fall of political leaders entitled *The Mirror for Magistrates* (1559–87), as well as Samuel Daniel's epic poem entitled *The Civil Wars between the Two Houses of York and Lancaster* (1595). Each of these non-dramatic writings represents a significant phase in both British and European historiography, practised as the political and religious divisions of the period generated a sense of patriotic nationhood which, in turn, created a demand for a written national past. Like these chronicles, Shakespeare's writing about England contributed an additional version of the nation. For early modern historiography was a creative affair, and in the course of writing, the historian's interpretation, the work's didactic purpose, as well as any political objective, could all rather unproblematically be made to prevail over what we have since come to recognize as one of the characteristics of historical writing, namely factual accuracy.

It is appropriate to speak of the Folio Histories as the English history plays. The standard topographical gaze in the Folio category is English, with London as its ideological centre. Yet numerous references set off England against the rest of Britain. These involve the shared past among the different parts of Britain, but also such markers of national identity as language and stereotyped character traits. Preparing his invasion of France, Henry

V is aware that the Scots represent a political reality fraught with danger to England. Hence the saying, repeated in *Henry V*: 'If that you will France win, / Then with Scotland first begin' (1.2.167–8). The Welsh in the history plays either speak their own language, which dissociates them from England (as in *1 Henry IV*), or they speak a curious stage accent, which is a broken and hence comic form of the English standard, suggesting the speaker's backwardness. Ireland manifests itself as a considerably more problematic native Other when Captain Macmorris in *Henry V* raises a question that rings all the way from the medieval past to Shakespeare's own Elizabethan present: 'What ish my nation?' (3.3.61–3).

Shakespeare recognizes the variety of peoples that inhabit the British Isles, just as he acknowledges their history in *Macbeth*, *King Lear* and *Cymbeline*. However, the English history plays also betray more than just an innocent tendency to subject marginal Britons to the English yoke. In *Henry V*, the military campaign against France and the dangers that the army encounters in battle may evoke the image of a united kingdom, but the soldiers from England, Wales, Scotland and Ireland also quarrel. In addition, the focus in *Henry V* is not merely on the war against France, but also on the Earl of Essex's colonizing move to control a subversive Ireland on behalf of Queen Elizabeth. This is what the only explicit reference to contemporary England in the history plays suggests, when the Chorus of the final act of *Henry V* invites us to imagine 'the General of our gracious Empress ... from Ireland coming, / Bringing rebellion broachèd on his sword' (5.0.30–2). The centripetal, expansionist English ideology subtly manifests itself in John of Gaunt's nostalgic praise of the nation in *Richard II*:

> This royal throne of kings, this sceptred isle,
> This earth of majesty, this seat of Mars,
> This other Eden, demi-paradise,
> This fortress built by Nature for herself
> Against infection and the hand of war,
> This happy breed of men, this little world,
> This precious stone set in the silver sea,
> Which serves it in the office of a wall
> Or as a moat defensive to a house,
> Against the envy of less happier lands,
> – This blessed plot, this earth, this realm, this England.
> (2.1.40–50)

On the face of it, this speech may seem to express a sense of proud isolationism. It should be noted, however, that England on its own is not an island: Gaunt has subsumed Scotland and Wales under the name of England in order to make up a 'sceptred isle'.

Even though Shakespeare did not write the history plays in the chronological order of English history, they nevertheless reveal a largely consistent design. This is especially the case with the early quartet, known as the first tetralogy (consisting of *1*, *2* and *3 Henry VI* and *Richard III*), and a later group of four, the second tetralogy (comprising *Richard II*, *1* and *2 Henry IV* and *Henry V*). The plays in each tetralogy cohere by carefully recalling past events and the genealogical background of the characters, but also by means of prophecies that foreshadow later events. In the Epilogue that ends *Henry V* – fittingly, a Shakespearian sonnet in which the actor refers to the 'bending author' (Epilogue, 2) – Shakespeare even reminds the audience of the history of England after the death of Henry V, the history which he himself had dramatized, at the beginning of his career, in the plays of the first tetralogy which, as Shakespeare tells his audience, 'oft our stage hath shown' (Epilogue, 13). Early modern drama, however, is never absolutely consistent. As a result, even when we make the move from *Henry V* to *Henry VI*, we see that Henry V, whose coffin graces the stage in the opening scene of *Henry VI*, is an unfamiliar monarch. To the early Shakespeare, he was not yet the man of the Agincourt victory of 1415 but the military leader in many battles of which, surprisingly, none is ever named in the first tetralogy. Nor is Henry's reputation that of the madcap Prince of Wales who surprised both the English and the French with his military prowess. In these early plays, young Henry is depicted as an apt and diligent pupil of the Earl of Salisbury, practising hard for a career in arms.

The first part of *Henry VI* monitors England's loss of its continental possessions due to the untimely death of King Henry V, who earned his military spurs in France. The death sets in motion a 'fatal prophecy' to the effect that 'Henry born at Monmouth should win all, / And Henry born at Windsor should lose all' (3.1.199, 202–3). England's weakness in France, however, is equally due to the domestic situation, as Humphrey of Gloucester, appointed Lord Protector to Henry's young heir, is not strong enough to contain the rivalling English nobles with an alleged claim to the throne. In *2* and *3 Henry VI*, Shakespeare traces the gradual disintegration of England's political order and the social network of family relations. Amidst the severe wranglings of the contending dynastic families, the pious and lethargic Henry VI attempts to rule by idealist Christian precepts rather than by force or diplomacy. Even as the battle of Towton rages and both strength and strategy are put to the test on either side, Henry VI withdraws from the field, indulges in poetic analogies to the battle instead and lets God decide the outcome:

> Now sways it this way like a mighty sea
> Forced by the tide to combat with the wind,
> Now sways it that way like the selfsame sea
> Forced to retire by fury of the wind.

Sometime the flood prevails, and then the wind;
Now one the better, then another best –
Both tugging to be victors, breast to breast,
Yet neither conqueror nor conquerèd.
So is the equal poise of this fell war.
(2 *Henry VI*, 2.5–13)

With his unsuccessful rule, Lancastrian Henry does not only nurture and justify the political ambition of the Yorkists, he also creates a rival in his ambitious wife, Margaret of Anjou, who eventually comes to 'rule the King' (*1 Henry VI*, 5.7.107). Her merciless and calculating statecraft already forshadows the Machiavellian successor to whom Shakespeare devotes much of the third and the entire fourth play of the first tetralogy, the Duke of Gloucester, later Richard III, who trades in his predecessor's moral ideals for empirical facts to guide his *Realpolitik*, making the end justify the means:

Why, I can smile, and murder whiles I smile,
And cry 'Content!' to that which grieves my heart,
And wet my cheeks with artificial tears,
And frame my face to all occasions.
I'll drown more sailors than the mermaid shall;
I'll slay more gazers than the basilisk;
I'll play the orator as well as Nestor,
Deceive more slyly than Ulysses could,
And, like a Sinon, take another Troy.
I can add colours to the chameleon,
Change shapes with Proteus for advantages,
And set the murderous Machiavel to school.
Can I do this, and cannot get a crown?
Tut, were it farther off, I'll pluck it down.
(3 *Henry VI*, 3.2.182–95)

As this medieval duke assumes the Renaissance identity of a Machiavellian to become king – something he manages with great panache in *Richard III* – he also aspires to be an orator who speaks well, and an actor who feigns well. The political mask and the identity of the masquer, however, blend so closely that eventually Richard can no longer tell which is which. At the point when the English nation is teetering on the verge of total disaster, Shakespeare presents us with the personal tragedy of a schizophrenic criminal, trapped between his own selves:

What do I fear? Myself? There's none else by.
Richard loves Richard; that is, I am I.
Is there a murderer here? No. Yes, I am.
Then fly! What, from myself? Great reason. Why?

Lest I revenge. Myself upon myself?
Alack, I love myself. Wherefore? For any good
That I myself have done unto myself?
O no, alas, I rather hate myself
For hateful deeds committed by myself.
I am a villain. Yet I lie: I am not.
(*Richard III*, 5.5.136–45)

The first tetralogy's dramatization of how a pious and unworldly king of the House of Lancaster is superseded by a Yorkist is hardly naive. For it is *virtù*, the Machiavellian skill at negotiating the destabilizing motions of fortune, that wins the day. For Richard III, it proves easier to obtain the crown than to keep it, and throughout *Richard III* the audience watch how Providence, that ever-elusive mode of divine intervention, steers the events leading to Richard's fall at Bosworth Field.

Richard III's victorious opponent, Henry Tudor, Earl of Richmond, is less colourful and engaging. But he is both pious and worldly, and in 1485 he achieves a lasting peace after decades of violence. Thanks to this Lancastrian's marriage to Elizabeth of York, the years of enmity between the two aristocratic households that have decimated each others' members for decades comes to an end. Henry Tudor, as Henry VII, becomes the first Tudor king of England, father to Henry VIII and grandfather to Shakespeare's own Queen Elizabeth I (whose auspicious birth marks the culmination of the playwright's *Henry VIII*). It is not surprising, perhaps, that many critics have interpreted the depiction of events in the first tetralogy as evidence of Shakespeare supporting the so-called Tudor Myth, the historiographical project started by Henry VII himself to have the history of England rewritten with diplomatic emphasis on the providentiality of the new royal house, while remaining silent about the remaining genealogical queries that could undermine the nation's peace and stability all over again. However, even though this was only Shakespeare's first tetralogy, his representation of the events from 1422 to 1485 is complex and shaded, and allows for many moments of identification with most of the characters involved – even with the often entertaining villain, Richard III – so that it is hard to mistake the plays for straightforward propaganda.

More than the first tetralogy, which shows the emergence of the ideal king only in the final acts of its last play, the second tetralogy may be described as a 'Mirror for Princes', after the medieval and early modern genre of writing that presented images of rulers from which one might learn statecraft, like *The Mirror for Magistrates* (1559–87), which Shakespeare used as a source for the history plays. In the second tetralogy, Shakespeare shows the slow rise to stardom of Henry V, whose death is mourned in the first tetralogy together with the national chaos which follows in its wake.

At the beginning of the second tetralogy, *Richard II* presents the reign of a profligate and hence flawed king who has inordinate confidence in the divine right of kings and the pomp that comes with his position. The neglectful Richard II is challenged by his subjects who – for the sake of the nation – seek to decide between obedience and revolt. When they rise up under the leadership of Henry Bolingbroke, the King abdicates during what is really an enforced deposition scene, from which Bolingbroke himself emerges as Henry IV. It is at the latter's insinuation that Richard is subsequently murdered in prison.

Intriguingly, as Richard leaves matters of state to his successor, his own poetic moments of introspection and vision generate our sympathy:

> I have been studying how I may compare
> This prison where I live unto the world;
> And for because the world is populous,
> And here is not a creature but myself,
> I cannot do it. Yet I'll hammer it out.
> My brain I'll prove the female to my soul,
> My soul the father, and these two beget
> A generation of still-breeding thoughts;
> And these same thoughts people this little world
> In humours like the people of this world.
> (*Richard II*, 5.5.1–10)

As the prisoner experiences a sense of freedom in the pursuit of simile and metaphor, one wonders if, in Shakespeare's history plays, politics and poetry are not mutually exclusive. The successful Machiavellian Bolingbroke is a realist to whom facts matter, but he is also emphatically apoetic. Unlike Richard II, he refuses to let simile and metaphor affect his perception of the material world of politics:

> O, who can hold a fire in his hand
> By thinking on the frosty Caucasus,
> Or cloy the hungry edge of appetite
> By bare imagination of a feast?
> (*Richard II*, 1.3.257–60)

It is ironic that this pragmatic king cannot end the play without acknowledging that certain things are beyond his control. It even seems a form of divine punishment for his deft usurpation that he should recognize in his eldest son and successor the very irresponsibility for which he dethroned his predecessor:

> Can no man tell me of my unthrifty son?
> 'Tis full three months since I did see him last.
> If any plague hang over us, 'tis he.

I would to God, my lords, he might be found.
Enquire at London 'mongst the taverns there,
For there, they say, he daily doth frequent
With unrestrainèd loose companions.
(*Richard II*, 5.3.1–7)

But the pragmatic Henry IV has really engendered a new Machiavel. The first time his son, Prince Hal, speaks to the audience in soliloquy, we learn that the image of him feasting with all and sundry that keeps his father awake at night is really part of a strategic plan to leave a lasting impression on English as well as world history. As we watch him manipulating his father, his subjects and his friends, we may begin to suspect a lack of humanity:

I know you all, and will awhile uphold
The unyoked humour of your idleness.
Yet herein will I imitate the sun,
Who doth permit the base contagious clouds
To smother up his beauty from the world,
That when he please again to be himself,
Being wanted he may be more wondered at
By breaking through the foul and ugly mists
Of vapours that did seem to strangle him
... My reformation, glitt'ring o'er my fault,
Shall show more goodly and attract more eyes
Than that which hath no foil to set it off.
I'll so offend to make offence a skill,
Redeeming time when men think least I will.
(*1 Henry IV*, 1.2.173–95)

Hal's confession significantly affects the way in which we interpret the rest of the second tetralogy. The dramatic irony creates a sense of complicity with the audience, and there is an inevitable appeal to our sense of responsibility. Though the design is deft, how do we cope with Prince Hal's public rejection, upon his coronation at the end of *2 Henry IV*, of his debauched though disarmingly carnivalesque drinking companion, Falstaff? On hearing Henry V's public dismissal of the man who was really his surrogate father, 'I know thee not, old man' (5.5.45), his political staff may utter a sigh of relief; to the audience, who were informed of this strategy long before, the end of the *Henry IV* diptych represents a sobering lesson in unsentimental statecraft. Even the comic ending of *Henry V*, with King Harry's successful courtship of the French princess, leaves us doubting whether the ideal mode of kingship, whose genesis we have been witnessing since *Richard II*, is preferable to the life-affirming pleasures abandoned with the rejection of Falstaff.

Given the enticing patterns that emerge both within and between the tetralogies, one understands why critics have found it more difficult to interpret the two remaining history plays in the Folio – *King John* and *Henry VIII* (also known as *All is True*), representing the earliest English history that Shakespeare dramatized, and the most recent. It is of interest that, more than in the tetralogies, both plays present material that would have been considered volatile in religious and political terms during the Reformation. Central to the plot of *Henry VIII*, which Shakespeare wrote in collaboration with John Fletcher, are the events involving Henry's divorce from Katherine of Aragon, the break in relations between England and Catholic Rome, the foundation of the Anglican Church, Henry's marriage to Anne Boleyn and the birth of Elizabeth I. It is complexity of character that prevents the play from veering into propaganda; so, too, does the near-martyrdom of Katherine of Aragon, which effectively compromises the audience's sympathy for the eponymous Protestant king and his anti-Catholic entourage.

A similar even-handedness may be found in *King John*. Before Shakespeare wrote the play, the life of this king had often been used to comment on the Reformation in England, on stage in plays like John Bale's *King Johan* (1538) and the two parts of the anonymous *Troublesome Reign of King John* (1591). In these histories the usurper king tended to gain audience sympathy at the moment when the nation that he represented came under pressure from the Church of Rome. Against the background of these models, we see how Shakespeare refused to generate propaganda via his underdog king. *King John* is a patriotic play, but never anti-Catholic. On one level, it is a study of the practical and psychological problems of an unrightful monarch. John's rule leads to internal division as the barons turn against him. As they seek political support from France, which is supported by the papal legate Pandolph, the safety of the nation is severely endangered. On another level, via the unhistorical character of Philip the Bastard of Falconbridge, the playwright explores how detachment and sympathy at the right moment may mould the model Englishman, who is ready to defend the nation with charismatic confidence in time of need. Finally, when John is succeeded by his son Henry, and the French prepare to return home, Falconbridge summarizes the events and their significance:

> This England never did, nor never shall,
> Lie at the proud foot of a conqueror
> But when it first did help to wound itself.
> Now these her princes are come home again,
> Come the three corners of the world in arms
> And we shall shock them. Naught shall make us rue
> If England to itself do rest but true.
>
> (*King John*, 5.7.112–18)

In recent years, there has been much debate over Shakespeare's Catholic sympathies. A closer analysis of *Henry VIII* and *King John* in their Reformation contexts is likely to yield further insight into this controversy. One thing is certain: Shakespeare was less concerned with the self-image of Protestant England as the Elect Nation than were a number of his contemporaries.

The history play was not a Shakespearian invention, nor were Shakespeare's the only plays of their kind on the early modern stage in London. Many of Shakespeare's histories were written in the wake of existing stage versions of similar events, like the *King John* plays, *Woodstock* (1592–3) and *The Famous Victories of Henry the Fifth* (1598), as well as a host of plays devoted to the life and adventures of Henry VIII. Moreover, the Shakespearian history plays were outnumbered by the stunning range of plays on the nation's history performed on the London stage during Shakespeare's own lifetime. Of importance in this respect is that these other plays communicated a vision of the English nation and its past which ideologically competes with Shakespeare's.

Among surviving early modern play texts are a host of Elizabethan Robin Hood plays celebrating a nation of yeomen and good fellows. With his largely monarchic gaze, however, Shakespeare-the-Historian seems to have had little interest in the merry members of this community, perceiving them rather as potentially disruptive. Prince Hal makes such fellowship secondary to his political interests when, in private with the audience, he proclaims his strategy to seem his friends' companion only as long as this may prove opportune.

In the Shakespearian histories there is little room for the suffering commoner. It is in vain that we search for instances of relief to the poor such as we find in, say, Thomas Drue's *Duchess of Suffolk* (c. 1623), or of empathy with the common people under the sway of a tyrannical ruler. The second part of *Henry VI* recognizes the tensions of social inequality, but the political relevance of the popular Jack Cade uprising is undermined by its comic representation on stage. The play introduces an element of social critique, but in the end errs on the safe side.

The nation's history has been significantly determined by potent and influential women. In the first tetralogy, Shakespeare presented these historical figures, including Joan of Arc and Margaret of Anjou, as unruly women. In the later plays, he contained the anxiety provoked there by safely removing the women from the active political arena, domesticating and marginalizing them, as with Princess Catherine of France in *Henry V*.

Unlike a number of his contemporaries in the genre, Shakespeare is hardly interested in urban or civic identities in the realm. Shakespeare's London is less sharply drawn, in terms both of its topography and its citizens. The

English capital functions as a backdrop to the royal histories that he narrates at the court there, and the Boar's Head tavern scenes in *Henry IV* – the only comic sequences that Shakespeare wrote with a London setting – are remarkably unspecific in urban terms. Rarely is the capital's population granted a dramatically relevant role, unless it be in *Richard III*, when the Duke of Gloucester manipulates the people, or in 2 *Henry VI*, with the uprising of Jack Cade. How different from the way in which the city is represented in the biographical history play of *Sir Thomas More* (c. 1603–4), which extensively deals with the London population's uprising against the resident aliens in familiar street locations. Interestingly, in the pages of the play attributed to Shakespeare, Thomas More effectively counsels the population to return home and be good, law-abiding citizens.

Shakespeare's histories are more king-oriented than the subject-oriented work of his contemporaries. As a consequence, Shakespeare's England was not 'even in his own time, the only way or perhaps even the most politically attractive way of imagining the English past'.[2] Even if we are charmed by Shakespeare's unparalleled artistry, we should not lose sight of the (often implicit) conservative political ideology of his plays, and of his history plays in particular.

With their complexity of vision and imaginative thrust, Shakespeare's English histories have eclipsed other contemporary histories presented on the London stage; they have also tended to make us forget that the history play was really an early modern European development. In the course of the sixteenth and seventeenth centuries we witness the production, across the European continent, through a stage genre that resembles its English counterpart, of a collective memory of the pasts of newly emergent nations of Europe. Some of these history plays drew on the work of Shakespeare himself, but countless continental dramas drew on their own historical chronicles.

With the exception of *Henry IV* and *Richard III*, the histories have been less popular than the other two Shakespearian stage genres, both in Britain and abroad. However, their impact should not be underestimated. The statesman John Churchill, the first Duke of Marlborough (1650–1722), is alleged to have said that he knew no English history but what he had learned from Shakespeare. Even if the Duke was being ironic, he nevertheless accurately captured the way in which Shakespeare has, for centuries, shaped the English sense of nationhood as well as its knowledge of monarchic history. The histories have mobilized support for the national as well as the royal cause, but they have also been used to question England's policy, both domestic and foreign.

Despite the pro-English and decidely monarchic bias of the histories, the individual plays, as well as single or combined tetralogies, have been read and staged the world over, often for reasons of a decidedly local nature. *Richard III* has been used to target tyrants including Napoleon, Hitler and Ceaucescu. In Japan, John of Gaunt's lament of England's past glory served to criticize Japanese economic malaise by simply changing the phrase 'This England' into 'This land'. *Henry V*, of course, has long provided a vital frame of reference for French culture. Over the centuries, the play has been revived in Britain to stir up anti-foreign sentiment whenever the country was at war with France, but when the nations were allies in World War I and World War II, matters were different, and to commemorate the tercentenary of Shakespeare's death in 1616 a combined Anglo-French *Henry V* was mounted at the YMCA Cinema Hut in Calais. In the United States, George W. Bush has been seen as the incarnation of an irresponsible Prince Hal turning into a belligerent Henry V.

Arguably the most remarkable foreign appropriation of the histories was that of the Polish Jan Kott. In *Shakespeare Our Contemporary* (published in Polish and French in 1962 and in English in 1964), Kott's exhortation to read the history plays in light of mid-twentieth-century political crises served as a catalyst for productions of the plays worldwide. More radical still was his identification in these plays of what he termed a 'grand mechanism', a cyclical process whereby the rise and fall of Shakespeare's medieval rulers continues in modern regimes. Under 1960s socialism – with its belief in the combined improvement of society and mankind – Kott's reading of the histories implied that mankind does not change, thus raising Shakespeare to the status of a cold-war warrior among opponents of totalitarianism.

Since Kott, our view of history has been repeatedly challenged, and our reading of the history plays has been enhanced accordingly. New Historicism has revolutionized the field and given the history plays a new lease of life with an anthropological approach that interprets these literary texts by reading them against their multiple early modern contexts, often revealing the complex way in which the plays were entangled with emergent ideologies of the English nation and the nation's empirical imperial ambitions. As an alternative to the New Historicism – one which maintains that the past may never be fully retrieved, that our image of that past will inevitably betray the ideology of the critic or historian and that we ought, therefore, to remain alert to unofficial versions of the past and counter-histories – we have also profited from the Presentist approach to the plays advocated by Terence Hawkes. Presentism studies, among other things, the cultural interaction between Shakespeare's 'Mirror for Princes' and the multiple historical appropriations of them precisely in an attempt to reveal our own ideology in the process.

No playwright has surpassed Shakespeare in the genre of the history play, though many have tried. The history plays have served as a model abroad from the seventeenth century to the present day, practitioners including Friedrich Schiller, Georg Büchner, Victor Hugo, Alfred de Musset, August Strindberg and Bertolt Brecht. In England Nicholas Rowe wrote his *Tragedy of Jane Shore* (1714) about an historical female whom Shakespeare mentions but never brings on stage in *Richard III*. Few readers of Shakespeare, however, recall that John Keats attempted to write a play on King Stephen, and that it was William Blake's unrealized ambition to complete another stage history of Edward III. However, Robert Bolt's dramatization of the relationship between Henry VIII and Thomas More in *A Man for All Seasons* (1906) and Alan Bennett's *The Madness of George III* (1991) have been extremely successful the world over.

In 1825, the neo-classical British artist Richard Westall (1765–1836) produced an allegorical representation of Shakespeare surrounded by the muses of Tragedy and Comedy. It is curious that even an artist who depicted scenes from Shakespeare's histories should not have given more credit to Clio, the muse who inspired Shakespeare to produce his unparalleled histories. Fortunately, this neglect is inversely proportional to the genre's current popularity. It seems as if – with the irreversible theoretical developments of recent years, but also with the unique experience of the new millennium, and the reality of new wars challenging both nations and creeds – Shakespeare's history plays represent a genre that has come into its own once again. Despite the focus on England, their impact continues to be not just local or national, but worldwide.

NOTES

1 Shakespeare may also have had a hand in *Edward III* (1595), written around the victory of Edward III and his son the Black Prince at the battle of Crécy (1346), early in the Hundred Years' War between England and France.

2 Richard Helgerson, 'Shakespeare and Contemporary Dramatists of History', in Richard Dutton and Jean E. Howard (eds.), *A Companion to Shakespeare's Works*, vol. II: *The Histories* (Oxford: Blackwell, 2003), pp. 26–47 (p. 45).

READING LIST

Cavanagh, Dermot, Stuart Hampton-Reeves and Stephen Longstaffe, eds. *Shakespeare's Histories and Counter-Histories*. Manchester: Manchester University Press, 2006.

Chernaik, Warren. *The Cambridge Introduction to Shakespeare's History Plays*. Cambridge: Cambridge University Press, 2007.

Dutton, Richard and Jean E. Howard, eds. *A Companion to Shakespeare's Works*, vol. II: *The Histories*. Oxford: Blackwell, 2003.

Greenblatt, Stephen. 'Invisible Bullets: Renaissance Authority and its Subversion, *Henry IV* and *Henry V*', in *Political Shakespeare: New Essays in Cultural*

Materialism, Jonathan Dollimore and Alan Sinfield (eds.). Ithaca, NY: Cornell University Press, 1991, 2nd edn, pp. 18–47.

Hattaway, Michael, ed. *The Cambridge Companion to Shakespeare's History Plays*. Cambridge: Cambridge University Press, 2002.

Hawkes, Terence. *Shakespeare in the Present*. London and New York: Routledge, 2002.

Helgerson, Richard. *Forms of Nationhood: The Elizabethan Writing of England*. Chicago: University of Chicago Press, 1992.

Hoenselaars, Ton, ed. *Shakespeare's History Plays: Performance, Translation and Adaptation in Britain and Abroad*. Cambridge: Cambridge University Press, 2004.

Holderness, Graham. *Shakespeare: The Histories*. Basingstoke: Macmillan, 2000.

Howard, Jean E. and Phyllis Rackin. *Engendering a Nation: A Feminist Account of Shakespeare's English Histories*. London and New York: Routledge, 1997.

Kott, Jan. *Shakespeare Our Contemporary*, trans. Boleslaw Taborski. London: Methuen, 1964.

Lindenberger, Herber. *Historical Drama: The Relation of Literature and Reality*. Chicago and London: University of Chicago Press, 1975.

Loftis, John. *Drama in England and Spain: Topical Allusion and History Plays*. Princeton, NJ: Princeton University Press, 1987.

Maley, Willy. '"This Sceptred Isle": Shakespeare and the British Problem', in *Shakespeare and National Culture*, John J. Joughin (ed.). Manchester: Manchester University Press, 1997, pp. 83–108.

Patterson, Annabel. *Reading Holinshed's 'Chronicles'*. Chicago and London: The University of Chicago Press, 1994.

Rackin, Phyllis. *Stages of History: Shakespeare's English Chronicles*. London and New York: Routledge, 1990.

Tennenhouse, Leonard. *Power on Display: The Politics of Shakespeare's Genres*. New York and London: Routledge, 1987.

Wikander, Matthew H. *The Play of Truth and State: Historical Drama from Shakespeare to Brecht*. Baltimore and London: Johns Hopkins University Press, 1986.

11

HEATHER JAMES

Shakespeare's classical plays

Shakespeare's classical heroes are ambitious to make names for themselves. The aspiring heroes of *Troilus and Cressida*, *Julius Caesar*, *Timon of Athens*, *Antony and Cleopatra* and *Coriolanus* seem drawn from the classical past to dramatize a will to power or lust for dominion (*libido dominandi*) without bounds. In this they resemble Alexander the Great, as recorded by Plutarch and repeated by the Italian humanist Baldassare Castiglione in *The Book of the Courtier* (1528), soon translated into English (1561):[1]

> Alexander the Great, upon hearing that in the opinion of one philosopher there were countless other worlds, began to weep, and when asked why, replied: 'Because I have not yet conquered one' – as if he felt able to conquer them all.

The broad theme of ambition is not particular to the classical plays: it permeates the English histories and the tragedies from *Richard III* to *Macbeth*. Yet the classical heroes differ from their English and Scottish counterparts in privileging the literal achievement of a *name* over the standard objects of ambition, the conqueror's laurels or earthly crowns. The characters that Shakespeare drew from English chronicle history aim for dominion in the here and now – i.e. in the England, Scotland, Wales, Ireland and France of their own day. Yet his classical heroes refuse geographical and temporal limitation. They want nothing more, or less, than to forge names for themselves that will hold sway for all time and not merely for the span of their natural lives.

Many of Shakespeare's classical heroes are success stories, if judged by their quest for fame, unbound by time or space. By Shakespeare's day, for example, the characters of *Troilus and Cressida* and *Julius Caesar* had entered into the languages, histories and customs of so many nations and historical periods that they had become both transnational and transhistorical figures. They no longer belonged strictly to any one people or period, not even the Hellenic world or Rome in the last days of the Republic. In

Shakespeare's plays, however, the triumph over time and place comes at a cost to a basic privilege of Shakespeare's dramatic characters: the classical heroes must subsist on a minimum of the generosity that Shakespeare extends even to his most flawed protagonists, such as Othello and Macbeth, and his self-celebrating villains, such as Aaron the Moor, Richard III and Edmund. Shakespeare has long been thought to add depth to the characters that he found in his sources. We expect him to do so as a rule. But he withholds the full benefits of the sympathetic imagination from his classical heroes. Shakespearian characters typically shuttle back and forth between the poles of antipathy and sympathy, but the classical heroes stick unusually close to the negative pole: while Coriolanus, Timon of Athens, Titus Andronicus and the warriors of *Troilus and Cressida* are extreme examples, they illuminate the failure of Shakespeare's Julius Caesar, Mark Antony and Octavius Caesar, as well as Brutus, to achieve the full share of charisma and affection granted to his non-classical heroes and even his villains.

Like Hamlet, as he stands in the graveyard and muses on the figures of Alexander and Julius Caesar, Shakespeare rejects elegy and panegyric and turns instead to parody and epigram. Setting down the skull of the king's jester, Yorick, Hamlet takes up the subject of kings: 'may not imagination trace the noble dust of Alexander till a find it stopping a bung-hole?' (5.1.187–9), he asks Horatio, in a mood his friend mistakes for melancholy. Hamlet playfully corrects him: 'Alexander died, Alexander was buried, Alexander returneth to dust, the dust is earth, of earth we make loam', he continues, 'and why of that loam whereto he was converted might they not stop a beer-barrel?' (5.1.192–5). Caesar is the next to fall prey to Hamlet's wit: 'Imperial Caesar, dead and turned to clay, / Might stop a hole to keep the wind away' (5.1.196–7). Like Hamlet, Shakespeare recalls great warriors and world-conquerors from the graveyard of the past only to reduce them to objects of satire but of little compassion, much less admiration.

Shakespeare's denial of the full greatness of Alexander and Caesar may be placed in certain historical contexts. One is a set of intellectual shifts in political thought at the time *Julius Caesar* and *Hamlet* were first performed: in late Elizabethan England, ideas of republicanism and resistance theory, which justified the killing of tyrants, were on the rise among the intelligentsia.[2] Another is their status as pagans, whose separation from Christ ironizes their immortal longings: divisions of faith brought on by time are at the heart of Hamlet's jest about Alexander, who died, was buried and returned to dust without hope of resurrection and eternal life. Also at stake are more secular concerns with the vast distance of the classical past from the present. How far back does cultural memory extend before it fragments and comes to resemble a collection of antiquities that can only gesture towards the wholeness of a lost era? Even the presence of Roman antiquities in London suggested uncertainty about the transmission of cultural memory: this is the central point made by the young Prince Edward of *Richard III* about the legend of the Tower of London, which was believed to have been built by Julius Caesar (3.1.68–78).

While topical concerns of Shakespeare's day feed the cultural ambivalence about great men of the classical past, they do little to illuminate a distinctive feature of Shakespeare's classical plays: namely, their philosophical and ethical aversion to men who violate decorum on a massive scale by refusing to accommodate themselves to history and local community. It is not unusual for Shakespeare and his contemporaries to direct anti-tyrannical sentiment at historical men who devoured the liberties of their fellow citizens even as they absorbed titles, offices and laws into their own persons. In what we might call the tyrant's scenario, the ambitious man vaults over earthly limits and assumes a place in the heavenly constellation as a god-on-earth. Shakespeare's small admiration for such men appears in his splendid jest about Alexander the Great that he routes through his captain, Fluellen, who remembers him as Alexander the Big and who transforms him, through his Welsh accent, into Alexander the Pig. For, as Fluellen insists, 'is not "pig" great? The pig or the mighty or the huge or the magnanimous are all one reckonings, save the phrase is a little variations' (*Henry V*, 4.7.13–15). Yet Shakespeare saved his particular scorn for those who deny the communal ties that locate them firmly in history. It is this pattern – the refusal of 'great' men to yield to history as necessarily shaping of their characters – that attracts Shakespeare's attention.

Given Shakespeare's reservations about his ambitious classical heroes, we might expect him to adapt his classical plays to the genre of *de casibus* tragedy associated with the Fall of Princes and the *Mirror for Magistrates*, in which over-reaching men ultimately meet with well-deserved calamity. This pattern is used to striking effect in *Richard III*, where the title character gleefully connives and murders his way to the throne only to suffer a precipitous fall, ushered in by a dream-vision in which his victims come back from the dead to curse him. Unlike Richard III, however, Shakespeare's classical heroes do not suffer a providential fall into conscience. Instead, they come either to a crossroads or a dead end in the narrative of their outsized ambitions. The more compelling of the classical heroes insert a voluntary element into their fall from power when they accept their contingent relations to history and community. These characters earn a place in tragedy: even a colossus may gain a share in the signature generosity that Shakespeare grants protagonists, but only when he gives up his dreams of transcending time and place.

Troilus and Cressida, which presents Shakespeare's most unrelenting critique of fame, offers a useful starting-place for a discussion of the classical plays. The legendary warriors of this play line up at Troy to fight out the question of their significance in time to come. The play's temporal situation is more complex than modern readers, trained up on Homer's *Iliad*, might expect, for the play presents not one but many versions of Troy. It is closer to a palimpsest of the Troy legend and its warriors – whose stories were told and retold in classical, medieval and early modern times – than it is to pretensions of origins and authenticity. The idea of complex and multi-faceted characters in fiction has long enjoyed primacy in literary reception. But expectations of depth through the accretion of experience in time might well founder when applied to Shakespeare's versions of Achilles, Ulysses, Nestor, Ajax and Agamemnon on the one side of Western civilization's oldest war, and Hector, Aeneas, Troilus, Paris and Helen on the other.

For his representation of the legendary warriors, Shakespeare tapped a range of authorities in the varied tradition of the Troy legend, from Geoffrey of Monmouth, Wace, Layamon, Benoît, Guido delle Colonne and Raoul Le Fèvre to Lydgate, Caxton, Chaucer, Henryson and Chapman. Sorting through the long legend of Troy, Shakespeare often chose the least favourable versions of these legendary figures. Ulysses is a political strategist, Ajax a blockhead, Nestor a windbag, Hector a gallant fool and Agamemnon, unforgettably, a general with 'not so much brain as ear-wax' (5.1.47), according to Thersites, the play's resident satirist. Even Achilles, the most illustrious warrior of all time, is a mere thug, who orders the assassination of his great opponent, Hector, rather than fight him in hand-to-hand combat. Achilles first commands his gang of Myrmidons to search the Trojan prince out on the battlefield and 'Empale him with your weapons round about. / In fellest manner execute your arms' (5.7.5–6), and, after Hector's death, he takes the credit: 'On, Myrmidons, and cry you all amain, / "Achilles hath the mighty Hector slain!"' (5.9.13–14). In this way, Shakespeare undermines the greatest warrior in Western tradition and, simultaneously, questions the heroic ethos that Achilles represents.

There is some hope, at the play's beginning, that its love plot will thwart the wholly reductive force of its military plot. Troilus promisingly rejects the rationale for the Trojan War in an early soliloquy (Helen 'must needs be fair' when the warriors of both sides use their blood to 'paint her thus', he says at 1.1.86–7) and embraces love as an antidote to the corrosive effects of the war. But he proves to be incapable of the leap of faith that would allow him to unite with his future reputation as a literary example of fidelity or with Cressida. Since he cannot *be* a true lover, as he confesses in his first love scene with Cressida, he hopes to become the poetic figure for one. He longs to be 'truth's authentic author to be cited' when, in the love poetry of the future, ' "As true as Troilus" shall crown up the verse / And sanctify the numbers' (3.2.168–70). Like his warlike peers, Troilus wants to make a name both for, and of, himself.[3]

Shakespeare's harsh critique of heroic exemplarity at the end of Elizabeth I's reign has something to do with the weight of a tradition that has been made 'tired with iteration' (3.2.163): sustaining faith in the waning Tudor dynasty seems to be hard work. At the time of the play's composition and staging, Elizabethan England had fallen into a gloom, ushered in by the rise of anti-Catholic spy-networks in the court and the fall of the dashing Earl of Essex, who held out promise of reform and religious toleration. The Troy legend, which was intimately associated with Tudor propaganda, seemed well suited to the exposure of its lost ideals. The cultural promise evoked by the cult of Good Queen Bess and Essex had failed. In the late 1590s, the celebrated Elizabethan settlement seemed less focused on restoring communal bonds than establishing a name for doing so.

Titus Andronicus, too, fosters a culture of political discontent. Whereas *Troilus and Cressida* wreaks havoc with the heroic exemplars of the Troy legend, *Titus Andronicus* focuses its assaults on the ideological representations of Queen Elizabeth found in classical myth: while the figures of Dido, Diana, the Venus armata and Astraea, virgin goddess of justice, all appear in the play, they are disconcertingly mapped onto the figure of Tamora, Queen of the Goths, foreign empress of Rome and chief enemy of the play's title character. In this play, too, Shakespeare holds up the images of Tudor authority as objects of polemical satire.[4]

Titus Andronicus represents Shakespeare's earliest experiment in staging classical heroes whose aspirations and ideals damage themselves and others. Like the warriors of *Troilus and Cressida*, Titus Andronicus shapes his actions in relation to the exemplary values associated with his name (he is 'surnamèd *Pius*', 1.1.23). Unlike the more unscrupulous warriors of *Troilus and Cressida*, Titus holds to a strict code of ethics, but even this virtue has its destructive side: through his rigid adherence to the most hierarchical and conservative of Roman political traditions, Titus reveals a wilful streak turned deadly. It is perhaps understandable that he denies his enemy, Tamora, Queen of the Goths, when she pleads for the life of her son, Alarbus. But his insistence that she accept the justice of his decision to kill her son in a ritual sacrifice gives weight to her outcry, 'O cruel irreligious piety!' (1.1.130). Titus does not relent, and 'Alarbus' limbs are lopped' (1.1.143). Titus is no easier on his own family. It is clear that Titus' family is surprised by the disastrous choices he makes in the play's first scene, when he declines the imperial diadem (his by popular election) and appoints Saturninus, the elder and worse of the last emperor's two sons, in his stead. But they are horrified when he also bestows his daughter Lavinia on Saturninus, too, since she is already betrothed to the younger and more virtuous son, Bassianus. In the melee that follows, Titus battles his own sons, whom he opposes on ideological grounds: while they defend the rule of law (Bassianus has the legal right), Titus insists on absolute power (the emperor's and his own). And Titus prosecutes his case even to the point of killing his youngest son, with the outraged cry, 'What, villain boy, / Barr'st me my way in Rome?' (1.1.286–7).

The play thus begins by asking what kind of man Titus is: a tragic hero or merely a colossus from the classical past? At the play's end, Titus prepares to settle just this question. His last act poses interpretative problems for readers of the play, because the hero, in his role as revenger, initiates a sweep of murders that ends with his enemy, the tyrannical Saturninus, but begins with his beloved daughter, Lavinia. By some lights, Titus has not changed enough from the play's first scene, when he killed his youngest son on what he takes to be principle, although others see it as a failure of mercy and paternity. Is it possible that Titus, to the bitter end, adheres so strictly to rules and precedents that he kills his children to make a point about his experience of piety and his right to be its embodiment? Recent performances, which have arisen alongside robust criticism, suggest that *Titus Andronicus* is a better play if its hero instead submits to his daughter's death wish – an interpretation supported by Lavinia's pleas for death at Tamora's hands rather than face the 'worse-than-killing lust' (2.3.175) of her sons.[5] In short, Titus may brush aside his longtime commitment to principled wrath (expressed in tyrannicide) in favour of his newfound compassion (revealed in his mercy killing).

At the end of the play, Titus Andronicus stands on the ruins of classical exemplarity, a situation he makes explicit when he questions the Emperor Saturninus about an apparently inconsequential proposition from the Roman past:

> My lord the Emperor, resolve me this:
> Was it well done of rash Virginius
> To slay his daughter with his own right hand
> Because she was enforced, stained, and deflowered?
> (5.3.35–8)

Saturninus duly affirms the justice of the Roman precedent, noting that 'the girl should not survive her shame, / And by her presence still renew [her father's] sorrows' (5.3.40–1). And Titus leaps into action:

> A reason, mighty, strong, effectual;
> A pattern, precedent, and lively warrant
> For me, most wretched, to perform the like.
> Die, die, Lavinia, and thy shame with thee,
> And with thy shame thy father's sorrow die.
> (5.3.42–6)

Within mere lines, Titus kills Tamora, Saturninus kills Titus and Lucius kills Saturninus. Titus amply fulfils his duties as the protagonist of a grisly revenge play: after all, he kills the Empress's two sons, Chiron and Demetrius, and cooks them up in the pie that he serves to Tamora as her last supper. The open question is what Titus has in mind by tending to his daughter's implicit death wish and her revenge (Tamora's sons raped and mutilated Lavinia, with their mother's full approval). We expect him to get to the business of tyrannicide, which he leaves undone, because he knows his son Lucius will do it for him or because he has no room in his heart for political grievances. In privileging Lavinia over Saturninus, Titus becomes the instrument of his daughter's needs. This decision, which comes to him with a full measure of struggle, inverts the duties that usually bind parent and child: the child is meant to carry out the wishes of the parent. Titus was willing to kill his son Mutius on this principle, and he administers his schoolmaster's lesson to Saturninus to review this article of political and familial order. The example of Virginius entitles paternal authorities, such as fathers and princes, to kill their dependants rather than suffer personal disgrace. In his last act, however, Titus empties out the cultural significance of this precedent in two ways: he becomes the instrument of Lavinia's apparent will to die and he precipitates the action that results in the killing of the Emperor, who grievously mistook the nature of his duties to his subjects. In submitting to the needs of his weakest dependant, Titus becomes, at last, a tragic hero of the Shakespearian stage.

Shakespeare's Julius Caesar faces similar choices between imperial self-fashioning and submission to the desires of his dependants, such as the Roman people, his wife Calpurnia and Brutus (possibly his natural son). At the beginning of the play, however, he seems to be a textbook case of ambition to concentrate 'empire without end' (*imperium sine fine*) in his own person, unlike his more successful heir, Augustus, who transferred this idea to Rome's mission of global conquest. Often figured in sixteenth-century moral critiques of ambition, Caesar is even its voice in one Latin poem, in which he identifies himself as 'I who alone was all things' in Rome.[6] Plutarch's Caesar, presented at length in *The Lives of the Noble Grecians and Romans*, Shakespeare's chief authority on classical history, reveals a similarly acquisitive sense of self. In one anecdote, he fell to weeping while he was 'reading the history of Alexander's acts':[7]

> he was sorrowful a good while after, and then burst out weeping. His friends seeing that, marvelled what should be the cause of his sorrow. He answered them, Do ye not think said he, that I have good cause to be heavy, when king Alexander being no older than myself is now, had in old time won so many nations and countries: and that I hitherunto have done nothing worthy of myself?

Plutarch's Caesar both fights and weeps in a competitive spirit: his tears unmistakably recall those of Alexander, who wept to hear there were other worlds, when he had yet to conquer one.

Shakespeare's Caesar, however, craves an immortal name more than he longs for an imperial crown. Shakespeare dwells on the scene in the marketplace, when Antony offers the crown to Caesar three times, only to be roared down by the Roman commons. But he chooses to present the scene only through the report of a witness, and a biased one: Casca delivers his 'blunt' account of Caesar's bid for power to Cassius, who puts it to immediate use in his own efforts to sway the loyalties of Brutus from Caesar. Despite the dramatic potential of the marketplace scene, Shakespeare saves the action scenes for the moment in which Caesar invents what we might call the 'third-person immortal'. When Caesar first enters the stage, he remarks to Antony that he counts Cassius among those envious men who 'be never at heart's ease / Whiles they behold a greater than themselves' (1.2.209–10). But Caesar shunts aside his insight on the grounds that he can ill afford to take his own fears to heart: 'if my name were liable to fear', he says, oddly, 'I do not know that man I should avoid / So soon as that spare Cassius' (1.2.200–2). His experience of fear is irrelevant, he concludes, 'for always I am Caesar' (1.2.213).

Caesar's objectification of his name suggests a heroic effort (in Stoic terms) to embody a range of abstract ideas in a material object: not his all-too-vulnerable body but his deathless and impassive name. Caesar returns to the third-person immortal with even more intensity in a later scene, in which he prepares for his triumphal march to the senate-house, where the conspirators await him. In this scene, Caesar is put through his rhetorical paces, confronted with his wife's fears and the augurs' prophecies, which oblige him to think of his mortality (an impossibility for 'Caesar') and his duties to his dependants (a challenge, considering how close imperial command is to his grasp). To yield to their premonitions would be a betrayal of his role as 'Caesar': 'Yet Caesar shall go forth' (2.2.28), he says, 'Caesar should be a beast without a heart / If he should stay at home today for fear. / No, Caesar shall not' (2.2.42–4). By the end of the scene, having used the third person more profusely than is becoming – critics have yet to forgive him for it – Caesar proceeds to the senate-house to undergo the fatal trial of his name.

From the perspective of the conspirators, there is no positive case to be made for Shakespeare's Caesar, for the good reason that he denies them a share in his considerable magnanimity and, worse, bestows it on the common citizens of Rome. The senators are on the receiving end only of Caesar's imperious side, which they actively provoke, goading him to make ever more hyperbolic assertions of his self-assurance and fixed ideas (e.g. 'I am as constant as the Northern Star, / Of whose true fixed and resting quality / There is no fellow in the firmament', 3.1.60–2). The people, by contrast, actually welcome his political rigour. The historical Caesar, as Plutarch notes, attempted reforms of the senate's historic abuses and named the people in his will. Shakespeare's Antony unforgettably reveals the conditions of the will in his speech over Caesar's body, while the senators and tribunes themselves expose the bond between the reformist Caesar and the people. Throughout the play's early acts, they repeatedly identify the people's liberties with Caesar's monarchical ambitions: feeling squeezed in both directions, above and below, they can scarcely contain their anxieties about the limits placed on their own liberties.

Caesar's close bond with the people and strained relations with the senators emerge clearly in Casca's report of the failed coronation in the marketplace. Casca's satirical remarks disclose more than he knows about Caesar's political and personal commitments. He has no idea why the people so loudly applaud Caesar's third refusal of the coronet, when it seems obvious to Casca that Caesar 'would fain have had it' and was 'very loath to lay his fingers off it' (1.2.239–41) on the first two occasions it was offered to him. Casca has no idea what it means to the people, or Caesar, to be tied by such a close bond that their fortunes rise and fall together. It annoys him to think that Caesar allows 'the tag-rag people' to 'clap him and hiss him, according as he pleased and displeased them, as they use to do the players in the theatre' (1.2.256–8). It amuses him to say that Caesar 'fell down in the market-place, and foamed at mouth, and was speechless' (1.2.250–1) because he had inhaled so much 'bad air' (1.2.248) generated by the people's shouts and hoots that he perforce fell to the level of the groundlings: 'the rabblement hooted, and clapped their chapped hands, and threw up their sweaty nightcaps, and uttered such a deal of stinking breath because Caesar refused the crown that it had almost choked Caesar; for he swooned and fell down at it' (1.2.243–6). What disgusts Casca is not the people's breath, diet or hygiene, but their exercise of public voice. For Casca, Cassius and Brutus, the popular voice represents social contagion, not the political inspiration it is to Caesar.[8]

Although Brutus claims no bond with the people – he prefers identification with Rome in her more abstract forms – he ultimately discovers that Caesar is willing to fall, even die, for him in precisely the same manner that he collapsed before the people. In the marketplace Caesar falls and, when he comes to consciousness, offers his neck to the people to slit, if he has offended them for reasons of weakness or ambition. In the senate-house he fights like a cornered animal, according to Plutarch, manfully resisting his attackers, 'but when he saw Brutus with his sword drawn in his hand, then he pulled his gown over his head, and made no more resistance'.[9] In the marketplace and the senate-house Caesar is overwhelmed by the will of those who depend on him. He can more or less cope with aristocratic resentment, but he cannot ignore the disaffection of his friends. As Shakespeare's hero unforgettably says, '*Et tu, Bruté*? – Then fall Caesar' (3.1.76).

While Shakespeare's Julius Caesar makes a fairly good end, in that he gives up his pretensions to being 'Caesar', as constant as the Northern Star, the same cannot be said of Brutus or Antony. Neither man dies well. Having failed as Rome's redeemer, in the tradition of his ancestor Junius Brutus, who overthrew the monarchical rule of the Tarquins and helped to establish the Roman Republic, Brutus becomes increasingly detached from his environment. Not even the news of his wife's death or the appearance of Caesar's ghost on the eve of the battle at Philippi is enough to tear him from self-preoccupation. It is as if, in giving up his hope to preserve Rome's republican institutions and thus shape Roman history, he loses his sense of belonging to anyone or any place. When the Roman Republic falls, Brutus comes to be (or see himself as) an anachronism – the embodiment of a noble but no longer viable idea. In *Antony and Cleopatra*, Antony loses his sense of fixed identity when he faces a similar crisis. From the play's early scenes, Antony anticipates that he will lose to Octavius in any contest of luck (2.3.31–6). But the weight of his personal failure is brought home to him only after the naval battle of Actium, at which he shamefully abandoned his soldiers to follow Cleopatra's retreating ship. In a haunting scene of introspection, Antony assesses the damage he has done to himself in an extended self-comparison to the imaginary shapes in cloud formation. Noting to his servant Eros that 'Sometime we see a cloud that's dragonish, / A vapour sometime like a bear or lion, / A towered citadel, a pendent rock, / A forkèd mountain, or blue promontory' (4.15.2–5), all forms that 'even with a thought / The rack distains, and makes it indistinct / As water is in water' (4.14.9–11), Antony painfully concludes: 'now thy captain is / Even such a body. Here I am Antony, / Yet cannot hold this visible shape' (4.15.12–14). Never a great believer in Stoicism, with its pose of indifference to the world, Antony cannot, as Brutus did, maintain a sense of self that is powered by flat denial. On the contrary, Antony imagines himself dissolving into thin air.

If Antony recovers his shattered heroic identity, it is because Cleopatra puts the pieces back together in a loving act of remembrance and imagination. In her exchange with Dolabella, whom Caesar has sent to lure her from her monument, she parries his efforts at negotiation with her lavishly described dream of the Emperor Antony:

CLEOPATRA. His face was as the heav'ns, and therein stuck
A sun and moon, which kept their course and lighted

The little O o'th' earth.
DOLABELLA Most sovereign creature –
CLEOPATRA His legs bestrid the ocean; his reared arm
Crested the world. His voice was propertied
As all the tunèd spheres, and that to friends;
But when he meant to quail and shake the orb,
He was as rattling thunder. For his bounty,
There was no winter in't; an autumn 'twas
That grew the more by reaping. His delights
Were dolphin-like; they showed his back above
The elements they lived in. In his livery
Walked crowns and crownets. Realms and islands were
As plates dropped from his pocket.
DOLABELLA Cleopatra –
CLEOPATRA Think you there was, or might be, such a man
As this I dreamt of?
DOLABELLA Gentle madam, no.
(5.2.78–93)

The queen of rhetoric and performance, Cleopatra uses her dream to prevail on Dolabella to disclose Caesar's intentions (to lead her in triumph). How does she succeed in dividing the loyalties of Caesar's own man? Although he clearly is moved by her dazzling sovereignty, as Roman men tend to be, Dolabella seems also to be stirred by the image she creates of an enduring Roman dream of imperial magnanimity. There is no such man as the one she describes: not Antony and not his master, the future Augustus Caesar.

Antony and Cleopatra is the only one of Shakespeare's classical plays to present a positive cast of characters who aim to be 'marble-constant' or assume heroic identities on a colossal scale. Exceptions to the rules of Shakespearian classicism, Antony and Cleopatra succeed *only* when they take themselves out of historical time and place and assume transhistorical and transnational identities. Their success depends on their willingness to assume roles in imaginative fiction, having lost their historical battle for worldly empire.

Timon of Athens and *Coriolanus* deal with two legendarily difficult men: Timon, an Athenian benefactor, and Coriolanus, Rome's fiercest warrior, both turn on their native cities in response to monstrous ingratitude. Timon, who sustains Athens' flattering self-image as a city as prosperous in its civic institutions as its arts, ruins himself through his unstinting generosity, but is serially rebuffed when it is his turn to ask for benefits to stave off crippling debts and even homelessness. Disabused of his fond notion that the gifts flowing from him bought him love, he dramatically spurns his false friends, declares his hatred for all men ('I am Misanthropos', he says at 4.3.53) and goes into voluntary exile in the woods near Athens, where he finds yet more money (he has the Midas touch), which he puts to immediate use in making good on his curses. His instrument is Alcibiades, the warrior and nobleman who has declared war on Athens and needs only to find funding in order to carry out one of his three historical acts of treason.

Coriolanus, who is Rome's chief warrior, has fought in cruel wars for Rome from his adolescence, returning each time with as many wounds as honours, and even earning his name, 'Coriolanus', by defeating the city of Corioles almost single-handedly. When social relations fray in Rome (as they did in Timon's Athens), Coriolanus finds that he is denied the office of consul (for failing to show his wounds to the people, as required by custom), condemned for treason (for rejecting the authority of the people's tribunes) and sentenced to exile from Rome. Whereas Timon curses the walls of Athens on his way out of the city, Coriolanus plans to destroy the walls of Rome when he returns, like an avenging god, at the head of the enemy's army. Rejecting judgement, he volunteers for exile, cursing the Roman citizens and proudly – if improbably – declaring, 'I banish you' (3.3.127).

Despite the similarities of the two plots, Timon and Coriolanus at first appear to have little in common. Timon is all affability, delighted to solve his friends' and clients' financial problems and determined to create a circle of Athenians tied to him by the bonds of love. Coriolanus, by contrast, bristles with discontent and wrath, which he frequently turns on the common people of Rome, whose faults he lambasts and whose fellowship he strenuously denies. Both men, however, have a common goal, which Timon pursues through gifts and blessings and Coriolanus through martial deeds and curses: each man aspires to divinity, one through economic largesse and the other through military service. No man can touch Timon for bounty: flattered as a god, he seeks to elevate, free and redeem others, without accepting repayment (even when two noblemen attempt to provide him gifts, he pays for them at 1.2.177–86). And no man can touch Coriolanus for martial prowess: he is a pitiless 'thing of blood' (2.2.105) and 'an engine' (5.4.16) of war mowing down all in sight, who finally 'sits in his state as a thing made for Alexander' and 'wants nothing of a god but eternity and a heaven to throne in' (5.4.18–20). What neither man seeks, or even accepts, are the reciprocal bonds of fellowship.

Of the two classical heroes, Coriolanus is the one who at length relents his anger and submits to his civic and familial bonds. In most readings of the play, the hero gets no credit for kneeling to his mother, Volumnia, when she comes – with his wife, son and family friend Valeria in tow – in the last of Rome's three embassies to its warlike son. He is sometimes thought merely to capitulate to the superior force of his mother, who has never held back her opinion that he is *her* warrior, whom she 'holp to frame' (5.3.62–3), and without whom he has no more moral or martial agency than an infant. He cannot be 'author of himself' and know 'no other kin' (5.3.36–7), but must be his mother's 'corrected son' (5.3.57).

We might think of this account as Volumnia's story: she uses it to gain her son's attention and bring him to his knees, as if he were the suppliant rather than his mother or Rome. With considerable poise, she publicly lays out her three-fold argument to her son: his invasion of Rome divides the loyalties of his household between family and state; his reputation in the historical record hangs in jeopardy; and mercy might be regarded as a worthy alternative to victory. Logical as her points may be, they make no difference to Coriolanus: none of these reasons is sufficient to make him break off the experiments in divinity he has been conducting since he first went into exile. For duress, after all, is mother's milk to Coriolanus. Volumnia herself used to 'load' her son '[w]ith precepts that would make invincible / The heart that conned them' (4.1.9–11); she taught him from boyhood that 'extremities' are 'the trier of spirits' (4.1.4).[10]

What, then, makes Coriolanus yield and kneel to his mother, to Rome, and to the outer world of determinism and fate that he has struggled to deny? Since going to war against Rome, he has refused any external form of determination, even forbidding 'all names', preferring instead to be 'a kind of nothing, titleless, / Till he had forged himself a name o'th'fire / Of burning Rome' (5.1.12–15). What makes him kneel to Volumnia is not his weakness, but hers. When logical persuasions fail, Volumnia is forced to reveal the depth of her own vulnerability, even if she does so with savage irony. Rallying Virgilia and Valeria to participate in a mock display of feminine submission, she cries, 'Down ladies: let us shame him with our knees' (5.3.170). Volumnia intends to shame her son with a charade of familial dependence, when she seems to believe that the reverse is true: 'There's no man in the world / More bound to's mother, yet here he lets me prate / Like one i'th'stocks' (5.3.159–61). For his part, Coriolanus must finally recognize that his once formidable mother has come to depend on him: she really has mistaken the duty of parent to child all this while, as she had said early in the scene (5.3.55–6), without meaning it.

At the end of his play, Coriolanus comes to man's estate by assuming the humbling responsibilities he owes to the members of his household and, by extension, the citizens of Rome. He is the only character in the play, it would seem, who grasps that his is a tragic role:

> O mother, mother!
> What have you done? Behold, the heavens do ope,
> The gods look down, and this unnatural scene
> They laugh at. O my mother, mother, O!

You have won a happy victory to Rome;
But for your son, believe it, O believe it,
Most dangerously you have with him prevailed,
If not most mortal to him. But let it come.
(5.3.183–90)

The speech is remarkable for the compassion it shows to his mother, who can see no tragic consequences to her actions and cannot take his words on faith. Abandoning the principle of strict justice by which he strove to live, Coriolanus now acts to protect his mother from the knowledge of her dependency on him and, more horrifyingly, the outer world of determinism and fate that he believed she sent him out to combat. Rather than force upon her the unbearable knowledge of her vulnerability and illusions, he gives her what he denied to the people: permission to think well of herself.

For most of the play, Coriolanus seems to be the very type of classical hero that Shakespeare favours least: longing to be 'author of himself' (5.3.36), he strenuously denies his ties to community, time and place. He does everything in his power, it would seem, to earn his current reputation as the least sympathetic and least self-reflective of all Shakespeare's tragic protagonists. When he chooses to kneel to his mother and yield to Rome, however, he fully accepts his contingent relation to history and community. At this moment, Coriolanus arrives at man's estate and, simultaneously, approaches the threshold of Shakespearian tragedy, as Julius Caesar and Titus Andronicus did before him. What brings him there is his consent to identify with the members of society who are forced to depend on others. Had he learned this lesson earlier, perhaps he might have revealed his wounds to the people of Rome.

NOTES

1 Baldassare Castiglione, *The Book of the Courtier*, trans. Charles Singleton and ed. Daniel Javitch (New York and London: Norton & Company, 2002), 1.18, p. 26.

2 See Andrew Hadfield, *Shakespeare and Republicanism* (Cambridge: Cambridge University Press, 2005).

3 Linda Charnes, *Notorious Identity: Materializing the Subject in Shakespeare* (Cambridge, MA: Harvard University Press, 1993), discusses the phenomenon of Shakespeareian characters who want to be what they already are: famous.

4 See Heather James, *Shakespeare's Troy: Drama, Politics, and the Translation of Empire* (Cambridge: Cambridge University Press, 1997).

5 Jonathan Bate, ed. *Titus Andronicus* (London: Arden Shakespeare, 1995), provides a useful discussion of stage productions of the play.

6 The poem, written by the aptly named Julius Caesar Scaliger, appears in a collection of Latin verses on classical men entitled *Heroes* (1546).

7 *The Liues of the Noble Grecians and Romanes* (1579). All references are to Geoffrey Bullough, *Narrative and Dramatic Sources of Shakespeare* (London and New York: Routledge and Columbia University Press, 1964), vol. V.

8 See Oliver Arnold, *The Third Citizen: Shakespeare's Theater and the Early Modern House of Commons* (Baltimore: Johns Hopkins University Press, 2007).

9 Bullough, *Narrative*, vol. V, p. 86.

10 My discussion of the tragic relationship between Coriolanus and his mother is drawn from '*Coriolanus*: A Modern Perspective', in Barbara A. Mowat and Paul Werstine (eds.). Folger Shakespeare Library (New York: Washington Square Press, 2009), pp. 297–308.

READING LIST

Adelman, Janet. *The Common Liar: An Essay on 'Antony and Cleopatra'*. New Haven: Yale University Press, 1973.

Arnold, Oliver. *The Third Citizen: Shakespeare's Theater and the Early Modern House of Commons*. Baltimore: Johns Hopkins University Press, 2007.

Bullough, Geoffrey, ed. *Narrative and Dramatic Sources of Shakespeare*, 8 vols. London and New York: Routledge and Kegan Paul and Columbia University Press, 1957–75.

Burkhardt, Sigurd. 'How Not to Murder Caesar', in *Shakespearian Meanings*. Princeton, NJ: Princeton University Press, 1968, pp.3–21.

James, Heather. *Shakespeare's Troy: Drama, Politics, and the Translation of Empire*. Cambridge: Cambridge University Press, 1997.

Kahn, Coppélia. *Roman Shakespeare: Warriors, Wounds, and Women*. London and New York: Routledge, 1997.

Miles, Gary. 'How Roman Are Shakespeare's "Romans"?' *Shakespeare Quarterly*, 40 (1989), pp. 257–83.

Miola, Robert. *Shakespeare's Rome*. Cambridge: Cambridge University Press, 1983.

Paster, Gail Kern. *The Idea of the City in the Age of Shakespeare*. Athens, GA: University of Georgia Press, 1985.

Spencer, T. J. B. 'Shakespeare and the Elizabethan Romans', in *Shakespeare Survey*, 10 (1969), pp. 27–38.

12

JANETTE DILLON

Shakespeare's tragicomedies

'*Exit, pursued by a bear*' (*The Winter's Tale*, 3.3.57). This is one of the most famous stage directions in Shakespeare. It makes us laugh, while at the same time giving us a sense of puzzlement and wonder. What did that moment really feel like for early modern audiences at the Globe or Blackfriars? Was it a real bear or a man in a bear suit?[1] Was it comic? Scary? Weird? Or all of these at once? We may begin by exploring something of the particular quality of Shakespeare's late plays through this stage direction and the rest of the scene that follows it in *The Winter's Tale*. Antigonus, who is the man pursued by a bear, has just laid down a baby, Leontes' child Perdita, whose life he has saved against Leontes' command. Her name tells us she is lost; yet her survival here as Antigonus himself meets violent death is a miracle. A shepherd comes on, finds the baby and 'take[s] it up for pity' (3.3.72–3); at which point his son comes on, amazed by the dark side of this wonder: 'I have seen two such sights, by sea and by land! But I am not to say it is a sea, for it is now the sky. Betwixt the firmament and it you cannot thrust a bodkin's point' (3.3.79–81). Why does Shakespeare give the shepherd's son all these words to say that he has seen something amazing? All he is saying, in fact, is that the sea meets the sky at the horizon, which is as ordinary and predictable an observation as can be. And yet in context the words seem to take on an emblematic quality, because they speak of two radically different things coming together, and of the way this can seem both natural and miraculous. The astounded shepherd's son thus becomes an unwitting mouthpiece for a statement that sums up tragicomedy as a genre, through the coming together, the collision even, of tragedy and comedy.

The two things the shepherd's son has seen by sea and land are the shipwreck and the bear eating Antigonus, and his story brings together the cries of both the shipwrecked souls and Antigonus, as well as the roaring of the sea and of the bear: 'first, how the poor souls roared, and the sea mocked them, and how the poor gentleman roared, and the bear mocked him, both roaring louder than the sea or weather' (3.3.91–4). The tone of this is hard to judge: it somehow sounds both innocent and callous. Even more difficult in tone, however, is the son's response to his father's question of when this happened: 'Now, now. I have not winked since I saw these sights. The men are not yet cold under water, nor the bear half dined on the gentleman. He's at it now' (3.3.96–8). The idea that the bear is still 'at it now', and indeed the very terminology of 'dini[ng] on the gentleman', is simultaneously horrifying, grotesque and ludicrous. An audience barely knows how to respond, until the shepherd himself dispels that vision of what is offstage with a reminder of the heart-warming sight that is onstage, and in terms that again emphasize the coming together of like with unlike, of birth with death: 'Heavy matters, heavy matters. But look thee here, boy. Now bless thyself. Thou metst with things dying, I with things new-born. Here's a sight for thee' (3.3.103–5). This is again an epiphanic moment, representing the classic tragicomic move from death to life.[2]

Tragicomedy

As the title of this chapter makes clear, there is no real critical consensus on what generic name to give to the group of Shakespeare's late plays comprising *Pericles*, *Cymbeline*, *The Tempest* and *The Winter's Tale*. Approaches that concentrate on their tragicomic aspect usually cite definitions of tragicomedy originating with either the Italian poet and dramatist Battista Guarini or his English follower, John Fletcher. Guarini, whose play *Il Pastor Fido* was first printed in 1590 and translated into English in 1602, defined tragicomedy as 'mixed ... not so grand that it rises to the tragic nor so humble that it approaches the comic'.[3] Fletcher, whose play *The Faithful Shepherdess* (1608) was an adaptation of Guarini's, wrote that 'A tragicomedy is not so called in respect of mirth and killing, but in respect it wants deaths, which is enough to make it no tragedy, yet brings some near it, which is enough to make it no comedy'.[4]

Though these definitions have an obvious bearing on Shakespeare's late plays, they make problematic starting-points for a discussion of them. Already, from our brief look at *The Winter's Tale*, we can see that it does not 'want deaths'. Nor is Antigonus' death the only one in the play, which also sets a son who dies against the daughter who miraculously lives. Chronology is an issue too. Shakespeare's *Pericles* may well predate *The Faithful Shepherdess* by a year or so; the term 'tragicomedy' in English was in use from at least Sidney's deploring of 'mongrel tragic-comedy' in his *Apology for Poetry* (circulating in manuscript from the early 1580s);[5] and the word 'tragicomical' is recorded from 1567. Nor was the concept of tragicomedy in England prior to Fletcher a matter of pure theory. Already by the 1560s plays such as *Damon and Pythias* (1564–5) and *Apius and Virginia* (c. 1567) had been defined as 'tragical comed[ies]'. Furthermore, if we apply the definitions of Fletcher and Guarini to Shakespeare's plays, we find that they fit plays written considerably earlier than either *Pericles* or *The Faithful Shepherdess*, or even than the English translation of *Il Pastor Fido* (1602).[6] Tragedy seems narrowly avoided, for example, in *The Merchant of Venice* (1596–7) and *Much Ado About Nothing* (1598). Indeed, in that both these plays 'want deaths' but 'bring some near it', they arguably fit Fletcher's definition of tragicomedy better than the later group. Shakespeare's fellow-actors, John Heminges and Henry Condell, classified *Cymbeline* as a tragedy when they included it in the First Folio.

Romance

So tragicomedy as a category does not define this group in a way that distinguishes them generically from all Shakespeare's other plays. What, then, are the distinguishing features of these plays that both bring them together as a group and differentiate them from earlier tragicomic forms? Part of the answer is 'romance': the kind of plot that included lost children, mistaken identity, gods and prophecies and miraculous reunion. Ben Jonson, Shakespeare's contemporary, had various contemptuous phrases for this form of writing: he called *Pericles* a 'mouldy tale'; he poured scorn on '*Tales*, *Tempests*, and such-like drolleries'; and he was self-congratulatory about his own refusal to 'make nature afraid in his plays'.[7] But the tradition ran long and deep in English writing, which in turn drew on classical Greek comedy and romance, often via French and Italian intermediary sources. English plays had long drawn on romance traditions for plot material; even religious drama in the form of miracle plays had affiliations to secular romance; and some of Shakespeare's most famous and respected contemporaries, such as Sidney and Spenser, had displayed a strong preference for it in non-dramatic poetry during the closing decades of the sixteenth century. In introducing the fourteenth-century poet John Gower as a choric figure into *Pericles* Shakespeare was acknowledging the ancient roots of this tradition in English writing.

Even the category of romance, however, first used by Edward Dowden to group the four late plays in 1875, does not quite single out these plays against any others in the Shakespearian canon.[8] Many earlier comedies have elements of romance: *The Comedy of Errors* (1594) reunites lost children and their parents; a god descends in *As You Like It* (1599); and mistaken identity is a recurrent comic motif. Yet the combination of romantic elements and tragicomic structure together does go some way to identify and differentiate the grouping. Having said that, romance also pulls against the way tragicomedy is developing in the seventeenth century by effectively banning satire, which was becoming associated with tragicomedy. Two companies were especially known for producing tragicomic plays in the early seventeenth century: the King's Men and the Children of the Queen's Revels. As Lucy Munro's recent study of the Queen's Revels Children highlights, satire is the hallmark of their style, and some of the tragicomedy performed by the King's Men, notably Fletcher's, shares this same satiric perspective. Shakespeare's tragicomedy differs from them in its refusal of satire. Though it produces moments that hover around the grotesque or burlesque and take risks with tone, it pulls back from the cynical worldview of satire.

The description of Antigonus being eaten by a bear, as we have seen, is brought away from potential burlesque and back to romance by the shepherd's turn towards the abandoned baby; and other moments that seem to be similarly heading towards the anti-romance of parody are also arrested rather than developed. The moment when Innogen discovers the headless Cloten lying next to her and mistakes it for her beloved husband, Posthumus, is one such moment. Early modern and contemporary audiences alike must surely cringe as Innogen first touches the body of her clownish step-brother, then claims to recognize each of his limbs one by one, and finally falls upon him in a mistaken embrace (*Cymbeline*, 4.2.295–332). But the martial entry of the Romans swiftly cuts across it with serious matter, and it is here that the soothsayer tells of the vision which, fulfilled, is to become the apotheosis of the play:

> Last night the very gods showed me a vision –
> ...
> I saw Jove's bird, the Roman eagle, winged
> From the spongy south to this part of the west,
> There vanish'd in the sunbeams ...
>
> (4.2.348–52)

The soothsayer reads the meaning of this to be that the Roman army will be successful; but in fact the descent of Jupiter in the play heralds a sequence that marks out the fulfilment of another prophecy. While Posthumus lies on the ground, visually echoing the supine bodies of the scene above (where Innogen sleeps and Cloten lies dead), he has a vision that culminates in Jupiter descending on an eagle to literally lay the truth on Posthumus' breast. On waking, Posthumus reads the true prophecy that foresees his reconciliation with Innogen as the jointing of a lopped branch onto the old stock of the tree. Posthumus, unlike the soothsayer, does not try to unravel its meaning, but simply recognizes its likeness to his life (5.5.241–3). Typically for these plays, true reconciliation is epiphanic and imagistic, seeming to stop time. As Innogen embraces him, Posthumus speaks briefly, echoing the terms of the tablet of truth: 'Hang there like fruit, my soul, / Till the tree die' (5.6.263–4). Thus the parodic moment of Innogen's misrecognition leads directly into the visionary path towards true recognition and reconciliation.

The gods

The role of the gods in these plays brings them together as a group and distinguishes them to some degree from Shakespeare's other plays. Though the god Hymen descends in *As You Like It*, as noted above, that moment is interestingly different from the descent of Jupiter in *Cymbeline*. Above all, Hymen's descent is confirmatory and celebratory, not interventionist. By the time Hymen enters, with '*Still music*' (*As You Like It*, 5.4.97), Rosalind has already resolved most of the difficulties and prepared the ground for this climactic set of unions. Indeed, even though Hymen enters singing with Rosalind and Celia, it is again Rosalind who begins the speeches that script coming together ('To you I give myself ...' 5.4.106), and Hymen has to silence her in order to take on the role of celebrant: 'Peace, ho, I bar confusion. / 'Tis I must make conclusion / Of these most strange events' (5.4.114–16).

In *Cymbeline*, by contrast, Posthumus is imprisoned and despairing at the point where Jupiter appears, and Jupiter's role is decisive: 'He shall be lord of Lady Innogen, / And happier much by his affliction made' (5.5.201–2). Diana's appearance in a dream to Pericles is decisive, like Jupiter's, bringing a clear instruction designed to bring about reunion:

> My temple stands in Ephesus. Hie thee thither,
> And do upon mine altar sacrifice.
> There when my maiden priests are met together,
> At large discourse thy fortunes in this wise:
>
> With a full voice before the people all,
> Reveal how thou at sea didst lose thy wife.
> To mourn thy crosses, with thy daughter's, call
> And give them repetition to the life.
> Perform my bidding, or thou liv'st in woe;
> Do't, and rest happy, by my silver bow.
> Awake, and tell thy dream.
>
> (21.225–35)

The gods speak even more decisively, at a much earlier point, and with negative impact, in *The Winter's Tale*, and it is Leontes' refusal to accept their word that sets near-tragedy in motion. The oracle pronounces Hermione chaste; Leontes simply dismisses this statement as 'mere falsehood' (3.2.139); and the result is the immediate death of his son. Leontes recognizes this as a punishment from the gods: 'Apollo's angry, and the heavens themselves / Do strike at my injustice' (3.2.143–4).

The Tempest has similarities with all three other late plays and with *As You Like It*. When the gods descend to bless the union of Ferdinand and Miranda, their appearance, like Hymen's, seems affirmative, but with one important difference: they are explicitly summoned by Prospero. Indeed, they may not even be gods at all, but rather mere effects of Prospero's magic. In speaking to Ariel, Prospero describes the vision of the gods he is about to summon as 'Some vanity of mine art' (4.1.41).

In all four plays the descent of gods allows for some spectacular stage effects, and the influence of court masque on these late plays is widely recognized. Court entertainment had always had the resource and potential for highly elaborate staging, and Henry VIII had spent lavishly on costumes, props and effects for masques and disguisings. Royal entries, such as coronation processions and receptions of visiting monarchs, had used descent machinery since at least the fourteenth century, and Henslowe had installed a descent mechanism at the Rose in 1595, so the technology for such effects had long been in place.[9] Elizabeth, who was more concerned to save money than to spend it, relied routinely on playing companies like the Chamberlain's Men to entertain the court. From 1603, however, when James VI of Scotland acceded to the English throne, taking the Chamberlain's Men directly into his service as the King's Men, the Twelfth Night masque again became a highlight of the court year, and money was poured into creating ever more astounding spectacles. Here is just one example of the kinds of effect Inigo Jones was developing in the early years of James' reign. Ben Jonson, who wrote the text for *The Masque of Queens*, describes how the scene moves from a witches' dance to the House of Fame:

> *In the heat of their dance, on the sudden, was heard a sound of loud music, as if many instruments had made one blast; with which not only the hags themselves but the hell into which they ran quite vanished and the whole face of the scene altered, scarce suffering the memory of any such thing. But in the place of it, appeared a glorious and magnificent building figuring the House of Fame, in the upper part of which were discovered the twelve masquers sitting upon a throne triumphal erected in form of a pyramid and circled with all store of light.*[10]

In creating spectacles such as the descent of Jupiter on an eagle or the vanishing banquet in *The Tempest*, therefore, Shakespeare was bringing to popular audiences a taste of the latest fashion in court performance.

Spectacle in stillness

Yet these plays also bring to the fore stage effects which are simultaneously inspired by masque yet antithetical to its values. Their revelatory moments are by no means all dominated by stage machinery and special effects. One of the characteristic features of the late plays is the creation of held tableaux, of spell-binding moments that engage the audience's gaze and attention in a very intense way without any recourse to mechanical spectacle. These moments are created almost entirely by actors' bodies used in particular ways in the stage space of the Globe or Blackfriars. When Prospero '*discovers* Ferdinand *and* Miranda, *playing at chess*' (*The Tempest*, 5.1.174) he may be pulling back a curtain in front of the discovery space at the rear centre of the stage, so that the framing of a stage within a stage works in conjunction with the still bodies of Ferdinand and Miranda to construct the lovers as an emblematic tableau. Even more simply, when Prospero solemnly abjures his 'rough magic', it is the actor's command of the space and the powerfully assertive and lyrical language he utters that primarily create the tableau effect (5.1.50). In addition, the props of staff and book, and the '*solemn music*' that follows, underline the sense that this is a moment of epiphany (5.1.58).

'Solemn' or 'soft' music are frequent accompaniments at such moments, sometimes substituting for speech and giving the moment a prolonged sense of stillness that seems to take it out of time. *Pericles* is especially full of dumb-shows, the effect of which is cumulative. There is no space here to examine this feature of the play very fully, but we may look selectively at the extended final sequence, beginning with Pericles' mourning of his seemingly dead daughter, Marina.

> *Enter* Pericles, *at one door with all his train,* Cleon *and* Dionyza [*in mourning garments*] *at the other.* Cleon [*draws the curtain and*] *shows* Pericles *the tomb, whereat* Pericles *makes lamentation, puts on sack-cloth, and in a mighty passion departs.* (*Pericles*, 18.23)

The tableau of Pericles wasting away with grief, '*undecent nails on his fingers, and attired in sack-cloth*' is re-presented in Scene 21, and he is described there as one who has become nothing but an unmoving and silent tableau: 'A man who for this three months hath not spoken / To anyone, nor taken sustenance / But to prorogue his grief' (21.18–20). Marina, not known to be his daughter, is brought to him as one likely to be a healing presence, and she sings to him, bringing him to speech after long silence. An initially halting and arhythmic dialogue gradually becomes more lyrical as recognition slowly comes closer, and Marina's past is recalled as a silent tableau that parallels Pericles' own:

She would never tell
Her parentage. Being demanded that,
She would sit still and weep.
(21.175–7)

At the same time, the quality of Pericles' own stillness is changing:

O Helicanus, strike me, honoured sir,
Give me a gash, put me to present pain,
Lest this great sea of joys rushing upon me
O'erbear the shores of my mortality
And drown me with their sweetness!
(21.178–82)

The culmination of the sequence, when Pericles finally accepts the kneeling Marina as his daughter, brings music that only Pericles can hear:

PERICLES But what music?
HELICANUS My lord, I hear none.
PERICLES None? The music of the spheres! List, my Marina.
LYSIMACHUS [*aside to the others*] It is not good to cross him. Give him way.
PERICLES Rar'st sounds. Do ye not hear?
LYSIMACHUS Music, my lord?
PERICLES I hear most heav'nly music!
It raps me unto list'ning, and thick slumber
Hangs upon mine eyelids. Let me rest. (21.213–21)
[*He sleeps*]

Editors vary as to where they script stage directions for music to play; but the absence of stage directions here from the quarto text of 1609 suggests that *Pericles* may have no audible music at all at this point, merely silence.

The final sequence of *The Winter's Tale*, in which the seeming statue of Hermione comes to life, culminates in music to 'awake' Hermione (5.3.98), but first explicitly scripts silence, as Paulina tells Leontes: 'I like your silence; it the more shows off / Your wonder' (5.3.21–2). And the reunion of Innogen and Posthumus clearly scripts a silence which Cymbeline finally interrupts:

POSTHUMUS Hang there like fruit, my soul,
Till the tree die.
CYMBELINE [*to Innogen*] How now, my flesh, my child?
What, mak'st thou me a dullard in this act?
Wilt thou not speak to me? (*Cymbeline*, 5.6.263–6)

Lyric mode

The pointing of these tableaux with music, silence and intensely poignant speech is indicative of a pervasive lyrical texture to the plays. This is partly a matter of language; partly a matter of music and song; and partly a matter of setting. Lyrical language is evident much more widely than merely in these moments of tableaux. We might quote speech upon speech to make this point, but perhaps one of the most memorably lyrical is Caliban's account of the island in *The Tempest*:

> Be not afeard. The isle is full of noises,
> Sounds, and sweet airs, that give delight and hurt not.
> Sometimes a thousand twangling instruments
> Will hum about mine ears, and sometime voices
> That if I then had waked after long sleep
> Will make me sleep again; and then in dreaming
> The clouds methought would open and show riches
> Ready to drop upon me, that when I waked
> I cried to dream again.
>
> (3.2.130–8)

Its lyricism stands out in the memory for two reasons: because it is spoken by a brutish creature and because its subject is the mysterious musicality of the island. Even more telling, perhaps, in relation to tragicomic form, is the paradoxical lyricism of Caliban's description of how he first learned language. It is embedded in contraries, beginning with the totally banal: 'I must eat my dinner', continuing with piercing and rhythmic sweetness:

> This island's mine, by Sycorax my mother,
> Which thou tak'st from me. When thou cam'st first,
> Thou strok'st me and made much of me, wouldst give me
> Water with berries in't, and teach me how
> To name the bigger light, and how the less,
> That burn by day and night; and then I lov'd thee,
> And showed thee all the qualities o'the'isle,
> The fresh springs, brine-pits, barren place and fertile –

and cutting suddenly to vitriolic abuse:

> Cursed be I that did so! All the charms
> Of Sycorax, toads, beetles, bats, light on you;
> For I am all the subjects that you have,
> Which first was mine own king, and here you sty me
> In this hard rock, whiles you do keep from me
> The rest o'th' island. (1.2.335–47)

Elsewhere in the late plays, as here, language is as mixed in mode as is genre. Lyrical simplicity contrasts with different kinds of opposite: violence; banality; and knotty complexity.

Song, though very often present in Shakespeare's plays across the whole period of his writing, has a resonant and often symbolic quality in these late plays. Not only the words of Ariel's song, 'Full Fathom Five', for example, but also the way Ferdinand hears it, make the case for this peculiar resonance. The song itself is very brief, but looks forward as well as back in the play, to transformations, healing and enrichment yet to come, as well as to losses and changes past:

Full fathom five thy father lies.
Of his bones are coral made;
Those are pearls that were his eyes;
Nothing of him that doth fade
But doth suffer a sea-change
Into something rich and strange.
Sea-nymphs hourly ring his knell.
(1.2.400–6)

Even more enchanting and strange, however, is Ferdinand's attempt to articulate the inexplicable way he 'hears' this music:

Where should this music be? I'th' air or th'earth?
It sounds no more; and sure it waits upon
Some god o'th' island. Sitting on a bank,
Weeping again the King my father's wreck,
This music crept by me upon the waters,
Allaying both their fury and my passion
With its sweet air. Thence I have followed it –
Or it hath drawn me rather. But 'tis gone.
No, it begins again.
(1.2.391–9)

The Kneehigh production of *Cymbeline* in 2006 built on and extended this pervasive texture of music and song, but none of the company's additions could match the sheer beauty of the famous dirge 'Fear no more the heat o' the sun', sung over an Innogen thought, as she herself thought Posthumus, to be dead (4.2.259–82).

Settings

Settings contribute to the lyrical quality of these plays, but they also make a more complex and wide-ranging contribution than this and serve to mark important distinctions between these plays, as well as some elements in common. The island setting of *The Tempest* provides the most consistently lyrical environment, as Caliban's description above emphasizes. It is not merely pastoral, but also magical and inherently musical. This could not be said of any of the other plays in this group, where pastoral usually has a part to play, but where its part can be more or less extended and lighter or darker. In all these other three plays, there are important shifts of location, linked to a change in both plot direction and mood. *The Tempest*, unusually for Shakespeare, observes the unities of time and place by occupying a fictional period of a few hours in a single location. Its shift of location, framed as it is by a past and future in Naples, is merely implied.

In *The Winter's Tale*, the scene where the shepherds find Leontes' abandoned daughter marks the shift of location from the court of Sicily to the imaginary seashore of Bohemia. The place-names are evocative and romantic, not based on any real reference to the countries concerned. As critics have often noted since, Bohemia (now part of the Czech Republic) has no seashore. But the move from the increasingly dark and poisonous world of Leontes' court to 'the white sheet bleaching on the hedge' (4.3.5) and the harvest home of a simple country life is necessary in order for the plot to turn around and the move towards reconciliation and forgiveness to begin. So too is the long gap in time between Acts 3 and 4, a strategy wholly opposite to that of the unities that structure *The Tempest*, and the butt of Jonson's jokes.[11] The distinction between the two worlds, however, is neither simple nor total. The seeming idyll of Bohemian rural life also includes the rogue peddler Autolycus, who merrily cuts the purses of the innocent country-dwellers as they buy his goods and terrifies the shepherds with an extended fantasy of the punishments that await them:

> He has a son, who shall be flayed alive, then 'nointed over with honey, set on the head of a wasps' nest, then stand till he be three-quarters-and-a-dram dead, then recovered again with aqua-vitae, or some other hot infusion, then, raw as he is, and in the hottest day prognostication proclaims, shall he be set against a brick wall, the sun looking with a southward eye upon him, where he is to behold him with flies blown to death.
>
> (*The Winter's Tale* 4.4.758–65)

Even country lives are tainted by fear, corruption and deceit. It is Autolycus who sings the song that celebrates 'the white sheet bleaching on the hedge'.

Similarly Wales, in *Cymbeline*, though a place of refuge from the wicked court, is also wild and fearful. The young princes, brought up in this wilderness far from court, combine gentleness with roughness:

> They are as gentle
> As zephyrs blowing below the violet,

> Not wagging his sweet head; and yet as rough,
> Their royal blood enchafed, as the rud'st wind
> That by the top doth take the mountain pine
> And make him stoop to th' vale.
>
> (4.2.172–7)

Their life has sweetness and nobility, but their cave-dwelling is 'pinching' and often 'freezing' (3.3.38–9). Innogen sets out for it as a 'blessed' place, wondering 'how Wales was made so happy' as to own the 'haven' (Milford Haven) that will receive her beloved Posthumus, but the letter from Posthumus that invites her to follow him there is in fact designed to create the opportunity for Pisanio to kill her.

Pericles moves restlessly from one location to another, ranging over Antioch, Tyre, Tarsus, Pentapolis, Ephesus and Mytilene. Each journey holds out the possibility of happiness or rest, but the threat of corruption or distress regularly contests that outcome. There is no binary opposition of court and country, but instead a peripatetic structure that emphasizes the idea of life as a journey and recalls the shape of medieval romance more strongly than does any of the other three plays in this group. Thaisa's death takes place at sea, as the journey moves from one place to another; and, if there is a parallel in this play to the seeming idyll of the natural or magical world, it is the briefly represented Ephesus, where Thaisa's coffin washes up and the physician Cerimon uses his skills to enable her to 'blow / Into life's flow'r again' (13.92–3).

Realism and romance

A world where the seeming dead come back to life and where physicians, magicians and resourceful women are all represented as having the power to avert tragedy may seem to be a world where romance, with all its implications of fantasy and implausibility, truly holds sway. Yet these plays are also grounded in the real world in important ways. All share some interest in political questions of rule, in the rights and duties of rulers and subjects and the possibility of resistance, and all, though they may resolve difficulties in fantastical ways, take a hard look at the difficulties themselves first.

The image of the state is present and insistent from the opening scene of *The Tempest*. Despite the heightened realism of its staging (the stage direction has the mariners enter '*wet*' (1.1.46)), the ship would almost certainly also have been read allegorically by an early modern audience as a ship of state. Certainly it presents conflicted relations between different levels of social hierarchy. The aristocrats attempt to tell the sailors their business and the Boatswain roughly orders them to stay below and stop interfering with the task of keeping the ship afloat. The emblematic quality of the conflict is acutely focused in the Boatswain's rhetorical question, referring to the waves: 'What cares these roarers for the name of king?' (1.1.15–16).[12] As the play continues, first revealing the history of Prospero's rule of Milan, moving on to examine the power relations between Prospero and the full range of others on the island and creating opportunities for speeches such as Gonzalo's imagining of the ideal state, its concern with political realities cannot be missed.

Cymbeline, overtly located in ancient Britain at a time when James I was trying to use the name of Britain to force political unity between England and Scotland, and giving Innogen and Posthumus the names of the wife and grandfather of Brut, the mythical founder of Britain, is the most overtly topical of these plays.[13] Its movement towards peace with the Roman Empire, furthermore, also allows it to pay homage to James' pacifist foreign policy and to flatter his preference for an imperial image of power. James was known to favour representations of his reign that figured him as a new Augustus, and quasi-imperial arches built for his postponed coronation entry into London in 1604 had added a new element to the English tradition of royal entries. The role of Wales in the play was probably even more specific to the moment of *Cymbeline*'s production c. 1610, since James' eldest son, Henry, was invested with great ceremonial as Prince of Wales in June of that year. The play's topicality, however, does not especially entail a more realist slant, and its political dimension, such as it is, is more narrative and allusive than propagandist.

Constance Jordan has argued that *Pericles* also engages with James' confrontations with parliament over his wish to create the political entity of Great Britain, but the case is less persuasive than for *Cymbeline*.[14] *Pericles*, as the truest inheritor of romance-form among these plays, is also the least concerned with political questions. This is not to say, however, that it is not grounded in the real world. Its brothel scene (19) is as gross as anything Shakespeare ever wrote, and brings the threat of worldly corruption into shockingly close proximity to the virgin purity of Marina. It is a juxtaposition akin to Innogen's encounter with Cloten's body or Miranda's memory of Caliban's attempted rape, and all three moments are characteristic of tragicomedy. But in presenting Marina's purity as triumphant over this brutal encounter, the scene is also reminiscent of the medieval genre of the saint's play, which in turn has a natural affinity with romance. The Digby *Mary Magdalen* (1480–1520), for example, displays Mary's sanctity through an extended journey that has much in common with that of Pericles, and includes a tavern scene (where Mary succumbs to, rather than resists, the temptation to lechery), a heathen temple and a storm at sea in which the mother dies giving birth and is cast off upon a rock. Paradoxically, however, it may have been precisely this seemingly apolitical echo of an archaic form of religious drama that gave the play its strongest political potential at the time. In 1609–10 it was performed by recusant actors in Yorkshire, almost certainly highlighting its ties to the old religion with deliberately inflammatory intent.[15]

The Winter's Tale, though at first glance seemingly as atopical as *Pericles*, presents an unflinching picture of the consequences of absolutism at a time when King James was locking horns with the English parliament over the power and status of the monarch. Leontes' irrational jealousy may seem a purely personal matter, but as the play progresses and he reaches the point of openly defying the law, in the form of the oracle, it becomes evident that when a ruler is the perpetrator of such folly, there are consequences for the whole country. And this play, though its representation of reconciliation and forgiveness is perhaps the most magical and overwhelming of all these late plays, also departs from them in representing deaths that truly are final. Though Hermione returns and Perdita is found, Mamillius and Antigonus do not return, and their deaths are not forgotten. As noted above, it is thus technically not a tragicomedy.[16] Yet the breathtaking quality of its return to comic form at the end is the measure of its real engagement with the form. It is as though in this play Shakespeare really wants to go as close as he dares to tragic form in order to see whether he can still make a comic resolution work. Literal, unresurrected death surely constitutes the hardest and least romanticized encounter with the real world; but even this, this play seems to say, can be overcome. This is the ultimate marriage of realism and romance, and the ultimate test of how far the stage can go to transform audiences' ways of seeing the world. 'It is required', as Paulina says, 'You do awake your faith' (5.3.94–5). The play consciously offers up romance, but invites us to take it for possibility:

> That she is living,
> Were it but told you, should be hooted at
> Like an old tale. But it appears she lives.
> (5.3.116–18)

The echo here of the only scene in which Mamillius plays an active part, telling old tales to his mother, is not accidental. Mamillius' line 'A sad tale's best for winter' (2.1.27) is deliberately written to signify beyond its immediate context. In recalling it here, the play is gracefully remembering the child who has to die to bring his father to his senses and seeking to incorporate his death into the renewal of life now celebrated in this most daring of tragicomedies.

NOTES

1 Teresa Grant, following a suggestion by George F. Reynolds, has argued that two real polar bear cubs were in theatrical use in 1610–11. See 'White Bears in *Mucedorus*, *The Winter's Tale*, and *Oberon, The Fairy Prince*', in *Notes and Queries*, 48 (2001), 311–13.

2 As Andrew Gurr has shown, furthermore, the shepherd's words echo Evanthius' well-known definition of tragedy and comedy: *in tragoedia fugienda vita, in comedia capessanda exprimitur* ('in tragedy the ending of life is expressed, in comedy, the beginning'). See 'The Bear, the Statue, and Hysteria in *The Winter's Tale*', *Shakespeare Quarterly*, 34 (1983), 421.

3 Lucy Munro, citing Guarini's 'Compendio', in *Children of the Queen's Revels: A Jacobean Theatre Repertory* (Cambridge: Cambridge University Press, 2005), p. 105.

4 *The Faithful Shepherdess*, ed. Florence Ada Kirk (New York: Garland, 1980), To the Reader, ll. 22–6.

5 *An Apology for Poetry*, ed. Geoffrey Shepherd (Manchester and New York: Manchester University Press, 2002), 3rd rev. edn. R. W. Maslen, p.112.

6 *Il Pastor Fido* was first printed in 1590 and must have been known to some in England before Edward Dymock translated it in 1602. But 1602 was also a key moment in terms of the dissemination of the Italian text, since it was published that year in an edition that included engravings, extensive notes and a treatise on tragicomedy.

7 'Ode to Himself', in Ian Donaldson (ed.), *Poems* (London: Oxford University Press, 1975), p. 355; *Bartholomew Fair*, ed. Suzanne Gossett (Manchester: University of Manchester Press, 2000), 'Induction', ll. 132–3.

8 Edward Dowden, *Shakspere: A Critical Study of His Mind and Art* (1875; London: Routledge and Kegan Paul, 1948).

9 See Janette Dillon, 'Chariots and Cloud Machines: Gods and Goddesses on Early English Stages', in Lloyd Edward Kermode, Jason Scott-Warren and Martine van Elk (eds.), *Tudor Drama before Shakespeare 1485–1590: New Directions for Research, Criticism, and Pedagogy* (Basingstoke: Palgrave, 2004), pp. 111–29.

10 Ben Jonson, *The Masque of Queens*, in *Renaissance Drama: An Anthology of Plays and Entertainments*, ed. Arthur Kinney (Oxford: Blackwell, 2005), 2nd edn, ll. 358–68.

11 In the Prologue to *Every Man in his Humour*, written for the revised edition of the play published in 1616, Jonson made clear his dislike of dramatists who 'make a child, now swaddled, to proceed / Man, and then shoot up, in one beard and weed, / Past threescore years': *Every Man in his Humour*, ed. Gabriele Bernhard Jackson (New Haven and London: Yale University Press, 1969), ll. 7–9; cf. *The Magnetic Lady*, ed. Peter Happé (Manchester: Manchester University Press, 2000), Act 2, Chorus, ll. 15–17.

12 David Norbrook takes this quotation as the title for his very thoughtful exploration of some of the political nuances of the play: '"What Cares These Roarers for the Name of King?": Language and Utopia in *The Tempest*', in Gordon McMullan and Jonathan Hope (eds.), *The Politics of Tragicomedy: Shakespeare and After* (London and New York: Routledge, 1992), pp. 21–45.

13 See Martin Butler (ed.), *Cymbeline* (Cambridge: Cambridge University Press, 2005), p. 37. As Butler points out, Shakespeare drew these names and others in the play from Holinshed's account of the founding of Britain.

14 *Shakespeare's Monarchies: Ruler and Subject in the Romances* (Ithaca, NY and London: Cornell University Press, 1997), chapter 2.

15 Information about these actors and their repertory comes from a Star Chamber case brought by a puritan Yorkshireman against his Catholic neighbour, in whose home the actors performed. See further Suzanne Gossett's introduction to her edition of the play (London: Arden Shakespeare, 2004), pp. 87–8.

16 It is not the only one of these four plays to represent a death (Cloten dies in *Cymbeline*), but the death of innocent characters, and especially the death of a child, creates a more problematic tone generically than the death of a villain.

READING LIST

Bishop, T. G. *Shakespeare and the Theatre of Wonder*. Cambridge: Cambridge University Press, 1996.

Bolam, Robyn. *Stage Images and Traditions: Shakespeare to Ford*. Cambridge: Cambridge University Press, 1987.

Cooper, Helen. *The English Romance in Time: Transforming Motifs from Geoffrey of Monmouth to the Death of Shakespeare*. Oxford and New York: Oxford University Press, 2004.

Gossett, Suzanne. 'Political *Pericles*', in *World-wide Shakespeares: Local Appropriations in Film and Performance*, Sonia Massai (ed.). London: Routledge, 2005.

Gurr, Andrew. 'The Bear, the Statue, and Hysteria in *The Winter's Tale*', *Shakespeare Quarterly*, 34 (1983), 420–5.

Henke, Robert. *Pastoral Transformations: Italian Tragicomedy and Shakespeare's Late Plays*. Newark and London: University of Delaware Press; Associated University Presses, 1997.

Jordan, Constance. *Shakespeare's Monarchies: Ruler and Subject in the Romances*. Ithaca, NY and London: Cornell University Press, 1997.

Lyne, Raphael. *Shakespeare's Late Work*. Oxford: Oxford University Press, 2007.

McMullan, Gordon and Jonathan Hope, eds. *The Politics of Tragicomedy: Shakespeare and After*. London: Routledge, 1992.

Mowat, Barbara A. *The Dramaturgy of Shakespeare's Romances*. Athens, GA: University of Georgia Press, 1976.

Munro, Lucy. *Children of the Queen's Revels: A Jacobean Theatre Repertory*. Cambridge: Cambridge University Press, 2005.

Palfrey, Simon. *Late Shakespeare*. Oxford: Oxford University Press, 1997.

Pettet, E. C. *Shakespeare and the Romance Tradition*. London: Staples Press, 1949.

Sokolova, Boika. *Shakespeare's Romances as Interrogative Texts: Their Alienation Strategies and Ideology*. Lewiston, NY: E. Mellen, 1992.

Warren, Roger. *Staging Shakespeare's Late Plays*. Oxford: Clarendon Press, 1990.

Wells, Stanley. 'Shakespeare and Romance', in *Later Shakespeare*, John Russell Brown and Bernard Harris (eds.). Stratford-upon-Avon Studies 8. London: Edward Arnold, 1966, pp. 49–79.

White, R. S. *Let Wonder Seem Familiar: Endings in Shakespeare's Romance Vision* New Jersey and London: Humanities; Athlone, 1985.

13

CLAIRE McEACHERN

Shakespeare, religion and politics

That 'religion' and 'politics' are largely overlapping domains in Tudor-Stuart England does little to curtail the vastness of the terrain they denote. The history of their conjunction for this period begins nearly sixty years prior to Shakespeare's arrival on the London theatrical scene, when Henry VIII threw off papal control of the church, proclaiming in the 1534 Act of Supremacy that 'the King our Sovereign Lord, his heirs and successors, kings of this realm, shall be taken, accepted, and reputed the only Supreme Head on earth of the Church of England, called *Anglicana Ecclesia*'.[1] The king's immediate goal was legitimacy for his divorce and remarriage, rather than wholesale reform of how his subjects worshipped. The act nonetheless declares that the monarch may henceforth 'repress, redress, reform, order, correct, restrain, and amend all such errors, heresies, abuses, offences, contempts and enormities, whatsoever they be' – or, from now on, heresy would also be treason. This act would be both repealed and reinstated by those 'heirs and successors', and historians continue to debate how Protestantism transformed medieval Catholic English society. But it is indisputable that by the time of Shakespeare's boyhood the royal assertion of power over spiritual matters had re-imagined English life in both corporate and intimate aspects, in ways that were not lost upon Shakespeare's plays.

The Church and the nation

The Tudor-Stuart church provided the principal lexicon of community in its time. Not only was the parish the primary unit of most people's affiliations, but the English church was the first official institution to imagine a larger nation as a homogenous space, time and tongue. The centralized state was still very much coming into being in the sixteenth century. England had no standing army or police force. The judicial presence was largely a local matter of resident gentry mediator, circuit-riding justices of the peace and neighbourhood constabularies (whose efficacy Shakespeare spoofs in plays such as *Much Ado About Nothing* and *Measure for Measure*). A less visible but perhaps more effective form of social accountability was provided through the informer. In fact, the only 'government official' most people ever encountered was their local clergyman. Complicating the development of any systematic state practices was the fact that the territory of England and Wales included a variety of geographies, modes of sustenance and corresponding cultural differences. It also comprehended many dialects and two distinct languages; if we include Ireland as part of the crown's domain (it did), there were three. James VI of Scotland's accession to the English throne in 1603 added highland and lowland Scottish terrains, cultures and languages, a different legal system and a different form of Protestantism to the archipelagic jumble whose integration the monarch was meant to represent.

So it was revolutionary that, when Elizabeth I came to the throne in 1558, among her first official acts was the Act of Uniformity mandating use of the Book of Common Prayer. (This book had previously been formulated for use under her brother, Edward VI, although the young king's short reign meant that it had had only a brief trial.) Common prayer offered a vision of a standardized corporate identity: 'where heretofore there hath been great diversity in saying and singing in churches within this realm, some following Salisbury use, some Hereford use, some the use of Bangor, some of York, and some of Lincoln, now from henceforth all the whole realm shall have but one use'.[2] In theory, henceforth all inhabitants of Elizabeth's dominion could (and should) be praying in unison on any given Sunday, and in English.

A chief mission of the Book of Common Prayer was to provide a calendar for reading over the course of the liturgical year. Shakespeare grew up hearing the Old Testament read annually, the New Testament three times a year and the Psalter once a month. The seven sacraments of the Roman Catholic Church were now reduced to three, but the Book of Common Prayer provided the language for them and other ceremonies marking life's major passages: Baptism, Confirmation, Matrimony, Thanksgiving after Childbirth, Visitation of the Sick and Burial. Ministers were ordered by law to employ the book, and parishioners were compelled under pain of a twelvepence fine to attend church on Sundays and holy days, and forbidden to 'derogate, deprave, or despise' said book in 'interludes, plays, songs, rhymes, or by other open words'.[3]

Also now subject to a government standard was the behaviour of the congregation. Accompanying the Prayer Book was a set of fifty-two Injunctions, instructions detailing comportment for both minister and flock. To be read quarterly by the minister, these warned in solid Protestant fashion against idolatry, purgatory, relics and miracles. They offered reminders of the true source of grace, emphasized the importance of pulpits, English bibles and attentive listening, and discouraged attendance at other parishes. At the same time, some of the age-old practices were retained: music, kneeling, tithing and almsgiving, albeit the latter now not as a means towards but a testament to their donor's receipt of divine grace. The overarching concern of the *Injunctions* is the prevention of 'discord among the people ... whereby charity, the knot of all Christian society, is loosed', whether such discord stemmed from perennial tensions within and between communities or from religious changes. Should dispute arise over the Prayer Book (or anything else), it was to be referred to the preacher, then to the bishop, and then the archbishop, a chain of command that led ultimately to the monarch.

Religion was not limited to what you did on Sundays. Soon joining the Prayer Book and the Injunctions was a collection of Homilies, or ready-penned sermons for ministers to read, preferably in lieu of their own compositions, whether they were incapable of writing them or (more threateningly) far too eager to demonstrate their inspiration. The *Homilies*' reach was theological, certainly: the new doctrines of salvation by divine grace and faith alone, as opposed to the human strivings of good works, were laid out. But the everyday applications of these doctrines were also specified, in sermons against adultery, gluttony, idleness, drunkenness, excess in apparel, and 'strife and contention'. Church was where you were told to obey state power and exhorted to preserve social harmony.

The divinely ordered nature of all Tudor-Stuart experience is perhaps best summed up in the opening paragraph of the 1569 *Exhortation Concerning Good Order and Obedience to Rulers and Magistrates*: 'Almighty God hath created and appointed all things in heaven, earth, and waters, in a most excellent and perfect order.'[4] Ranks of angels, of temporal governments, disposition of the seasons, the weather, plants, animals and even human anatomy are congruent in their hierarchies: 'some are in high degree, some are in low, some kings and princes, some inferiors and subjects, priests and laymen, masters and servants, fathers and children, husbands and wives, rich and poor'.[5] Tudor-Stuart social order is ideally divine, organic, patriarchal and linked to land and rank and even language, such that 'noble' and 'vilein' (from the French for 'serf') were not just categories of caste but of ethics (good; vile). Sumptuary laws fitfully if futilely decreed that apparel – cloth, cut, colour – should be keyed to one's social station. These laws were frequently violated – and not just by actors – but their premise was that a person's rank should be clear from his appearance. Should preaching on these themes fail to curb anti-social behaviour, ecclesiastical courts served to investigate and chastise infractions – not just blasphemy and the like, but also those having to do with social and sexual relations, such as slander and adultery. It is not so much that the culture of early modern England was religious, but that religion *was* culture in early modern England.

On the other hand, as Shakespeare's plays demonstrate time and time again, when it comes to state ideology there is theory, and then there is practice. Government descriptions of society can be as idealized as those of any play or poem. Shakespeare's comedies, with their plot movement of communal regeneration engineered through romantic coupling, may come closest to affirming the *caritas*-based communion urged by official texts and protocols, their passing snubs to order notwithstanding. His history plays, on the other hand, are full of kings insisting on their divinely authorized rule even as civil order disintegrates around them; it is telling that of two of his own exhortations to order, one (in *Henry V*) is put into the mouth of a cleric urging a monarch into foreign war so as to shoo him away from ecclesiastical property, and the other deployed by a crafty cynic (Ulysses, in *Troilus and Cressida*).

The call-and-response dialogic requirements of drama perhaps mean that no proposition in a play ever goes unchallenged. But what is clear is that Shakespeare is aware of the persuasive rather than descriptive status of claims to divinely sanctioned nature and culture, as well as of the importance of rhetorical skill in claiming and maintaining power. His most successful kings, if success is measured in terms of their ability to seize and wield control, display an ability to deploy the language of power, to opportunely rewrite conventional myths such that they sanction their own reigns. Richard II attempts to bolster his weakening rule by emphasizing the God-given identity of monarch and his land over and against the claims of a disaffected nobility, and Richard's rival, Bolingbroke, overpowers the myth by bringing a greater number of soldiers to bear. The reliance on *Realpolitik* does not stop the latter from attempting to use the same idiom of divine right once he has deposed Richard and ascended the throne.

This is not just a case of a lone artist slyly speaking truth to power, or mining dramatic irony from the fissures between policy and practice. Tudor-Stuart officialdom was made keenly and frequently aware in other quarters of just how idealized idealizations of a uniform nation could be. Departures from the vision of homogeneity and hierarchy laid out in the Book of Common Prayer arose not just from below, but within the government itself. Nor were the scriptural doctrines that were invoked to underwrite social order always consistent. 'Render unto Caesar the things which are Caesar's' might underscore a government's power, but the remainder of the verse – 'and unto God the things that are God's' (Matthew 22:21) – suggests that temporal and spiritual realms may enjoin differing claims upon the soul and the society.

Political culture provided plentiful instances of the gap between ideal and real, as well as contradictions internal to ideology. Defenders of the Roman Catholic Church delivered frequent rebukes to the Elizabethan contiguity of state and church, and were vigorously answered. These exchanges were conducted in print throughout Shakespeare's lifetime; they tended to configure the difference between churches (and their allied temporal polities) as a stark choice between Christ and Anti-Christ, both sides claiming to be on the side of the angels. Events also contributed to the sense of an English church under perpetual threat from the international Catholic superpower. The Papal Bull of 1569 declared Elizabeth I a heretic and absolved her subjects of their obedience to her under threat of excommunication. English Catholic seminaries founded at Douai in 1568 and Rome in 1579 trained priests to minister to English Catholics. A fomenting focal point for Catholic insurrection was provided through most of the 1580s by Elizabeth's cousin and potential heir, Mary Stuart of Scotland. Elizabeth herself dallied through the early 1580s with the prospect of marriage, possibly with a Catholic foreign prince (a prospect haunted by the memory of her sister Mary Tudor's marriage to Philip of Spain, during which hundreds of English Protestants were martyred as heretics). Troubling military events included the continental wars of religion and the ongoing campaign to subdue Catholic Ireland, the narrow escape from the Spanish Armada in 1588 and the Gunpowder Plot of 1605, a failed attempt by English Catholics to assassinate King James in Parliament.

All of these factors fuelled a sense of England as an elect underdog threatened from without. Elizabeth I's self-styling as the 'Virgin Queen' powerfully embodied the island integrity of 'this precious stone set in the silver sea' (*Richard II*, 2.1.46), so much so that when James VI of Scotland ascended the English throne as James I in 1603, his proposed plans for the legal union of England and Scotland were met with vigorous protests about the chastity of English cultural and legal identities. This, despite the fact that it was only upon James' accession – a male, with the outlying reaches of said island in tow – that the crown could claim the entire island as its domain; as James put it, only 'now become like a little world within itself, being entrenched and fortified round about with a natural, and yet admirable strong pond or ditch'. However, the English parliament remained unconvinced and, alienated by the assertion of royal dominion, countered geographic integrity with the allegedly even more inviolate cultural purity of English common law.

Shakespeare's history plays capitalize on this 'us-versus-them' paradigm of patriotic feeling. *Henry V* is the most obvious instance where a common enemy unites, although what is remarkable is how its appeals to unity (e.g. the famous St Crispin's Day speech, 4.3.18–67) jostle alongside portraits of internal dissent, such as the arguments among the English, Welsh, Irish and Scottish captains, or between the disguised king and his subjects. Conflict between England and France seems the least of it. In fact, given that most of Shakespeare's material in the history plays concerns the civil wars prior to the accession of Henry Tudor (Elizabeth I's grandfather), the more frequent threat to English integrity comes from warring factions within the polity. *Henry V* provides a fleeting taste of triumphalism in its portrait of underdog England's unlikely victory over a foreign power, but the overriding tone of the history plays is elegiac and their communities fragile. Indeed in the 1590s England must have felt vulnerable, beset by a longstanding war in Ireland, threats from the Catholic powers abroad, an ageing and heirless queen, and increasingly vocal sectarian challenges to well-bounded communal homogeneity and harmony.

Despite the overriding polarities of Tudor-Stuart political polemic, these plays rarely address explicitly the fact that the English past they represent was a Catholic one. *King John*'s battles with the pope come closest to echoing the anti-Catholic discourse that animated much national posturing at this time, but *Henry VIII*'s Reformation (like Henry VIII's) is a marital rather than doctrinal or political event. Falstaff is more riotous knight than proto-Protestant hero, and the fever that finally consumes him comes from a 'burning quotidian-tertian' (*Henry V*, 2.1.107–8), not a Lollard martyr's fire. Wily Italian friars rove throughout some plays (*Measure for Measure*), but so do well-intentioned ones (*Much Ado About Nothing*, *Romeo and Juliet*), and given that the sources and setting of many of Shakespeare's plays are continental, friars lie far thicker on the ground than the odd Puritan (*Twelfth Night*). In fact, given that the scheming and hypocrisy of the clergy is a literary convention that both pre- and post-dates the Reformation, and crosses national boundaries, and also given the extreme tone of contemporary religious polemic, Shakespeare's portraits of the cloth are probably more temperate than they could have been. His religious satire, such as it exists, tends towards the gentle, the sole exception perhaps being his portrait of *Twelfth Night*'s disagreeable Malvolio, who, as 'a kind of Puritan' (2.3.125), represents the hypocrisy of an ostentatious servility; his tormentors, however, are also revealed as repellent in their own way.

Whether the lack of direct confrontation with the Reformation is due to the fact that it posed a less remarkable breach with the past to those who lived through it than it does to historians, or whether it was so sensitive a political subject that it was best skirted, or whether, as some have argued, Shakespeare was secretly a Catholic and disapproved of it (see Chapter 1), in general his plays address the cultural shift from a community bound together under one code to a universe of competing claims chiefly through the medium of mortal kingship.

No doubt because his words were written for the voices and bodies of actors, Shakespeare primarily invokes the idea of England not through a focus on institutions (parliament, church, law), but on the interaction of personalities (royal counsellors, bishops, Justices Shallow and Silence). The monarch's person in particular becomes a focal point, both of the plays and for the community they conjure. The Christian paradigm of a god made flesh – and hence vulnerable to human feeling – is the model for many of his kings, whether it is Henry VI, plaintive on his molehill, or Richard II, lyrically powerful in his prison cell, or Henry V, claiming it's lonely at the top on the night before his greatest battle. Canny Elizabeth I herself realized the political utility of humanizing the powerful; her own versions of 'a touch of Harry in the night' included both sentimental and strategic styling of herself as mother or spouse of her people (in order to counter parliamentary pressure for marriage-and-heir), or summoning popular sympathy by allegedly wishing herself a carefree milkmaid.

Elizabeth's personifications of monarchy tended to mute her power, whereas her successor's magnify it. James I also appealed to the 'natural' body of the king, although the fact that he had first done so (in 1598) while attempting to assert the relatively weak power of the Scottish monarch over and against the bullying of local magnates meant that his use of the trope emphasized law rather than love, a subject's duty to his father king rather than feeling for his mother country. When this rhetorical emphasis was joined in the early 1600s by the heavy-handed tone and terms of James' increasing frustration with resistance to his plans for British union, the notion of a king's outsized passions became a spectral presence in English politics: 'I am a man of flesh and blood, and have my passions and affections as other men. I pray you, do not too far move me to do that which my power may move me to.'[6] To a degree that can be difficult for the modern reader to grasp, let alone sympathize with, Tudor-Stuart opinion considered monarchy and its attendant hierarchies not only the most indigenous form of English government, but also the most comforting and (in its replication of divinity) the most virtuous; at the same time, this regard was not unalloyed by a healthy scepticism of power when it went unfettered either by wise counsel or a monarch's humble need to account to his own Lord.

The proportions of divine and human melded in a king clearly caught Shakespeare's eye and ear, not just in his portraits of a ruler's more sympathetic 'human' qualities – loneliness, fear, love – but also in representations of more ruthless aspects of human nature, all the more rapacious when backed by presumptions of absolute political power. His first portrait of a tyrant in a play is the villainous political impresario Richard III, whose unscrupulous yet nonetheless audacious rise to power tugs an audience between condemnation and chagrined admiration. In *Macbeth* Shakespeare revisits the scene of a reputedly heinous will to power, yet this time grants his tyrant a haunting capacity for self-inquiry. King Lear is of course the character who most asks us to think about the psyche of a ruler from the inside out, of what it must be like to consider yourself godlike even as your body and your children betray you; again we are shocked by the overpowering force and rapacity of such larger-than-life passions even as we are asked to sympathize with them. Gauging whether Shakespeare's plays support order or challenge it often comes down to whether we judge the empathy they summon to demystify authority or bolster it.

The narrative poem *The Rape of Lucrece* deserves some mention in this company as a reflection upon what happens when persons of absolute power go unchecked by conscience or good counsel – in this case, providing the pretext of Rome's conversion to republicanism. So too in *Julius Caesar*, Shakespeare ponders the ways in which power depends upon possession of a rhetoric, whether in Brutus' struggle to rationalize his pending betrayal of Caesar, or in Mark Antony's show-and-vote-stealing eulogy for him. Despite the fact that both parliament and royal counsellors were longstanding institutions in England's government, a political community not primarily secured in and by divinity or monarchy was only a theoretical and exotic possibility in Tudor-Stuart England, something to be read about in histories of other (mostly ancient) peoples. But republican models clearly interested Shakespeare, perhaps precisely because they lacked the simple organizing principle/al of the monarchic person and hence forced consideration of what other bonds of community might inhere, as well as what scope thereby remained for individual greatness (*Coriolanus*).

The church and the subject

The Tudor-Stuart church not only shaped collective identity in this period. Its presence also raised questions about how the most local component of the whole – a person – was best made and known. These questions arose not so much from tensions between the church and external antagonists as from dissent internal to *Anglicana Ecclesia*, between the official position and Protestants who wished the English church to put yet more distance between itself and Rome. A sense of a nation imperilled was nonetheless also a feature of this indigenous debate. However, in this instance the danger was imagined not as coming from an external threat but from the failure of internal homogeneity. In standard anti-Catholic polemic, the stereotypical villains were equivocating Jesuits, recusant Catholics who refused to fall in line, or even worse, 'church-Papists', those just pretending to go along in public but privately loyal to the old ways, even at the risk of lost property or lives. But far more disruptive of social harmony may have been those dissatisfied reforming voices invested in winnowing the elect from the damned among the English. Their targets were less church-Papists than church-Protestants, those more or less acquiescent to the governmental programme if not especially fervent (at least according to the standard of reformers) on behalf of their own salvation.

As with the conflict with Rome, these internal tussles over religious identity – both internal to the church and about the interior of a person – accompanied the church from its inception and boiled to the surface at frequent intervals. They begin with debates over clerical vestments in 1569, or the question of whether preachers should differentiate themselves from their congregants by means of their clothing. If the Vestiarian Controversy concerned costume, the Admonition Controversy of the early 1570s turned on the role of a script, and brought the Prayer Book front and centre, where it would remain for decades as a source of conflict. If the high water marks of the Catholic threat were provided by the Armada in 1588 and the Gunpowder Plot of 1605, the controversy among Protestant voices reached its initial climax in the satiric *tour-de-force* of the Marprelate tracts of the late 1580s – the moment when Shakespeare arrives on the London scene. During the reign of Elizabeth such tensions did not result in the overt splitting-off of sects or parties; on the contrary, reformers insisted on their full membership in the national church. But James I was en route to his English throne when he was met with a petition from reformers hopeful of a new king's willingness to hear their cause, particularly a king who came to them from the relatively more reformed Scottish kirk. So next came the Hampton Court Conference in January 1604, a meeting between bishops and the dissatisfied 'puritan' ministry, for whom the sole resulting consolation was James' authorization of a new translation of the Bible. The English Civil War between puritan and royalist was still decades away, but the fiction of a unitary and internally harmonious and homogenous church population had become one degree more fictional.

The ostensible issue of the sustained debate was the role of standardized ceremony, or ritual behaviour, in shaping faith. For the more ardent reformers, the Book of Common Prayer was not a means to consensual harmony achieved through synchronized actions and words but 'an unperfect book, culled and picked out of that popish dunghill, the Mass book full of all abominations'.[7] The basic grievance with the ritual forms was that the rote recitation of state-prescribed, mass-produced and standardized texts usurped the role of inspired preaching and the qualified preachers capable of it: 'Reading is not feeding, but it is as evil as playing upon a stage'.[8] According to this perspective, a ritual performance of corporate homogeneity was uninspired and hence uninspiring; a recited script, far from inscribing social harmony or spiritual rectitude, permitted deviant individuals to cloak themselves behind the mask of gesture: 'One he kneeleth on his knees, and this way he looketh, and another he kneeleth himself asleep, another kneeleth with such devotion, that is he so far in talk, that he forgetteth to arise till his knee ache ... another bringeth a book of his own, and though he sit when they sit, stand when they stand, kneel when they kneel, most of all he intendeth his own book. Is this praying?'[9] Instead, the reform-minded advocated preaching that would 'prick' the conscience and 'pierce the heart', so that 'the Prince may be better obeyed, the realm flourish in more godliness'.[10] The government for its part understood harmonious common prayer as not merely skin- or gesture-deep but as something quite spiritually profound, and inspired preaching as unlikely to generate peace either politically or psychologically.

Reformers might have seemed naive in their belief in preaching's power to shape a politically peaceful soul or polity, but their critique of the official church also pointed out the idealism of the latter's position. The idea that 'now the whole realm would have one use' may have had a certain beauty, but the realities of personnel, communications, customs and cultures meant that in truth orthodoxy was unevenly developed throughout the realm. The further the London–Cambridge axis was left behind, the less likely it was to find parishes formed in the official image, and, as all parties admitted, it could be just as difficult to find doctrinaire Christians even close to the centre of the polity. Shakespeare writes plays (*The Merchant of Venice*, *Othello*) that foreground the conspicuous religious alien, and scholars have often responded with a search for the numbers of actual Jews or Muslims in early modern London. But it may be that sufficient inspiration for the 'Other within' was excavated by the disputes about how best to shape an English Protestant.

Central to this debate are questions also central to Shakespeare's plays and practice, and it is here more than in any other register that we should look for the effect of the Tudor-Stuart spiritual polity upon them. *What is the relationship between actions and feelings, outsides and insides? Are people what they seem to be, or does the inner man dissent from the representation he presents to the world?* Hamlet claims to 'have that within that passes show' (*Hamlet*, 1.2.85); his uncle Claudius fears that his prayers are insufficiently propelled heavenwards by inner conviction. Othello's plot pivots on a villain who is universally believed honest by fellow-characters even as he confesses his villainy to us. Prince Hal discloses in soliloquy his plan to stage-manage his own political debut by the use of the tavern foil, warning us not to trust appearances – or him. His father – an actor in a king's costume – wins a battle by the military tactic of dressing others in the king's costume.

Can actions shape insides? The cross-dressed comic heroines feel in themselves a new boldness, whereas Bottom, transformed to an ass on the outside, seems irresolutely himself despite a new taste for provender. *When an actor speaks words, to what extent do they transform his self – does he remain separate and unmoved, or does he become what he plays?* Did, as in *Twelfth Night*, a boy actor playing a girl playing a boy wooing a girl remember his gender? Antony and Cleopatra cross-dress; Enobarbus fears it has unmanned his master. Does Hamlet believe his own madness; did Burbage feel himself becoming Hamlet? What's Hecuba to either of them?

When an actor speaks words, to what extent do they transform his audience? Iago plays upon Othello with words that frame representations; Hamlet seeks to discover guilt in his uncle's response to a play; Rosalind pretends to be a boy partly in order to reform Orlando's style of loving; Benedick and Beatrice are prompted to love each other by means of charades; Claudio is persuaded that Hero is unfaithful by the same means. Puritan opponents of the stage criticized the immorality of pretending to be someone other than you are, both because of its power to transform the actor himself, but also lest the spectacle move spectators to imitation. This fear belies the reformers' claim about the inertness of mere recitation, that 'Reading is not feeding, but it is as evil as playing on a stage.' None knew the power of representation better than they, for the premise of an inspired reading and preaching of the good book was that words could and should shape the soul. Perhaps the reformers' animus against the theatre may have had to do with the way the imaginative experience of playgoers mimicked the habits of believers. Competition for the Sunday afternoon audience was intense not because theatre and church offered alternative kinds of imaginative engagement, but the same kind.

Getting to heaven

Lurking within the debate about how best to reform a soul is an anterior dispute pertinent to Shakespeare's plays, namely, on whether it is possible or even proper to do so. While theatre is not theology, debate on this question also informed how personhood, and perhaps literary character, was understood in this moment. And just as it is important for an understanding of this period's political culture to imagine a mindset that found solace in hierarchy, it pays here to keep in mind the importance for Tudor-Stuart imaginations of an afterlife.

This afterlife was by no means an uncontested site. Different stripes of Christianity defined the nature of the connection between now and later in different ways. Scepticism about the afterlife's very existence was also present in this period, as was indifference or insouciance. Jewish tradition put very little emphasis upon one. Alternative models were also available. Classical Stoicism voiced a notion of a largely undifferentiated eternity: Elysium was for exceptional heroes like Achilles, but Hades served for the rest, whether good or bad. Stoicism also urged a model of affective neutrality towards one's fate, or the idea that a person should face both good fortune and bad – including death – with equal dispassion. Many of Shakespeare's heroic figures, from Juliet onwards, can display versions of this bravery. But the idea that the consequences of earthly behaviour could extend beyond this world into a next, or that earthly existence if properly interpreted indicated one's eventual destination, influenced the ethics of action in a way it may no longer do for many of us.

For all the differences among confessions, there was a broad Christian consensus on the presence of original sin. We are all fallen; the question is, what to do about it? – if, indeed, anything can be done. Sin's expiation was partly addressed by Christ's sacrifice, but clearly work remained to clean up its effects. Differences of opinion on how to and who should do this work was what distinguished not only Catholics from Protestants, but Protestants from each other. Under Catholicism, for instance, a person was meant to do as much of this work as possible; if he or she did not manage to eradicate it during a lifetime of good works and penance, the soul would reside for a term in purgatory (a place just as unpleasant as hell, but temporary rather than eternal), the eventual removal to heaven ideally hastened by continuing efforts of one's descendants on one's behalf. While it was presumptuous to assure salvation, which was ultimately at God's discretion, a good faith effort was required of the person and gave them a measure of voluntary participation in the project of their own salvation.

In Protestantism as formulated by Luther, this effort was reassigned to God alone: it was a merciful gift from a beneficent deity to his unworthy creature, to be accepted with gratitude and relief. Any resulting good works were more evidential than efficacious, proof of one's salvation rather than a way to work one's way into God's good graces, which was not humanly possible. The more austere theologian Calvin breathed new life into the Augustinian notion of predestination, the theory that God had decided an individual's ultimate fate prior to his birth (maybe even prior to Creation itself). What follows from such a proposition firstly is scepticism of whether a person even *could* affect his status, either for better or worse. Was the will free? Secondly, and perhaps more disturbingly: what kind of a God is it that not only makes us suffer for another's sin but condemns souls out of hand without hope of reprieve?

From the point of view of social order, the extremity of this formulation is clearly problematic: with no reward in sight, what incentive did a reprobate (or for that matter even an elect) soul have not to indulge his most base desires, given that his ultimate fate was already sealed? What, indeed, was the point of inspired preaching, if it was only to those always already saved? Historians describe early modern English Protestantism as generally Calvinist in flavour, Calvin's austerity being somewhat modified over the course of its naturalization. This mellowing was no doubt partly as a consequence of the social ramifications of predestinarian thinking: consigning a portion of humankind to hell might be fine for God, but he didn't have to live with them meanwhile. Hence some theologians believed in a degree of human collaboration in salvation, although insisting that the impulse to the good itself ultimately derived from above. Others ventured that knowledge of one's own salvation was possible, and that curiosity about and a desire to test for one's ultimate destination was itself evidence of salvation. Crucially, however, the testing grounds were not so much one's actions in the world as the often inscrutable and ambivalent feelings in which they originated.

Protestant understandings of salvation tended thus to render human experience according to at least two basic plots. According to the more comic perspective, the saving force of divine grace was liberating, a release from the ethical accounting processes of medieval Catholicism, whereby one would perpetually wonder whether one's good deeds had finally outstripped the bad. Understandings of divine grace as shaping both the means and the ends of human life, rewarding good and punishing evil (if not necessarily as soon as we would prefer), argued for a largely beneficent and attentive deity. On the other hand, the possibility of predetermined damnation was a tragic one, and enquiry into the prospects for salvation opened up a whole new introspective dimension of suspense and anxiety about human value.

These kinds of concern resonate throughout Shakespeare's work. Their darkest inflection is in the tragedies. If Macbeth is fated to sin, either by the witches or his own divinely apportioned character, is he seizing his fate or a mere pawn? If God has for some predetermined reason endowed him with a will to power which requires that he sin, why inflict upon him the further cruelty of having so fine an ethical sensibility with which to apprehend but not resist his own evil? Hamlet too struggles with a predestined path, although it is a ghost and not witches that describes it to him: how can he resist the imperative of his father and the mode of vengeful manhood prescripted for him, and what might the consequences be for his own soul?

King Lear is the play that most presses these questions of the relations between humans and the supernatural. While the setting is pre-Christian Britain, many Reformation concerns haunt the play. It proposes a variety of theories of the supernatural: Lear summons Nature (a goddess he shares with the villain Edmund) to punish his enemies; Albany can only muster a conditional apprehension of the divine response to human plights: 'If that the heavens do not their visible spirits / Send quickly down to tame these vild offenses, / It will come, / Humanity must perforce prey on itself, / Like monsters of the deep' (4.2.47–51). Most invocations of the heavens concern its punishing and retributive function, justice rather than mercy: Edgar argues that his father's adultery 'cost him his eyes' (5.3.172). Yet despite all the calls for divine vengeance, the play questions the notion that human behaviour deserves anything: that goodness will be rewarded, or evil punished. Cordelia's forgiveness of her father is the play's rare gesture towards solace, human or otherwise. Edgar also comforts a parent who has wronged him, but we tend to wonder whether he might not have cured his father's despair less sadistically, not by insisting Gloucester submit to suffering but by revealing his identity to him and reassuring him of a son's forgiveness. Edgar's disguise as a 'Bedlam beggar' whose spectacle of mortification 'enforce[s]' the charity of others, and the Fool's apocalyptic rhetoric voice a Christian critique of social inequity, but it is one that goes nowhere. Human society, and human nature, may be corrupt, but there is no alternative (including a compensatory afterlife). Lear may wish to escape society into a storm that is both scourging and blessedly indifferent to human emotions, but he is driven back indoors. Gloucester may think he is giving his purse to a stranger; in fact it is his lawful heir, the person whom the system sanctions. Such redemptions or challenges to the system as the play offers prove as illusory as Lear's dying imagination of his dead daughter's breath.

In its bleakness *King Lear* is an extreme case; it demonstrates the range of Shakespeare's imaginative reach but perhaps not its usual province. Both early and late in his creative career Shakespeare writes plays that rely on the providential and are more concerned to bless than blast. Its workings are clearly more fluid in the comedies, where the stumbling impediments presented by human evil are typically rendered as small-scale adolescent rebellion and lust, easily and playfully channelled into the socially regenerative forms of lawful matrimony. In the later comedies the challenge to grace grows, given the increasing psychological complexity of the lovers, and hence the darker components of humanity: jealousy, betrayal, fear of the opposite sex, even incompatibility are the challenges the comic plot must overcome. *Much Ado About Nothing* and *All's Well That End's Well*, for instance, both contain bridegrooms whose fallen nature is left unfinessed at the play's close: while we can hope that their characters will improve with age and the love of a good woman, evidence for hope is scant. In *Measure for Measure* and *Troilus and Cressida* the less savoury aspects of humankind become less idiosyncratic and more systemic.

The plays Shakespeare writes at the end of his career resurrect human nature to some degree, although the challenges posed by human fallibility remain. As in the tragedies, human error unfurls, sometimes at terrible costs: dead children, loss of political power, marital harmony and the passage of time itself. Unlike in the tragedies, however, sometimes new hope can be pieced together from the wreckage, founded on the capacity to forgive and forget, and the serendipity of good fortune (or at least near-misses with bad). While Shakespeare hardly seems to propose the perfectibility of human nature, he hints at its capacity to bend and learn rather than break.

NOTES

1 In Gerald Bray (ed.), *Documents of the English Reformation* (Cambridge: James Clarke and Co., 1994), pp. 113–14.
2 John Booty (ed.), *The Book of Common Prayer* (Charlottesville: University of Virginia Press, 1976), p. 16.
3 Bray, *Documents*, p. 331.
4 *Exhortation Concerning Good Order and Obedience to Rulers and Magistrates* (1570), p. 1.
5 Ibid.
6 *Commons Journals* (1803), vol. I, p. 367.
7 John Field and Thomas Wilcox, *An Admonition to Parliament* (London, 1572), in W. H. Frere and C. E. Douglas (eds.), *Puritan Manifestoes* (New York: Lenox Hill, 1954), p. 21.
8 Ibid., p. 22.
9 Ibid., p. 24.
10 Ibid., p. 18.

READING LIST

Booty, John, ed. *The Book of Common Prayer*. Charlottesville: University of Virginia Press, 1976.

Bray, Gerald, ed. *Documents of the English Reformation*. Cambridge: James Clarke and Co., 1994.

Collinson, Patrick. *The Elizabethan Puritan Movement*. New York: Methuen, 1967.

Duffy, Eamon. *The Stripping of the Altars: Traditional Religion in England 1400–1580*. New Haven: Yale University Press, 1992.

Frere, W. H., and C. E. Douglas, eds. *Puritan Manifestoes*. New York: Lenox Hill, 1954.

Haigh, Christopher. *The Plain Man's Pathways to Heaven: Kinds of Christianity in Post-Reformation England*. Oxford: Oxford University Press, 2008.
Knapp, Jeffrey. *Shakespeare's Tribe: Church, Nation, and Theater in Renaissance England*. Chicago: University of Chicago Press, 2002.
Maus, Katharine Eisaman. *Inwardness and Theatre in the English Renaissance*. Chicago: University of Chicago Press, 1995.
McEachern, Claire and Debora Shuger, eds. *Religion and Culture in Reformation England*. Cambridge: Cambridge University Press, 1997.
Targoff, Ramie. *Common Prayer: The Language of Public Devotion in Early Modern England*. Chicago: University of Chicago Press, 2001.

14

JONATHAN GIL HARRIS

Shakespeare and race

Trying to understand race in Shakespeare's writing is an exercise fraught with difficulty. Even outside Shakespeare's work, the word *race* is a slippery one: its meaning can all too easily elude our grasp just when we think we know what it is. Take, for example, a Bollywood film called *Race* (2008). Set in South Africa, the film deals with a pair of brothers from that country's minority Indian community. Any prospective viewer aware of South Africa's history would expect the film's title to refer to themes of ethnic identity and racial tension. So we might be surprised to find that it refers instead to a tragic Cain-and-Abel struggle – the ongoing 'race' between the two brothers, waged first over horses and then with cars. This is an extreme example of *race*'s slipperiness. But when used to denote racial identity, the term's meaning can be still harder to pin down. To some, *race* suggests biological differences based in physiognomy and skin colour. Skin colour, however, was not the ground of anti-Semitic racism in Nazi Germany. And recent years have seen the resurgence of an anti-Islamic racism that is again less about skin colour than about religious difference. *Race* is thus not a transparent concept but a bundle of contradictions. It is at one and the same time visible and invisible, a component of biological identity and a trope of cultural or religious difference. It is, in other words, a cluster of problems. This is just as much the case in Shakespeare's writing, where *race* again poses profound problems of genealogy, colour and religion.

Problems of genealogy

The word *race* appears sixteen times in Shakespeare's works. In each case, its meaning deviates from the associations with skin colour or religion that we now tend to assign it. *Race* derives from the Latin *radix*, meaning 'root'; it retains this sense when the Clown refers to 'a race or two of ginger' in *The Winter's Tale* (4.3.43). Roots readily imply ancestry, and Shakespeare most often uses the term *race* to designate a notion of lineage that confers a specific social rank. Thus we hear of 'the Nevilles' noble race' in *2 Henry VI* (3.2.215) and a 'happy race of kings' in *Richard III* (5.3.152); Marina's pupils in *Pericles* are of 'noble race' (Chorus 20: 9); and Posthumus' line in *Cymbeline* is 'a valiant race' (5.5.177). In each of these instances, *race* demonstrates what one critic calls the 'genealogical idiom' of much pre-modern European thought.[1] The term's early modern European cognates – *razza* in Italian, *raza* in Castilian, *raça* in Portuguese and *race* in French – designated any group of plants, animals or humans that share traits through a common lineage. John Florio's Italian–English dictionary of 1598, for example, defines *razza* as 'a kind, a race, a brood, a blood, a stock, a name, a pedigree'.[2] *Race* and its cognates loom especially large in the language of horse pedigree. Edward Topsell's *Historie of Four-Footed Beastes and Snakes* (1607) speaks of 'mares appointed for race', that is, for breeding.[3] Shakespeare often uses the term in this equine sense. In *The Merchant of Venice* Lorenzo refers to 'a wild and wanton herd / Or race of youthful and unhandled colts' (5.1.71–2); in *Macbeth* Duncan's horses are 'the minions [i.e. darlings] of their race' (2.4.15). Shakespeare metaphorically develops the equine sense of *race* on two other occasions: in *Measure for Measure* Angelo gives his 'sensual race the rein' (2.4.160); and in the Sonnets the narrator's desire – made 'of perfectest love' – 'Shall neigh ... in his fiery race' (51.10–11).

As these instances suggest, Shakespeare's usages of *race* do not imply skin colour. He never employs the term in relation to 'black' characters such as Aaron the Moor in *Titus Andronicus*, the Prince of Morocco and the Moorish serving-woman in *The Merchant of Venice*, or Othello the Moor of Venice. He characterizes the Egyptian Queen Cleopatra's beauty as belonging to a 'race of heaven' (*Antony and Cleopatra*, 1.3.37), but the phrase suggests celestial lineage rather than dark skin. The one possible exception, at least to modern eyes, is when Miranda refers in *The Tempest* to the native islander Caliban's 'vile race' (1.2.361). Caliban, the son of the Algerian witch Sycorax and (possibly) the devil, is famously characterized by Prospero as a 'thing of darkness' (5.1.278). Yet Miranda's and Prospero's epithets arguably refer less to Caliban's skin colour than to his breeding, in the twin sense of his (bastard) lineal descent and his lack of civilized decorum. Still, Miranda's rejection of Caliban pushes in the direction of modern racism inasmuch as it enforces the divide between human and 'savage' (1.2.358), between noble and base kinds. This divide is suggested also by *Timon of Athens* when Timon separates the world, which he refers to as 'the whole race of mankind', into 'high and low' (4.1.40).

For Miranda, Caliban's 'vile race' manifests itself in his desire to produce offspring by raping her, a desire that raises the spectre not only of sexual violence but also of mixture and adulteration. This spectre haunts another of Shakespeare's usages of *race*. When Antony denounces Cleopatra for preventing him from 'getting of a lawful race' with his Roman wife, Octavia (3.13.107), he implies, like Miranda, that illegitimate sexual union – in this instance, adultery rather than rape – produces adulterated offspring: the 'race' sprung from Antony and his Roman wife is lawful, whereas his children with his Egyptian mistress are bastards. Here *race* presumes even as it abhors the possibility of mixture and adulteration. This presumption contributes to the contradictory early modern meanings of *race* and its cognates. Sebastián de Covarrubias y Orozco's Spanish dictionary, published in 1611, initially defines *raza* as 'The breed of thoroughbred horses, which are branded with an iron so that they can be known'. But Orozco's dictionary complicates this vision of pure-breeds, distinguishable only by an arbitrary mark, with an additional definition: 'Race in [human] lineages is understood pejoratively, as having some Moorish or Jewish race.'[4] *Raza*, in its sense of pedigreed (equine) genealogy, is here supplemented by the additional sense of 'race' as an adulteration of pure blood.

Orozco's adulterating 'Moorish or Jewish race', like Shakespeare's spectres of adulterated 'race' in *The Tempest* and *Antony and Cleopatra*, speak to important developments that transformed Europe over the course of the fifteenth to the seventeenth centuries. This period witnessed the rise of Western European imperialism, global trade and colonialism – processes that both exposed Europeans in unprecedented ways to foreign cultures and prompted a hardening of their conceptions of racial difference. In 1492, the same year that Columbus 'discovered' America and its 'Indian' inhabitants, Christian Spain drove the last Moorish king out of the Iberian Peninsula and expelled all Jews; subsequently, Christians of Moorish and Jewish 'race' or ancestry attracted the suspicious attention of the Spanish Inquisition. During the sixteenth century, as Spain conquered much of the Americas and large numbers of its native inhabitants perished by the sword or by disease, Portugal established not only the transatlantic African slave trade but also eastern trading colonies such as Goa in India and Amboyna in Indonesia. England, having already begun its own colonial experiment in Ireland, fantasized about following the Portuguese example in both the West and East Indies. Shakespeare participates in such fantasies. *A Midsummer Night's Dream* simply imagines merchant ships sailing through the 'spiced Indian air' (2.1.124). But his later plays fantasize a twinned mercantile and sexual conquest of the Indies: in *Troilus and Cressida* Troilus is the 'merchant' and his would-be lover's 'bed is India' (1.1.99, 96), and Falstaff in *The Merry Wives of Windsor* says of his anticipated double conquests, Mistress Ford and Mistress Page, 'They shall be my East and West Indies, and I will trade to them both' (1.3.61–2). This fantastic blurring of sex and trade found a real-life corollary in the new colonies of the Americas, India and Indonesia, where European contact with native peoples often produced mixed-blood children of uncertain ancestry.

The irony is that, for Shakespeare, the English were themselves less a pure race than the product of mixture. In *Henry V*, the French Dauphin characterizes the English as 'Our scions, put in wild and savage stock' (3.5.7); the English have emerged from the grafting of noble Frenchman and 'savage' British after the Norman Conquest of 1066. Here Shakespeare applies to the English a horticultural understanding of race that appears more explicitly in *The Winter's Tale*, where he represents grafting as the hybridization of the 'bark of baser kind / By bud of nobler race' – a mixture that, in this case, 'does mend nature' (4.4.94–6). Such a view is clearly in conflict with what we see in *The Tempest* and *Antony and Cleopatra*, where racial mixing does not so much 'mend' as deviate from nature. To underscore the unnatural deviance of mixing, those of 'vile race' are sometimes represented in Shakespeare's plays as a separate species: Caliban, for example, is mistaken by the European castaways Trinculo and Antonio for a fish (2.2.24, 5.1.269). Coupling with those of 'vile race' could thus be readily refigured as interspecies sex. This strategy is most apparent in *Othello*, when Iago tells Desdemona's father, Brabanzio, that if she marries the black Othello, 'you'll have your daughter covered with a Barbary horse, you'll have your nephews neigh to you, you'll have coursers for cousins and jennets for germans' (1.1.112–15). With this poisonous fantasy, Iago implicitly conflates the two early modern senses of *raza* in Orozco's dictionary – that is, the pedigreed horse here shades into an adulterating alien kind.

Problems of colour

Othello shows that even if Shakespeare did not use the term *race* as a marker of skin colour, he was possessed of a strong colour consciousness – or, more specifically, a black-and-white consciousness. Throughout his work, he juxtaposes characters of 'fair' and 'black' complexion. In *A Midsummer Night's Dream*, the fair Helena (who is compared to a white 'dove') contrasts with the dark Hermia (who is compared to a black 'raven' (2.2.120)). The Sonnets contrast a fair youth with a dark lady, whose blackness also contrasts with the 'false borrowed face' of other women who make themselves 'fair' with cosmetics (127.6). The juxtaposition of 'fair' and 'black' can even occur in one character. Rosaline in *Love's Labour's Lost* is presented as 'black as ebony' (4.3.244), but, like the dark lady, her refusal of cosmetics makes her beautiful: 'therefore she is born to make black fair' (4.3.257).

These instances trade in traditional colour symbolism, where blackness is either damned as evil – 'Black is the badge of hell', observes the King in *Love's Labour's Lost* (4.3.250) – or, in the manner of Petrarchan poetic convention, converted by true love to fairness. As a result, some readers have argued that we should resist reading Shakespeare's black-and-white antinomies as racial. But although we cannot know whether or not the dark lady was based on a real African woman, it is clear that Shakespeare's use of black-and-white symbolism often depends on conceptions of colour that are racially inflected. Neither Hermia nor Rosaline is presented as African. But Hermia's lover, Lysander, denounces her in racial terms – 'Away, you Ethiope!' (*A Midsummer Night's Dream*, 3.2.258) – when she no longer pleases his eye. Similarly, the King questions Rosaline's black beauty by observing that 'Ethiops of their sweet complexion crack' (*Love's Labour's Lost*, 4.3.264). And Shakespeare presents another pair of female characters, Silvia and Julia in *The Two Gentlemen of Verona*, in terms that again evoke racial difference: 'Silvia – witness heaven that made her fair – / Shows Julia but a swarthy Ethiope' (2.6.260). Whereas *Ethiope* serves in these instances as racial shorthand for physical ugliness, Shakespeare resorts to an additional generic term applied to black Africans, *Moor*, to mark moral darkness. Hamlet excoriates his mother for marrying Claudius after the death of his beloved father, asking her how 'Could you on this fair mountain leave to feed, / And batten on this moor?' (*Hamlet*, 3.4.65–6). The power of this remark derives from Hamlet's pun on 'moor', which allows him to make a simultaneous topographical contrast (his father is a lofty 'mountain', whereas Claudius is a base, marshy 'moor' in the lowlands) and contrast of colour (his father is 'fair' in virtue, while Claudius the 'moor' is morally if not physically dark).

The complex interdependence of black-and-white symbolism and racial difference is most apparent in *Othello*. The play's language is full of antinomies of fair purity and black pollution that draw much of their power from the skin colours of Othello and Desdemona, even as they cannot be made synonymous with them. The Duke tells Brabanzio that in terms of virtue, Othello is 'far more fair than black' (1.3.289); once Othello becomes convinced that Desdemona has sexually betrayed him, he asks: 'Was this fair paper, this most goodly book, / Made to write "whore" upon?' (4.2.73–4). Each remark draws attention to the skin colour of Othello or Desdemona but also brings that colour into tension with the moral qualities conventionally associated with it. Othello's 'fair' virtue supposedly countermands his 'black' complexion; 'fair' is the colour also of the chaste Desdemona's skin, but the writing of 'whore' upon that 'goodly book' represents her supposed sexual blackening, not just because of Othello's allegation of her sexual betrayal, but also because of his implied image of black letters inscribed on and sullying her previously 'fair paper'.

With *Othello*, Shakespeare reproduces a centuries-old literary tradition of black-and-white symbolism grounded in interracial coupling. Medieval romances often feature a black Saracen princess courted by a white Christian knight. One such, Wolfram von Esenbach's thirteenth-century Arthurian romance *Parzival*, includes an interlude between Gahmuret, a noble Arthurian knight, and Belecane, a black Moorish queen. After converting to Christianity, Belecane gives birth to Gahmuret's son, Feirefiz, whose skin is black with white spots. Later, Feirefiz joins forces with his white half-brother Parzival to search for the Holy Grail. Although Wolfram pronounces black to be 'the colour of hell' and white 'the colour of heaven', Belecane's and Gahmuret's miscegenation does not present the threat to social order that the adulterations of race imagined by Iago do.[5] If anything, a Christianity that had initially rebelled against notions of ethnic exceptionalism sought to include blackness within its universal church, as is suggested by the medieval legends of the black Magus and the Indian Christian King Prester John. Still, these supposedly inclusive representations of blackness presume the subjection of dark alien to white Christian authority – Moorish Belecane to white Gahmuret, the mixed-race Feirefiz to his pure-blood half-brother Parzival, the black Magus and the Indian King to the putatively white Jesus.

Whereas medieval writers used the black-and-white antinomy to depict the unity-in-diversity of the Christian polity, early modern playwrights made it serve somewhat more exclusionary ends. Ben Jonson's *The Masque of Blackness*, performed at court for King James in 1605, featured Queen Anne and her courtiers disguised, in blackface, as Africans; they presented themselves to the king in order to be cleansed, a process completed in the entertainment's sequel, *The Masque of Beauty*. Here blackness was no longer validated by its docile submission to white authority: it was now an unacceptable deviation from order requiring expulsion by the monarch. The emergence of the transatlantic slave trade in the sixteenth century – which transported Africans not only to America, but also to England – was partly responsible for this more negative attitude to blackness. Antipathy to the country's growing African population is evidenced by Queen Elizabeth's repeated orders in the last years of her reign to deport 'blackamoors' from England. And it is striking that 'slave' is already a metonymy for blackness in *Titus Andronicus*, when Aaron says of his baby son, 'Look how the black slave smiles upon the father' (4.2.119).

If England's growing contact with Africans served to harden the perceived difference between black and white, the early modern theatre arguably hardened it yet further by playing up the visual contrast between black and white characters. In his famous 1595 drawing of a scene from *Titus Andronicus* – the only contemporary illustration of a performance of a Shakespeare play – Henry Peacham chose to foreground the contrast between black Aaron and the white characters, especially Tamora, who kneels close to him. Aaron himself allegorizes his black countenance in opposition to his white lover, Tamora:

> What signifies my deadly-standing eye,
> My silence, and my cloudy melancholy,
> My fleece of woolly hair that now uncurls
> Even as an adder when she doth unroll
> To do some fatal execution?
> No, madam, these are no venereal signs.
> (2.3.32–7)

Aaron's black face and curly hair bear no 'venereal signs' – that is, signs of love, which he attributes instead to white Tamora. The difference between Aaron's and Tamora's skin colours may have been even more visually pronounced in the earliest performances than Peacham's drawing or Aaron's speech suggest. Shakespeare's company may have made the black-and-white antinomies of plays like *Titus Andronicus* and *Othello* starkly apparent by its use of stage make-up: for if the part of a Moor demanded the application of cosmetic colour to the face, so too may have the part of a woman, which some theatre records suggest were performed by a boy actor with whitened face. The representation of gender on the all-male stage, then, may have been an important factor in transforming race from a matter of genealogy to one of radically opposed complexions.

But it is also important to note that blackness on Shakespeare's stage is not just about visible antinomies: it is also about language. Shakespeare's English contemporaries associated the term *barbarous* specifically with African speech, thanks to the etymologically dubious but popular myth recorded by the rhetorician George Puttenham. Noting that the term derives from the ancient Greeks, Puttenham acknowledges that some of his contemporaries believe it to describe 'the rude and barking language of the Africans now called Barbarians', otherwise known as the Berbers, from North Africa's Barbary Coast.[6] In Miranda's account, 'rude and barking language' is precisely what distinguishes Caliban's 'vile race': 'thou didst not, savage, / Know thine own meaning, but wouldst gabble like / A thing most brutish' (*The Tempest*, 1.2.358–60). The Prince of Morocco in *The Merchant of Venice* speaks a version of 'rude and barking language' when, wooing Portia, he promises to 'Pluck the young sucking cubs from the she-bear, / Yea, mock the lion when a roars for prey, / To win the lady' (2.1.29–31); his harsh consonants, pounding spondees and violent animal imagery are at odds with the romantic scene he wishes to perform. But if Morocco is 'rude' when he aspires to civility, Othello is the opposite. He characterizes his ability with language in terms that paraphrase Puttenham's remark: 'Rude am I in my speech, / And little blessed with the soft phrase of peace' (1.3.81–2). Othello's words, like Morocco's, point back to his blackness, but in an ironic register: his eloquence undercuts his claim to 'rude' speech. Nick Bottom's synaesthetic malapropism in *A Midsummer Night's Dream*, 'I hear [a] face' (5.1.191), seems oddly appropriate for Shakespeare's Moors. How an audience 'sees' each character's black face, in the sense both of 'looking at' and 'understanding' it, depends on how the audience hears each character's use of language.

Indeed, Shakespeare keeps encouraging his audience to 'look at' skin colour in ways that also 'understand' it. There is a long history, dating back beyond Pliny, of attributing dark hues to hot climates. Cleopatra claims that she is 'with Phoebus' [i.e. the sun's] amorous pinches black' (*Antony and Cleopatra*, 1.5.28). And the Prince of Morocco asks Portia to 'Mislike me not for my complexion, / The shadowed livery of the burnished sun' (*The Merchant of Venice*, 2.1.1–2). 'Complexion' here does not just mean skin colour, as it does now. Derived from the Latin *complexio*, or 'mix', 'complexion' referred specifically to the body's internal mix of four 'humours' or liquids – red blood, yellow choler, green phlegm and black melancholy (also known as black bile) – that physicians from antiquity to the time of Shakespeare understood as the basis of skin colour and psychological disposition, depending on which humour is most in abundance. Aaron's 'cloudy melancholy' (2.3.33), which features in his anatomy of his blackness, typifies how Africans were often thought to be susceptible to an excess of black bile, thanks to the burning-up of their other humours by the heat of the sun. This typifies 'geohumoralism', the conviction that geography determines racial complexion and temperament. Even Othello's jealousy may have been subjected to geohumoral interpretation by his earliest audiences. Although Desdemona insists that 'the sun where he was born / Drew all such humours from him' (*Othello*, 3.4.28–9), Robert Burton says in *The Anatomy of Melancholy* that jealousy is characteristic of husbands in 'hot countries', including 'Africa'.[7]

Geohumoralism presumes a conception of race that, in its dependence on location, might seem to be mutable. Change your climate, and you change your skin colour and personality too. Yet blackness was rarely read as mutable. According to a common saying of the time, it was impossible 'to wash the Ethiope white' – just as Aaron says, in his defence of blackness, that it is impossible for the 'water in the ocean' to 'turn the swan's black legs to white' (*Titus Andronicus*, 4.2.100–1). For him, blackness is immutable. By contrast, Aaron regards whiteness as an easily wiped away superficiality, evidenced in his denunciation of Tamora's white sons as 'Ye whitelimed walls' (4.2.97). Aaron's assumption of whiteness's susceptibility to mutation was echoed in a quasi-scientific discourse of blackness as an hereditary infection. In 1578, George Best speculated of Ethiopians that their 'blackness proceeds of some natural infection of the first inhabitants of that Country, and so all the whole progeny of them descended, are still polluted with the same blot of infection ... by a lineal descent they have hitherto continued thus black'.[8] Here Best obviously feels no need to explain the origins of whiteness, which he regards as normative. Like Best, Shakespeare seems to recognize that blackness is an hereditary corruption independent of climate when Aaron fathers a black child in Rome with Tamora, the Queen of the Goths. Tamora and her nurse see the child's darkness as not just a pathological adulteration of her noble white lineage, but also a bestial deviation from geohumoral normalcy: for them, the baby is 'as loathsome as a toad / Amongst the fair-faced breeders of our clime' (4.2.67–8).

Best's conception of blackness as a lineal 'infection', however, is ultimately couched not in scientific but in theological terms. To explain the origins of the infection, he invokes the story of Cham (or Ham), Noah's disobedient son. Best asserts that Cham's crime was not seeing his father naked, as the Bible states, but his copulation with his wife on board the Ark. This crime, Best claims, was punished by the blackness of the son Cham fathered, Chus, who settled in Africa and became the ancestor of the Moors. The story of Cham's curse proved popular during the heyday of the transatlantic slave trade. But the notion that Chus was black and the ancestor of the Moors lacked scriptural authority. The colour of Cham's son is not specified in the Bible, nor was he always understood to be the ancestor of black Africans; in some cases, he was alleged to have sired the peoples of greater Asia, including the Mongolian great Khan or 'Cham', whose beard Benedick refers to in *Much Ado About Nothing* (2.1.233). Shakespeare was familiar with the Cham story. In *The Merchant of Venice*, we learn that one of Shylock's fellow Venetian Jews is called Chus (3.2.284), the namesake of Cham's son. Does Shakespeare seek here to blacken Jews? Or is he merely associating Jews with an antique lineage? In any case, the name of Chus the Jew hints at how Shakespeare's conceptions of race, whether genealogical or coloured, were implicated in notions of religious identity.

Problems of religion

Some critics have argued that religion, not skin colour, was the major marker of difference in early modern Christian Europe. However, the history of religious discrimination has been distinguished too drastically from the history of antipathy to dark skin, which means that Christian interactions with Jews and Muslims have often been neglected in colour-centred studies of race in Shakespeare, just as colour has sometimes been neglected in studies of religious difference in Shakespeare. But these different markers of difference overlapped in significant ways. This was especially so in the Iberian Peninsula, where the Christian Reconquista (or reconquest) of previously Muslim kingdoms and the expulsion of the Jews helped produce conceptions of religious identity that, in privileging *limpieza de sangre* or 'pure blood' over blood adulterated by Moorish and Jewish ancestry, were simultaneously racial.

The term *Moor* probably derives from the Greek *mauros*, meaning dark. But it could refer to light- as well as dark-skinned people, and more generically to Muslims in Spain and Ottoman Turkey as well as Africa and India. As we have seen, Shakespeare often treats *Moor* as a synonym for black. He has 'blackamoors' play music in *Love's Labour's Lost* (5.2.156); in both *Titus Andronicus* and *Othello* the 'Moor' is black, though the stage direction at the beginning of the second act in *The Merchant of Venice* introduces the Prince of Morocco as a 'tawny [i.e. brown] Moor'. Elsewhere in Shakespeare's writing, however, *Moor* evokes Islam or a generic anti-Christianity. One of the most recurrent hand properties of stage-Moors is the sword: Aaron brandishes one in Henry Peacham's illustration. But often the sword-bearing Moor is less a black African than a warrior Muslim, like the Turkish mercenary soldier Brusor in the anonymous play *Soliman and Perseda* (c. 1590), who boasts of slaying the Sophy and Persians with his sword. Shakespeare remembered Brusor in the Prince of Morocco, who likewise swears noisily by his 'scimitar / That slew the Sophy and a Persian prince' (*The Merchant of Venice*, 2.1.24–5). Shakespeare's Turkish/Moorish conflation persists in *Othello*: at play's end, making the final stand that culminates in his identification with 'a malignant and turbaned Turk' (5.2.362), Othello too starts brandishing his 'sword of Spain': 'Behold, I have a weapon' (5.2.260, 266). This suggests how *Moor* could denote a pan-Muslim and even an anti-Christian identity as much as a specifically black one. In this context, we might note the epithets that accompany Aaron's supposedly racial identity: 'irreligious Moor' (*Titus Andronicus*, 5.3.120), 'misbelieving Moor' (5.3.142), 'damned Moor' (5.3.201). Aaron is understood in terms of his religion (or lack of it) as much as his colour. Even his name, which is of Jewish origin, puts him outside the pale of Christian tradition.

The cross-hatching of religious and racial otherness on the early modern English stage depended on several markers of bodily difference, some of which took the visible form of hand properties and prostheses. We have already seen how the stage-Moor conventionally brandished a sword. Early modern stage-Jews like Barabas in Christopher Marlowe's *The Jew of Malta* and Shylock in *The Merchant of Venice* probably wore the red beard sported by Judas in medieval mystery plays, as well as a 'Jewish gaberdine' or long coat (1.3.108). But the most significant markers of embodied religious difference were usually invisible to audiences. In the case of Jewish and Muslim men, that marker was circumcision, as Othello's reference to the 'malignant and ... turbaned Turk' as a 'circumcised dog' (*Othello*, 5.2.362, 364) makes clear.

If circumcision marks the unseen bodily difference of Jew and Muslim from Christian, Shylock's conversion at play's end cannot eradicate that hidden mark. In this he differs from his daughter Jessica, who bears no such sign on her body. Her conversion to Christianity is thus less vexed; when she declares of Shylock that 'though I am a daughter to his blood, / I am not to his manners' (*The Merchant of Venice*, 2.3.17–18), that 'blood' is no obstacle to her conversion, for her new Christian identity is more a matter of culture (or 'manners') rather than biology. But on one occasion, *The Merchant of Venice* suggests that Jessica's conversion is enabled by her racial 'blood' as much as her cultural 'manners'. Using language that evokes the black-and-white antinomies of other Shakespeare plays as well as Reconquista Spain's obsession with bloodlines, Salerio recasts Shylock and Jessica as racially divergent: 'There is more difference between thy flesh and hers than between jet and ivory; more between your bloods than there is between red wine and Rhenish' (3.1.33–5). Shylock's body is aligned here with black 'jet' and the wine of dark grapes, Jessica's body with white 'ivory' and 'Rhenish', i.e. white wine.

The blackening of the Jewish male in *The Merchant of Venice* is suggested not only by Chus the Jew, the namesake of Cham's son, but also by Shylock's parable about Jacob. In this speech, Shylock compares his thrift and profit to Jacob's in winning a flock of sheep by making the white ewes conceive 'parti-colored', i.e. black-and-white, lambs (1.3.84). Shylock associates Jacob – otherwise known as Israel and hence as father of the Jewish nation – with processes of adulteration. His parable thus recalls Orozco's two definitions of *raza* as an animal lineage and as an adulteration of pure pedigree. Later, Shylock metaphorically adulterates the Christian Antonio, who, by defaulting on his debt to Shylock, becomes a version of Jacob's 'parti-colored' sheep – he is, in his own words, a 'tainted wether of the flock' (4.1.113). The term 'tainted' does powerful work here: it means both diseased and darkened, thereby recalling Best's explanation of blackness as an infection or pollution. The fear of Jewish pollution of the body politic – through poison, disease, circumcision or usury – was deep-seated in early modern England and on at least one occasion sponsored violent retribution by the state. Although England's Jewish community had been expelled by Edward I in 1290, a small and mostly undercover community lived in Shakespeare's London. It included the Portuguese Jew Dr Roderigo Lopez, Queen Elizabeth's personal physician; with little evidence, he was accused and executed in 1593 for a supposed plot to poison her. In *The Merchant of Venice*, the fear of Jewish tainting is averted instead by Shylock's forced baptism, which removes him from the play, and Jessica's willing conversion, which allows her a place in its conclusion.

The supersession of Shylock the tainting black father by Jessica the converted white daughter inverts Jacob's movement from white ewes to 'parti-colored' lambs. That youthful Jessica's 'ivory' should triumph over old Shylock's 'jet' suggests also how temporal positioning is a subtle yet important tactic in the demarcation of racial difference, especially when colour alone cannot do the trick. Time, of course, is an important dimension of *race* in its genealogical guise: one derives one's identity from ancestors who have come before. But races are also frequently distinguished according to where they are relative to each other on a single timeline. Such a distinction is something we might associate more with European thought over the last two centuries, particularly the belief in a progressive history that culminates in the West and puts non-Western cultures and peoples in the 'waiting-room of history'.[9] Yet the distinction between a primitive culture of the past and a more perfect culture of the present was a feature of Christian thought from its inception. In particular, the exegetical method known as typology, according to which the events and people of the 'Old' Testament of the Jews allegorically foreshadowed those of the more perfect 'New' Testament of the Christians, worked to refashion Judaism as the prologue ('BC') to the Christian epoch ('AD'). Jews who coexisted with Christians were thus cut from the present, or made into living anachronisms. Shakespeare resorts to typological thought in *The Merchant of Venice*. Lorenzo, enriched by Portia's alienation of 'old' Shylock's estate, tells her that 'you drop manna in the way / Of starved people' (5.1.292–3); here archaic Jewish matter ('manna' or bread from heaven) serves as a metaphor for the sustenance of present-day Christians, a process of typological conversion that parallels the economic conversion of 'old' Shylock's wealth for 'new' Christian use.

Admittedly, Christian theology also complicates the belief in progressive history by presuming an original state of grace in paradise interrupted by the Fall. As Europeans encountered the native inhabitants of America, some asked: are they closer than we are to an original paradise? This question assumed that being antique is an advantage rather than a deficiency. Michel de Montaigne certainly thought as much when he described Brazilian Indians as unadulterated by civilization. And so does *The Tempest*'s Gonzalo, who has read Montaigne and describes the people of Shakespeare's island as 'gentle-kind' spirits living in a Golden Age (3.3.32). But such a view also potentially banished native Americans to a past from which modern Europeans have evolved. In his 1590 *True and Briefe Report of the New Found Land of Virginia*, for example, Thomas Harriot and his illustrator Theodore de Bry resort to exactly this tactic by comparing Algonquian Indians to the savage Picts of British antiquity.

Shakespeare often uses the term *Indian* or *Men of Ind* (as when Trinculo speculates that Caliban comes from a breed of 'savages and men of Ind' (2.2.55–6)) to figure a primitive people who are temporally and religiously backward. Occasionally the term seems designed to connote a primitive nakedness: in *Henry VIII*, we hear of a 'strange Indian with the great tool' (5.3.32–3). Elsewhere, Shakespeare presents the Indian as a backward pagan, like the 'rude and savage man of Ind' in *Love's Labour's Lost* who 'bows ... his vassal head' and 'kisses the base ground' when the sun rises (4.3.218–21), or Helen in *All's Well That Ends Well*, who describes her love for Bertram as 'Indian-like': 'Religious in mine error', she complains, 'I adore / The sun' (1.3.188–90). In one famous textual crux, the primitive connotations of Shakespeare's *Indian* blur into the ancient associations with the typological Jew. While the quarto edition has Othello compare himself to 'a base Indian who threw a pearl away / Richer than all his tribe' (*Othello*, 5.2.356–7), the Folio edition substitutes 'Judaean' for 'Indian'. Othello thus damns himself as either racially primitive or temporally ancient. In any case, 'Indian' and 'Judaean' are both forms of religious error that Othello associates with the beliefs of a 'tribe' – a term, like *race*, that suggests genealogy, but in this case a specifically pre-Christian, and even pre-societal, lineage.

Critics often note how, in his last speech, Othello is split between the roles of Christian defender of Venice and Turkish traitor. But he is also split in time, between Christian present and Indian or Judaean past. These splits distil the many contradictions of Shakespeare's treatment of race. Over the course of the play, Othello's race slides between pure pedigree ('I fetch my life and being / From men of royal siege' (1.2.21–2)) and impure adulteration (he is a 'devil' who will make a 'grandsire' of Desdemona's father (1.1.91)), visible colour ('I am black' (3.3.267)) and hidden religious difference (he is a 'circumcised dog' (5.2.364)), present convert and backward primitive. If we respond to the contradictions of race in Shakespeare simply by seeing them as typical of a dark time cut off from the more enlightened world we now inhabit, we repeat one of the strategies of a racializing knowledge that seeks to erect temporal as well as spatial partitions between a primitive 'them' and a modern 'us'. We might instead allow the contradictions of race in Shakespeare to speak back to us in the present – not just to reveal the genealogy of our habits of thought, but also to suggest alternatives to them. And one of those alternatives may be the proposition that what we think we know about *race* now is every bit as fraught as what Shakespeare knew then.

NOTES

1 Robert Bartlett, 'Medieval and Modern Conceptions of Race and Ethnicity', *Journal of Medieval and Early Modern Studies*, 31:1 (2001), 39–56 (esp. 44).

2 John Florio, *A Worlde of Words, or Most Copious, and Exacte Dictionarie in Italian and English* (1598), p. 313.

3 Edward Topsell, *A Historie of Four-Footed Beastes and Snakes* (London: 1607), p. 234.

4 Sebastián de Covarrubias y Orozco, *Tesoro de la lengua castellana o española* (Madrid: 1611); English translation in Margaret Greer, Walter Mignolo and Maureen Quilligan (eds.), *Rereading the Black Legend: The Discourses of Religious and Racial Difference in the Renaissance Empires* (Chicago: University of Chicago Press, 2007), pp. 12–13.

5 Wolfram von Esenbach, *Parzival*, ed. Albert K. Winner, trans. Helen M. Mustard and Charles E. Passage (London: Vintage, 1998), 3rd edn, p. 3.

6 George Puttenham, *The Arte of English Poesie: 1589* (Menston: Scolar Press, 1968), p. 210.

7 Robert Burton, *The Anatomy of Melancholy: What it is, With all the Kindes, Causes, Symptomes, Prognostickes, and Seuerall Cures of It* (1621), vol. III, p. 264.

8 George Best, *A True Discourse of Discoverie, for the Finding of a Passage to Cathaya*, in Richard Hakluyt, *The Principal Navigations, Voyages, Traffiques & Discoveries of the English Nation* (1600), 12 vols., ed. Walter Raleigh (Glasgow: James MacLehose & Sons, 1903–5), vol. VII, pp. 261–71 (esp. p. 263).

9 Dipesh Chakrabarty, *Provincializing Europe: Postcolonial Thought and Historical Difference* (Princeton NJ: Princeton University Press, 2000), p. 8.

READING LIST

Alexander, Catherine M.S. and Stanley Wells, eds. *Shakespeare and Race*. Cambridge: Cambridge University Press, 2000.

Callaghan, Dympna. *Shakespeare without Women: Representing Gender and Race on the Renaissance Stage*. London and New York: Routledge, 2000.

Floyd-Wilson, Mary. *English Ethnicity and Race in Early Modern Drama*. Cambridge: Cambridge University Press, 2003.

Goldberg, Jonathan. *Tempest in the Caribbean*. Minneapolis: University of Minnesota Press, 2004.

Greer, Margaret, Walter Mignolo and Maureen Quilligan, eds. *Rereading the Black Legend: The Discourses of Religious and Racial Difference in the Renaissance Empires*. Chicago: University of Chicago Press, 2007.

Hahn, Thomas, ed. 'Race and Ethnicity in the Middle Ages', *Journal of Medieval and Early Modern Studies*, 31:1 (2001), 1–37.

Hall, Kim F. *Things of Darkness: Economies of Race and Gender in Early Modern England*. Ithaca, NY: Cornell University Press, 1995.

Hendricks, Margo, ed. 'Forum: Race and the Study of Shakespeare', *Shakespeare Studies*, 26 (1998), 19–79.

'"Obscured by Dreams": Race, Empire, and Shakespeare's *A Midsummer Night's Dream*', *Shakespeare Quarterly*, 47:1 (1996), 37–60.

and Patricia Parker, eds. *Women, 'Race', and Writing in the Early Modern Period*. London and New York: Routledge, 1994.

Loomba, Ania. *Shakespeare, Race and Colonialism*. Oxford: Oxford University Press, 2002.

McGiffert, Michael, ed. 'Constructing Race: Differentiating Peoples in the Early Modern World', *William and Mary Quarterly*, 54:1 (1997), 3–352.

Shapiro, James. *Shakespeare and the Jews*. New York: Columbia University Press, 1995.

Smith, Ian. 'Barbarian Errors: Performing Race in Early Modern England', *Shakespeare Quarterly*, 49:2 (1998), 168–86.

15

STEPHEN ORGEL

Shakespeare, sexuality and gender

At the conclusion of *Twelfth Night*, as part of the long-awaited and heavily overdetermined reconciliation scene, comes a revelation that modern audiences would surely find disconcerting if they paid attention to it. Sebastian, in the course of catechizing his disguised twin sister Viola, gives their age at the death of their father as 13 (5.1.237–41). They cannot be much older than this during the course of the play: they are prepubescent, constantly mistaken for each other; Sebastian's voice has not yet changed, and his facial hair has not begun to grow. Even for Shakespeare's audience, their youthfulness would have been striking, an index at the very least to the precociousness of sexuality in Illyria. Indeed, if they are still 13, it means that, though Sebastian and Olivia have by this time married, the husband has not yet even reached the age of consent, which at this period in Shakespeare's England was 14 for men, 12 for women. We find this moment unnoticeable because Sebastian and Viola, in modern productions, are roles for mature actors, not children. Sebastian's combative energy and erotic readiness suggest at the very least advanced adolescence, and would have suggested it to Shakespeare's audience as well: the physiologists of the age placed the onset of active male sexuality at 15 or 16.

The idea of a 13-year-old husband was a fantasy, though doubtless a culturally significant one. But Olivia's propensity for falling in love with prepubescent youths – she falls in love with two – was, if not normative, at least not uncommon. The fact that a young man has retained his boyishness, which is generally equated with looking feminine, is often represented as a strong incentive to erotic pursuit, by either men or women. Shakespeare's beloved young man in Sonnet 20, for example, has all the attractions of a woman without her drawbacks:

> A woman's face with nature's own hand painted
> Hast thou, the master-mistress of my passion;
> A woman's gentle heart, but not acquainted
> With shifting change as is false women's fashion.
>
> (1–4)

Similarly, Orlando in *As You Like It* is praised because 'He hath but a little beard' (3.2.188), and Adonis in *Venus and Adonis* is 'more lovely than a man' (9). A particularly cynical view of the preference for beardless boys is expressed in Thomas Middleton's *No Wit, No Help Like a Woman's*: a character named Sir Gilbert Lambston, who has been wooing a rich widow only to see her give herself in marriage to a smooth-faced youth who is, in fact, a cross-dressed woman, complains of the erotic preferences of the age:

> Rich widows, that were wont to choose by gravity
> Their second husbands, not by tricks of blood,
> Are now so taken with loose Aretine flames
> Of nimble wantonness and high-fed pride
> They marry now but the third part of husbands,
> Boys, smooth-fac'd catamites, to fulfill their bed,
> As if a woman should a woman wed.
>
> (4.2)

In this society, Olivia is not alone; and though it is unclear whether Sebastian has been Antonio's 'smooth-fac'd catamite', he is as attractive to Antonio as to Olivia.

But why does Shakespeare make his twins so young? The twins in Shakespeare's source, Barnabe Rich's *Apollonius and Silla*, on whom Sebastian and Viola are based, are considerably older: at the tale's opening Silvio, the character who became Sebastian, is already away at the wars. Indeed, why does the play raise the issue of the twins' age at all? Their precocious sexuality at least brings their characters into coincidence with the actors impersonating them: beneath their costumes Viola and Olivia are prepubescent boys, and to make Viola's male twin the same age made theatrical and logical, if not physiological, sense. Still, there must be more to it than this. Shakespeare similarly revised the age of Juliet, which appears to be about 16 in Arthur Brooke's *Romeus and Juliet*, downward to 13. This again is specified very precisely, and seemingly quite unnecessarily: Juliet's nurse says that Juliet is not yet 14, and even specifies her birthday, the next Lammas Eve, 31 July (1.3.15, 23). Juliet's mother, moreover, says that she herself gave birth to Juliet when she too was 14 (1.3.74–5), and Paris, undertaking to persuade Juliet's father to accept him as a son-in-law, bases his plea on the claim that women are sexually mature even earlier: 'Younger than she are happy mothers made' (1.2.12). Were there enough 12-year-old mothers in Shakespeare's England to make this anything more than another pederastic fantasy about the sexual precociousness of Mediterranean societies?

It is most of all an index to a powerful sexual fantasy that in both its positive and negative versions pervades the plays: the dream of a wife or husband just emerging from childhood, inexperienced, endlessly pliable, not yet hardened into adulthood – the opposite of those frighteningly mature spouses who fill the plays that deal not with the fun of wooing but with life after marriage, figures like Paulina, Lady Macbeth, Goneril and Regan; or Othello, Macbeth, Leontes. The corollary to this fantasy is one in which young people in love evade the patriarchal imperatives by escaping to a world without parents, where they can arrange their own marriages: the fantasy of *As You Like It*, *A Midsummer Night's Dream*, and of Jessica and Lorenzo in *The Merchant of Venice*; or one in which the controlling father is dead, as in the cases of Olivia, Viola and Sebastian in *Twelfth Night*, Beatrice in *Much Ado About Nothing*, Helen in *All's Well That Ends Well* – though even the dead father can constitute a considerable impediment to sexual fulfilment, as is the case for Portia in *The Merchant of Venice*.

The normative ending of comedy is marriage, but Shakespeare characteristically works a significant variation on the norm. Shakespeare's comedies typically end just before the marriage, sometimes, as in *Love's Labour's Lost* and *Twelfth Night*, with an entirely unexpected delay or postponement. The play that begins where comedy ends, with the father defeated and the lovers married, is *Othello*. What happens after marriage? Very little in the way of sexual satisfaction, to begin with: the lovemaking of Othello and Desdemona is relentlessly interrupted on the only two nights they spend together before he murders her on their wedding sheets. Even in those few marriages in Shakespeare that are are depicted as sexually happy – in *Hamlet* and *The Winter's Tale*, for example – the sexuality of women is represented as profoundly unsettling. Hamlet deplores the fact that his mother enjoys 'the rank sweat of an enseamèd bed' (3.4.82) with her husband and even disapproves of her previous sexual interest in his father: 'she would hang on him / As if increase of appetite had grown / By what it fed on' (1.2.143–5). Leontes' paranoid fear of cuckoldry is merely an extreme case of the age's cultural assumptions about the nature of women.

How different, then, were women from men? Early modern gynaecology offered widely varying accounts of the aetiology of gender, but the most persistent, descending from Galen, cited apparent homologies in the genital structure of the sexes to show that male and female were versions of the same unitary species. The female genitals, it was argued, were simply the male genitals inverted and carried internally rather than externally. Sexual experience was conceived to be the same in both: during coitus, both experience orgasm and ejaculate, and female ejaculation with its component of female seed is as essential for conception as male ejaculation. Both male and female seeds are present in every foetus. A foetus becomes male rather than female if the male seed is dominant and generates enough heat to press the genital organs outwards – that is, if the foetus is stronger, strength being conceived as heat.

In this version of anatomical history, we all begin as female, and masculinity is a development out of and away from femininity; the female is an incomplete male. The medical literature from classical times onwards confirms the theory by recording various examples of women completing the physiological process and, under the pressure of some great stress or excitement, turning into men. The most famous of the early modern accounts, often cited, describes a shepherd named Germain Garnier, who had been a woman named Marie until the age of 15, when, as she was chasing her pigs, her genitals turned inside out, transforming her into a man. Garnier was still alive in Montaigne's time; when Montaigne visited his town, Garnier was away, but he questioned the townspeople about the man and made him an exemplary case in his essay *Of the Power of the Imagination*. He had no doubt about the authenticity of the transformation and observes that 'this sort of accident is frequently met with'.[1]

At the same time, the alternative theory maintaining that the anatomical differences between male and female are definitive and that women are not incomplete men but have their own kind of perfection is also found, sometimes in tandem with the homological theory, even though they are contradictory and should be mutually exclusive. Sir Thomas Browne, for example, in *Pseudodoxia Epidemica*, asserts on the basis of his anatomical studies that Galen was wrong and that the male and female genital organs cannot be inverted versions of each other. Nevertheless, shortly afterwards he declares his conviction concerning 'the mutation of sexes, or transition into one another' that 'not only mankind, but many other animals may suffer this transexion, we will not deny, or hold it at all impossible'. Beside this passage Browne places the marginal gloss, 'Transmutation of Sexes, viz. of Women into Men, granted.'

From a cultural point of view, the critical element in the argument is less the fluidity of gender than the assumption that its movement works in only one direction, from female to male, which is conceived to be upwards, towards completion; in this construction, the masculine is what the human strives to be. The most frightening part of this teleology was the fantasy of its reversal, the fear that men can turn into – or be turned into – women; or perhaps more precisely, can be turned *back* into women, losing the strength that enabled the male potential to be realized in the first place. The fear of effeminization pervades the moral literature of the age: boys must be trained to be men, and to remain manly required constant vigilance. Associating with women, falling in love, was inherently dangerous to the masculine self: lust, it was said, effeminates, makes men incapable of manly pursuits;

hence the pervasive antithesis of love and war throughout the age. The classic Shakespearian example is Mark Antony, transformed by love from 'the triple pillar of the world' into 'a strumpet's fool' (1.1.12–13); and Cleopatra, playing her own entirely conventional role, completes his effeminization:

> Ere the ninth hour, I drunk him to his bed,
> Then put my tires and mantles on him whilst
> I wore his sword Philippan.
>
> (2.5.21–3)

Similarly, Romeo, berating himself for his unwillingness to harm Tybalt, cries:

> O sweet Juliet,
> Thy beauty hath made me effeminate,
> And in my temper softened valour's steel.
>
> (3.1.108–10)

Such formulations are all but axiomatic in the period. In the *Anatomy of Melancholy*, Robert Burton elucidates the matter with uncharacteristic directness: love is 'full of fear, anxiety, doubt, care, peevishness, suspicion, it turns a man into a woman'.[2]

What is manhood that the most natural and universal of human emotions can undo it? The age is full of warnings implying that masculinity is not something to be taken for granted. We find this puzzling because for modern physiology the sexual organs constitute the bottom line, the ultimate truth of gender. Nevertheless, a modern father who urges his timid son to 'be a man' is perfectly comprehensible, despite the fact that this commonplace exhortation assumes precisely that masculinity is achieved not through biology but through an effort of will. In the same way early modern moralists continually reminded their charges that manhood was not a natural condition but a quality to be striven for and maintained only with great difficulty. And the greatest danger to manhood was women.

Needless to say, the persistence of homological gynaecology has little to do with science. Renaissance ideology had a vested interest in defining women in terms of men – the point was to establish the parameters of maleness, and those of womanhood only in relation to men. Of course, this pertains solely to the Galenic model and not to the alternative that saw the female as distinct. But there is nothing egalitarian about the notion that women and men are versions of each other, that women are almost men and can even become men. Most of the scientific opinion codified by Ian Maclean in his essential study *The Renaissance Notion of Women* assumes the correctness of the homological thesis, but nevertheless stresses the differences between men and women, not their similarities, and these differences are invariably prejudicial.[3] Women are more passionate, less intelligent, less in control of their affections and so forth. The difference in degree of perfection becomes in practical terms a significant difference in kind, and such arguments are used to justify the whole range of male domination over women.

But it needs to be emphasized that throughout the period the performative aspects of gender figure far more significantly in discussions of the subject than does physiology. The disguises of Rosalind, Viola, Portia, Innogen, seem to us whimsical fantasies, but if we consider them in relation to some real cases they will look rather different. In 1605 Elizabeth Southwell, one of Queen Anne's maids of honour, eloped with her lover, Sir Robert Dudley. The elopement was scandalous. Dudley already had a wife and family, and had recently converted to Roman Catholicism. He was the illegitimate son of the Earl of Leicester, but after Leicester's death he challenged the legitimacy of his father's heirs and presented evidence that Leicester had been secretly married to Dudley's mother. This was an explosive allegation; the suit was not allowed to proceed, and on behalf of Leicester's widow and family Dudley was charged in the Star Chamber with criminal conspiracy. Dudley and Elizabeth fled, escaping to the Continent with Elizabeth making the entire trip disguised as Dudley's page. The couple lived openly in Lyons and, despite the bigamy, received a papal dispensation to marry. They settled in Florence, and Dudley was thereafter lucratively employed as a military and naval engineer by the Duke of Tuscany. Few Shakespearian disguise plots end so happily.

Lady Arbella Stuart was the heroine of a more tragic transvestite plot. Her mother, the daughter of the famous Bess of Hardwick, Countess of Shrewsbury, had married the uncle of James VI, the king of Scotland who was to become James I of England. Arbella was therefore the king's first cousin, and any marriage she might contract had to be approved by the crown. Needless to say, no suitor was ever deemed satisfactory: the king had no interest in increasing the number of possible claimants to his throne. Arbella finally took matters into her own hands. In 1610, at the age of 35, she secretly, and illegally, married William Seymour, a grandson of the Earl of Hertford with a distant claim to the throne. When the match became known, Seymour was imprisoned in the Tower and Arbella placed under house arrest, initially at Lambeth. But when it was found that this made it too easy for her to communicate with her husband, she was ordered to be sent to Durham. As the journey began, she took ill, and the party stopped at Barnet, in north London, for some weeks. As the move once again seemed imminent, Arbella took action. She persuaded one of her attendants that she was stealing out to pay a final visit to Seymour and would return before morning. She disguised herself as a man, with trousers and boots, a doublet and a black cloak. She wore a man's wig that partially concealed her features, and a black hat, and she carried a rapier. In this disguise she fled, successfully deceiving an innkeeper and an ostler as to her sex, and headed for the coast for a rendezvous with Seymour, where they intended to take a boat to freedom in France. Seymour escaped from the Tower through an equally ingenious disguise plot.[4] For Arbella this comedy did not end happily: the couple missed their rendezvous, and though both took ships separately for Calais, Arbella's was pursued; she was arrested at sea and spent the remaining five years of her life imprisoned in the Tower. Seymour, however, disembarked safely in France and lived abroad until Arbella's death. He then returned to England and within the year married the daughter of the Earl of Essex – an astonishingly happy ending for him, under the circumstances.

The disguises of Shakespearian drama look less like theatrical convention if we consider them with these cases in mind. It is scarcely hyperbole to say that disguise offered Arbella Stuart the only hope of an escape from the intolerable situation her paternity had placed her in – Innogen's case in *Cymbeline* is hardly more melodramatic. And both Elizabeth Dudley's and Arbella Stuart's disguises were genuinely impenetrable – quite as impenetrable as any in Shakespeare. Arbella had a long, hard ride from Barnet to the coast, during which she and her servant stopped at an inn and changed horses. The ostler later reported only that the young man seemed unwell, and had difficulty with the horse (Arbella would have been accustomed to riding side-saddle), but he had no inkling that there was a woman beneath the clothing and hair. These cases are a good index to how much the sense of who one was in the period depended precisely on externals, on costume, wigs, facial hair, accessories such as jewellery – on everything that comprised the representation of a social role. But beyond this, there must be a presumption in the culture that such superficies represent realities and are the closest we can come to knowing somebody.

One can imagine a romance in which the plot does not ultimately undo itself in the removal or penetration of the disguise, where disguise becomes the reality, the true expression of the self – where the impersonation becomes the person. This actually happens in Beaumont and Fletcher's play *Philaster*, in which the embattled heroine Euphrasia, disguised as the page Bellario, decides to remain permanently in drag and serve her lord and lady as an epicene youth, equally attractive to men and women. There are gestures towards this sort of essentialization of costume in Shakespeare. In *As You Like It*, when Rosalind disguises herself as the youth Ganymede to accompany Celia in their flight into the forest of Arden, it is for practical reasons: women on the road are always in danger, and the presence of a man – any kind of man, even a prepubescent youth – is a sufficient deterrent to predators. The disguise subsequently becomes a cover for her meetings with Orlando; but why is the cover necessary? It would appear, indeed, to be self-defeating: by the middle of the play, when Orlando is tacking love-poems to Rosalind on every tree, Rosalind is perfectly well aware of his feelings for her. She even acknowledges the pointlessness of continuing her disguise: 'Alas the day, what shall I do with my doublet and hose?' (3.2.199–200). Why not at this point reveal herself and consummate the love? But the play is scarcely half over; for another two acts, always as Ganymede, she puts Orlando through a series of tests and catechisms, good for comedy but only serving to delay the ultimate erotic satisfaction. Disguise here is the essence of romance, and when the disguise is discarded the romance has ended – here in marriage, though if we think about what happens afterwards, for example in *Othello* and *Romeo and Juliet*, it is not clear that abandoning the disguise necessarily constitutes a happy ending.

In *Twelfth Night* Viola initially regards her transvestite disguise as correspondent to her inner state. It will be, she says, 'the form of my intent' (1.2.51). By the middle of the play she has changed her mind, calling disguise 'a wickedness / Wherein the pregnant enemy [Satan] does much' (2.2.25–6): she is now trapped in a costume that misrepresents the form of her intent, that makes it impossible for her to express her feelings. But she too maintains the disguise long after its utility in the plot has been exhausted. In the middle of Act 3, when Antonio intervenes in her duel with Sir Andrew and calls her Sebastian, it is clear to her that her brother is alive and in Illyria – she concludes the scene with the recognition 'That I, dear brother, be now ta'en for you' (3.4.340). The resolution, the unmasking, could occur at any point after this; but she retains her disguise for another two acts, even in the final confrontation with her twin, putting him through a pointless exercise comparing details about their parentage. The eventual unmasking, moreover, does nothing to change the terms on which the play has operated throughout: appearances remain of the essence. Olivia has fallen in love with the cross-dressed Viola, and when Sebastian appears, identically costumed, she instantly, effortlessly, transfers her feelings to him – the twins are, for Olivia, interchangeable. But if falling in love with a cross-dressed woman is the same as falling in love with a man, what is a man except the costume?

There are very few plays that suggest gender may be more than the costume – that that part of the self which is defined by sexuality is ultimately and absolutely real and knowable. Viola, challenged by Sir Andrew, laments that 'a little thing would make me tell them how much I lack of a man' (3.4.268–9), invoking in that lack a very old anatomical fantasy that women are men with something missing (the fantasy is as old as Galen, but it is still present in Freud). The play alludes to this assumption elsewhere, in its puns on 'cut' and 'cunt' (2.3.166; 2.5.77–81). This is obviously a male fantasy, not a female one, though in this case Viola's failure of nerve is not merely a function of the missing genital organs: in the duel, Sir Andrew turns out to be no more of a man than Viola. In a much more substantial example, John Fletcher's strange play *The Honest Man's Fortune*, a very attractive young man named Veramour is propositioned by an elderly lecher. To repel his attentions Veramour claims he is really a woman and proceeds to dress accordingly. This stratagem is only marginally successful, since the lecher is equally attracted to women, and as the play nears its climax a good deal of discussion takes place over the difficulties of distinguishing attractive boys from women. The argument is short-circuited when one of the participants tartly observes that a hand thrust into the subject's underpants would easily settle the matter – a piece of common sense that would demolish a good many disguise plots.

Even in the real world, however, common sense is not always the bottom line, and the boundaries of mimesis are far more extensive than they are in the theatre. The witnesses who were deceived by Arbella Stuart saw nothing more intimate than her hair and her clothing, but they also detected nothing in her manner to suggest that any surprises might lie hidden beneath the clothing: gender here was a matter of behaviour and costume. There are a number of famous cases of people who successfully lived cross-gendered for years, for example the Chevalier d'Éon as a woman, and the jazz pianist Billy Tipton as a man. Tipton's sex was discovered only after his death, by the medical examiner; his wife and children (the children were adopted) had been entirely unaware of it. This means, obviously, that the marriage was without the usual sorts of intimacy, but his wife explained that this suited both of them, and the marriage was long and happy. This all sounds quite inconceivable, but Diane Middlebrook's superb biography of Tipton renders the story both credible and touchingly human. Initially Tipton passed as a man because in the 1930s for a woman to perform in jazz clubs as anything but a vocalist was simply impossible. The band members from her early years, whom Middlebrook tracked down and interviewed, said they of course knew she was a woman; her cross-dressing was what made the band viable. Gradually the impersonation became the person. Tipton's wife, a stripper, said she was initially attracted to him precisely because he was unlike the other men she had known, gentle and affectionate, and not eager for sex – an unusual kind of man, in her experience, and since she had been badly mistreated by sexually aggressive men in the past, she was grateful for his manner and found him easy to fall in love with. He explained his physical aloofness by saying he had been seriously injured in an accident and was obliged to wear heavy elastic bandages around his chest all the time; obviously they never saw each other naked. Out of this fiction Tipton constructed an entirely satisfactory life with a wife, and later with adopted children, for whom the fiction was fact.

It would be incorrect here to say that all Tipton's family knew of him was his costume. The costume represented an inner truth. That truth was constructed, but aren't all our selves constructed? The Billy Tipton story is no more incredible than the innumerable stories of people with aristocratic pretensions who turn out to have come from humble origins – the facts of gender seem to us much more basic and undeniable than the facts of social class, but surely this is an illusion. Billy Tipton's or Arbella Stuart's sexual anatomy would have been the ultimate reality only for the purposes of one particular type of sexual intercourse. For other forms of interaction, however – indeed, for most of what constitutes life – gender is not a matter of anatomy but of self-presentation.

The performative elements of gender of course took on an additional complexity in the Elizabethan theatre, where the women's roles were played by men. There are no simple explanations for why the culture wanted to exclude women from the stage. It relates to a whole complex of Renaissance attitudes towards women, and it is always explained in the period by saying that actresses were tantamount to prostitutes: for a woman to display herself on stage was to violate all the canons of female modesty and chastity. Such assumptions about women were universal in the Renaissance, on the Continent as well; but the English were the only culture in Europe to attempt to solve the problem by maintaining a transvestite public theatre. The practice, however, was genuinely naturalized in England. Thomas Coryat travelling in Italy was surprised to find that the actresses he saw there were as good at playing women's roles as boys in England were.[5]

At the same time, moralizing attacks on the Elizabethan theatre tend to focus particularly on the transvestism of the stage, and consider it an enticement to and cover for sexual, and particularly homosexual, activity. The charge rarely pretends to be supported by evidence and appears preposterous to modern eyes, but it does register something about the extent to which homoeroticism was institutionalized in Elizabethan culture. Three-quarters of Shakespeare's Sonnets are love-poems to a young man, a fact that was unproblematic in Shakespeare's time, but one that criticism has only recently been willing to acknowledge. How much of an issue, then, was homoeroticism in the age?

To begin with the legal situation, sodomy was a capital crime, and fulminations against the act were a staple of polemical literature of all kinds.

Anti-theatrical tracts assumed that the boys who played the women's roles on stage played them in life as well; anti-Catholic invective declared ecclesiastical celibacy to be a cover for institutionalized buggery; judicial indictments for political or religious crimes often included additional charges of sodomy. Indeed, sodomy tended to serve as a gloss on whatever the culture considered worst or most threatening: those accused of atheism or sedition were almost invariably declared also to be sodomites. The corollary, however, is that the charge is almost never found in isolation; in fact, the legal definition of sodomy was exceedingly narrow. According to the Lord Chief Justice, Sir Edward Coke, the sex had to be non-consensual, a rape; the prosecution had to be able to prove that there had been both anal penetration and an ejaculation ('*emissio seminis*' alone, Coke observes, 'maketh it not buggery'); [6] the courts also required a witness, and there were strict rules about who could serve as a witness in such cases. The law as elucidated by the Lord Chief Justice said nothing about sex between consenting male partners, about sex between men other than anal sex, about homosexual activity of any sort performed in private: none of these legally constituted sodomy. In the popular mind the term covered a multitude of horrendous sins, not all of them by any means involving homosexuality; but precisely for that reason it is significant that sodomy was legally construed in such a way that it could hardly ever be prosecuted. Bruce Smith's study of the Assize courts in the home counties reveals a total of only six sodomy trials in the entire reign of Elizabeth; all but one involved the rape of a minor, and five of the six resulted in acquittals.[7] Heterosexual fornication and even sex with animals were prosecuted much more energetically.

How can Shakespeare's Sonnets, with their open declarations of the poet's love for the beautiful young man, 'the master-mistress of my passion', be part of this cultural scene? The most direct answer is that sodomy was not equivalent to homoeroticism, and English Renaissance culture did not, in fact, display a morbid fear of homoeroticism as such. On the contrary, the love of men for other men was both a fact of life and an essential element in the operation of the patronage system. The love of men for other men tended to be idealized, whereas the love of men for women was often presented as dangerous and destructive – as it is in the Shakespeare sonnets. The rhetoric of male friendship in the period is precisely that of passionate love – the line between the homosocial and the sodomitical was a firm but exceedingly fine one, and could, of course, lie dangerously in the eye of the beholder. And though female homoeroticism was in less danger of being construed in sexual terms, by the 1590s a term for lesbianism – 'tribadry' – had entered the language, and both Jonson and Donne allude to women practising it.[8]

One's point of view on these matters was everything. The association of the stage's transvestite boys with homosexual prostitution is found not only in puritan polemicists but in the playwrights themselves; in the latter cases, however, the attitude implied tends to be neither anxious nor outraged, but liberal and permissive. In Thomas Middleton's *Father Hubburd's Tales*, a budding London rake is advised 'to call in at the Blackfriars, where he should see a nest of boys able to ravish a man';[9] this is not a warning, but a recommendation. At the opening of Ben Jonson's *Epicoene*, the fashionable Clerimont appears with a pageboy who is described as 'his ingle' – his catamite, or boy-lover – but the fact is offered merely as one of a number of indications of the pleasant life of a London playboy.[10] In *The Alchemist*, the case is cited of a bankrupt captain who has, through the magician's art, been able to:

> Arrive at competent means, to keep himself,
> His punk, and naked boy, in excellent fashion,
> And be admired for't.
>
> (3.4.80–2)

The punk and naked boy are female and male prostitutes respectively. None of these good-natured invocations of homosexual activity displays any animus whatever against sodomy.

For the readers of Shakespeare's age, the locus classicus for the idealization of homosexual feeling was Christopher Marlowe's *Hero and Leander*, published (twice) in 1598, but circulating in manuscript for at least five years before that. Indeed, one of the most striking aspects of the poem is its overt sexuality. There are Italian poems like this, but almost none in English until the next century; it is emotionally very daring. It is also very open about its sexual interests – the tradition that says that Marlowe was gay gets a good deal of support from *Hero and Leander*. Nevertheless (or perhaps therefore), it became an instant classic.

Marlowe describes both Hero and Leander as infinitely desirable; but the praise of Leander is much more frankly sexual than that of Hero, and specifically homosexual. Gods and men pine away for Hero, but the measure of Leander's beauty is not that women desire him, but that men do: 'Jove might have sipped out nectar from his hand' (I.62)[11] – he is as desirable as Ganymede; had Hippolytus seen him he would have abandoned his chastity; 'The barbarous Thracian soldier, moved with naught / Was moved with him, and for his favour sought' (I.81–2) – rough trade solicits him. None of this comes from Marlowe's source, Musaeus, where Leander is not described; in the Greek original, Hero is beautiful, and Leander is all desire, the validation of her beauty.

Marlowe is certainly daring, though less so in a Renaissance context than he seems now – for adult men to be attracted to good-looking youths was quite conventional. Still, there is no way of arguing that Marlowe is being *merely* conventional, that he does not really mean it, or does not mean it the way it sounds. The first sestiad includes a teasing description of how beautiful Leander's body is:

> How smooth his breast was, and how white his belly,
> And whose immortal fingers did imprint
> That heavenly path, with many a curious dint,
> That runs along his back
>
> (I.65–6)

and the second sestiad has an extraordinary passage about Neptune making passes at Leander as he swims the Hellespont. Nothing here suggests that Marlowe feels, or expects his readers to feel, any anxiety over the enthusiastic depiction of a man making love to another man. The scene is not moralistic, but appreciative and comic.

The closest analogue to Shakespeare's Sonnets to the young man is Richard Barnfield's overtly homoerotic series of sonnets to a beloved youth, published in *Cynthia, With Certaine Sonnets* in 1595. Love poetry in the 1590s included celebrations of the love of men for men:

> Sometimes I wish that I his pillow were,
> So might I steal a kiss, and yet not seen
>
> (viii, 1–2) [12]

Barnfield's long poem *The Affectionate Shepherd* (1594), celebrating the poet's love for a youth inevitably called Ganymede, confronts the cultural ambivalence implicit in idealized homoeroticism:

> If it be sin to love a sweet-fac'd boy, ...
> If it be sin to love a lovely lad;
> Oh then sin I, for whom my soul is sad.
>
> (8–12)[13]

A letter written by King James to his favourite, the Duke of Buckingham, gives a good sense of how much the homoerotic was part of the currency of social relationships in Shakespeare's age:

> I cannot content myself without sending you this present, praying God that I may have a joyful and comfortable meeting with you and that we may make at this Christmas a new marriage ever to be kept hereafter; for, God so love me, as I desire only to live in the world for your sake, and that I had rather live banished in any part of the earth with you than live a sorrowful widow's life

without you. And so God bless you, my sweet child and wife, and grant that ye may ever be a comfort to your dear dad and husband. James R.[14]

The metamorphic quality of the king's sexuality in this rhetoric is notable: he proposes marriage to Buckingham and then imagines himself in succession as widow, father and husband, and Buckingham as his child and wife. Gender here is entirely permeable; the king proposes an image of an endlessly mutating family.

The rhetoric of patronage, and of male friendship generally, was precisely the language of love, and it rendered all such relationships literally ambiguous. Such language does not necessarily imply a sexual relationship; but it is important to add that, by the same token, nothing in the language precludes it either – James *was* accused of making his favourites his lovers. The language of love in the age implies everything but tells nothing.

NOTES

1 *Essays*, Book 1, 21, trans. Donald Frame, *The Complete Works of Montaigne* (Palo Alto: Stanford University Press, 1948), p. 69.
2 *Anatomy of Melancholy*, 3.2.4.1 (1660), p. 510.
3 Ian Maclean, *The Renaissance Notion of Woman* (Cambridge: Cambridge University Press, 1980).
4 Sarah Gristwood, *Arbella* (London: Bantam, 2003), pp. 302–3.
5 For a full discussion, see my *Impersonations: The Performance of Gender in Shakespeare's England* (Cambridge: Cambridge University Press, 1996).
6 Cited, with other relevant material, in Bruce Smith, *Homosexual Desire in Shakespeare's England* (Chicago: University of Chicago Press, 1991), p. 50.
7 Ibid., p. 47.
8 The essential works on male homosexuality in England in the age of Shakespeare are Bruce Smith, *Homosexual Desire* (cited above), and Alan Bray, *Homosexuality in Renaissance England* (London: Gay Men's Press, 1982), and, on lesbianism, Valerie Traub, *The Renaissance of Lesbianism in Early Modern England* (Cambridge: Cambridge University Press, 2002).
9 Thomas Middleton, *The Collected Works*, general eds. G. Taylor and J. Lavagnino (Oxford: Oxford University Press, 2008), p. 159.
10 *Ben Jonson*, 11 vols., ed. C. H. Herford and Percy and Evelyn Simpson (Oxford: Clarendon Press, 1925–52), vol. V, 1.1.23.
11 Line references are to the text of *Hero and Leander* in my own edition, *Marlowe: The Complete Poems and Translations* (New York: Penguin Books, 2007).
12 Richard Barnfield, *The Complete Poems*, ed. George Klawitter (Selinsgrove, PA: Susquehanna University Press, 1990), p. 126.
13 Ibid., pp. 79–80.
14 *Letters of King James VI & I*, ed. G. P. V. Akrigg (Berkeley: University of California Press, 1984), p. 431.

READING LIST

Bray, Alan. *Homosexuality in Renaissance England.* New York: Columbia University Press, 1995, 2nd edn.

Breitenberg, Mark. *Anxious Masculinity in Early Modern England.* Cambridge: Cambridge University Press, 1996.

DiGangi, Mario. *The Homoerotics of Early Modern Drama.* Cambridge: Cambridge University Press, 1997.

Fisher, Will. *Materializing Gender in Early Modern Literature and Culture.* Cambridge: Cambridge University Press, 2006.

Foucault, Michel. *The History of Sexuality.* New York: Vintage, 1990.

Goldberg, Jonathan. *Sodometries: Renaissance Texts, Modern Sexualities.* Palo Alto: Stanford University Press, 1992.

Ingram, Martin. *Church Courts, Sex and Marriage in England, 1570–1640.* Cambridge: Cambridge University Press, 1987.

Jones, Ann Rosalind and Peter Stallybrass. *Renaissance Clothing and the Materials of Memory.* Cambridge: Cambridge University Press, 2001.

Laqueur, Thomas. *Making Sex: Body and Gender from the Greeks to Freud.* Cambridge, MA: Harvard University Press, 1990.

Maclean, Ian. *The Renaissance Notion of Woman.* Cambridge: Cambridge University Press, 1980.

Newman, Karen. *Fashioning Femininity and English Renaissance Drama.* Chicago: University of Chicago Press, 1991.

Orgel, Stephen. *Impersonations: The Performance of Gender in Shakespeare's England.* Cambridge: Cambridge University Press, 1996.

Sedgwick, Eve Kosofsky. *Between Men: English Literature and Male Homosocial Desire.* New York: Columbia University Press, 1985.

Smith, Bruce. *Homosexual Desire in Shakespeare's England.* Chicago: University of Chicago Press, 1991.

Stone, Lawrence. *The Family, Sex and Marriage in England 1500–1800.* New York: Harper and Row, 1977.

Traub, Valerie. *The Renaissance of Lesbianism in Early Modern England.* Cambridge: Cambridge University Press, 2002.

Woodbridge, Linda. *Women and the English Renaissance: Literature and the Nature of Woman Kind, 1540–1620.* Champagne-Urbana: University of Illinois Press, 1986.

16

ANTHONY DAWSON

Shakespeare on the stage

The actor

The most important element that distinguishes Shakespeare on the stage from Shakespeare on the page is the presence of the living actor. Shakespeare was well aware of this; he built into his plays an extraordinary attentiveness to the physical being of the actor, or, to be more precise, the actor/character. The body on the stage belongs to the actor but is in a sense the character as well. At the end of *King Lear*, for example, the distraught king and father carries the dead body of his daughter Cordelia on stage. He is an old man ('four score and upward') and she a mature woman. It is no easy feat to carry her (here our awareness of the actor's burden may very well cross with our sense of the character's). But her very weight is part of the point – a physical manifestation of the burden of pain that so many of the people on stage have at this point to shoulder, Lear more than any other. He lays her down, mourning her fate. Briefly he revives, hoping for, perhaps believing in, a reprieve from all this pain: 'This feather stirs; she lives!' For a moment he seems to believe she breathes, but then distraction takes over as the others try to speak to him. At the end, though, his concentration on her prone body is totally absorbing:

> And my poor fool is hanged. No, no no life ...
>   Thou'lt come no more.
> Never, never, never, never, never!
> Pray you undo this button. Thank you, sir.
> Do you see this? Look on her, look, her lips,
> Look there, look there!
>
> (5.3.264, 304–10)

The passage is fraught with interpretative difficulties that can be resolved only in the theatre and will be resolved differently in different performances. There is, for example, the matter of the button – is it his own, perhaps too tight at the neck, so that he feels suffocated? Or is it Cordelia's, preventing her from drawing that all-important breath which a moment ago he had hallucinated stirring the feather? And what of the last two lines, which are present in the Folio but absent from the quarto version of the play? Should they be included at all? One thing is clear about them: in a specific theatrical way, they direct the gaze of the spectators to what is going on in front of them. The lines are spoken to the onstage observers, but they apply equally to us who watch from outside the circle. The potential for distraction in the audience, always present in an open-air theatre such as Shakespeare's Globe, is thus controlled by the actor commanding us to look. And we are asked to watch for minute physical signs. The bodies, even particular parts of the bodies (lips, neck), of both main participants are made the object of our most intense scrutiny.

At such moments Shakespeare seems to offer a kind of *close-up*, long before the invention of cameras or the zoom lens. And I take this as exemplary of what we mean when we talk about Shakespeare on the stage. It has become a critical commonplace that Shakespeare wrote his plays to be acted, that they are incomplete on the page and need enactment to bring them fully to life. But what exactly does this claim mean, and how has it been put into practice over the centuries? These are the issues that I wish to address in this chapter. I began with an example of how what is written on the page seems to demand a certain kind of theatrical attention. This is paradigmatic, since it represents the way Shakespeare thinks about meaning: he typically starts on the stage, in the theatre.

Early modern audience members seemed to sense the emotional power of such close encounters; at least, they reacted precisely to the evocative physicality of actors. A well-known moment from the early history of Shakespeare criticism is a short account of a performance of *Othello* written by an Oxford cleric, Henry Jackson, after a production at the University in 1610.[1] In it Jackson praises the young male actor who played the role of Desdemona. He calls attention especially to the death scene, in which, he says, she (he uses feminine forms even though the actor is male) 'implored the pity of the audience' through her posture, as she lay across the bed, and especially by her facial expression. What is remarkable here is the attention to physical detail, the 'close-up' effect that the performance encourages and makes affective use of. The idea is to *move* the audience, and the medium for doing so is the actor's physical being, his/her exploitation of the body and its myriad ways of generating meaning and emotion, even when the character the actor is playing is dead.

The history of Shakespeare on the stage is to a large extent a history of embodiment. Let us take a look at a couple of other early examples. In an elegy for Richard Burbage, the leading actor in Shakespeare's company, the author writes of Burbage's mastery of various important Shakespearian roles, one of which is 'Young Hamlet'. The elegist goes on to praise Burbage's skill:

> Oft have I seen him leap into the grave,
> Suiting the person which he seemed to have
> Of a sad lover with so true an eye
> That there, I would have sworn, he meant to die.

Once again we note a concentration on the physical: the impulsive leap into the grave, the despairing eye of the lover. The scene described is probably the graveyard scene from *Hamlet*, during which, as one early text (the least reliable) has it, the distraught hero leaps into Ophelia's grave to confront Laertes and assert the superiority of his grief over that of her brother. Critics have been divided over whether to accept this as evidence for how Hamlet was performed during the period – is it not inconsistent with his princeliness, some wonder, that he should stoop to such undignified behaviour? But the key point for me is not Hamlet's dignity but the writer's insistence on physical movement and facial expression, especially the eyes, and their links to the interpretation of character.

Other commentary from the period also suggests a concentration on the power of the actors' bodies to evoke strong emotion. Thomas Nashe, a writer and friend of the theatre in the 1590s, talks of how Shakespeare's *1 Henry VI* resurrects the historical Lord Talbot on stage through the physical presence of 'the tragedian that represents his person' and how the actor, who seemed actually to be Talbot again alive and 'fresh bleeding', drew the tears of 'ten thousand spectators at least'. Elizabethan astrologer Simon Forman in a private diary writes of the effect that plays he saw at the Globe had on him; his accounts ramble, but at times he recalls a striking moment that allows us to imagine once again that crucial theatrical embodiment. Of Macbeth, for example, he writes, 'the blood on his hands could not be washed off by any means, nor from his wife's hands which handled the bloody daggers in hiding them, by which means they became both much amazed and affronted'; and later, obviously haunted by Lady Macbeth, he speaks of how she 'did rise in the night in her sleep and walk[ed] and talked and confessed all and the doctor noted her words'.[2] This last detail draws attention to staging – perhaps the doctor held a 'table' or commonplace book, and most probably he stood to the side, an observer, like the audience, of Lady Macbeth's tormented self-incrimination. If we flash forward almost 200 years, to the great performances of Sarah Siddons as Lady Macbeth at Drury Lane in the 1790s, we encounter something similar, though in other respects the stage values could hardly have been more different (male actor as opposed to female, outdoor amphitheatre with little scenery and no artificial lighting as opposed to grand indoor theatre with candelabra and elaborate stage machinery, etc.). For one spectator, the effect of Siddons' sleepwalking scene was so directly physical that he reported to a friend, 'Well, sir, I smelt blood. I swear I smelt blood.'[3]

This suggests a kind of continuity in the history of Shakespeare on stage despite the enormous shifts in style and scenic representation that have marked the way the plays have been performed over the centuries. What ultimately underpins that sense of continuity, I think, is character, the bedrock of Shakespearian effect. What we call character, the Elizabethans called 'person' (from *persona*, the Latin word for 'mask' and by extension for role or character represented by the mask). In Nashe's formulation, it is the 'person' of Talbot that is 'represented' by the actor, so that the effect is generated by a complex mix of presence and absence – the actor is present but also absent, in that he is not himself but the character, and the character is absent (because fictional) but also present in the actions and words of the actor. Part of the effect, then, derives from the audience's awareness of make-believe (the *persona*), but the fictional carries within it a sense of the reality of the person represented (he or she is 'like us' in certain ways). The actor's physical being is the ligature between these two levels, the basis of what William Archer called the spectator's 'dual consciousness' (we know it's 'only' a play, and yet we accept it as real).[4]

Thus, though characters are not the same as real people, they resemble them in important ways, and audiences react to them as though they were. This has sometimes raised the ire of literary critics such as L.C. Knights, who in 1933 published a little book entitled, mockingly, *How Many Children Had Lady Macbeth?*, in which he attacked as naive the treatment of literary artifacts as though they were people and argued that the right way to read Shakespeare was to regard the plays as highly complex verbal constructs (poems, in a word) whose internal relations are the basis of their meaning. With the advent of post-modernism, more radical scepticism has been levelled at the idea of character, since, it is argued, to concentrate on character is to assume, falsely, that individual subjectivity is coherent, stable and autonomous, whereas the truth is precisely the opposite – human beings are 'subjects' in the sense that they are subjected to countless external determinants that constitute them, and thus are fractured and mobile, shifting and unstable. Despite such demurrals, it is character over the centuries that has caught the attention of actors and audiences alike, character that has been the main driver of meaning and effect.

But character is not static or fixed. Personhood is defined by actorly movement and language and the corresponding emotions that are thereby produced, and it is also affected materially by the scenic components of the performance, including the stage space itself. This was true in the open amphitheatres like the Globe for which Shakespeare conceived his plays, but it is no less true for the theatre of David Garrick in the eighteenth century or Laurence Olivier in the twentieth. Character in this sense is a process, something that unfolds during the performance. How actors over the years have handled the challenge of embodying character, what the Elizabethans called 'personation', within a particular stage space, constitutes the essence of Shakespeare on the stage.

Garrick offers a splendid example; Hamlet was one of his most famous roles, and one of his most avid fans was a young German traveller and scientist, Georg Lichtenberg, who wrote detailed reports of the great actor's performance. His description of Hamlet's encounter with his father's ghost captures both Garrick's brilliantly calculated movements and the effect they had on the audience. Playing on the spacious stage of the Drury Lane theatre, which had the scenic capability to suggest actual battlements, Garrick moved to one side, near the proscenium pillar, in order to draw the audience's attention away from the part of the stage where the ghost would soon appear. He could thus whirl around when Horatio alerts both Hamlet and the audience to the ghost's sudden presence. In Lichtenberg's account, he 'turns sharply and at the same moment staggers back two or three paces with his knees giving way under him ... his mouth is open: thus he stands rooted to the spot, with legs apart ... His whole demeanour is so expressive of terror that it made my flesh creep even before he began to speak'.[5] Indeed, the whole audience, absorbed by the actor's intensity of movement, is 'terror-struck' even before the actual appearance of the ghost. Garrick's intensely physical style was a matter of the most calculated art. It was said that he had contrived a mechanical wig for this very scene, so that upon the ghost's uncanny appearance his hair actually began to lift off the back of his head. Such details, while clearly artificial, were part of the bodily technique that Garrick employed, which served his aim of representing a certain kind of Hamlet, a man of feeling with a profound love of his father.

Garrick's way of using and displaying the body in performance, while it may seem too studied to us, is noteworthy not only for the fact that it was seen at the time as a triumph of naturalism, but also because it to a large extent defined the way actors approached roles for centuries. Even now, the traditional Anglo-American approach to Shakespearian character owes more to Garrick than it might acknowledge. His attention to physical detail as a way to express the inner life of the character, his attunement to the quick, sometimes imperceptible, sometimes violent, shifts from one emotion to another, his understanding of Shakespeare as liberal, sensible and morally serious, these qualities still, in different ways, underwrite most performances in the English-speaking world.

But there have been and still are quite different approaches to representing persons on stage. Let me jump from eighteenth-century London to late twentieth-century Germany, where experimental approaches to Shakespeare's plays have been the norm rather than the exception. These productions have often sought to radically destabilize and invert traditional ways of staging Shakespeare and hence of understanding character. A production of *Timon of Athens*, for example, directed by Franz Patrick Steckel in Bochum in 1990, went to extraordinary lengths to externalize most of the characters, Timon especially, who was transformed into a dark and melancholic emblem. All the characters wore huge, distorted masks and heavy robes designed by Berlin artist Dieter Hacker; the masks evoked the greed and hypocritical self-interest of the false friends who surround Timon, whose mask resembled a hollowed-out crater. The stage itself was uncluttered, a bare platform in autumnal colours. Monstrous and grotesque, the figures inhabiting that space were clearly allegorical, as was the actorly movement, slow, balletic and ritualistic. But this did not prevent a precise sense of character emerging from 'behind each depersonalized figure';[6] it's just that the characters, in tune with the overall tenor of this strange play, were like those of a modern morality drama, more fixed and less unpredictable than we are used to in Shakespeare.

The production ended with a pointed visual effect, one that reveals a great deal about the actor's relation to his role. Instead of a curtain call, the actors stepped forward in sequence, took off their masks and placed them ceremonially on the stage. This put actual human faces into dialogue with their grotesque counterparts and also produced an 'uncanny feeling of witnessing a demonstration of the theorem that people are both identical and not identical with their masks'.[7] All together, the large number of 'heads' arranged on the stage floor challenged the audience to think about the intimate relation between the actor's body and the person he depicts. The masks added a dimension to the kinds of interplay I spoke of earlier, since they supplemented the body itself so that there were three elements instead of two contributing to the complex figure of the person. This tends to be true of masked performance in any culture or time, but what distinguished Steckel's production was a certain self-consciousness about the process, a kind of 'alienation effect' represented graphically in the final tableau, and provoking the question, where indeed *is* the person and what constitutes him (or her)?

The scene

In discussing the making of character, I have inevitably glided into discussing scenography, the overall look of a production and how that contributes to meaning and effect. Character and scene are inextricably woven together, and have been since Burbage appeared on the open platform of the Globe in close touch with the surrounding sea of spectators. In order to pursue this idea somewhat more systematically, I want to consider the origins of the kind of radical scene-painting featured in the *Timon* production just described. To do so, we have to think back to the nineteenth century, when a vivid pictorialism ruled the stage, together with a taste for detailed, historical, even archaeological, accuracy; thus the assassination and forum scenes in *Julius Caesar* might be played in front of a vast replica of the Roman senate-house and Forum, effected through a subtle blending of architectural elements and perspective scene-painting. In England, it was Charles Kean, the son of the great Romantic actor Edmund Kean, who, in the 1850s, brought this style to its apex; designers preparing a production of *The Merchant of Venice*, for example, were shipped off to Venice to ensure that their rendition of St Mark's Square was authentic. Hermione's trial in *The Winter's Tale* was set in a reproduction of the Greek theatre at Syracuse; the painted backdrop featured a huge crowd in the stands, the artificial citizens blending with the real actors.[8] (See Figure 2.) This kind of thing tended to diminish the affective power of the actors, who were dwarfed by the sets. And it often led to rearrangement of Shakespeare's texts, so that scenes with the same settings could be run together. An even worse problem with such elaborate staging was that it seriously slowed down the action, often requiring 10- or 15-minute breaks between scenes as stagehands shifted the scenery.

Henry Irving, the greatest English actor-manager in the latter part of the century, was often guilty of such long interruptions, but they produced some of his most vivid scenic effects; he moved away from painted backdrops, using architectural features that took advantage of the great depth of his Lyceum stage, enhanced by subtle lighting effects (Irving preferred gas to the new fashion of electric light). His Venice, with its bridges and palazzi, reproduced the city, and the invented, shadowy scene when, as Shylock, he returned from dinner with the Christians and knocked futilely on the locked door, only to find his daughter gone, gained force from the stage picture: it made manifest an element of melancholy in the character that was new and insightful – and frequently imitated since. In his hands, Shylock became a tragic figure, a move that was facilitated by the removal of the entire fifth act. Such text-bending was neither new nor uncommon; in the seventeenth century, Nahum Tate re-wrote *King Lear* with a happy ending, a version that held the stage for 150 years, and in the eighteenth, Garrick made sweeping changes to the last third of *Hamlet*, eliminating what he called 'the rubbish of the fifth act', in order to enhance his reading of Hamlet as active and unyielding in his revenge.[9] Such moves have always been the prerogative of

2 While painted multitudes look on, Hermione, supported by her women, appeals to her enthroned husband during the trial scene of *The Winter's Tale*, as staged by Charles Kean, Princess's Theatre, London, 1856.

producers, from Shakespeare's time (the early quartos of *Hamlet* and *King Lear* attest to this) to our own.

Inevitably, pictorial elaboration such as Irving's spawned a reaction. As the nineteenth century progressed, a few producers sought ways to get out from under the crushing burden of scenery by thinking their way back to the original conditions of Shakespearian staging. The new emphasis was on getting rid of multiple sets and replacing them with a platform that jutted out beyond the proscenium, thus bringing the actors closer to the audience. This unlocalized space allowed rapid movement, and easy transition from one scene to another. In the 1880s, William Poel launched a campaign for rapidly spoken, uninterrupted Shakespeare on a (relatively) bare stage.[10] Poel was an enthusiast (some might call him a crank), but his influence is undeniable. His was a quest for a different kind of authenticity – not to reproduce the places where Shakespeare's plays are set, but to reproduce how they were played at the Rose or the Globe. This meant an open platform, Elizabethan costumes and unvaried lighting that simulated the outdoor light of the Elizabethan public theatres, as well as rapid verse-speaking and continuous movement. 'We are less conscious of the artificiality of the stage where a few well-understood conventions, adroitly handled, are substituted for attempts at an impossible verisimilitude', wrote George Bernard Shaw apropos of one of Poel's productions.[11] But those productions, unfortunately, tended to be amateurish, and his desire to return to Elizabethan modes of staging often lost sight of the immediacy and vitality of theatrical life.

Still, Poel's general approach was taken up by more skilled producers such as Harley Granville-Barker, who succeeded in finding ways to 'invent a new hieroglyphic of scenery', as he wrote at the time, without losing the urgency and appeal of Shakespeare's texts.[12] For Granville-Barker, Poel's method was overly 'archaeological' – 'there is something too much of the Elizabethan letter, as contrasted with the Elizabethan spirit'.[13] In his own productions of *The Winter's Tale*, *Twelfth Night* and *A Midsummer Night's Dream,* staged between 1912 and 1914, Granville-Barker sought ways to reproduce that spirit in a modern, but unlocalized, style. In *A Midsummer Night's Dream*, for instance, his fairies were strange, golden, mechanical creatures who moved like figures in an exotic ballet through a stylized and dreamlike forest; forgoing the sorts of illusionism that had brought live rabbits unto the greensward in productions of the play just a few years previously, Granville-Barker deliberately undermined stage illusion by re-imagining the fairies as something strange and otherworldly. He also dispensed with Mendelssohn's music, which had become de rigueur, and replaced it with English folk tunes. Granville-Barker was influenced by the modernist experiments that were changing the face of art across Europe in the first decades of the twentieth century, both in the theatre and more broadly (see Figure 3); the trend was towards simplification, abstraction and non-illusionism, using lighting as well as scene design to give a new meaning to stage illusion – no longer naturalistic but abstract and self-contained. In some ways lighting was the most important innovation of all; for Gordon Craig, a radical designer/director and son of the great Victorian actress Ellen Terry, light was 'the true and sole *material* of the Art of the Theatre'.[14] It was the expressionistic, sculptural potential of lighting that most fascinated innovators like Craig, and this has had an influence on productions, even relatively conventional ones, to this day. The downside was that even more than pictorialism, this had the potential to reduce the actor's role to what Craig called an *Übermarionette* (i.e. super-puppet).

If, in Germany, expressionism, with its brooding play of shadows, its huge, stark staircases and its melodramatic, stylized acting became the dominant trend in the 1920s, in England the big news was the move to modern dress. '*Hamlet* in plus-fours', staged in London in 1925 by the Birmingham Repertory Theatre under the general direction of Barry Jackson, while not the first modern-dress production, was by far the most notorious.[15] Though there was a tremendous fuss in the press testifying to the shock of such innovation, the main effect of the modern costumes (dinner jackets, cloche hats, bobbed hair and the like) was not in the end to shock the audience but to liberate the actors, and hence to give them the centrality that they frequently lacked during the reign of pictorialism and that of its modernist reaction. The actor playing Claudius, for example, remarked that the siphon bottle from which he added a squirt of soda to his tumbler of whisky after the play scene gave him a naturalistic grip on the moment. The actors could render their characters in terms familiar to their audience, and their success in doing so can be measured by the fact that several of the ideas about those characters that are now commonplace can be traced back to this production: Claudius as well-groomed, charming, 'foxily diplomatic',[16] Polonius as shrewd and politic, Ophelia as sexually explosive in her madness scene and Hamlet (reduced to being one of an ensemble and not a major star) as disenchanted and anti-Romantic, 'loose-tongued' and 'bawdy-minded'.[17] (See Figure 4.) Here is a clear example of cooperation between the look of a production and its representation of character; the costumes and props led the way, and the simple set, while somewhat more traditional in look (painted backdrops were used), enabled rapid movement and continuity between scenes, so that the actors could concentrate on making their characters speak directly to the spectators.

As the century progressed, there emerged various performative strains, all rooted in the developments of the early decades. On the Continent, a strongly

3 Modernist design, merging the onstage audience (foreground) with offstage audience, during the 'play-within-the-play' scene of *A Midsummer Night's Dream*, as staged by Harley Granville-Barker, 1914.

4 The notorious modern-dress production of *Hamlet* with Ophelia (Muriel Hewitt) and Hamlet (Colin Keith-Johnston), as staged by the Birmingham Repertory Theatre, the Kingsway Theatre, London, 1925.

politicized Shakespeare was often on display, particularly in Germany and Eastern Europe. Brecht's openly non-illusionist, politically challenging 'epic theatre' was influential, as was the brooding expressionism of figures such as Leopold Jessner in Berlin or Karel Hilar in Prague. The latter's *Hamlet*, mounted in 1926 in a dark and almost colourless environment, harshly lit and with screens and massive pieces of furniture appearing and disappearing on moveable platforms, featured an alienated, youthful prince, impotent and inexperienced, 'alternately confused and vehement',[18] distant from the centres of power. As in Jessner's openly anti-monarchical version in the same year, Hamlet, played by Edouard Kohout, was a sensitive poetic figure crushed by the machinery of power. It is striking how similar this conception is to the version presented by the RSC at Stratford almost forty years later (directed by Peter Hall in 1965), when David Warner, tall, gangly and unformed, a long reddish scarf thrown loosely around his neck, also spoke directly to the alienation and resentment of a (different) post-war generation; like Kohout, he found himself trapped and rendered impotent by a well-oiled political apparatus, made visible in John Bury's sets, which were constructed largely of gleaming black Formica and bespoke an efficient, glossy and impenetrable court.

In the intervening years in Britain, a somewhat more conservative approach to the meanings of Shakespeare's texts held sway, due partly to the inevitable reverence towards his language in the English-speaking world. In other countries and languages, directors often felt freer to experiment and confront, to use Shakespeare for their own, often overtly political, purposes. Nevertheless, through the 1930s and into the 1940s, a succession of important directors, actors and designers at the Old Vic and Stratford carried on the work begun by Granville-Barker. Of these, Theodore Komisarjevsky, John Gielgud and Tyrone Guthrie are probably the most important. Komisarjevsky directed a number of dazzling and unconventional shows at Stratford between 1932 and 1938, in unlocalized and sometimes whimsical settings; using elements from a number of different periods which were hung together in an almost 'hallucinogenic' manner,[19] he took a 'metaphoric' approach, designed to deliver 'a context for interpretation', that would not be seen again in Britain till the 1960s and 1970s.[20] Gielgud's style was more cautious: he, like his favourite design team (called 'Motley'), preferred localized settings, but with a basic, single-unit adaptable set, easily altered for different scenes, and a good-sized open playing space downstage, which gave increasing prominence to the actors.[21]

Tyrone Guthrie took this latter feature the furthest by overseeing, with designer Tanya Moiseiwisch, the construction of the first fully equipped, modern 'Shakespearian' stage – that at Stratford, Ontario. Housed first under a tent in 1953, and then incorporated into the permanent building that followed a few years later, Moiseiwisch's open stage was a kind of translation of the Elizabethan theatre into a modern shape; surrounded by spectators on three sides, it featured a spacious playing area encircled by a few wide stairs, a neutral back wall and a simple central balcony held up by pillars, with an entrance-way underneath. This has proved the model for dozens of stages since, just because it offers the flexibility, the freedom from the conventions of realistic illusion and the opportunity for continuous performance missing from the traditional proscenium theatre. On it, the actor can reclaim his centrality and command from the audience a kind of intimacy and attention similar to that which prevailed on the Elizabethan stage. Guthrie, always restless and even iconoclastic in his thinking, became its champion almost by accident. In 1937, he mounted a controversial production of *Hamlet* at the Old Vic, with Laurence Olivier in the main role, an interpretation that took its cue from Freudian theory by stressing Hamlet's Oedipal fixation on his mother. After a successful London run, the company took the production to Elsinore in Denmark, where the plan was to perform it in the castle courtyard. But terrible weather on the opening night, together with the arrival of royalty to see the show, forced a different expedient on the company. Having decided to move to the ballroom of the hotel where they had been staying, they erected a small makeshift stage fronted by steps leading to an open space on the ballroom floor. 'The effect aimed at', says Guthrie in an article written shortly afterwards, 'was the atmosphere of a café chantant with the audience in the most informal and closest contact with the actors.' The actors bravely improvised their way through, keeping invention going till near the end, when they began to flag. Nevertheless, the experience convinced Guthrie that 'intimacy between the audience and the players is the first essential'[22] and started him on the quest that ended at Stratford Ontario (which, in turn, inspired a host of similar projects, perhaps most importantly the Swan at Stratford-upon-Avon).[23]

During the post-war years, especially after the formation of the Royal Shakespeare Company under Peter Hall in 1961, Stratford became the dominant venue for Shakespeare. In the 1960s and 1970s, the English theatre to some extent played catch-up relative to its continental neighbours, moving frequently to scenographically daring and politically challenging performances. Of these, the most famous, if least political, was Peter Brook's endlessly inventive version of *A Midsummer Night's Dream* at Stratford in 1970. Brook, looking for ways to free the play from the weight of romantic tradition, took his inspiration from the art of the circus and the acrobat, because, he said, 'they both make purely theatrical statements. We've worked through a language of acrobatics to find a new approach to a magic that we know cannot be reached by 19th-century conventions.'[24] The stage, designed by Sally Jacobs, was a brightly lit white box, its emptiness beckoning the audience to use imagination in bringing to life this play that is in many ways *about* imagination. Puck and Oberon, dressed in brilliantly coloured satin, flew on trapezes. (See Figure 5.) At one dazzling point, Puck, asked to bring the magic flower, swung down on his trapeze while spinning a plate on a rod, and then passed it, still spinning, to Oberon. As one critic noted, 'The plate does not *become* the flower. Instead, the act of passing it becomes the *magic* of the flower.'[25] The lovers, though remaining on the ground, were fiercely acrobatic tumblers, sometimes directed by Puck on stilts (recalling Granville-Barker's anti-illusionist use of Puck almost sixty years previously). The forest, at times literally tangling the lovers, was made of coiled wires manipulated, in full view of the audience, by the fairies on the catwalk above. At the end, the curtain call became a gesture that forced the audience to think about its own role in the theatrical enterprise. On the final lines of Puck's epilogue ('Give me your hands if we be friends / And Robin shall restore amends'), the company advanced into the audience and shook hands with as many spectators as they could reach. The effect was to emphasize the fact of performance, and to stimulate questions about the relations between the performers, their roles and the 'persons' they play.

While Brook was reinventing a familiar play, other RSC directors began to take on plays rarely seen previously, giving them a strong political spin. Of these *Troilus and Cressida* is exemplary, partly because of its openness to both a distinctly anti-war interpretation, which chimed with the growing opposition to American involvement in Vietnam, and a bold investigation of the subterranean relations between violence and sex (both hetero- and homosexual).[26] *Troilus* became a signature play for the rest of

5 Oberon (Alan Howard), observed by Puck (John Kane), applies the magic wand/potion to Titania (Sara Kestelman) in Peter Brook's ground-breaking production of *A Midsummer Night's Dream* at Stratford, 1970.

the century – after two more RSC revivals in the 1980s, it was given four major productions during the following decade, three by the RSC and one at the National, more than any other Shakespeare play at those venues.[27] All four of these latter featured eclectic settings and up-to-date political commentary; in 1999 at the National, the Greeks were vaguely Homeric, the Trojans exotic and Middle Eastern, their differences highlighted by the use of black actors for the latter and white actors for the former. Other productions unabashedly mixed past and present in post-modernist style (coffee mugs and desk lamps on the table jostling with ancient-looking swords and bracelets – 1990), or mixed images of internecine conflict (contemporary Ireland and the Balkans with a dash of Lorca's Spain – 1998). And one seemed deliberately to evoke the bare flesh, leather jockstraps and camp eroticism of Barton's productions of the 1960s, suggesting that sex and war, like everything else, had become nothing but performance; thus was the political critique that motivated those earlier versions attenuated and undermined. Such 'post-modern' eclecticism has become the mark of most Shakespearian performance these days, time and location often fractured by the mixture of styles.

Another noteworthy feature of these productions was the prominence they gave to Cressida; in Trevor Nunn's version, after an unscripted attempt to reconnect with Troilus at the end, she stood rigid while Pandarus delivered his epilogue and the scabrous Thersites hovered at the back; the two men exited and the six huge doors of the set clanged shut, so that Cressida was imprisoned, a lonely victim of lust and war. This move to highlight woman's experience is a mark of Shakespearian performance (as indeed of much else) since at least the 1980s. A production of *Troilus* that I saw in 2006 brought all the women's roles to the forefront, especially that of Cassandra, who became a kind of chorus and appeared in almost every scene. It is, as well, not uncommon nowadays to see women taking on men's roles or to find men's roles being re-written as roles for women. I've lately seen a *Titus Andronicus* where Bassianus was played as a woman, so that his/her desire for Lavinia was reconfigured as an attempt at same-sex marriage. This of course is extreme, and it didn't work, but, besides exemplifying the director's prerogative (discussed above) to do what he/she wants with the text, it bespeaks a trend highlighted by events such as Fiona Shaw's celebrated appearance as Richard II in 1995, or the transforming of *King* into *Queen Lear* (1990). There have, in the last two decades, been a large number of such experiments, all of which indicate that women, after a long wait that began with the boy players of Elizabethan England, have moved closer to the centre of the Shakespearian stage. And in doing so, they have brought into view something that has always been there, if not always acknowledged – a complex set of interactions played out through the representation of bodies.

I want to end with one such representational moment, once again involving a bodily close-up – this time, not on the professional stage but in a humble classroom. The occasion was a performance of *Othello* by students (whom I regularly require to prepare abridged versions of particular plays). The scene was an ordinary industrial classroom with hard linoleum floors and fluorescent lighting, but transformed into Desdemona and Othello's bedchamber by the simple addition of a few props: the front desk moved to the middle of the room, canopied with a gauzy curtain and spread with a white duvet; a candle; the intrusive house lights turned off; Desdemona prone. 'Who's there? Othello?' – 'Ay, Desdemona.' – 'Will you come to bed, my lord?' (5.2.23–5). And out through the diaphanous curtain she reached her hand, lingeringly, the same 'liberal hand' she had extended to her distraught husband just minutes before (in a sequence from 3.4, when Othello demands, 'Give me your hand', and she complies, recalling ''twas that hand that gave away my heart'). That earlier gesture was here repeated in an evocative moment of grave theatrical embodiment. Despite the unpropitious environment, the extended hand, which spoke so eloquently of her tragic failure to comprehend, gave me a profound chill. I felt a little like the gentleman who 'smelt blood' as Sarah Siddons struggled to cleanse her guilty hands, or the Oxford scholar so deeply moved by the facial expression of that same Desdemona.

My point is that the sense of embodiment with which I began, and which I take to be a fundamental ground of Shakespearian meaning, can be engendered in the most unlikely circumstances. The key is to tap into a play's multiple registers – performative certainly, but also literary and psychological; to do them justice we need to mark as precisely as possible how physical performance, the movement of bodies on stage, concretizes a set of complex relations that we can identify as products of Shakespeare's wide-ranging and yet physically grounded intelligence. At its most intense, Shakespeare's thought begins in close-up, the body always out front ('Pray you, undo this button'). In that way it is always performative, always embedded in persons whose fortunes matter to us, deeply.

NOTES

1 Jackson's notice, written in Latin, is available in the original and in translation in the *Riverside Shakespeare* (Boston: Houghton Mifflin, 1997), 2nd edn, p. 1978.

2 Ibid., pp. 1966–7 (modernized).

3 Sheridan Knowles, quoted in A. C. Sprague, *Shakespearian Players and Performances* (Cambridge, MA: Harvard University Press, 1953), p. 67.

4 I have discussed this complex interplay around the idea of person in greater detail in Anthony B. Dawson and Paul Yachnin (eds.), *The Culture of Playgoing in Shakespeare's England* (Cambridge: Cambridge University Press, 2001), pp. 20–37.

5 Georg Lichtenberg, *Lichtenberg's visits to England, As Described in His Letters and Diaries*, trans. and annotated by Margaret L. Mare and W. H. Quarrell (Oxford: Clarendon Press, 1938), p. 10.

6 Wilhelm Hortmann, *Shakespeare on the German Stage: The Twentieth Century* (Cambridge: Cambridge University Press, 1998), p. 321.

7 Ibid., p. 322.

8 Dennis Kennedy, *Looking at Shakespeare: A Visual History of Twentieth Century Performance* (Cambridge: Cambridge University Press, 2001), 2nd edn, p. 27.

9 See G. W. Stone, 'Garrick's Long-Lost Alteration of *Hamlet*', *PMLA*, 49 (September 1934), 890–921.

10 A similar reaction was afoot in Germany, where, in 1889, a Shakespearian stage was established in Munich, designed by Karl Lautenschlager; it was used periodically till 1906. See Simon Williams, *Shakespeare on the German Stage 1586–1914* (Cambridge: Cambridge University Press, 1990), pp. 185–90.

11 Quoted in J. L. Styan, *The Shakespeare Revolution* (Cambridge: Cambridge University Press, 1977), p. 59.

12 Quoted in J. C. Trewin, *Shakespeare on the English Stage 1900–1964* (London: Barrie and Rockcliff, 1964), p. 56. In his still widely respected *Prefaces to Shakespeare*, Granville-Barker wrote: 'Gain Shakespeare's effects by Shakespeare's means if you can … But gain Shakespeare's effects, and it is your business to discern them' (London: Sidgwick & Jackson, 1927, rept. 1940), 1st series, p. xl.

13 *Evening News*, 3 December 1912, quoted in Dennis Kennedy, *Granville Barker and the Dream of Theatre* (Cambridge: Cambridge University Press, 1985), p. 151.

14 F. J. and L.-L. Marker, 'Craig and Appia: A Decade of Friendship and Crisis, 1914–1924', *Essays in Theatre*, 3:2 (May 1985), 69.

15 The same company had staged *Cymbeline* in modern dress a couple of years before. For a full account of this production, see my *Hamlet: Shakespeare in Performance* (Manchester: Manchester University Press, 1995), pp. 83–96.

16 Ivor Brown, *Saturday Review*, 29 August 1925.

17 Ibid., and J. T. G., *Sketch*, 2 September 1925.

18 Jarka Burian, '*Hamlet* in Postwar Czech Theatre', in Dennis Kennedy (ed.), *Foreign Shakespeare* (Cambridge: Cambridge University Press, 1993), p. 197.

19 Ralph Berry, 'Komisarjevsky at Stratford', *Shakespeare Survey*, 36 (1983), 81.

20 Kennedy, *Looking*, p. 132. An example of such a 'metaphoric' setting is the large octagonal sand-pit that was used as the main setting for John Barton and Peter Hall's ground-breaking production of *Troilus and Cressida* in 1960.

21 Ibid., p. 139.

22 Tyrone Guthrie, '*Hamlet* at Elsinore', *London Mercury*, 213 (July 1937), 248. For a fuller account, see my *Hamlet*, pp. 110–16.

23 Such theatres need to be distinguished from actual replicas, the most famous of which is 'Shakespeare's Globe' on the South Bank of the Thames, not far from where the original Globe stood. Constructed to be as authentic as possible, the

Globe was an experiment that turned into a commercial success – and has been most successful when it has moved away from the authenticity imperative and mounted productions with a more contemporary feel.

24 Interview with John Barber in the *Daily Telegraph*, 14 September 1970.

25 Peter Thomson, 'Shakespeare: Theatre Poet', *Shakespeare Survey*, 24 (1971), 126.

26 The play was presented three times between 1960 and 1976, all directed by John Barton: on his own in 1968, with Peter Hall in 1960 and with Barry Kyle in 1976.

27 At the RSC, Sam Mendes directed in 1990, Ian Judge in 1995 and Michael Boyd in 1998, while Trevor Nunn directed at the National in 1999. See my edition of *Troilus and Cressida* (Cambridge: Cambridge University Press, 2003), pp.52–64.

READING LIST

Barton, John. *Playing Shakespeare*. London and New York: Methuen, 1984.

Bate, Jonathan and Russell Jackson, eds. *Shakespeare: An Illustrated Stage History*. Oxford: Oxford University Press, 1996.

Bulman, James C., ed. *Shakespeare,Theory, and Performance*. London and New York: Routledge, 1996.

David, Richard. *Shakespeare in the Theatre*. Cambridge: Cambridge University Press, 1978.

Dawson, Anthony B. and Paul Yachnin. *The Culture of Playgoing in Shakespeare's England*. Cambridge: Cambridge University Press, 2001.

Foakes, R. A. *Illustrations of the English Stage*. Aldershot: Scolar Press, 1985.

Granville-Barker, Harley. *Prefaces to Shakespeare*. London: Sidgwick & Jackson, 1927–37.

Gurr, Andrew. *Playgoing in Shakespeare's London*. Cambridge: Cambridge University Press, 1987.

Hodgdon, Barbara and W. B. Worthen, eds. *A Companion to Shakespeare and Performance*. Oxford: Blackwell, 2005.

Holland, Peter. *English Shakespeares: Shakespeare on the English Stage in the 1990s*. Cambridge: Cambridge University Press, 1997.

Holland, Peter, ed. *Shakespeare, Memory and Performance*. Cambridge: Cambridge University Press, 2006.

Hortmann, Wilhelm. *Shakespeare on the German Stage: The Twentieth Century*. Cambridge: Cambridge University Press, 1998.

Kennedy, Dennis. *Looking at Shakespeare: A Visual History of Twentieth-Century Performance*. Cambridge: Cambridge University Press, 2001, 2nd edn.

Players of Shakespeare: a series published by Cambridge University Press,1988–, and edited by Robert Smallwood, with others; performers talk about their roles.

Rutter, Carol Chillington. *Enter the Body: Women and Representation on Shakespeare's Stage*. London and New York: Routledge, 2001.

Shakespeare in Performance series, 24 vols., general eds. J.R. Mulryne, J.C. Bulman and Margaret Shewring (Manchester: Manchester University Press, 1984–2006); individual volumes devoted to single plays.

Sprague, A.C. *Shakespearian Players and Performances*. Cambridge, MA: Harvard University Press, 1953.

Stern, Tiffany. *Rehearsal from Shakespeare to Sheridan*. Oxford: Oxford University Press, 2000.

Styan, J. L. *The Shakespeare Revolution*. Cambridge: Cambridge University Press, 1977.

Trewin, J. C. *Shakespeare on the English Stage 1900–1964*. London: Barrie and Rockcliff, 1964.

Wells, Stanley, ed. *Shakespeare in the Theatre: an Anthology of Criticism*. Oxford: Oxford University Press, 1997.

Wells, Stanley and Sarah Stanton, eds. *The Cambridge Companion to Shakespeare on Stage*. Cambridge: Cambridge University Press, 2002.

17

EMMA SMITH

The critical reception of Shakespeare

So much has been written about Shakespeare since Robert Greene's first dismissive reference to that 'upstart crow' in 1592 that it may seem perverse to deploy the trope of absence or loss to try to make sense of the volume of commentary.[1] Shakespeare's critical reception seems marked by the phenomenon of too much, rather than too little. But Shakespeare studies is littered with much-missed absences: *Love's Labours Won* (the mysterious play named in Francis Meres' *Palladis Tamia* of 1598), Shakespeare's private letters or diary, satisfactory drawings of the Globe or of any of Shakespeare's plays in contemporary performance, the records for the grammar school in Stratford for the relevant period, the holograph manuscript of *Hamlet* or indeed any of the plays or poems, the identity of Mr W.H., the dedicatee of the Sonnets published in 1609, the meaning of 'scamels', Caliban's unglossable word in *The Tempest* (2.2.17).[2] These literal unknowns mark the critical enterprise with the signs of loss. In the intervening centuries since Shakespeare, the critical tradition has tried to address this loss through literary tactics that closely resemble those of two familiar literary genres: the elegy, through which the lost is mourned and commemorated, and the detective story, by which the lost is reconstructed through the painstaking reading of evidence. Shakespeare studies has toggled between the detective and the elegiac as the most appropriate genres for its retrieval and construction of the lost object.

In what follows I attempt first to group critical responses to Shakespeare not chronologically but in terms of the particular identification of what it is critics are looking for: the lost text; the lost context; the lost plenitude; the lost performance. A final section takes stock of current critical approaches and gestures towards possible critical futures. At the end of the chapter I suggest some further reading, organized along a chronology of critical reception.

Text

'twere a paper lost
(*Cymbeline*, 1.3.3)

That no holograph manuscript of a work of Shakespeare exists might be thought to be the founding crisis of the discipline of Shakespeare studies. Fervent work to attribute to Shakespeare 'Hand D' in the collaboratively authored manuscript drama *The Book of Sir Thomas More* attests to the passionate scholarly desire to find this lost origin.[3] Generations of editors from Heminges and Condell in the 1623 Folio onwards have worked to establish a text of Shakespeare which in some way attends to or bodies forth the missing written text, and theories of bibliography have conjured up 'foul papers', 'bad quartos' and other textual phantoms to stand in place of what is lost. Fredson Bowers' memorable summary in 1959 describes the bibliographic aim of 'penetrating the veil of print and recovering the characteristics of the lost manuscript'; setting out issues with which all editors of Shakespeare must grapple, Bowers gives primary importance to the question, 'What was the nature of the lost manuscript which served as printer's copy?'[4]

When Heminges and Condell presented their edition of Shakespeare to the public in 1623, they claimed close kin with those working papers of their author. Whereas before, readers were 'abused with divers stolen and surreptitious copies' (eighteen of their plays had already been published), here they and their fellows are 'cured and perfect of their limbs ... as he conceived them. Who, as he was a happy imitator of Nature, was a most gentle expresser of it. His mind and hand went together: And what he thought, he uttered with that easiness, that we have scarce received from him a blot in his papers.'[5] That Shakespeare's own expression was effortless and, implicitly, that disruptions to that textual ease must therefore be attributed to denigrated outside agents – compositors, printers, actors, pirates – was a guiding principle of much editorial practice until the late twentieth century, which aimed to rescue the authentic words of the playwright from this collaborative corruption. Early editors also inherited Heminges and Condell's faith in the Folio texts, as transmitted through subsequent editions in 1632, 1663 and 1685, even while they cherry-picked from other early texts 'to select from thence whatever improves the Author'.[6] Thus Theobald's 1733 edition vowed to present 'the greatest Poet in his Original Purity', asserting that the quarto texts were pirated 'from piece-meal Parts surreptitiously obtain'd from the Theatres, uncorrect, and without the Poet's knowledge'.[7] For editors in the twentieth century, the theatrical provenance assigned to the quartos was the basis of their textual authority: discussing the principles for *Re-Editing*

Shakespeare for the Modern Reader (1984), Stanley Wells prepared the way for his substantive new Oxford edition (1986) because of an 'excessive [editorial] reliance on those texts which seem closest to Shakespeare's original papers rather than to the texts reflecting the theatre practice of his time', thus attempting to derive authority for something lost – Shakespeare's manuscript – from something else lost – 'the theatre practice of his time'.[8]

Towards the end of the twentieth century, critics re-examined some of bibliography's favoured narratives: Laurie Maguire on the fallacy of Greg's speculative theory of memorial reconstruction; Randall McLeod and Paul Werstine on Pollard's 'bad quartos'; Peter Blayney on the beguiling myth of piracy; Margreta de Grazia and Peter Stallybrass on paratextual features and apparently neutral editorial regularization.[9] Even Heminges and Condell's vision of Shakespeare's working practices was decisively revisited in a ground-breaking collection of essays on *King Lear* edited by Michael Warren and Gary Taylor as *The Division of the Kingdoms* (1983). The subtitle says it all: 'Shakespeare's Two Versions of *King Lear*'. In place of a lost original, the contributors to the volume substitute two authoritative printed texts, the 1608 quarto *History of King Lear and his Three Daughters* and the 1623 Folio *The Tragedie of King Lear*, each with 'independent dramatic integrity'.[10] The rapid mainstreaming of this new bibliographic orthodoxy in the *Oxford Shakespeare* (eds. Stanley Wells and Gary Taylor) and the *Norton Shakespeare* (general ed. Stephen Greenblatt) which provide edited versions of Q and F has had an effect on other contested play texts. In 2006 Arden published a two-volume *Hamlet* providing edited texts of Q1, Q2 and F.[11] Edited quarto texts have gone from the self-consciously maverick and provocatively titled *Shakespearian Originals* series published by Harvester Wheatsheaf to the canonized, blue-liveried *New Cambridge* texts, via Internet and other multiple editions.[12] Depending on your viewpoint, then, Shakespeare's text remains lost, or has been found in spades.

Context

'Tis won as towns with fire – so won, so lost

(*Love's Labour's Lost*, 1.1.144)

Lily B. Campbell opens her *Shakespeare's Histories: Mirrors of Elizabethan Policy* (1947) with an attack on Mark Van Doren's assumption – which she and we may take as symptomatic of a certain and prevalent critical approach – that Shakespearian interpretation needs no more scholarly equipment or knowledge 'beyond those which a whole heart and a free mind abundantly supply'.[13] Campbell's thesis is quite the contrary: that to understand

Shakespeare's history plays one must understand the scholarly and sometimes arcane principles and methods of sixteenth-century historiography – and have access to a major centre for the study of intellectual history such as, in her case, the Huntington Library in California – since her Shakespeare is 'a man among men, a man who can be understood only against the background of his own time'.[14] That background is largely intellectual. Her Shakespeare, like A.D. Nuttall's a half-century later, is a man among books[15] – rather as it is for Campbell's better-known English contemporary, E.M.W. Tillyard, who also draws on early modern historiography and discusses the 'remote and queer ... political doctrines' of pre-Shakespearian chronicle history plays at some length before analysing the plays as expressive of a political 'scheme fundamentally religious, by which events evolve under a law of justice and under the ruling of God's Providence and of which Elizabeth's England was the acknowledged outcome' (1944).[16]

What is striking about both these turns to history is the way in which they mimic the very plays they analyse. Just as Shakespeare's inscription of his own historical moment is often unacknowledged and complicated by looking backwards, so too is that of his wartime critics, who reflect without comment their own time's particular investment in its past. This view of Campbell and Tillyard helps us see that their historical past is a creature both of the archive and of the imagination: fugitive, illusory and forever connected to the present. As Hugh Grady and Terence Hawkes firmly assert in a 2007 introduction to the current school of 'presentism': '[We must] acknowledge that the questions we ask of any literary text will inevitably be shaped by our own concerns, even when these include what we call "the past".'[17] The most abiding context for Shakespeare, even for the most historical of scholars, is always the receding, multiple present.

'I began with the desire to speak with the dead.' When Stephen Greenblatt opened his book *Shakespearian Negotiations* (1988) with that echoing phrase, the late twentieth-century's preoccupation with the reconstruction of Shakespearian contexts had found its spokesman.[18] The old historicism of Campbell and Tillyard had given birth to its Oedipal son, historicism Jr, just as almost simultaneously a more literal reconstruction of 'Shakespeare's Globe' theatre had begun on London's Bankside, fathered by the energy and commitment of the American actor Sam Wanamaker.[19] For Greenblatt, the desire was to understand the 'unmistakeable pleasure and interest in the literary traces of the dead' in a 'poetics of culture': 'I want to know how cultural objects, expressions, and practices – here, principally, plays by Shakespeare and the stage on which they first appeared – acquired compelling force.'[20] Greenblatt's New Historicism thus combines the element of empathic human connection that Campbell scorns in Van Doren, with something of her archival energy. Others of the emerging New Historicist tendency further contextualized literary texts with a close attention to material detail: to the meanings of 'race' and difference in the early modern period;[21] to cultural ideas about death and mourning;[22] to gender roles and the construction of early modern sexualities;[23] to ideas of identity and subjectivity;[24] to the early modern London context;[25] to religious affiliations and inscriptions:[26] it is possible to trace in these close and revealing analyses of Shakespeare's own period many of the preoccupations of our own.

Before New Historicism, responses to Shakespeare tended to adduce historical evidence to excuse perceived deficiencies in the text. Thus Nicholas Rowe explains that Shakespeare's 'way of tragic-Comedy was the common mistake of that age' (1709–10); 250 years later, G.K. Hunter argues about the significance of Othello's race by demonstrating 'how mindlessly and totally accepted in this period was the image of the black man as the devil'.[27] A reluctance to adduce 'common' or 'totally accepted' views about the past has been an abiding preoccupation of late twentieth-century Shakespeare studies. New, more recent material contexts for Shakespeare's plays have also been important to his critical reception. In studying Victorian stagings of Shakespeare, for example, or the use of Shakespeare in debates about the Jewish Naturalization Act of 1753, or the wartime context of Laurence Olivier's film of *Henry V* (1944), for instance, critics have been keen to shape Jonson's idea of an historically transcendent Shakespeare 'not of an age but for all time' (1623) into a kind of serial topicality: a Shakespeare endlessly adaptable to historical circumstance in place of one soaring free from history.[28]

Plenitude

> It is not lost; but what an if it were?
>
> (*Othello*, 3.4.83)

Contextual or historical criticism, as discussed above, has found meaning in Shakespeare's works by reinstating them in their original cultural milieu, or in densely materialized subsequent time periods. Other scholars in all periods, though, have sought meaning and value in Shakespeare precisely because his work is thought to transcend immediate circumstances to offer philosophical or human truths of a more enduring kind. The basis of Dryden's affection for Shakespeare was that 'of all Modern and perhaps Ancient Poets, [he] had the largest and most comprehensive soul' (1668).[29] Following Milton's Shakespeare 'warbl[ing] his native Wood-notes wilde' in 'L'Allegro' (1645) it became a standard defence of Shakespeare's perceived linguistic and structural irregularities to cite him as a poet of nature, whose significance was more philosophical – more humanistic – than strictly aesthetic, and this attitude still prevails for many defences of Shakespeare's privileged place in English-speaking cultures. Samuel Johnson's version in his 'Preface' to his edition of 1765 is indicative in its attribution of absolute value to Shakespearian non-specificity:

> *Shakespeare* is above all writers ... the poet of nature; the poet that holds up to his readers a faithful mirror of manners and of life. His characters are not modified by the customs of particular places, unpractised by the rest of the world, by the particularities of studies or professions, which can operate but in small numbers; or by the accidents of transient fashions or temporary opinions; they are the genuine progeny of common humanity, such as the world will always supply, and observation will always find. His persons act and speak by the influence of those general passions, and the whole system of life is continued in motion.[30]

More than two centuries later Harold Bloom's admiration for Shakespeare's plays as 'the outward limit of human achievement: aesthetically, cognitively, in certain ways morally, even spiritually', that his major dramatic characters do not merely represent but 'invent' the human, partakes of the same enthusiasm for an ineffable and essential Shakespeare (1998).[31]

If Shakespeare's plays exceed their context, according to such approaches, it is by the appeal to transcendent ideas – the human, the moral, the social, the structural. Writing in the 1960s, Northrop Frye saw Shakespeare's significance as a structuralist iteration of mythic archetypes, in which, for example, Shakespearian comedy draws on Judaeo-Christian tropes of preparation, on carnival and Saturnalian rituals of release, and on the idea of the revel that 'normally begins with an anticomic society, a social organization blocking and opposed to the comic drive, which the action of the comedy evades or overcomes'.[32] Identifying large-scale structural devices such as the 'wheel of fortune' or mythemes such as the killing of the father and the sacrifice of the son,[33] Frye's work sidesteps both close verbal analysis and specific contextualization, identifying instead structure and parallel and echo within the Western literary tradition. For G. Wilson Knight, the focus of interest is something different again, as he distinguishes his own preferred form of 'poetic "interpretation"' from the activity of criticism:

> The critic is, and should be, cool and urbane, seeing the poetry he discusses not with the eyes of a lover but as an object; whereas interpretation deliberately immerses itself in its theme and speaks less from the seats of judgment than from the creative centre.[34]

For Knight, 'the persons of Shakespeare are compact of poetic colour, poetic association' (1931). Like William Whiter's Lockean *Specimen of Commentary on Shakespeare* (1794) before him, and Patricia Parker's *Literary Fat Ladies* (1987) afterwards, Wilson Knight's Shakespeare is linguistic and rhetorical. For A.C. Bradley's influential account in *Shakespearian Tragedy* (first published in 1904), the focus was different: the recognizable psychology of character. As John Bayley writes in 1991 of Bradley in a revealing coupling which itself collapses the real and the fictive, 'he talks about Shakespeare and Shakespeare's characters as if he were discussing friends or colleagues, or the people he has met with in a memorable novel'.[35] His 'persons' are compact of flesh and blood, not Knight's 'poetic colour'. Writing about *Hamlet*, Bradley understands and sympathizes with its troubled hero's disgust at Gertrude's 'eruption of coarse sensuality, "rank and gross", speeding post-haste to its horrible delight', and its effect on him: 'It brings bewildered horror, then loathing, then despair of human nature. His whole mind is poisoned. He can never see Ophelia in the same light again: she is a woman and his mother is a woman.'[36]

Hamlet is a play of particular attraction for critics finding essential, ahistorical significance in Shakespeare's work. Some indicative examples will have to stand for a vast critical history: 'I have a smack of Hamlet myself, if I may say so';[37] 'the strange void at the center of *Hamlet* becomes a symbolic expression of the Western and modern malaise ... our "symptoms" always resemble that unnameable paralysis of the will, that ineffable corruption of the spirit, that affect not only Hamlet but other characters as well';[38] 'Shakespeare's dramas, like Freud's, propose our coming to know what we cannot just not know; like philosophy';[39] 'femininity functions as the lost object, divided subject and alienating Other of *Hamlet*'s generic and discursive practice';[40] 'a tragedy of thought inspired by the continual and never-satisfied meditation on human destiny and the dark perplexity of the events of this world, and calculated to draw forth the very same meditation in the minds of the spectators'.[41] I quote briefly not to make the claims sound laughably grandiloquent deracinated from their argumentative context, but to illustrate the range of significance critics have wanted, and been able, to find in the play. As Freud notes at the end of his discursus on *Hamlet* in the section 'Typical Dreams' in *The Interpretation of Dreams* (1900), 'every neurotic symptom, even the dream, is capable of over-interpretation, indeed, demands it': it's hard not to apply this to the play, and to Shakespeare himself.[42]

Performance

> it were lost sorrow to wail one that's lost
>
> (*Richard III*, 2.2.10)

What Peggy Phelan identifies as the ineluctable critical and psychic lure of the 'lost archives of the performances we also missed' gives performance studies and the history of Shakespeare on the stage its particular version of ghostliness.[43] From historical studies of the Elizabethan and Jacobean stages, audiences and personnel to which Shakespeare wrote, to analysis of the semiotics of recent performances in the theatre and on film, the search for the lost performance, or the construction of a platonic ideal of performance, has been prominent in twentieth-century approaches to Shakespeare. Earlier attitudes to the theatre by editors and textual critics tended to be derogatory. As we have seen, theatre was often judged a necessary but tainting agent of the transmission into print. Later Shakespearians identified themselves firmly as readers, not viewers, of Shakespeare, substituting for the ephemeral theatre production the private experience of reading. Charles Lamb's essay 'On the tragedies of Shakespeare, considered with reference to their fitness for stage representation' (1811) was clear they were not fit. The difference between the inadequacies of the stage and the empathic communion of the sensitive reader were articulated in relation to *King Lear*: 'On the stage we see nothing but corporal infirmities and weakness, the impotence of rage; while we read it, we see not Lear, but we are Lear – we are in his mind, we are sustained by a grandeur which baffles the malice of daughters and storms.'[44] Lamb's contemporary William Hazlitt was likewise adamant that 'we do not like to see our Author's plays acted'.[45]

It was not until A.C. Sprague's modest suggestion in 1944 that 'Shakespeare's plays were written for performance, and surely, through performance, light has been shed on many dark places in them' that the academic study of performed Shakespeare really took off.[46] Since then it has come almost to dominate the academy, and, while it has developed its own methodologies, increasingly its insights have been integrated with those from other critical fields.[47] Interrogating inherited histories of early modern theatre practice to provide new insights into ideas of geographical and psychological space is the intellectual parallel to the attempts at original staging in the rebuilt Globe theatre.[48] Part of the attempt to record lost performances from archival records is registered as stage histories of particular plays, or of the theatre practice of a particular era.[49] Actors' own recollections of and insights into roles and productions have also been prominent.[50] So too have analyses, taxonomies and appreciations of Shakespeare on film, where the apparent fixity of the medium has gone some way to recuperating the theatre's transience.[51] But it is in acknowledging the experiential, ephemeral unrecoverability of the plays on the stage that recent theoretical critics have perhaps come closest, amid Shakespeare's long history of interpreters, to embracing the texts' radical contingency and multiplicity. W. B. Worthen's sophisticated interrogation of 'dramatic performativity' combines work on performance, on philosophy and on the text (2003): Bridget Escolme deconstructs ideas of text, performance and audience in her challenging *Talking to the Audience* (2005).[52] Each proposes stages – intellectual and theatrical – on which the text, or a text, can be provisionally secured.

The twenty-first century

> what remains will hardly stop the mouth
> Of present dues: the future comes apace
> (*Timon of Athens*, 2.2.144–5)

Early in the twenty-first century, Shakespeare's critical reception continues to produce and reproduce more and more monographs and articles, as documented by the invaluable *World Shakespeare Bibliography Online*.[53] Our dominant methodology now is plurality – text becomes texts, performance becomes performances, Shakespeare becomes Shakespeares – as if by adding the plural 's' we can fill up our critical bereavement with multiplicity. A range of important approaches jostle for our attention. Post-colonial readings of the plays attend to their implication in hierarchical and imperialist contexts old and new;[54] theorists of sexuality and gender explore the ongoing impact of Shakespeare on modern and early modern categories;[55] historians of theatre develop new insights about the theatres for which Shakespeare wrote and to which he has been adapted.[56] Recent introductory guides approach Shakespeare via the close reading brio of Simon Palfrey, the thematic insight of Laurie Maguire or the critical history of Lisa Hopkins, as if each, or all, of these distinct encounters might be most suitable for Shakespeare's many student readers.[57] Current titles such as *Green Shakespeare*, *Shakespeare and Republicanism* and *Looking for Sex in Shakespeare* continue to confirm the adaptability of both Shakespeare and his critics: the character of what we find in our critical searches changes to reflect our current preoccupations, as it has always done.[58] Gary Taylor writes that 'we find in Shakespeare only what we bring to him or what others have left behind; he gives us back our own values. And it is no use pretending that some uniquely clever, honest, and disciplined critic can find a technique, an angle, that will enable us to lead a mass escape from this trap.'[59] Stockholm-like, it's not even clear we'd want to escape; we've become institutionally and culturally dependent on and strangely fond of Shakespeare our captor.

Predictions are always dangerous. New Historicism's dominance of Shakespeare studies over the last three decades can't go on for ever, perhaps particularly now the capitalist economic model from which it drew its own methodology of exchange and circulation has itself apparently gone pop.[60] Hindsight – what you have as reader but I can't have now – will tell whether Mark David Rasmussen's nudge towards 'a fuller and more self-conscious engagement with questions of form' or Madhavi Menon's call for *Unhistorical Shakespeare* will have the kind of critical impact of Greenblatt's sonorous séance.[61] What is certain, however, is that even the twenty-first century's new interest in large-scale editions of other early modern dramatists, including claims for Middleton as 'our other Shakespeare' will not knock Shakespeare from his position.[62] Just as Dryden's Neander predicted the course of critical debate when he preferred Shakespeare over Jonson in 1668, so we all know now the answer to Nigel Smith's forlorn question *Is Milton Better than Shakespeare?*[63] Neither the critical detective work nor the elegiac memorial to Shakespeare is complete: this chapter of the *Companion* is the one whose obsolescence, happily, is guaranteed.

FURTHER READING

On early responses to Shakespeare from 1623 to 1801, see Brian Vickers, *Shakespeare: The Critical Heritage* (London: Routledge and Kegan Paul, 1974–81). Michael Dobson's account of *The Making of the National Poet* covers the century after the Restoration (Oxford: Clarendon Press, 1992); Jonathan Bate discusses *Shakespeare and the English Romantic Imagination* (Oxford: Clarendon Press, 1986) and gives generous excerpts from Romantic writings on Shakespeare in the collection *The Romantics on Shakespeare* (London: Penguin, 1992). Nineteenth-century Shakespeare is addressed in two volumes of *Victorian Shakespeare* edited by Gail Marshall and Adrian Poole (Basingstoke: Palgrave Macmillan, 2003). Hugh Grady's *The Modernist Shakespeare* (Oxford: Clarendon Press, 1991) discusses the early twentieth century, as does Terence Hawkes in *That Shakespeherian Rag* (London: Methuen, 1986). Michael Taylor covers *Shakespeare Criticism in the Twentieth Century* (Oxford: Oxford University Press, 2001); my *Blackwell Guides to Criticism* on Shakespeare's comedies, histories and tragedies (Oxford: Blackwell, 2004) and Russ McDonald's *Shakespeare: An Anthology of Criticism and Theory 1945–2000* (Oxford: Blackwell, 2004) anthologize key recent critical interventions.

NOTES

1 Robert Greene, *Groats-worth of Witte, bought with a million of Repentance* (1592), quoted and discussed in Stephen Greenblatt, *Will in the World: How Shakespeare Became Shakespeare* (London: Jonathan Cape, 2004), pp. 212–15.
2 Stanley Wells and Gary Taylor (eds.), *The Oxford Shakespeare* (Oxford: Clarendon Press, 1988), emend 'scamels' to 'seamews'.
3 See A. W. Pollard *et al.*, *Shakespeare's Hand in the Play of Sir Thomas More* (Cambridge: Cambridge University Press, 1923); Scott McMillin, *The Elizabethan Theatre and 'The Book of Sir Thomas More'* (Ithaca, NY: Cornell University Press, 1987); Jeffrey Masten's insights and challenges in 'More or Less: Editing the Collaborative', *Shakespeare Studies*, 29 (2001), 109–31.

4 Fredson Bowers, *Textual and Literary Criticism* (Cambridge: Cambridge University Press, 1959), p. 18; *On Editing Shakespeare and the Elizabethan Dramatists* (London: University of Pennsylvania Library, 1955), p. 8.
5 *Mr William Shakespeares Comedies, Histories and Tragedies* (1623), sig. A3.
6 Edward Capell (ed.), *Mr William Shakespeare his comedies, histories, and tragedies* (1768), vol. I, p. 21.
7 Lewis Theobald, *The works of Shakespeare: in seven volumes* (1733), vol. I, p. xxxviii.
8 Stanley Wells, *Re-Editing Shakespeare for the Modern Reader* (Oxford: Clarendon Press, 1984), pp. 3–4. On the theatrical interest of the quarto texts, see Kathleen O. Irace, *Performing the 'Bad' Quartos* (Newark: University of Delaware Press, 1994).
9 See Laurie E. Maguire, *Shakespearian Suspect Texts: The 'Bad' Quartos and Their Contexts* (Cambridge: Cambridge University Press, 1996); Random Cloud, 'The Marriage of Good and Bad Quartos', *Shakespeare Quarterly*, 33 (1982), 421–31; Paul Werstine, 'Narratives about Printed Shakespeare Texts: "Foul" Papers and "Bad" Quartos', *Shakespeare Quarterly*, 41 (1990), 65–86, 421–31; Peter W. M. Blayney, 'The Publication of Playbooks', in John D. Cox and David Scott Kastan, *A New History of Early English Drama* (New York: Columbia University Press, 1997), pp. 383–433; Margreta de Grazia and Peter Stallybrass, 'The Materiality of the Shakespearian Text', *Shakespeare Quarterly*, 44 (1993), 255–83.
10 Gary Taylor and Michael Warren, 'Preface', *The Division of the Kingdoms: Shakespeare's Two Versions of 'King Lear'* (Oxford: Clarendon Press, 1983), p. vii.
11 Ann Thompson and Neil Taylor, *Hamlet* (London: Arden Shakespeare, 2006).
12 *Shakespearian Originals: First Editions*, general eds. Graham Holderness and Bryan Loughrey (10 plays printed, Hemel Hempsted: Harvester Wheatsheaf, 1992–6); *The New Cambridge Shakespeare: The Early Quartos*, general eds. A. D. Braunmuller and Brian Gibbons (12 plays printed, Cambridge: Cambridge University Press, 1998–2008); for example, Bernice W. Kliman's 'The Enfolded Hamlet', www.leoyan.com/global-language.com/ENFOLDED/enfolded.intro.html (accessed 5 September 2008).
13 Mark Van Doren, *Shakespeare* (New York: Random House, 1939), quoted in Lily B. Campbell, *Shakespeare's Histories: Mirrors of Elizabethan Policy* (San Marino, CA: Huntington Library, 1947), p. 3.
14 Ibid., p. 6.
15 A. D. Nuttall, *Shakespeare the Thinker* (New Haven and London: Yale University Press, 2007).
16 E.M.W. Tillyard, *Shakespeare's History Plays* (London: Chatto and Windus, 1944), pp. 146, 320–1.
17 Hugh Grady and Terence Hawkes, 'Introduction: Presenting Presentism', in Grady and Hawkes (eds.), *Presentist Shakespeares* (London: Routledge, 2007), pp. 1–5 (p. 5).
18 Stephen Greenblatt, *Shakespearian Negotiations: The Circulation of Social Energy in Renaissance England* (Oxford: Clarendon Press, 1988), p. 1.
19 'About the Globe', Shakespeare's Globe website, www.shakespeares-globe.org/information/abouttheglobe/ (accessed 2 September 2008).
20 Greenblatt, *Shakespearian Negotiations*, pp. 3, 5.

21 See for example Ania Loomba, *Gender, Race, Renaissance Drama* (Manchester: Manchester University Press, 1989); Kim F. Hall, *Things of Darkness: Economies of Race and Gender in Early Modern England* (Ithaca, NY and London: Cornell University Press, 1995); Emily C. Bartels, *Speaking of the Moor: From Alcazar to Othello* (Philadelphia: University of Pennsylvania Press, 2008).
22 See for example Robert N. Watson, *The Rest is Silence: Death as Annihilation in the English Renaissance* (Berkeley and London: University of California Press, 1994); Michael Neill, *Issues of Death: Mortality and Identity in English Renaissance Tragedy* (Oxford: Clarendon Press, 1997).
23 See for example Karen Newman, *Fashioning Femininity and English Renaissance Drama* (Chicago and London: University of Chicago Press, 1991); Frances E. Dolan, *Dangerous Familiars: Representations of Domestic Crime in England 1500–1700* (Ithaca, NY and London: Cornell University Press, 1994); Stephen Orgel, *Impersonations: The Performance of Gender in Early Modern England* (Cambridge: Cambridge University Press, 1996); Valerie Traub, *The Renaissance of Lesbianism in Early Modern England* (Cambridge: Cambridge University Press, 2002).
24 See for example Catherine Belsey, *The Subject of Tragedy: Identity and Difference in Renaissance Drama* (London: Methuen, 1985); Katharine Eisaman Maus, *Inwardness and Theatre in the English Renaissance* (Chicago and London: University of Chicago Press, 1995).
25 See for example Lawrence Manley, *Literature and Culture in Early Modern London* (Cambridge: Cambridge University Press, 1995); Jean E. Howard, *The Stage and Social Struggle in Early Modern England* (London: Routledge, 1994); Lena Cowen Orlin (ed.), *Material London, ca. 1600* (Philadelphia: University of Pennsylvania Press, 2002).
26 See for example Alison Shell, *Catholicism, Controversy and the English Literary Imagination, 1558–1660* (Cambridge: Cambridge University Press, 1999); Peter Lake with Michael Questier, *The Antichrist's Lewd Hat: Protestants, Papists and Players in Post-Reformation England* (New Haven and London: Yale University Press, 2002).
27 Nicholas Rowe, *The Works of Mr William Shakespear* (1709–10), vol. I, p. iv; G.K. Hunter, '*Othello* and Colour Prejudice', in *Dramatic Identities and Cultural Tradition: Studies in Shakespeare and His Contemporaries* (Liverpool: Liverpool University Press, 1978), pp. 31–59 (p. 39).
28 See for example Richard Foulkes, *Performing Shakespeare in the Age of Empire* (Cambridge: Cambridge University Press, 2002); James Shapiro, *Shakespeare and the Jews* (New York: Columbia University Press, 1996); James N. Loehlin, *Henry V* (Manchester: Manchester University Press, 1996).
29 John Dryden, *Of Dramatic Poesie, 1668* (Menston: Scolar Press, 1969), p. 47.
30 Samuel Johnson (ed.), *The plays of William Shakespeare* (1765), vol. I, sig. A3.
31 Harold Bloom, *Shakespeare: The Invention of the Human* (New York: Riverhead Books, 1998), p. xvii. Among the many disagreeing with Bloom's contentions, see Marjorie B. Garber, 'What did Shakespeare Invent?', in *Profiling Shakespeare* (New York: Routledge, 2008), pp. 271–7.
32 Northrop Frye, *A Natural Perspective: The Development of Shakespearian Comedy and Romance* (New York: Columbia University Press, 1965), p. 73.

33 Northrop Frye, *Fools of Time: Studies in Shakespearian Tragedy* (Toronto: University of Toronto Press, 1967), pp. 17ff.
34 G. Wilson Knight, 'Prefatory note', *The Imperial Theme* (1931; London: Methuen, 1954), pp. vi, 19–20.
35 John Bayley, 'Foreword' to A.C. Bradley, *Shakespearian Tragedy: Lectures on 'Hamlet', 'Othello', 'King Lear', 'Macbeth'* (Harmondsworth: Penguin, 1991), p. 1.
36 Ibid., p. 118.
37 S.T. Coleridge, *Table Talk* (2nd edn. 1836), repr. in Jonathan Bate (ed.), *The Romantics on Shakespeare* (London: Penguin, 1992), p. 161.
38 René Girard, *A Theatre of Envy: William Shakespeare* (New York and Oxford: Oxford University Press, 1991), p. 284.
39 Stanley Cavell, *Disowning Knowledge in Six Plays of Shakespeare* (Cambridge: Cambridge University Press, 1987), p. 191.
40 Julia Reinhard Lupton and Kenneth Reinhard, *After Oedipus: Shakespeare in Psychoanalysis* (Ithaca, NY and London: Cornell University Press, 1993) p. 57.
41 A.W. Schlegel, *A Course of Lectures on Dramatic Art and Literature* (1815), repr. in Bate, *The Romantics*, p. 307.
42 Sigmund Freud, *The Interpretation of Dreams*, trans. Joyce Crick (Oxford: Oxford University Press, 1999), p. 204n.
43 Peggy Phelan, personal communication quoted by Barbara Hodgdon, 'Introduction: A Kind of History', in Barbara Hodgdon and W. B. Worthen (eds.), *A Companion to Shakespeare and Performance* (Oxford: Blackwell, 2005), pp. 1–10 (p. 8).
44 Charles Lamb and Mary Lamb, *The Works of Charles and Mary Lamb* (London: Methuen, 1903), p. 124.
45 William Hazlitt, *The Selected Writings of William Hazlitt*, ed. Duncan Wu (London: Pickering & Chatto, 1998), p. 148.
46 Arthur C. Sprague, *Shakespeare and the Actors: The Stage Business in his Plays (1660–1905)* (Cambridge, MA: Harvard University Press, 1944), p. xxv.
47 On performance studies as a separate discipline, see for example Hodgdon and Worthen (eds.), *A Companion to Shakespeare and Performance* and Stanley Wells (ed.), *Shakespeare in the Theatre: An Anthology of Criticism* (Oxford: Oxford University Press, 2000); on integrated approaches see for example Pascale Aebischer, *Shakespeare's Violated Bodies: Stage and Screen Performance* (Cambridge: Cambridge University Press, 2004) and Stephen Orgel, *Imagining Shakespeare: A History of Texts and Visions* (Basingstoke and New York: Palgrave Macmillan, 2003). For an important counter to the prevalence of performance studies, see Lukas Erne's controversial *Shakespeare as Literary Dramatist* (Cambridge: Cambridge University Press, 2003).
48 See for example Andrew Gurr, *The Shakespearian Playing Companies* (Oxford: Clarendon Press, 1996); Henry S. Turner, *The English Renaissance Stage: Geometry, Poetics, and the Practical Spatial Arts 1580–1630* (Oxford: Oxford University Press, 2006).
49 Play-centred stage histories include the *Shakespeare in Production* series, 13 vols., general eds. J. S. Bratton and Julie Hankey (Cambridge: Cambridge University Press, 1996–2005) and the *Shakespeare in Performance* series, 24 vols., general eds. J. R. Mulryne, J. C. Bulman and Margaret Shewring (Manchester: Manchester

University Press, 1984–2006), individual volumes devoted to single plays; period histories include G. C. D. Odell, *Shakespeare from Betterton to Irving* (New York: Scribner, 1920); Cary M. Mazer, *Shakespeare Refashioned: Elizabethan Plays on Edwardian Stages* (Ann Arbor: UMI Research Press, 1981); Pauline Kiernan, *Staging Shakespeare at the New Globe* (Basingstoke: Macmillan, 1999).

50 See for example Michael Dobson, *Performing Shakespeare's Tragedies Today: The Actor's Perspective* (Cambridge: Cambridge University Press, 2006) and Michael Pennington, *Twelfth Night: A User's Guide* (London: Nick Hern Books, 2000).

51 See for example Russell Jackson (ed.), *The Cambridge Companion to Shakespeare on Film* (Cambridge: Cambridge University Press, 2007).

52 W. B. Worthen, *Shakespeare and the Force of Modern Performance* (Cambridge: Cambridge University Press, 2003); Bridget Escolme, *Talking to the Audience: Shakespeare, Performance, Self* (London: Routledge, 2005).

53 *World Shakespeare Bibliography Online*, published by Johns Hopkins Press for the Folger Shakespeare Library, at www.worldshakesbib.org/ (accessed 2 September 2008).

54 See for example Ania Loomba and Martin Orkin (eds.), *Post-Colonial Shakespeares* (London: Routledge, 2003), 2nd edn, and Natasha Distiller, *South Africa, Shakespeare, and Post-Colonial Culture* (Lewiston, NY: Edwin Mellen Press, 2005).

55 See for example James C. Bulman (ed.), *Shakespeare Re-Dressed: Cross-Gender Casting in Contemporary Performance* (Madison: Fairleigh Dickinson University Press, 2008); Mary Bly, *Queer Virgins and Virgin Queans on the Early Modern Stage* (Oxford: Oxford University Press, 2000).

56 Simon Palfrey and Tiffany Stern, *Shakespeare in Parts* (Oxford: Oxford University Press, 2007); Richard Schoch, *Not Shakespeare: Bardolatry and Burlesque in the Nineteenth Century* (Cambridge: Cambridge University Press, 2002); Judith Buchanan, *Shakespeare on Film* (Harlow: Pearson Longman, 2005).

57 Simon Palfrey, *Doing Shakespeare* (London: Arden Shakespeare, 2005); Laurie Maguire, *Studying Shakespeare: A Guide to the Plays* (Oxford: Blackwell, 2004); Lisa Hopkins, *Beginning Shakespeare* (Manchester: Manchester University Press, 2005).

58 Gabriel Egan, *Green Shakespeare: From Ecopolitics to Ecocriticism* (London: Routledge, 2006); Andrew Hadfield, *Shakespeare and Republicanism* (Cambridge: Cambridge University Press, 2005); Stanley Wells, *Looking for Sex in Shakespeare* (Cambridge: Cambridge University Press, 2004).

59 Gary Taylor, *Reinventing Shakespeare: A Cultural History, from the Restoration to the Present* (New York: Weidenfeld and Nicolson, 1989). p. 411.

60 On New Historicism's relation to capitalism, see Stephen Greenblatt, 'Towards a Poetics of Culture', in H. Aram Veeser (ed.), *The New Historicism* (London and New York: Routledge, 1989), pp. 1–14, and Richard Wilson, 'Introduction: Historicising New Historicism', in Richard Wilson and Richard Dutton (eds.), *New Historicism and Renaissance Drama* (London and New York: Longman, 1992), pp. 1–18.

61 Mark David Rasmussen (ed.), *Renaissance Literature and its Formal Engagements* (London and New York: Palgrave, 2002), p. 1; Madhavi Menon,

Unhistorical Shakespeare: Queer Theory in Shakespearian Literature and Film (London: Palgrave, 2008).

62 Gary Taylor, 'Lives and Afterlives', in Taylor and John Lavagnino (general eds.), *Thomas Middleton: The Collected Works* (Oxford: Clarendon Press, 2008), p. 58.

63 John Dryden, *Of Dramatick Poesie 1668* (Menston: Scolar Press, 1969), p. 50; Nigel Smith, *Is Milton Better than Shakespeare*? (Cambridge, MA: Harvard University Press, 2008).

18

PAUL PRESCOTT

Shakespeare and popular culture

Shakespeare? Popular culture?

What sense does it make to couple Shakespeare – Bard of Avon, icon of genius, highbrow *extraordinaire* – with 'popular culture'? If his writings are widely valued for their complexity, timelessness and universal human truths, popular culture is for many synonymous with banality, the ephemeral and the trivial. If Shakespeare is deep and difficult, the typical products of popular culture are shallow and all too accessible. To enjoy Shakespeare, the argument might run, requires training, time and long-term investment; the consumption of popular culture, by definition, requires little or no effort. From the perspective of these stark contrasts, 'Shakespeare and popular culture' looks like a dead-end of incompatibility.

Yet Shakespeare is everywhere in contemporary culture. His presence is not confined to the 'official' locations of classrooms, universities and theatres, but permeates popular mass media such as cinema, television, tabloid journalism, computer games, pop music, comics and advertisements. Shakespeare's face sells products and is familiar to millions, many of whom may never have read or seen his work; any bald-headed, bearded man need only don a ruff and grab a quill to be instantly recognizable as 'Shakespeare'. Someone this easily impersonated is a major celebrity. Shakespeare's words are quoted and misquoted (intentionally or otherwise) to amuse, persuade and impress. Many of Shakespeare's characters have been plucked from their plays to become free-standing cultural stereotypes of amorousness (Romeo), indecision (Hamlet) or steely 'un-feminine' ambition (Lady Macbeth). Shakespeare's plots are plundered to provide storylines for films, science fiction and soap operas. Shakespeare scholars have increasingly sought to analyse and theorize what Douglas Lanier has called 'Shakespop', the presence, citation and appropriation of Shakespeare across a range of popular mass media.

Many Shakespearians, professional or amateur, might view the study of 'Shakespop' with scepticism. Why write about Hamlet cigars when you could be writing about *Hamlet*? Why watch *A Midsummer Night's Cream* (one of many pornographic film adaptations) when you could, more wholesomely, re-read the play itself? Chris Offutt's satirical *Guide to Literary Terms* defines a 'Pop Culture Essay' as a piece 'written by someone who prefers to shop or watch television'; prefers, that is, these lazy, consumerist pleasures to the more taxing task of serious scholarship.[1] This chapter suggests that there is far more to the study of Shakespeare and popular culture than shopping or watching television. Critics for centuries have been interested in the symbiosis between Shakespeare and popular culture, though they might not have described their interest in those terms.[2] Much depends on definitions. Raymond Williams described 'culture' as 'one of the two or three most complicated words in the English language'.[3] To Elizabethans, it was a noun of process describing the tending of something, usually crops or animals, but it was also, more rarely, applicable to the process of human development. Shakespeare never used the word. Operative meanings have since proliferated to such a degree that the word risks meaning all things to all people, without meaning the same thing to any two. 'Popular' is not much more straightforward.[4]

We might begin with a definition of popular culture as an umbrella term for the social practices, patterns of consumption and daily experiences of the *majority* population of a society at any given point in time. This definition is controversial and begs many questions, but it has been selected to give the reader the widest possible sense of the applications of 'Shakespeare and popular culture'. From this perspective, the field of study is vast and fertile, stretching from the early modern period to the present. At one end of the spectrum, we might seek to understand Shakespeare's position as a playwright who drew on popular theatrical and social traditions, and whose drama is filled with allusions to and representatives of the popular culture of his time. Alternatively, we might focus on the way in which Shakespeare is quoted, commodified or refashioned by popular culture in the post-modern present, whether in advertising, mainstream cinema, rap music or on YouTube. In between the early modern 'then' and the post-modern 'now' lie myriad histories of reception and reproduction, as the popular culture of each generation – and of different countries and continents – inherits and inflects 'Shakespeare'.

All of this now strikes most teachers and critics as worthy of study. No extreme cultural or aesthetic relativism need be implicit in this approach; to argue that the analysis of popular culture is a legitimate academic undertaking is not to neuter discrimination or value judgements, let alone argue that Mickey Mouse or Lily Allen are in some way as important or as valuable as *Measure for Measure*. What explicitly underpins a popular cultural studies approach is the less controversial observation that the value and meaning of texts changes from generation to generation, from place to place and between different social groups. To observe the historical fluctuations of Shakespeare's value is to be reminded of the contingency of our *own* readings of the texts. To focus on the reception of Shakespeare by the majority of people is not only fascinating in itself, but also applies pressure to the received idea that Shakespeare belongs exclusively to high or elite culture. There is a two-way relationship between popular culture and Shakespeare: popular culture shaped Shakespeare's art, but Shakespeare's art continues to shape popular culture.

Shakespeare and early modern popular culture

Scholars of early modern history and literature have used the term 'popular culture' to refer to very different objects of study. We might isolate three key definitions: 1) the beliefs and social practices of the vast majority of the population below the level of gentry; 2) a form of oppositional politics at odds with mainstream or elite ideology; 3) the participation in the traditional festive practices of a pre-modern 'Merrie England'.[5] Each of these definitions is helpful in thinking about the relationship between Shakespeare's plays and early modern popular culture.

Popular audiences

Shakespeare wrote (largely) popular plays for largely popular audiences. The exact social composition of early modern England can never be known, but historians are in broad agreement that the gentry and aristocracy formed a small minority and that the common populace – a combination of the middling sort and lower-status groups, all excluded by law and practice from any voice in the major affairs of the state – comprised as much as 95 per cent of the population.[6] The survival of the large open-air amphitheatres of the 1590s must have depended largely on the daily patronage of this populace. Although his non-dramatic poetry might have been aimed at a more socially exclusive readership, Shakespeare's plays had to appeal to as many elements as possible of London's heterogeneous population. Robert Cawdrey's *A Table Alphabetical* (1604) defines 'popular' as 'seeking the favour of the people by all means possible'; by this definition, playwriting in early modern England was a popular art form.

What was Shakespeare's attitude to this popular audience on which much of his livelihood depended? The question has prompted much critical speculation. Shakespeare uses the word 'popular' (or a variant of it) eight times, half of them in *Coriolanus*, his great anatomy of political power and the pressures of popularity. Each time, 'popular' carries negative connotations: Henry IV says that his predecessor Richard II 'enfeoffed himself to popularity' (*2 Henry IV*, 3.2.69); Hal's errant youth is retrospectively described as 'fill'd up with riots, banquets, sports', and as one incapable of shunning 'open haunts and popularity' (*1 Henry IV*, 1.1.90); conversely, Prospero's back-story is of a man who neglected worldly ends, bettered his mind and, thus 'o'er-priced', became too precious for 'all popular rate' (*The Tempest*, 1.2.92). Coriolanus' banishment from Rome is described, by a non-partisan Volscian watchman, as the result of 'a violent popular ignorance' (5.2.41). This disdain for popularity seems to be reinforced by Hamlet's sneers at the groundlings who are 'capable of nothing but inexplicable dumbshows and noise' (3.2.10–11). In Sonnet 111, the speaker laments:

> O, for my sake do you with Fortune chide,
> The guilty goddess of my harmful deeds,
> That did not better for my life provide
> Than public means which public manners breeds.
> Thence comes it that my name receives a brand,
> And almost thence my nature is subdued
> To what it works in, like the dyer's hand.
>
> (1–7)

Some critics – too readily, as with Hamlet's words, assuming the speaker to be Shakespeare himself – have fastened on these lines as evidence of Shakespeare's contempt for his popular profession. Correspondingly, a long tradition in Shakespeare criticism holds the popular audience responsible for lapses of taste, tone and quality in the plays. Given the choice, these critics argue, Shakespeare would never have written so many dirty jokes, low comic routines, sword fights and other crowd-pleasing spectacles. He was shackled to his trade, forced to prostitute his talent to gratify the base tastes of the 'rank-scented many' (*Coriolanus*, 3.1.70). As Robert Bridges wrote in 1927: 'Shakespeare should not be put into the hands of the young without the warning that the foolish things in his plays were written to please the foolish, the filthy for the filthy, and the brutal for the brutal.'[7] But if one tradition has criminalized Shakespeare's popular audience, another has idealized it as consisting of cheerful and decent folk whose ears, attuned by an aural-oral culture, were more capable than their twentieth-century counterparts of following the complexity of Shakespeare's writing. This popular audience, according to Alfred Harbage, 'must be given much of the credit for the greatness of Shakespeare's plays'.[8]

Straightforward binaries of high and low, elite and popular will only get us so far in understanding the appeal and power of the plays to their first audiences. We should be wary of describing moments of action, let alone whole plays, as either populist or caviar for the general, as we can never know for sure which sections of the Globe audience reacted favourably to which moments of the performances, or indeed how much that audience thought of itself as unified in the experience of theatre-going or, conversely, was always aware of its social divisions. A common-sense approach might recognize that artistic taste can be mysterious and does not always neatly correspond to social status.[9] Formal education does not inevitably lead to intelligence; posh people enjoy dirty jokes; a working-class upbringing need be no bar to the understanding, enjoyment or production of sophisticated art.

Shakespeare's perceived attitude to the popular elements in his audience continues to inform critical and editorial practice. One of the more radical decisions taken by the editors of the *Oxford Shakespeare* (1986) was to cut the ending found in both authoritative early texts of *Troilus and Cressida* and to conclude the play not with Pandarus' scabrous epilogue but with Troilus' nobly restrained grief. The logic behind this decision is sophisticated, but rests in part on an assumption about what a popular audience would be able to tolerate. Elsewhere, the shadow of the Dyer's Hand continues to fall on the popular sense of who Shakespeare was, above all in the desire to have him someone other than a man from the 'middling sort'. 'Anti-Stratfordian' is the collective name for the belief that someone other than the man from Stratford wrote the plays commonly attributed to him. Anti-Stratfordian authorship candidates are legion, but are almost invariably aristocrats and/or university-educated (Shakespeare, grammar-school boy and son of a glove-maker, was neither). An antagonism to popular culture is implicit in nearly all anti-Stratfordian literature and thought. Perhaps surprisingly – given the elitist bent of anti-Stratfordianism – the notion that someone else wrote Shakespeare is now quite common in popular culture.

Popular voices

Shakespeare's popular audiences paid to see and hear plays which dramatized all levels of early modern society. But the social composition of the *characters* that populate Shakespeare's dramas did not reflect that of his audience in the public theatres. Shakespeare's drama is disproportionately concerned with the imagined lives of elites – Kings, Queens, Dukes, Counts and so on – and it is revealing that Shakespeare largely avoided writing in the mode of the City Comedy, that most mimetic and journalistic of early modern dramatic genres. Yet Shakespeare's art was socially diverse and polyphonic – in his plays we also hear and see citizens, soldiers, cobblers, servants, hired assassins, bellows-menders, shepherds, fishermen, ballad-mongers, bawds, boatswains and apothecaries. To the disgust of many later critics, particularly eighteenth-century neo-classicists, Shakespeare chose to mingle high with low, dramatizing the interaction between the powerful and the powerless, the elite and the ordinary. Shakespeare's clowns are not confined to his comedies, but make telling cameos throughout the tragedies: Prince Hamlet speaks with, and mostly listens to, a gravedigger; a Clown delivers the fatal asp to Cleopatra, and, in *Macbeth*, acts as Porter at the hellish gate of Glamis castle. In *A Midsummer Night's Dream*, the Fairy Queen Titania passionately dotes on Bottom the earth-bound, working-class weaver.

Any assessment of the ways in which Shakespeare staged popular culture leads to the question: what were his politics? Many critics, of the left as well as the right, have concluded that Shakespeare was an instinctive conservative whose dramas broadly endorsed strict social hierarchy and the privileges of rank. High-born characters frequently reflect on the mutability and childlike gullibility of the masses. Democracy, what Coriolanus calls the 'popular shall', is dangerous. In the Jack Cade rebellion in 2 *Henry VI* or the forum scene in *Julius Caesar*, Shakespeare depicts this volatile and manipulable populace in action. We hear much about the divine rights of kings, far less about the divine rights of the people. But these anti-popular moments and sentiments are counter-balanced by many occasions on which Shakespeare gives sympathetic airtime to the oppositional voices of popular culture. As Annabel Patterson sensibly observes:

> Given what we know of Shakespeare's status as the most popular playwright at a time when the theatre was popular as never before or since – at its peak the London theatre attendance ranged between 8,000 and 10,000 per day – it seems folly to assume that his plays, by assuming an elitist social perspective, knowingly insulted a large proportion of their audience.[10]

Patterson's *Shakespeare and the Popular Voice* (1989) is one of many studies that have sought to rescue Shakespeare from the charge of elitism and redefine him as a playwright attuned to the proto-democratic desires of early modern popular culture.

Less controversially, it is clear that the infinite variety of Shakespeare's soundscape owed much to the richness of the demotic, the vernacular and the linguistic registers of the base, common and vulgar. The popular voice, sometimes oppositional and radical, sometimes acquiescently docile or merely comic, but always vivid, forms one of the keynotes of Shakespearian drama.

Popular festivity

Elizabethan professional drama emerged from a complex fusion of popular dramatic forms (including mystery cycles, morality plays and the Italian *commedia dell'arte*) with higher cultural themes and modes of expression (whether derived from classical, courtly or humanist sources). From the indigenous popular drama, Shakespeare inherited the pivotal figures of the Vice, the Clown and the Fool, and an actor–audience relationship that was intimate, flexible and spontaneous. But no less influential to Shakespeare's art, according to some critics, were the rich popular traditions of festivity. The early modern English calendar was organized around a succession of festivals and holy-days which served to punctuate the working, secular year with days of celebration, festivity and the joyous suspension of labour. These days often had their origin in the pre-Christian beliefs of a rural popular culture which attended to seasonal rhythms and the related cycles of fertility. Thus the early modern sense of time was different from our own. Our experience of leisure and holidays is flexible and individual – there will always be someone else working when we're on holiday – and the ways in which we spend our time off are, in theory, almost endlessly diverse. In early modern England, a festival marked a day off for all workers and tended to unite a community through the collective enactment of games and rituals. Indeed the 'merry wars' between the sexes in *The Taming of the Shrew* or *Much Ado About Nothing* may have struck some of Shakespeare's audience as variations on the traditional Hocktide games that pitted men and women against each other in Shakespeare's own county of Warwickshire at Easter. Falstaff's humiliation as Herne the Hunter at the close of *The Merry Wives of Windsor* recalls the Skimmington ride or charivari, a festive tradition in which a community made public its objection to a prospective marriage, in this case Falstaff's greedy attempts to seduce both Mistress Page and Mistress Ford.

A key concept is that of the carnivalesque. Following Michaïl Bakhtin's influential *Rabelais and his World* (1965; English translation 1968), many critics have argued that the spirit of carnival suffuses Shakespearian drama. Carnival was the popular festival that preceded Lent in much of medieval Europe. It was characterized by topsy-turvy inversions of social hierarchy: men dressed as women, a boy might be pronounced bishop, and the village idiot would become king or Lord of Misrule. The lower stratum of the body (the bowels, belly and genitals) was indulged and ruled the head; it was a period of bacchic blow-out before the privations and self-disciplines of Lent. We might here think of scenes in Shakespeare in which ordinary gradations of rank somersault under the influence of alcohol: Iago the ensign tricks Cassio the lieutenant into career-threatening inebriation; drunk Lepidus, one-third of the triumvirate that rules the ancient world, must be carried to bed; Christopher Sly, presumably drunk, is conned into believing himself to be a lord. We might also interpret whole plays as symbolic enactments of the Battle between Carnival and Lent: *Love's Labour's*

Lost begins with four men swearing off sensual and bodily delights, only to learn that, in the words of the popular clown Costard, it 'is the simplicity of man to hearken after the flesh' (1.1.214–15); *Measure for Measure*, in a very different key, offers a comparable struggle between puritanical prohibition and popular pleasure. Falstaff – the personification of carnivalesque appetite and vice – spends two plays vying with the dour Henry IV for Hal's affection and allegiance, a contest Falstaff will ultimately lose as the Prince must put away frivolity ('I know thee not, old man') in order to rule as Henry V.

In assessing the importance of popular traditions, forms and customs to Shakespeare's drama, we should remember that the text we read captures only part of the performance experienced by its first audiences. Popular sub-literary forms such as songs, dances and jigs, all common features of early modern drama, often went unrecorded. Even so, the printed texts of Shakespeare's plays retain so many instances of popular song and calls for dance that we can only assume that these were seen as central to the dramatic experience. How we interpret the presence of popular culture in Shakespearian drama will inevitably depend on our own prejudices and on the peculiar dynamics of the context of the moment in which the popular is staged or voiced. We can, however, provisionally conclude that without popular audiences, Shakespeare's plays might never have been written. And without the active and dynamic influence of popular culture, they would have been infinitely poorer.

Shakespeare and contemporary popular culture

To fast-forward 400 years from the early modern to the post-modern is to be struck by a welter of radical discontinuities, upheavals both in the status of Shakespeare and in the constitution of culture(s), popular and otherwise, that would have been unimaginable to the play's first audiences. Four hundred years ago, Shakespeare's plays provided pleasure and perhaps instruction to a few thousand people mainly located in the capital city of a small island in western Europe; now, Shakespeare is a global phenomenon, pleasing, boring or leaving indifferent millions of readers and viewers across the planet. (See Chapter 19.) Where Shakespeare was once optional – shall we go to the Globe this afternoon or not? – he is now, for many, mandatory, the ability to read and analyse his plays being one of the ways numerous education systems use to measure intelligence. Four hundred years ago, only a few dozen people made money directly out of Shakespeare; now professional Shakespearians are legion. Shakespeare has been canonized, placed at the pinnacle of Western high culture; he has been exported through soft and hard colonialism, his passage somewhat eased by the emergence (equally colonial) of English as the world's lingua franca. His medium, the public theatre, is – depending on one's outlook – either in surprisingly good health or a marginal, middle-class art-form in the last throes of a demise made inevitable by the inventions of cinema, television and the Internet. (See Chapter 17.)

As striking as these changes may be, we are also haunted by some abiding questions: how popular is the audience for Shakespeare? To whom does Shakespeare belong? Does 'Shakespeare' stand for stasis or change? Are his works produced and received as reactionary or revolutionary? Is popular culture Shakespeare's natural element, or are his works contaminated by contact with the palms of the vulgar? Again, we are confronted by the complexity of the term 'popular culture'. 'The popular', Robert Shaughnessy writes, 'is itself hardly a singular or uncontested term or frame of reference: seen from some angles, it denotes community, shared values, democratic participation, accessibility, and fun; from others, the mass-produced commodity, the lowest common denominator, the reductive or the simplified, or the shoddy, the coarse, and the meretricious.'[11] Most cultural historians have sought to distinguish twentieth- and twenty-first-century popular culture from the folk and popular cultures of pre-industrial societies such as early modern England. In his influential essay 'A Theory of Mass Culture' (1957), Dwight Macdonald insists on just such a stark distinction:

> Folk art grew from below. It was a spontaneous, autochthonous expression of the people, shaped by themselves, pretty much without the benefit of High Culture, to suit their own needs. Mass Culture is imposed from above. It is fabricated by technicians hired by businessmen; its audience are passive consumers, their participation limited to the choice between buying and not buying.[12]

In this narrative of decline, where once the populace made its own art and customs it now merely passively consumes those products engineered by profit-mongering elites.

Some critics have located the beginnings of this decline as coincidental with, and partly precipitated by, the founding of the first professional theatres in England. This culture industry, in which Shakespeare was the key player, 'almost certainly helped to accelerate the shift from direct skilled engagement in the production of cultural experience to the more passive habits of cultural consumption'.[13]

As these accounts suggest, much of the argument about the place of Shakespeare in post-modern popular culture revolves around the politics of production and consumption. Who makes and sells 'Shakespeare' in the present? Who's buying? What are they buying into? So ubiquitous is Shakespeare's presence both in global popular culture and in a range of popular sub-cultures around the world that the student and critic are spoiled for choice. Douglas Lanier's *Shakespeare and Modern Popular Culture* (2002) offers a wide-ranging and even-handed analysis of allusions, parodies and adaptations with particular attention to American popular television, film and music. Richard Burt's interest lies even lower down the cultural food chain, focusing on Shakespeare's pairing with the so-called 'trash' genres of pornography, horror and action films, comic-book fantasy and so on, a pairing that he argues typically produces 'Schlockspeare'. As a rule, Burt argues, these hybrids have little to say that is meaningful about Shakespeare's texts, nor do they offer the potential for any critique of the dominant consumerist and conservative values of post-modern American society. Scepticism towards popularized Shakespeare is also common to many academic analyses of mass-market films such as Baz Luhrmann's *Romeo+Juliet* (1996), John Madden's *Shakespeare in Love* (1999) and the Shakespeare adaptations directed by Kenneth Branagh. (See Chapter 20.)

In what follows, I describe some recent collisions between Shakespeare and contemporary popular culture in order to sketch out potential avenues for future research. The examples are mostly drawn from British and American culture over the first decade of the twenty-first century, but the material selected and the questions that arise from them should be internationally applicable, even if the cultural concerns and contexts vary according to location.

Popularity contests: 'Your voices!'

How do we determine cultural significance? How do we measure popularity? In December 1999, Shakespeare was voted British 'man of the millennium' by listeners to BBC Radio 4's 'Today' programme. Shakespeare received just over a quarter of 45,000 votes, narrowly beating his nearest contender – Sir Winston Churchill – to take the crown. These 'best of' lists are festive fixtures, ways through which contemporary British culture marks the passing of time; they appear most prolifically in or around the twelve days of Christmas, a 'silly season' in which real news is notoriously thin on the ground. At the end of the second millennium, they were especially legion. But what, if anything, did this festive ritual prove? In another poll conducted in April 2008, YouGov asked 2,032 respondents to name four things they most associated with England: 61 per cent said the monarchy, 58 per cent said fish and chips, 50 per cent said William Shakespeare and 43 per cent said roast beef. Put together, the two polls present a tantalizing glimpse of a culture which cherishes the pre-eminence of what Tony Blair might have called 'the people's playwright'. But there are major caveats. First, the sample of people consulted in both cases was fractional and, in the case of the Radio 4 poll, presumably skewed by an 'educated', middle-class demographic. Second, and crucially, we don't know *why* Shakespeare gathered these votes. Third, what are we to make of the fact that in 2002, BBC TV conducted another such exercise, this time asking the public to vote on their '100 Greatest Britons', and Shakespeare, man of the millennium, came merely fifth?

Perhaps the culturally revealing question is not 'Is Shakespeare the greatest?', but 'Who should represent Shakespeare?' In February 2009, the Shakespeare Birthplace Trust in Stratford-upon-Avon announced that it was to open a Shakespearian 'Hall of Fame' featuring thirteen individuals whose induction would recognize their contribution to the championing of Shakespeare's works. Twelve were selected by the Trust, but the thirteenth would, in the fashion of popular TV shows such as *Strictly Come Dancing* and *Big Brother*, be decided by a public vote. Ten further candidates were offered for the play-off place; the poll, hosted by the *Guardian* newspaper website, was open to anyone anywhere in the world with access to the Internet. Three of the ten candidates received a combined 92 per cent share of the vote. While Goethe, Virginia Woolf and Sarah Siddons languished with less than 1 per cent of the vote each, actor David Tennant romped home with 65 per cent (his nearest rivals Boris Pasternak, 15 per cent, and John Gielgud, 12.3 per cent). Tennant's television performance as Dr Who had made him immensely popular, and his recent stage appearances for the RSC as Biron and, particularly, Hamlet had won critical and public acclaim. What is of interest to students of Shakespeare and popular culture is the *reaction* both to Tennant's victory and to the 'Hall of Fame' idea itself. Responses to the latter revealed anxieties about the 'dumbing-down' of high culture: the 'Hall of Fame' is an American sporting tradition; was there not something vulgar about treating artists like baseball players and subjecting them to a popular vote? Blog discussion about Tennant's victory also quickly revealed cultural faultlines. Those seeking to block Tennant's win were accused of a snobbish antipathy to popular culture. But Tennant's supporters wanted it both ways: they both defended the artistic value of the television series, but also stressed the actor's training and prior stage experience as a Shakespearian. In such moments, a reciprocal, if fraught, legitimation takes place: Shakespeare is popularized, but the popular also partakes of the prestige of 'legitimate' high culture.

Popular production: Shakespeare with a twist

If one index of popularity is statistical, the big numbers lie not in one-off polls or random street interviews, but in a world (wide web) elsewhere.

Eleven thousand people may have voted Shakespeare the man of the millennium, but fifty times that amount (and rising) have watched 'Shakespeare', a video by British hip-hop artist Akala, posted on YouTube in July 2006. The lyrics consist of Akala claiming that his music is in a different class from that of other hip-hop artists – so far, so predictable – but as we reach the first chorus, this macho rhetoric climaxes in a surprising comparison:

> I'm a whole different kettle of fish: Thou shalt not fuck with dis. My shit, I tell em like this: It's like Shakespeare with a nigger twist.

Akala's deployment of Shakespeare as a benchmark of (almost) peerless verbal sophistication is common to many pop cultural citations; the difference here is that Akala presents that sophistication not as remote or elitist, but as something with which a young black Londoner can claim kinship, albeit with a vital twist. Akala is not the first person to bring rap and Shakespeare together. The Reduced Shakespeare Company's *Complete Works* features a (borderline racist) *Othello* rap; *The Bomb-itty of Errors* (1999), an 'ad-rap-tation' of Shakespeare's early comedy, has successfully toured venues across North America. So clichéd is the association between Shakespeare and rap in the American school system – as teachers struggle to make Shakespeare 'relevant' – that in 2005 the satirical paper *The Onion* felt obliged to pen a spoof in which a fictional English teacher tries to street-talk her high-school class into liking 'Big Willie Shakes':

> Shakespeare had the tightest flow in the history of the English language. His iambic pentameter couldn't be touched by other MCs, although player-haters think he sampled heavily from Ben Jonson. In fact, were he alive today, I'm convinced he would be a rapper. Well, I guess he could be a playwright, too.[14]

But popular artists like Akala (or, indeed, Shelton Alexander, the New Orleans spoken-word performer who styles himself the 'African American Shakespeare') seem unfazed by this kind of satire, insisting instead that Shakespeare stands as a genuine precedent and inspiration for contemporary black music and culture. In 2008, Akala released 'Comedy, Tragedy, History', another Shakes-hip-hop track in which he alludes at high speed to as many of Shakespeare's plays as possible.

How does Akala's use of and identification with Shakespeare relate to his stated aim to be 'a generational voice for change, empowerment and salvation, for himself, his people, and for the streets'?[15] Will his subsequent foundation of the Shakespeare Hip-Hop Company in 2008 succeed in spreading his love of Shakespeare to 'hard-to-reach' inner-city teenagers?

This is just one of countless examples of Shakespeare citation in popular music. Its significance is complex and debatable; what is beyond doubt is that, for at least half a million people, Akala's tracks are now part of the repertoire of associations evoked by the name of 'Shakespeare'. This repertoire has been vastly expanded by the new platforms of the digital age. A site like YouTube not only makes it easier for professional cultural producers to disseminate their work, it also offers a potentially egalitarian space in which 'ordinary' people and amateurs can post their own versions of Shakespeare. In short, widespread availability of new technologies has made it easier than ever for consumers to become producers. Since 2006, for example, almost 3 million people have watched Cat Head Theatre's *Hamlet*, a short animation featuring three lively cat heads perched on cut-out Elizabethan costumes performing an extract from Hamlet's first meeting with Rosencrantz and Guildenstern (2.2). Many of the 'home-made' Shakespeare postings on YouTube feature similarly surprising metamorphic re-imaginings: *Troilus and Cressida* set in small-town slacker-youth America, the dialogue and plot bearing only an obscure – but intriguing – resemblance to the original; a pop-video pastiche of *Othello* experienced from Desdemona's point of view; a silent film loosely based on the opening act of *Julius Caesar* as seen through the eyes of Filipina schoolgirls.

In many other postings, Shakespeare's speeches serve as vehicles for self-expression, both outlets for and containers of the performer's emotion. In the great, Shakespeare-riddled film *Withnail and I* (1987), comic-tragic Uncle Monty reflects that 'it is the most shattering experience of a young man's life when one morning he awakes and, quite reasonably, says to himself: "I will never play the Dane".' But now, in the user-generated era, anyone with a camcorder can have a go at the soliloquies and play the Dane in cyberspace. At the time of writing, one of the most popular Shakespeare-related videos on YouTube features Craig Bazan, a young African American, delivering a passionate rendition of Hamlet's 'Oh what a rogue and peasant slave am I' on a derelict street-corner in Camden, New Jersey. Bazan's performance has received hundreds of viewer comments – most complimentary, some expressing surprise that he had not been shot mid-soliloquy in one of the United States' most crime-ridden neighbourhoods. In response, Bazan posted another video in which he thanked his far-flung fans whilst also defending the reputation of his home town. The message: that, despite media stereotyping, not all young African American men are snared in the guns-and-drugs spiral. Here – as with Akala – 'Shakespeare' is a marker of social optimism and identity politics: if he can happen here, channelled through this performer, on this corner, the town cannot be written off as just another demoralized and irredeemable ghetto.[16]

It is too early to say whether the proliferation of home-made Shakespeares marks a new stage in the history of popular culture's relationship with Shakespeare. What is clear is that many of these videos vividly challenge the pessimistic notion that contemporary mass culture has reduced most of us to the position of passive consumers, left only with the choice of whether to buy or not to buy. Alongside the Shakespeare of high culture – elite, aloof and impenetrable – exists Shakespeare the fertile (and un-copyrighted) source of accessible and malleable images, stories and character. Just as the playwright Shakespearianized the popular culture he inherited in the 1590s, so, in turn, Shakespeare will continue to be popularized in the decades to come. As ever, it will be relatively easy to see Shakespeare in popular culture, much harder to know what exactly he is *doing* there. That interpretative challenge awaits the student of this rich and controversial strand of Shakespeare studies.

NOTES

1 Chris Offutt, 'Extract from *Offutt's Guide to Literary Terms*', *Harper's Magazine*, October 2008, 26.

2 For example, see Dr Johnson's verdict in 1765 that Shakespeare 'has more allusions than other poets to the traditions and superstition of the vulgar; which must therefore be traced before he can be understood'. *Johnson on Shakespeare*, ed. Arthur Sherbo. Vols. VII–VIII of *The Yale Edition of the Works of Samuel Johnson* (New Haven: Yale University Press, 1968), vol. VII, p. 53.

3 Raymond Williams, *Keywords: A Vocabulary of Culture and Society* (London: Fontana, 1976), p. 87.

4 For a more thorough discussion of these issues than is possible here, see Douglas Lanier, *Shakespeare and Modern Popular Culture* (Oxford: Oxford University Press, 2002), pp. 1–20; for a good overview, see John Storey, *Cultural Theory and Popular Culture: An Introduction* (Harlow: Pearson, 2001), 3rd edn.

5 These are the three key definitions usefully identified by Mary Ellen Lamb, *The Popular Culture of Shakespeare, Spenser, and Jonson* (London: Routledge, 2008), p. 1.

6 Barry Reay, 'Popular Culture in Early Modern England', in Reay (ed.), *Popular Culture in Seventeenth-Century England* (Beckenham: Croom Helm, 1985), p. 1.

7 Robert Bridges, 'On the Influence of the Audience', *Collected Essays* (Oxford: Oxford University Press, 1927), p. 28.

8 Alfred Harbage, *Shakespeare's Audience* (1941; New York: Columbia University Press, 1969), p. 159.

9 This sentence would be anathema to Pierre Bourdieu, who argues, often convincingly, the exact opposite in *Distinction: A Social Critique of the Judgement of Taste*, trans. Richard Nice (1979; London: Routledge and Kegan Paul, 1986).

10 Annabel Patterson, *Shakespeare and the Popular Voice* (Oxford: Blackwell, 1989), p. 3.
11 Robert Shaughnessy, 'Introduction', in Shaughnessy (ed.), *The Cambridge Companion to Shakespeare and Popular Culture* (Cambridge: Cambridge University Press, 2007), p. 2.
12 Dwight Macdonald, 'A Theory of Mass Culture', in John Storey (ed.), *Cultural Theory and Popular Culture: A Reader* (Hemel Hempstead: Prentice Hall, 1998), 2nd edn, p. 23.
13 Michael Bristol, 'Theater and Popular Culture', in John D. Cox and David Scott Kastan (eds.), *A New History of Early English Drama* (New York: Columbia University Press, 1997), p. 248.
14 'Shakespeare was, like, the Ultimate Rapper', *The Onion*, 41:34, 24 August 2005.
15 Quotation taken from Akala's website: www.akalamusic.com/
16 Cat Head Theatre *Hamlet*: www.youtube.com/watch?v=DbK1eCt97ag. Craig Bazan: www.youtube.com/watch?v=Oa-cfEncd6Y. Luke McKernan's site, 'Bard-Box', helpfully offers a collection of the best and most interesting examples of original Shakespeare videos online: http://bardbox.wordpress.com/

READING LIST

Shakespeare and early modern popular culture

Barber, C. L. *Shakespeare's Festive World: A Study of Dramatic Form and its Relation to Social Custom*. Princeton, NJ: Princeton University Press, 1959.

Bevington, David. *From 'Mankind' to Marlowe: Growth of Structure in the Popular Drama of Tudor England*. Harvard: Harvard University Press, 1965.

Bristol, Michael. *Carnival and Theater: Plebeian Culture and the Structure of Authority in Renaissance England*. London: Methuen, 1985.

Gillespie, Stuart and Neil Rhodes, eds. *Shakespeare and Elizabethan Popular Culture*. London: Arden Shakespeare, 2006.

Knowles, Ronald, ed. *Shakespeare and Carnival: After Bakhtin*. Basingstoke: Macmillan, 1998.

Kott, Jan. *The Bottom Translation: Marlowe and Shakespeare and the Carnival Tradition*. Evanston, IL: Northwestern University Press, 1987.

Laroque, François. *Shakespeare's Festive World: Elizabethan Seasonal Entertainment and the Professional Stage*. Cambridge: Cambridge University Press, 1991.

Patterson, Annabel. *Shakespeare and the Popular Voice*. Oxford: Blackwell, 1989.

Weimann, Robert. *Shakespeare and the Popular Tradition in the Theatre: Studies in the Social Dimension of Dramatic Form and Function*. Baltimore: Johns Hopkins University Press, 1978. Originally published in German in 1967.

Shakespeare and modern popular culture

Burt, Richard. *Unspeakable ShaXXXpeares: Queer Theory and American Kiddie Culture*. New York: St Martin's Press, 1998.

Burt, Richard, ed. *Shakespeare after Mass Media*. New York: Palgrave, 2002.

Shakespeares after Shakespeare: An Encyclopedia of the Bard in Mass Media and Popular Culture, 2 vols. Westport, CT: Greenwood Press, 2006.

Lanier, Douglas. *Shakespeare and Modern Popular Culture*. Oxford: Oxford University Press, 2002.

Levine, Lawrence W. *Highbrow/Lowbrow: The Emergence of Cultural Hierarchy in America*. Cambridge, MA: Harvard University Press, 1988.

Shaughnessy, Robert, ed. *The Cambridge Companion to Shakespeare and Popular Culture*. Cambridge: Cambridge University Press, 2007.

Taylor, Gary. *Reinventing Shakespeare: A Cultural History from the Restoration to the Present*. London: Hogarth Press, 1990.

19

ANSTON BOSMAN

Shakespeare and globalization

The worldwide diffusion of William Shakespeare's works occurs today, as it has occurred for centuries, in the context of social processes of mobility and mediation. Since the 1960s these processes have been studied under the rubric 'globalization', but the term names a condition as ancient as the experience of empire and diaspora, of nations and the states they create. Such antiquity should not lead us, however, to equate classical Rome with Elizabethan England or modern Russia or Japan. On the contrary, if we can accept an influential definition of globalization as both 'the compression of the world and the intensification of consciousness of the world as a whole', then we should try to historicize that compression and that consciousness.[1] We might begin with Shakespeare himself, since he lived in the age when all the world's populated continents were first permanently linked by trade. Some economic historians have even argued that globalization began in the year 1571, when the Spanish established Manila as an entrepôt finally connecting Asia and the Americas, and William Shakespeare of Stratford-upon-Avon turned 7.[2] During his lifetime, cultural exchanges multiplied not only among European nations, but between Europe and the Atlantic and, more slowly, Pacific worlds. Many of these growing interdependencies left their mark on Shakespeare's writing and theatre, from advances in stage design to an explosion of literary sources in print.

In Shakespeare's day, moreover, English was taking its first steps towards its current status as a world language. Beginning with travellers and traders in the sixteenth century, English penetrated the Americas, Asia and the Antipodes in the seventeenth and eighteenth, enabled colonial developments in Africa and the South Pacific in the nineteenth, and was adopted in the twentieth as an official language by many newly independent states. Between the death of Elizabeth I and the closing years of the reign of Elizabeth II, the number of mother-tongue English speakers in the world increased at least fiftyfold, from around 7 million to over 350 million.[3] As English spread, Shakespeare's works travelled beyond Britain into the colonies and across the empire, settling in the United States and throughout the post-colonial world: thus the copyright page of the Oxford *Complete Works* locates the press in Oxford and New York but lists its publishing centres as follows: 'Auckland, Cape Town, Dar es Salaam, Hong Kong, Karachi, Kuala Lumpur', etc. To these nodes in the publishing economy we should add the global centres of theatre (London) or film (Los Angeles) from which Shakespeare radiates in English – or better, in 'Englishes', since a Hollywood adaptation or a West End production in Scots extends the rich variation within the English language itself.

Yet the scattering of Shakespeare is not coextensive with the advance of English. Dissemination of his work in foreign languages began in his lifetime, when so-called English players travelled the Continent, assembling multi-national troupes, mounting polyglot productions and seeding translations in European vernaculars.[4] Early Dutch and German versions were gradually overshadowed by French, in which the first foreign Shakespeare collection appeared (1745–6), and which dispersed Shakespeare as far as Russia and Turkey, via Spanish and Portuguese to South America, and via Italian into the cosmopolitan sphere of opera and ballet.[5] But French neoclassical Shakespeare was countered in its turn by the German Romantics, who produced their own canonical translation (1762–6, revised as the first foreign complete works in 1775–7), as well as a lively performance tradition. So forceful was this appropriation of Shakespeare for nationalistic purposes that German writers, scholars and theatre managers claimed the Bard as a compatriot, inspiring later political uses of Shakespeare in the Soviet Union and Eastern Europe. By the twentieth century the plays – and, at some delay, the poems – had found new homes in Icelandic and Greek, in Quebecois and Korean, in Arabic and Zulu. The complete works now appear in over thirty languages and individual texts in over eighty. And in our multi-lingual world it is not unusual to stage or film Shakespeare in a mix of tongues, expanding his own use of French or Welsh into a production like Tim Supple's 2006 *A Midsummer Night's Dream*, which blended English with a mixture of Hindi, Bengali, Tamil, Sinhalese, Malayalam, Marathi and Sanskrit.

The Shakespeare we confront today has been globalized beyond the confines of any single language or territory. As migrants and media exchange his works back and forth across national borders, a simple opposition between 'domestic' and 'foreign' Shakespeare grows ever less convincing, and to set down his fortunes country by country is to tour the empty pavilions of an abandoned world's fair. For this reason, it seems prudent to explore the subject of this chapter by ways other than the recitation of national theatre histories. Let us instead follow the worldwide dissemination of Shakespeare by distinguishing among three global networks: a theatrical network made up chiefly of performers and directors; a textual network comprising writers, editors and translators; and a digital network deploying a range of media and devices.[6] Needless to say, in practice these environments considerably and increasingly overlap, and it is therefore with some irony that I have named each section after what might initially seem the single numinous source of each network's power: the actor, the author and the aether.

Actors

The globalization of Shakespeare began with performance. Years before literary translations of the plays appeared, foreign versions took shape on stage and in real time as an actor, or, rarely, a spectator, mediated between English and a local tongue. Troupes crossing Europe before the Thirty Years' War (1618–48) used a bilingual clown to summarize and satirize the unfolding action for an audience that knew no English. And in the first Shakespeare recorded outside Europe, an English merchant ship off the coast of what is now Sierra Leone became in 1607 a stage for *Hamlet*, with an African guest providing a running translation in Portuguese (and possibly Temne).[7] Over time, as players abroad acquired new languages and drafted local partners, these spoken improvisations – comparable to today's sports commentary or simultaneous interpreting – developed into complete foreign-language stagings, scripts and printed books. But printing did not simply replace the authority of performers with that of writers. A 1620 German collection of the itinerant repertory, for example, cites no author but advertises the plays as having been 'acted and presented by the English in Germany'.[8] For some time, translations remained largely instrumental documents judged in terms of their accessibility to actors. And as late as 1899 a new French version of *Hamlet* made its mark not by the names of its translators, Marcel Schwob and Eugène Morand, but through the star power of the person who commissioned and starred in it – Sarah Bernhardt.[9]

To be sure, the time between the Baroque and the Belle Époque saw major shifts in theatre and drama, with consequences for international Shakespeare. First the early modern actor's sole governance over staging was redistributed across a performance network including producers, directors, designers and dramaturgs. In 1620, after all, a troupe of Anglo-European comedians comprised ten to fifteen actors plus musicians, headed by a leader who often played the crucial clown role; yet this leader was not responsible for ensuring the artistic unity of a production, and so performances tended to be free and quite uneven adaptations of their source. With the rise of the actor-manager in the eighteenth century and the director and producer in the nineteenth, aesthetic control became a controversial issue.

Actor-directors drove avant-garde innovation or putative returns to authenticity. When Bernhardt presented *Hamlet* in 1899, she unusually combined the roles of producer, principal actor and director. She also insisted that the alexandrine couplets and plot changes of earlier French versions be swept away by a landmark scholarly translation in prose. The new text's claim to fidelity – it sought to approximate Elizabethan English by concocting a pastiche of sixteenth-century French – makes a fascinating contrast with Bernhardt's experimental portrayal of Hamlet, against sentimental *travesti* norms, as a virile and volatile young man.[10]

The actor's role in transferring a play across cultures remains central today. In Taipei in 2001, for instance, the Taiwanese master Wu Hsing-Kuo premiered his solo work *Li Er zaici* (*Lear is here*), which fused materials from Western and Chinese theatrical traditions. Wu introduced Shakespeare's story by presenting Lear's Fool as refracted through the clown type of *jingju* theatre (also known as Beijing opera). Sporting the hallmark white-patched nose and crouching steps of the Chinese clown, Wu's Fool drew the audience into complicity using conventions of rhyme and mime:

> Ah ha! [An exclamation used by the clown type.]
> Just now I had a dream,
> Dreaming of my master sleeping in a dark hole.
> Giving up his position as a king and volunteering to be an inferior,
>
> How can I not feel distressed for him!...I really miss him when I don't see him; but I simply want to kick him whenever I do see him. You old fool, idiot! How can you be so out of your mind before you're really old?! [*To the audience.*] Do you know why? I'll tell you...[11]

This cross-cultural performance echoes the interventions of the earliest travelling clowns. While Wu is not concerned to present a word-for-word equivalent for a specific passage in *King Lear*, this moment is clearly an effort to translate some of the play's other theatrical 'languages', including intonation, movement, gesture and make-up, from one culture to another. (The show also incorporated versions of *jingju* costume, properties, singing, music and dance.) In this process of translation, neither Shakespeare nor the traditional Chinese genre went unchanged, and the transformations continued as Wu modified his play throughout its subsequent European tour. *Li Er zaici* reminds us that theatre is a syncretic and provisional art whose multiple dimensions are reconfigured before each new audience: like the Fool himself, a transcultural actor must improvise with verbal and physical agility, stretching the limits of convention and thereby revitalizing the theatre itself.

Though his play explored personal themes, Wu admitted that it harboured a cultural agenda. Describing *King Lear* as 'a bombshell ... capable of exposing human hypocrisy', he expressed the hope that *Li Er zaici* would in turn be 'capable of destroying the tombstone that has been prepared for traditional Chinese theatre'.[12] A hallmark of Shakespeare's intercultural entanglements is this tension between the apparently universal values of a story and the local motivations of its staging. The tension runs especially high in places where staging has itself been proscribed. Consider the difficult recent case of Afghanistan, where theatre was silent through decades of warfare, culminating in the repressive rule of the Taliban in the 1990s. Since the fall of the Taliban, however, Afghanistan has seen a theatrical revival at the national and regional levels, including projects jointly undertaken by Western and Central Asian practitioners. Perhaps the most remarkable such project was the truly global collaboration that led to a production of *Love's Labour's Lost* in a bomb-scarred Mughal garden in Kabul over five nights in September 2005.

For the Kabul *Love's Labour's Lost* eleven Afghan actors gathered under the direction of a Canadian actress and a US aid worker to perform a text adapted into Dari by two Afghan writers from a Farsi translation prepared by an Iranian scholar.[13] The play was chosen because the directors liked Shakespeare, because the actors preferred a comedy to a tragedy and because it could be adapted for an equal number of male and female roles. In the aftermath of Taliban rule, having women on stage at all was contentious, and those who joined the cast – forgoing veils or protective burqas – had to face some public disapproval. In this context the play's initial oath, by which the King and his three lords forswear female company and mandate punishments for women who approach the court and men who speak with them, acquired fresh urgency, as did the comically swift dissolution of their contract under the witty and level-headed interventions of the Princess and her ladies. Moreover, the Kabul production added to Shakespeare's plot new features targeted at specific Taliban prohibitions: towards the play's end, after mocking the lords' inconstancy, the Princess Shardakht-e-Herat called for conciliatory music, whereupon courtiers took up instruments and serenaded the ladies with an Afghan folk song – and the women promptly joined in, thereby putting the fundamentalist ban on public singing by women, which had until recently been in force, firmly in the past.

Nonetheless, the production's religious and political context imposed limits and changes. There was no touching between the sexes during the performance, but when the actors held hands at the curtain call some of the (mostly Afghan and male) audience demurred. And many of the comic types in *Love's Labour's Lost*, descended from the zanies of the *commedia dell'arte*, disappeared from the cast list in Kabul on account of their obscene jokes teeming with sexual and scatological innuendo. Most remarkably, the revels of the lords disguised as Muscovites bore too strong an association with the brutal Soviet invasion of Afghanistan and had to be rewritten. The fake Russians were turned into fake Indians, who entertained the ladies with song-and-dance routines from Bollywood films, which are hugely popular among Afghans. More is at stake here than a transfer of humour from Shakespeare's place and time into a new cultural context, complex though that operation is; rather, the Kabul team sought to translate Shakespeare's European stereotypes of foreign places, remapping them for an audience caught in a web of relations stretching throughout Asia and beyond, mediated by English drama and Hindi cinema alike.

I earlier proposed examining transnational performances of Shakespeare in terms of a tension between universal values and particular motivations. The Kabul *Love's Labour's Lost* might appear to endorse such a split, inasmuch as the American co-adaptor praised Shakespeare for writing 'truths of human experience' and was then excoriated online by an Afghan blog poster as an agent of 'imported theatre'.[14] Upon inspection, however, its adaptation process models neither global hegemony nor local resistance, but a complex give-and-take between sameness and difference. Sociologists have named this trade-off 'glocalization', and the term may serve to describe how the global flow of Shakespeare is filtered through local environments.[15] Performance, in particular, registers the inequities of world power but cannot be reduced to them. Under the British Raj, for instance, educational policy deployed Shakespeare as part of its so-called civilizing mission, and yet Indian adaptations on stage also helped to nurture an emerging nationalism; after independence had been won, moreover, actor-directors like Utpal Dutt pressed further by immersing the dramas in Bengali language and folk theatre, and touring the countryside with intercultural experiments such as his *Jatra Macbeth*.[16] At the same time, Shakespeare found a home in the Indian film industry, and twenty-first-century Bollywood continues to adapt the plays, which will doubtless soon appear on the television screens of Afghanistan. Such is the circuitry of 'glocal' culture.

It will be clear from the above examples that no single politics attaches to performances of foreign Shakespeare. But even when a production has political intent, its mission may or may not be fulfilled. Take the example of the Brazilian *Coriolanus* staged in 1974, a decade into military dictatorship. At a time when the arts were severely censored, this high-profile *Coriolano* was still protected by the standard case made for Shakespeare's classic status and his portrayal of universal values. In reality, however, it had been conceived by the actor Paulo Autran (who played the lead, produced the play and collaborated on the Portuguese translation) as an indictment of its hero as 'a right-wing extremist' and 'consummate villain'.[17] The production was inspired by Brecht's *Coriolan*, which adapted Shakespeare in order to rebut Nazi ideals of military heroism (German schoolbooks in the 1930s compared Coriolanus to Hitler) and on which the German playwright was working at his death. Like Brecht, Autran dramatized Coriolano's fall from grace by adding a scene in which his family requests funerary rites for his corpse but is bluntly denied. In spite of this, the Brazilian public saw Coriolano not as a villain, but as a tragic hero. Among the reasons for this aesthetic failure, Autran admitted, was his own identification with the protagonist – and, one might add, the context of a state-run theatre dominated by a traditional charismatic actor-manager.[18] In this instance, the performance itself revealed an internal contradiction: between a local intent to criticize and the universally shared desire of actors to be admired.

Authors

'Every engagement with a Shakespearian text', writes Antony Tatlow, 'is necessarily intercultural. The past really is another culture, its remoteness disguised by language that can occasionally appear as familiar as we seem to ourselves, whom we understand so imperfectly.'[19] This argument applies even more strongly when a Shakespearian work is translated into foreign languages. To translate a text is to disguise it anew, rendering it at once more familiar and more remote. In the case of Shakespeare, most translations evoke familiarity by updating the text's Elizabethan English to a modern version of the target language, so that non-Anglophone readers confront the plays and poems as contemporary works. On the other hand, this procedure occludes or effaces many of Shakespeare's bravura linguistic effects, forcing translators to invent awkward correspondences or relegate problems to footnotes. In general, however, translations successfully disguise not only the historical and cultural remoteness of their source, but the work of the translators themselves. And that work, though routinely described as a process of conversion, is better understood as a kind of conversation – one in which the translator responds to Shakespeare as well as to the symposium of interpreters who have echoed, contested and manipulated his voice across multiple languages, epochs and cultures.

Let us take a look at two recent bilingual editions of *A Midsummer Night's Dream*. The name of William Shakespeare appears on each cover, but so does the name of a translator: the German version, *Ein Sommernachtstraum*, was translated by Frank Günther, and the French, *Le Songe d'une nuit d'été*, by Jean-Michel Déprats.[20] Opening each book reveals more hands at work. In the course of their annotations both translators acknowledge their debts to their predecessors, Déprats tracing a path from the nineteenth-century translations of François-Victor Hugo to such recent versions as that of Pierre Messiaen, and Günther citing the now canonical work, from the 1760s to the 1820s, of Christoph Martin Wieland, August Wilhelm Schlegel and Ludwig Tieck. And we have still to consider whose English text lies on the verso pages: for its English half, the Günther edition draws on the Arden edition of Harold F. Brooks, whereas the French volume prints a text established by Gisèle Venet using sources up to the Oxford edition by Peter Holland. Each volume includes resources compiled by yet more scholars and critics. Clearly, the globalization of Shakespeare in print is a richly collaborative task.

If, as we have seen, Shakespeare's worldwide influence in the theatre depends on a complex international performance network, then his literary expansion outside Britain and the United States relies on a corresponding textual network consisting of writers, printers, publishers, editors and translators. And just as we recognized the actor as only one element in performance, so our concept of the author must share credit with a host of literary collaborators. The bilingual editions at issue here make this shared authority especially apparent. When reading a Shakespeare edition in English, we generally repress the extent to which editors 'modernize and punctuate, name characters, determine who is present on stage, print speeches in prose or verse, choose specific words at the expense of others, even decide when a character is or is no longer king – and in the process determine what constitutes Shakespeare's works'.[21] But an *en face* foreign-language version alerts us to precisely such changes, reminding us that translation is a kind of editing, and equally that editing is a kind of translation.[22] As a practical norm, moreover, translators work not from the quarto or Folio texts, but from English-language editions or intermediate versions in their own or a third language: not all Shakespeare translators have known English, and 'in certain situations, including eighteenth- and nineteenth-century Europe, indirect translation of Shakespeare was the rule rather than the exception'.[23] The textual network, in other words, is not everywhere connected, but instead characterized by interference, circuitous indirection and occasional loss.

Let us return to our bilingual editions for an example. Consider the famous line from *A Midsummer Night's Dream* spoken by Peter Quince on first seeing his much-changed comrade: 'Bless thee, Bottom, bless thee. Thou art translated' (3.1.105). Here is the line as it appears in the German and French versions:

> SQUENZ: Gott steh dir bei, Zettel, Gott steh dir bei! Du bist verwünschen! (73)
> QUINCE: Dieu te bénisse, Bottom, Dieu te bénisse! Tu es transfiguré. (138)

One difference between the versions lies in the names of the characters: Günther translates them into German, whereas Déprats opts to retain the English originals. An obvious problem is how to translate the name 'Bottom', which evokes the character's profession by denoting a weaver's implement – the spool on which yarn was wound – but also has bawdy connotations, even if different in the Renaissance from those picked up by modern ears.[24] No translation could capture this *double-entendre*. Günther's word *Zettel* designates the warp in a woven fabric, but lacks bodily resonance; it has been the standard translation since Wieland. Unlike German, French lacks a canonical Shakespeare text and has given Bottom various names, including *Navette* (a weaver's shuttle) or *Lefond* (the bottom in the sense of a base or depth). Despite this, Déprats reverts to the English, declaring it more elegant and familiar than a French invention. Yet this choice cancels out Bottom's later puns on his own name, such as his dream which 'hath no bottom' (4.1.209): whereas Günther can joke that 'Zettels Traum' is 'verzettelt' (wasted or warped), Déprats is saddled with the cipher that 'Le Rêve de Bottom' is 'un rêve insondable'. Both choices yield losses and gains. They exemplify opposing strategies of translation: the German option domesticates the source in the target culture while the French marks the source as foreign. Most choices in translation fall between these extremes, and the diffusion of Shakespeare's texts depends on innumerable compromises made by editors and translators between the poles of alienation and acculturation.

There is more to be said about the lines cited above: one might remark that both French and German exclamations specify the name of God where the English ('Bless thee') elides it, and that Shakespeare's term for Bottom's transformation – he is 'translated' – is notably modified by the terms 'verwünschen' (bewitched) and 'transfiguré' (transfigured, with inevitable echoes of Jesus on the Mount). Of course, 'translated' in Quince's use does not specify either a spell or a sacrament; its chief meaning, implied by its etymology as well as Helena's earlier use of the word to imagine trading places with Hermia (1.1.191), is metamorphosis by spatial displacement. That even the sense of 'translation' can be lost in translation is more than a joke in this play, which returns obsessively to the difficult interlocking of disparate worlds, such as an Athenian palace and a Warwickshire wood imperfectly compressed by a cosmopolitan who can 'put a girdle round about the earth / In forty minutes' (2.1.175–6). If Puck embodies global reach in *A Midsummer Night's Dream*, then the play's most local figure, unnamed and known only by a place, is the 'Indian boy' (3.2.376). No account of the world of the play or of the play in the world would be complete without considering India, which lies both in the text's mythical past and in its mercantile future.

The literary tradition from which Shakespeare drew associated Oberon with India by way of France. As *Le Songe d'une nuit d'été* makes sure to record, the fairy king of India first appears in a medieval *chanson de geste* translated into English in the 1530s (which inspired Spenser, Greene and later Jonson). But in Shakespeare's globalizing age, India was becoming less a fable and more a financial opportunity. To evoke 'the spicèd Indian air' (2.1.124) in the 1590s was to cite travel narratives and anticipate contracts for trade; by the decade's end the East India Company would be founded. And as Anglo-Indian relations shifted from the commercial to the colonial, Shakespeare took a central place in the theatres of the Raj, beginning in Bombay and Calcutta and spreading into the regions, in English and indigenous languages alike.[25] From around 1870, an efflorescence of literary adaptations and literal translations saw the printing of Shakespeare's dramas in Indo-Aryan languages (such as Hindi or Urdu) and Dravidian languages (including Tamil, Kannada and Telugu). In these versions, Oberon's Indian origins are cunningly reclaimed from Europe by South Asia, and transposed from an exotic romance to vernacular drama. In M. L. Srikantesha Gowda's Kannada translation, *Pranilarjuniyam* (1896), Oberon appears as Manmatha, churner of hearts, an avatar of a classical Indian love-god.[26] And in R. Krishnamachari's Sanskrit adaptation, *Vasantikaswapnam* (1892), he is named Pradosh or 'Night' as personified in classical texts like the *Mahabharata*.[27]

These translations pursued a familiar domesticating strategy by transporting Shakespeare's text into a complex new linguistic, cultural and political environment. But, unlike their French or German counterparts, Indian translators of *A Midsummer Night's Dream* also needed to confront the play's explicit references to their country. What, for instance, should a Sanskrit author make of Titania's reproof that Oberon has returned 'from the farthest step of India' (2.1.69)? The actors in the Afghan *Love's Labour's Lost*, discussed above, ingeniously solved a similar dilemma by replacing the play's comic Muscovites with Indians. But rather than relocate Oberon/Manmatha/Pradosh at some equivalent limit of travel, an alternative operation has been to mute the exotic setting entirely. Thus Krishnamachari rewrites 'the farthest step of India' simply as *maddesham* (my land), the 'spicèd Indian air' as *upavanapranta* ('the edge of a small forest') and the 'Indian boy', who Puck says was stolen from a king, as a mere *rajabala* ('a prince'). To close the gap in this way between Shakespeare's notion of India and the reality of the nineteenth-century subcontinent is a bold move in a text written at the height of colonialism, but the change deprives the drama of a crucial third location besides the city and the wood – a place that shimmers between fact and fiction and should therefore prove for its readers not idly imaginary but actively imaginative. On the one hand, erasing India as fantasy and grounding it in the play's geography makes Shakespeare's text newly global. On the other, such an appropriation also risks making the text newly provincial. After all, how India signifies in *A Midsummer Night's Dream* is a question to be posed rather than resolved or disguised, and what Theseus calls a poet's 'shaping fantasies' (5.1.5) ought to challenge the act of translation even, or perhaps especially, when the translator's own culture is implicated.

Aethers

Shakespeare's global dissemination is easy to track insofar as theatrical and textual processes generate recognizable material products, and most late twentieth-century stage and printing practices would not have struck even a time-travelling Elizabethan as the forms of things unknown: a company of managers and artisans still gathers around the body of one or more actors to produce a play; a network of editors and translators still labours over the text of one or more authors to generate a book. What would surprise an Elizabethan, however, is how modern technology has lately enabled a shift from physical objects to electronic carriers for the inscription and decoding of sound and images. The globalization of culture is now unthinkable without the media of mass communication, and radio, cinema and television have contributed hugely to the diffusion of Shakespeare across national boundaries. Yet scholarship on Shakespeare's transnationalization through popular media is not far along, and even studies of film often remain segmented by national categories, despite film's multi-national workforce and global audience.[28] One reason for this delay is that these media are derivative: though not immediately accessible to our senses, any analogue capture of a Shakespeare play carries a physical palimpsest of the bodies and books at its source.

By contrast, the emergence of digital media has begun to transform both the page and the stage, significantly blurring the historical distinction between them. When you read a play or poem on the Web in an electronic edition or a digital facsimile, or when you rent a DVD of that play from an online service via mail or streaming video, or when you download an audio file of that poem to a portable device, or when you preview a book or theatre performance online before buying that text or ticket without leaving your computer: in these and many other instances you are dealing with Shakespeare not as realized materially by an actor or author, but as distributed virtually across a spacious and volatile medium – a kind of aether. This metaphor has grown popular as early descriptions of the new information system as a fast and complex superhighway have given way to evocations of the system's increasing disembodiment and unpredictability through the image of a cloud.[29] By definition, this next generation of the Internet will operate transnationally: since 'vast virtualized computer systems and electronic services know no borders', the cloud has been termed 'the ultimate form of globalization'.[30]

To those who know Shakespeare's work, the rhetoric of cloud computing will recall *The Tempest*, which we may consider an anticipation of the joys and illusions of cyberspace. The play's unplaceable island pulses with aethereal phenomena. Caliban praises its ambient sounds and shimmering images, humming instruments and visions of 'clouds [that] methought would open, and show riches / Ready to drop upon me' (3.2.136–7); but this nebulous idyll fails to materialize, and even Prospero's multi-media 'pageant' turns out to be a 'baseless fabric' which, like 'the cloud-capped towers' and 'the great globe itself', melts 'into thin air' (4.1.150–5). This analogy between a swift-moving cloudy mass or 'rack' (151) and the mode of performance itself is one that each production of *The Tempest* is bound to reinvent. In 2005, for instance, a Montreal company called 4D art staged *La Tempête* as a 'mixmedia creation' whose cast was divided between islanders, who were played by normal actors, and shipwrecked Italians, who appeared on stage as ingenious holograms.[31] These 'virtual characters' appeared sometimes as life-sized images, sometimes as towering close-ups, their taped voices perfectly synchronized with the live action. The staging presented the wayfarers as mere projections of Prospero's imagination, with one exception: when the virtual Ferdinand touched the hand of Miranda, he miraculously assumed corporeal form. Swirling light and sound effects (including chanting in indecipherable languages) permeated the auditorium, and above the French dialogue an edited version of Shakespeare's script appeared as supertitles.

Lost in an electronic cloud of text, video, music and theatre, the audience at *La Tempête* experienced the post-digital condition that performance theorists have termed 'intermediality.'[32] This buzzword suggests the capacity of newer media to unfix and recombine older forms, which in Shakespearian terms means unsettling the familiar dualism by which the drama has been fissured into writing and playing. In what follows, I sketch out two developments of this intermedial type which are likely to support the transnationalization of Shakespeare in the twenty-first century. The first, the electronic supertitle, already has a record of turning foreign-language performances into multi-lingual texts; the second, the digital translation, is barely underway but has the potential to convert bilingual print editions into macaronic archives – texts from which each user fashions a unique interpretative performance.

Modelled on the cinema subtitle used since sound films reached international audiences, the theatrical supertitle has recently developed from a translation tool to a means of aesthetic innovation. In a study of mixed-language theatre, Marvin Carlson has charted the supertitle's promotion 'from a feature of the experimental stage and occasionally of the opera to a major feature of international performance', where supertitles can now provide 'not simply a device for duplicating the spoken text, but a separate communicative channel in the theatrical experience'.[33] The trick has been to turn the obvious defects of captioning – visual distraction and enforced selectivity, not to speak of the partiality of any translation – into unexpected virtues. Compare 4D art's *La Tempête*, whose scrolling tickertape of Shakespearian lines served merely as a digital libretto for English-speaking audiences, with *King Lear* as produced by the Belgian troupe Needcompany in 2000, where the supertitles added both a language and a new theatrical code. While Needcompany's actors performed in Flemish, French and bits of English, the supertitles appeared in the language of the audience (German for Carlson in Berlin, but English when performed in New York). Nor did the titles always run parallel to the action: on the contrary, the play opened with Kent and Gloucester scoffing at their projected lines, and in the chaotic battle an actor shouted out speech prefixes while text flashed by unspoken overhead. During the final scene the supertitles degenerated into fragments, then went dark, as though the script itself had strained and shattered beneath the tragedy's weight.

Beyond the European avant-garde, the new supertitles are enhancing the work of cultural translation surveyed early in this chapter. One example is the writing and performance of the Anglo-Kuwaiti director Sulayman Al-Bassam, who has been staging Shakespearian adaptations in Arabic and English since 2001. Al-Bassam uses an unusual layering technique: he first adapts Shakespeare's text into modern English with an Arabic twist; this version is translated into Arabic for performance; supertitles convert the Arabic into the primary language of the audience; and the Arabic script is finally turned back into English for the purposes of publication.[34] In the following supertitles for *Richard III – An Arab Tragedy* (Stratford, 2006), Clarence rejects his assassins' hypocritical order that he pray:

> – Dare you counsel me to pray to God yet would war with God by murdering me? … He who kills without due reason, it is as though he kills the whole of humanity (Q.);
> – Pray!
> – *And do not shed blood that is sacred by Allah's law* (Q.);
> – Pray!
> – Al Rawindi in the sources says: *beware of shedding innocent blood* –
> – Pray![35]

Much can be said about Al-Bassam's shift of *Richard III* from a Christian to a Muslim world, but here we can only observe that the supertitles clearly mark Quranic allusion and italicize quotations from Islamic scripture and scholarship. To grasp the crucial change of register, then, a foreign-language audience needs this text – but what sort of text is it? The video screens display neither what is being spoken nor what will ultimately be printed, but something provisional and virtual. In a flash, each supertitle opens a channel between languages, media and cultures, and through its translation and annotation the theatrical experience is recharged.

If the supertitle provides, as it were, the lightning between a production's cloud of versions and meanings and the ground of individual points of reception, what could be its equivalent in textual terms? A plausible answer is: the hyperlink. We cannot yet predict how digital media will renovate the translation of Shakespeare's writings, but that process will surely draw on English-language projects currently underway to transfer the plays and poems from printed books into hypertext. The most advanced of these are the Internet Shakespeare Editions and the Shakespeare Electronic Archive, founded in the 1990s in Canada and the United States respectively.[36] Whilst their names signal different goals – editions versus an archive – the projects create similar environments that benefit from editorial selection and structure as well as archival completeness and searchability. Both provide a wealth of resources in text, image, video and sound formats, and both ensure that users can easily navigate these media via a network of hyperlinks. This network has the capacity to link a single Shakespearian word not merely to a textual gloss but to an essay or concordance or photograph or audio file or film clip. Digital animation may even allow onscreen text to dance between multiple variants, so that options for dialogue or stage directions flicker alternately before the eye.[37]

A Shakespeare text this full, open and dynamic offers an ideal template for future work in translation. The raw material for that work is already accessible in digital libraries such as Project Gutenberg, which currently provides Shakespeare online in English and eight European languages. Where sites affiliated with Project Gutenberg spring up across the world, there Shakespeare translation appears as well: the first of these, Sweden's Project Runeberg, explains why even a site devoted to Scandinavian literature had to include an author of his stature – and adds that since *Hamlet* derives from a Danish myth, the influence has been reciprocal.[38] What is more, the gap between foreign e-texts and the English-language archives is closing fast: the Shakespeare Electronic Archive features clips from Svend Garde's German-made *Hamlet* (1920) and is building a new collection on Shakespeare performance in Asia, while the Internet Shakespeare Editions site has mounted a growing collection of essays under the rubric 'Shakespeare Around the Globe'.[39] It is no longer difficult to imagine a digital archive of Shakespeare translations and adaptations that would collect and configure the range of texts, performances and commentaries sampled in this chapter. Whatever the form of that cloudy future, it will require the collaborative energies of Shakespearians worldwide, the same energies of which 400 years of globalization yield fine and ample evidence.

NOTES

1 Roland Robertson, *Globalization: Social Theory and Global Culture* (London: Sage, 1992), p. 8.
2 Dennis O. Flynn and Arturo Giráldez, 'Globalization began in 1571', in Barry K. Gills and William R. Thompson (eds.), *Globalization and Global History* (London: Routledge, 2006), pp. 232–47.
3 David Crystal, *The Cambridge Encyclopedia of the English Language* (Cambridge: Cambridge University Press, 1995), p. 92.
4 See my essay 'Renaissance Intertheater and the Staging of Nobody', *ELH*, 71:3 (2004), 559–85.
5 See Dirk Delabastita, 'Anthologies, Translations, and European Identities', in Dirk Delabastita, Jozef De Vos and Paul Franssen (eds.), *Shakespeare and European Politics* (Newark: University of Delaware Press, 2008), pp. 343–68.
6 I adapt this tripartite scheme from W. B. Worthen, 'Shakespeare 3.0, or Text versus Performance, the Remix', in Diana E. Henderson (ed.), *Alternative Shakespeares 3* (London: Routledge, 2008), pp. 54–77.
7 See Gary Taylor, '*Hamlet* in Africa 1607', in Ivo Kamps and Jyotsna G. Singh (eds.), *Travel Knowledge* (New York: Palgrave, 2001), pp. 223–48.
8 See my essay 'History Between Theatres', in Peter Holland and Stephen Orgel (eds.), *From Performance to Print in Shakespeare's England* (New York: Palgrave Macmillan, 2006), pp. 191–207.
9 See Romy Heylen, *Translation, Poetics, and the Stage: Six French 'Hamlets'* (London: Routledge, 1993), pp. 61–91.
10 For a full treatment, see Gerda Tardanow, *The Bernhardt 'Hamlet'* (New York: Peter Lang, 1996).
11 Ruru Li, '"Who is it that can tell me who I am? / Lear's shadow": A Taiwanese Actor's Personal Response to *King Lear*', *Shakespeare Quarterly*, 20:20, 205. Translations from the unpublished Chinese script, provided by Wu, are by Ruru Li.
12 Quoted in Yong Li Lan, 'Shakespeare and the Fiction of the Intercultural', in Barbara Hodgdon and W. B. Worthen (eds.), *A Companion to Shakespeare and Performance* (Oxford: Blackwell, 2005), p. 548.
13 My account of the production is indebted to Irena R. Makaryk, "Afghanistan Brings back the Bard": Shakespeare, Gender, and Cultural Mediation', paper delivered at the International Shakespeare Congress, Stratford-upon-Avon, 2006.
14 www.worldchanging.com/archives/003446.html (accessed 16 December 2008).
15 The term was proposed by Roland Robertson in 'Glocalization: Time–Space and Homogeneity–Heterogeneity', in M. Featherstone, S. Lash and R. Robertson (eds.), *Global Modernities* (London: Sage, 1995), pp. 23–44.
16 See Jyotsna G. Singh, *Colonial Narratives/Cultural Dialogues* (London: Routledge, 1996), pp. 120–52.

17 Quoted and trans. in Roberto Ferreira da Rocha, 'Hero or Villain: A Brazilian *Coriolanus* during the Period of the Military Dictatorship', in Bernice W. Kliman and Rick J. Santos (eds.), *Latin American Shakespeares* (Madison: Fairleigh Dickinson Press, 2005), p. 38.
18 Ferreira da Rocha, 'Hero or Villain', p. 49.
19 Antony Tatlow, *Shakespeare, Brecht, and the Intercultural Sign* (Durham, NC: Duke University Press, 2001), p. 5.
20 *Ein Sommernachtstraum*, trans. Frank Günther (Cadolzburg: Ars vivendi, 2000); *Le Songe d'une nuit d'été*, trans. Jean-Michel Déprats (Paris: Gallimard, 2003). Subsequent references, to page numbers, will be parenthetical.
21 Lukas Erne, *Shakespeare's Modern Collaborators* (London: Continuum, 2008), p. 42.
22 See Balz Engler, 'The Editor as Translator', *Shakespeare Survey*, 59 (2006), 193–7. As a counterpoint, see Alessandro Serpieri, 'The Translator as Editor: The Quartos of *Hamlet*', in Ton Hoenselaars (ed.), *Shakespeare and the Language of Translation* (London: Arden Shakespeare, 2004), pp. 167–83.
23 Dirk Delabastita, 'Shakespeare Translation', in Mona Baker (ed.), *The Routledge Encyclopedia of Translation Studies* (London: Routledge, 1998), p. 224.
24 See Patricia Parker, 'The Name of Nick Bottom', in Claire Gheeraert-Graffeuille and Nathalie Vienne-Geurrin (eds.), *Autour du 'Songe d'une nuit d'été'* (Rouen: Publications de L'Université de Rouen, 2003), pp. 9–29.
25 See Dennis Kennedy, 'Shakespeare Worldwide', in Margreta de Grazia and Stanley Wells (eds.), *The Cambridge Companion to Shakespeare* (Cambridge: Cambridge University Press, 2001), pp. 258–61.
26 See G. S. Amur, 'Shakespeare in Kannada', in D. A. Shankar (ed.), *Shakespeare in Indian Languages* (Rashtrapati Nivas, Shimla: Indian Institute of Advanced Study, 1999), p. 118.
27 My source is David V. Mason, 'Who is the Indian Shakespeare? Appropriation of Authority in a Sanskrit *Midsummer Night's Dream*', *New Literary History*, 34 (2004), pp. 639–58.
28 On film, see Chapter 20 by Katherine Rowe in the present volume. On television and radio, see the chapters by Emma Smith and Susanne Greenhalgh in Robert Shaughnessy (ed.), *The Cambridge Companion to Popular Culture* (Cambridge: Cambridge University Press, 2007). A fine study of transnationalization through radio is Andreas Höfele, 'Reeducating Germany: BBC Shakespeare 1945', in Dirk Delabastita, Jozef De Vos and Paul Franssen (eds.), *Shakespeare and European Politics* (Newark, DE: University of Delaware Press, 2008), pp. 255–77.
29 See Jessie Holliday Scanlon and Brad Wieners, 'The Internet Cloud', *The Industry Standard*, 9 July 1999. Retrieved from www.thestandard.com/article/0,1902,5466,00.html
30 'Computers without borders', *The Economist*, 23 October 2008. Retrieved from www.economist.com/specialreports/displaystory.cfm?story_id=12411854
31 An archive of production materials, from which my citations are drawn, is accessible at www.4dart.com/
32 See the essays gathered in *Intermediality in Theatre and Performance*, ed. Freda Chapple and Chiel Kattenbelt (Amsterdam: Rodopi, 2006).

33 Marvin Carlson, *Speaking in Tongues: Language at Play in the Theatre* (Ann Arbor: University of Michigan Press, 2006), pp. 186, 200.
34 My account of Al-Bassam relies on Graham Holderness, '"Silence bleeds": *Hamlet* across borders', *European Journal of English Studies*, 12:1 (April 2008), 59–77.
35 Cited in ibid., 71.
36 Their websites are http://shea.mit.edu and http://internetshakespeare.uvic.ca
37 Sonia Massai, 'Scholarly editing and the shift from print to electronic cultures', in Lukas Erne and M.J. Kidnie (eds.), *Textual Performances* (Cambridge: Cambridge University Press, 2004), p. 95.
38 See http://runeberg.org/authors/shakewil.html
39 On the US project, see Peter S. Donaldson, 'The Shakespeare Electronic Archive: Collections and Multimedia Tools for Teaching and Research, 1992–2008', *Shakespeare*, 4:3 (September 2008), 250–60. The Canadian project's essay series and guidelines are available at http://isebeta.uvic.ca/Foyer/around-globe.html

READING LIST

Bartolovitch, Crystal. '"Baseless fabric": London as a "world city"', in *'The Tempest' and its Travels*, Peter Hulme and William H. Sherman (eds.). Pennsylvania: University of Pennsylvania Press, 2000, pp. 13–26.

Brusberg-Kiermeier, Stefani and Jorg Helbig, eds. *Shakespeare in the Media: From the Globe Theatre to the World Wide Web*. Frankfurt-am-Main: Peter Lang, 2004.

Carvalho Homem, Rui and Ton Hoenselaars, eds. *Translating Shakespeare for the Twenty-First Century*. Amsterdam and New York: Rodopi, 2004.

Chaudhuri, Sukanta and Chee Seng Lim, eds. *Shakespeare without English: The Reception of Shakespeare in Non-Anglophone Countries*. London: Pearson Longman, 2006.

Hoenselaars, Ton, ed. *Shakespeare and the Language of Translation*. London: Arden Shakespeare, 2004.

Holderness, Graham and Byran Loughrey. 'Arabesque: Shakespeare and Globalisation', *Essays and Studies*, 59 (2006), 24–46.

Kujawinska-Courtney, Krystyna and John M. Mercer, eds. *The Globalization of Shakespeare in the Nineteenth Century*. Lewiston, NY: Edwin Mellen Press, 2003.

Massai, Sonia, ed. *World-Wide Shakespeares: Local Appropriations in Film and Performance*. London: Routledge, 2005.

Orkin, Martin. *Local Shakespeares: Proximations and Power*. London: Routledge, 2005.

Schülting, Sabine, ed. 'Welttheater', special section of *Shakespeare-Jahrbuch*, 138 (2002), 11–98.

20

KATHERINE ROWE

Shakespeare and media history

The scholar Raymond Bellour once described film as 'an unattainable text', a phrase that has resonated in media studies since 1975, when he wrote it. At the time, the medium of film was largely synonymous with 'cinema', a collective experience in which audiences arrived at designated times to watch a multi-reel screening. For most viewers, movies were screened once and then revisited in memory. Bellour foresaw a different future, when 'film will find ... a status analogous to that of the book' and individuals may own and access movies at will.[1] Yet even then, he argues, films will remain unattainable in one important respect. For Bellour, the defining property of a 'text' is a specific kind of audience engagement: the ability to quote a text in its own medium, handle it as we do a novel or essay and thus make it imaginatively, aesthetically and intellectually our own. At the time, ordinary movie viewers did not have the ability to handle their movie-going experiences in this way: to interpret, select and re-make them in their own medium, as writers can do with the works of other writers. Many things have changed since Bellour made this argument. New technologies such as DVDs and video-editing stations now allow students to handle and quote clips and digital stills. New genres such as the remix and video mash-up make audio-visual sampling, quotation and interpretation a popular form of artistic play. It remains impossible to quote moving sequences in a paper-and-print essay such as this one. Yet we have drawn closer to Bellour's vision of aesthetic and intellectual access.

The consequence of such technological changes for Shakespeare studies is one focus of this essay. A second focus is the influential concept of textuality that Bellour invokes (drawn from Roland Barthes): the idea that a text is produced in audience engagement, use and re-use. A long historical view makes it clear that this holds true for all media. It was certainly true of drama as Shakespeare's audience saw it in early modern London theatres. In the Prologue to *Henry V* the Chorus makes this clear when he calls on the Globe audience to 'piece out our imperfections with your thoughts' and 'on your imaginary forces work' to conjure 'mighty monarchies' and confine them 'within the girdle of these walls' (ll. 18–23). In other words, the audience's collective imagination creates the sense of 'being there' mediated by the Globe.

Laurence Olivier invokes this idea again in his 1944 film, re-interpreting what the Chorus calls the 'puissance', or power, of the audience as a vision of English national unity during World War II (l. 25). His famous opening sequence tracks out of London and swoops down into the bustle of Elizabethan playgoers, rotating past the crowded circular stalls as it descends and settling us into their midst as the play begins. (See Figure 6. a–d.)

With its dynamic camera and realist scene, this sequence conveys a vital sense of imagined community within the 'wooden O' of the Globe, as the Chorus describes. But the full meaning of this cinematic address, with its claims on collective audition, emerges as later films recycle and re-make the sequence. *Shakespeare in Love* (dir. John Madden, 1998) replays it ironically, panning (rotating past) empty stalls and stage to set the scene of business competition, asking us to consider how works find audiences. Julie Taymor offers a darker vision of cultural repetition and re-use, resituating the stall pan in a coliseum (*Titus*, 1999). Whereas Olivier invites the audience into a protected community, Taymor repeats that gesture in a dangerous space, charging us with complicity in the cyclical violence committed there.

The field of media history reframes the last century of Shakespeare screen adaptations with this long historical view, connecting the cutting edge of what we can do with Shakespeare to many of the older media explored elsewhere in this volume. Accordingly, this chapter is organized around three key areas in which scholarly thinking has changed as a result. These are: 1) how we understand adaptation as a cultural process and what questions we ask about it; 2) what we mean by a 'medium', and how we see the relations between visual and verbal media; and 3) how we imagine screen audiences. The essay closes with recommendations for students and other readers: approaches to adaptation that have pay-offs for understanding older media, newer media and Shakespeare.

Rethinking adaptation

Over the past two decades, changes both within and outside the field of Shakespeare studies have reframed the phenomenon of adaptation as the normative way that Shakespeare's works have always been transmitted. Textual studies taught us to see works such as *Henry V* as evolving and emergent, an ever-growing series of editions and versions like those described above.[2] This was true in the Renaissance, when many of Shakespeare's plays originated in multiple versions. (See Chapters 3 and 5.) Now all the different

a) Olivier, *Henry V*, ‘thatch zoom’

b) Olivier, *Henry V*, ‘stall pan’

c) Madden, *Shakespeare in Love*, ‘stall pan’

d) Taymor, *Titus*, ‘stall pan’

6 Cinematic address to the audience. a) ‘Thatch zoom’, Laurence Olivier, *Henry V*, 1944 b) ‘Stall pan’, Laurence Olivier, *Henry V*, 1944 c) ‘Stall pan’, John Madden, *Shakespeare in Love*, 1998 d) ‘Stall pan’, Julie Taymor, *Titus*, 1999.

ways a work may be presented (staged, printed, edited, filmed, sketched as graphic novel, parodied in spin-offs, etc.) are understood as modes of adaptation. Adaptation is recognized as an act of interpretation and a primary means by which cultures around the globe revive and re-purpose earlier cultural matter. (See Chapter 19.)

This view of adaptation as a global cultural process has drawn attention to the ways Shakespeare has regularly been invoked, over the centuries, to authorize and validate new technologies of expression. As Peter Donaldson has shown, from the late nineteenth to the early twenty-first centuries, Shakespeare provided the launch content for a host of new technologies. These include: early voice recording (wax cylinder impressions of Edwin Booth reciting speeches from *Hamlet* and *Othello*); early silent film (Sir Herbert Beerbohm Tree's scenes from *King John* in 1899); telephony (Alexander Graham Bell transmitted 'To be or not to be' at the Centennial Exhibition in Philadelphia, 1876); television (the BBC's live broadcasts in the 1930s and later featured Shakespeare from the London stage); through to interactive CD-Roms and web archives.[3] To these might be added launches of radio and gramophone technologies. The pattern continues with virtual environments, such as the online game *Arden* and online theatre.

Across these varied launches of new media Shakespearian material provides continuity and a standard against which to measure innovation. If the words emerging from Bell's Centennial transmitter can be recognized as Shakespeare's, then the technology has passed a symbolic threshold, conveying meaningful language, not just noise. This function of Shakespearian language – as a standard of intelligibility, meaning and value – emerged as part of Western colonial expansion, industrialization and globalization, and has been a subject of much critical attention. (See Chapter 19.) For scholars of Shakespeare and film, it has also restricted analysis. From the early twentieth century on, commentators circled around the question 'Is it Shakespeare?', tracking the way Shakespeare's language does or does not translate into the language of film, measuring a movie by the degree of its *fidelity* to an idealized original.[4]

Measured against any source text, of course, all adaptations are by definition secondary, because 'the source texts will always be better at being themselves'.[5] But what audiences measure an adaptation against is really their own preconceptions about 'what Shakespeare intended'; the Romantic idea of Shakespeare's plays as works of universal genius makes it hard for audiences in later periods to recognize such investments as culturally specific rather than timeless.[6] A longer view is instructive. For example, *Titus Andronicus* was clearly popular in the early seventeenth century; we know this for a variety of reasons, including the fact that three editions were printed between

1594 and 1611, a relatively high number in such a short time. The play lost favour in the following century, and by the Victorian period it was deemed a crude starter tragedy, or possibly not Shakespeare's at all. The twentieth century saw it recuperated on stage by Peter Brook (1955) and Deborah Warner (1987). By the twenty-first century Taymor had confirmed it as a 'dissertation on violence' that teaches us to reflect on our collective history of brutality.[7]

From the early twentieth century onwards, Shakespearian film critics also sought to extract themselves from the impasse of 'Is it Shakespeare?' by asking more open-ended questions: 'Why is Shakespeare being enlisted here?' 'How is Shakespearian material being used?' 'What other source texts and genres are interwoven with Shakespeare, and how do these interact?' 'How does this new context illuminate and change our preconceptions about the Shakespearian material?'

In exploring these different questions, it can be helpful to think of adaptations as answering to multiple, sometimes competing, interests in *revival* on the one hand and *recycling* on the other.[8] The impulse to revive a Shakespeare play and make it relevant for modern audiences engages mainstream adaptors in complex trade-offs. For example, the demand of authenticity requires holding on to Shakespeare's language, whereas accessibility requires some translation for modern audiences. Kenneth Branagh, a prolific film reviver from the late 1980s to the present, solves some of these difficulties. By using long takes he helps audiences to focus on the unfolding language. Camera shots synchronized with dialogue pair archaic terms with objects that explain them, sometimes following the glance of the speaker (an 'eye-line match'). Alternatively, revivals may re-write in modern English entirely – or translate to a different modern language, as Grigori Kozintsev does with *Hamlet* (1964), offering those familiar with the play the complex experience of remembering familiar Renaissance lines and listening to Russian dialogue while reading subtitles that translate those lines back into modern English. Revival may also engage directors in recuperative strategies, to redeem 'problem' plays that violate modern values: *Othello*, *The Merchant of Venice* and *The Taming of the Shrew* are frequent examples. Addressing audiences sensitized by feminist ideals, for example, film and video adaptations of *The Taming of the Shrew* make Katherine's final submission seem knowing, or playful, to redress the misogyny that registers in this closing scene.

Recyclers, by contrast, re-work Shakespearian matter for non-Shakespearian uses, with less concern for authenticity and accessibility, often acknowledging their mixed sources. In this mode, Taymor mines *Titus Andronicus* as an archive of violent matter, but packs that archive with references to popular culture, modern film and art, and twentieth-century history. The soundtrack for *The Angelic Conversation* (1985), Derek Jarman's lyrical meditation on same-sex love, samples sources in a similar way. It interweaves the industrial band Coil and fourteen Shakespeare sonnets (read by Judi Dench) with mechanical 'found sound', natural sounds and opera.

The filmic preoccupations of such innovative auteurs – Orson Welles, Olivier, Jarman, Kozintsev, Franco Zeffirelli, Akira Kurosawa, Al Pacino, Kenneth Branagh, Baz Luhrmann, Taymor and others – have helped broach questions about the *appropriation* of Shakespeare and the cinematic movements, experimental and mainstream, that shape specific adaptations. It is important to remember, however, that to overemphasize the film-maker as the creative 'originator' is to repeat the problem described above by substituting one set of authorial intentions for another.[9] Like a Renaissance play, a film or television show is a complex collaboration: of screenwriters, funders, director, cinematographer, actors, editors, producers, post-production specialists and many others. Moreover, these industries are themselves part of larger economic networks. As the field of cinema and media studies has deepened its understanding of global production, distribution and exhibition, Shakespeare scholars too have been increasingly interested in the cultural work of specific adaptations and the ways in which they participate in, as well as critique, economic, social and political institutions.

Rethinking 'media': literary history is media history

Perhaps the most important transformative force in Shakespeare studies, at the beginning of the twenty-first century, has been the blossoming of digital archives and digital text. Changes in the way we understand texts and textuality have profoundly altered our thinking about other media. Through much of the twentieth century, for example, many literary scholars approached screen adaptations with the assumption that literature and film were in fundamental competition, aesthetic and intellectual opposites.[10] Literature was viewed as a verbal medium that sponsored critical thinking and the measured responses associated with independent thought and high culture. By contrast, film was often viewed as a visual medium characterized by speed and discontinuity: a domain of unthinking, uncritical response, associated with mass emotion and low culture. These oppositions were so entrenched that in the first full-length study of silent Shakespeare films (1968), Robert Hamilton Ball describes his work as a 'diversion': 'fun', 'recreation', and 'a distraction' from his 'customary' scholarship.[11] A similar attitude informs many 'how-to' guides to teaching film in the Shakespeare classroom. Because 'Shakespeare is hard but film is easy', the argument goes, film adaptations make Shakespeare accessible: they ease students into the less diverting but more valuable labour of reading the play texts.

What historians sometimes call the 'late age of print', our present moment of media transition, brought a renewed interest in media history that broke down such reductive oppositions and fostered a more nuanced view of media change in literary studies. Those who work closely with texts have seen rapid change in the reading and writing tools many of us use daily. That process has increased awareness of the ways apparently distinct media are always *converging*, sharing technologies and functions.[12] In this way, for example, the reference and indexing functions provided by the book converged in the late twentieth century with the electronic database. The codex, or bound book, was the first storage format to support non-sequential reading of large amounts of text. The electronic database supports non-sequential reading of much larger amounts of text, and in a dynamic, expanding way. Similarly, with the advent of videos and then DVDs, the way we view audio-visual works such as films and TV shows has converged with reading habits learnt from books. Rewind, pause, 'bookmarking' of scenes and chapters, screenshots: all these features offer codex-like functions to viewers interested in non-sequential study of, handling of and quoting from audio-visual texts.

As technologies converge, new formats also *remediate* older ones. That is, newer technologies not only borrow from earlier ones but also compete to supply their social functions and gain their commercial positions by imitating their styles and formats.[13] In this way, television remediated the cultural role of live theatre in the mid-twentieth century, casting itself as 'home theatre' for the living-room.[14] Looking back to the seventeenth century, the print history of Shakespeare's plays reveals remediation as a long-standing phenomenon. We know, for example, that the popularity of early editions had in part to do with how effectively stationers (publishers and printers) used book formats to invoke, rehearse, surpass and even critique what might be found in the theatre, repurposing performance content for a market of readers.[15]

We can see the same dynamic in Olivier's opening sequence for *Henry V*, which both imitates and rivals seventeenth-century perspectives of London. (See Figure 7.) These engraved and printed images give us a commanding perspective on time as well as space: we view the thickly populated Bankside from a high angle and from years later. (This was true even in the seventeenth century: Merian's *View* conjures a landscape from a quarter-century earlier.) Olivier's opening sequence claims the same panoramic sweep, but also the power to enter that time and space. When it zooms from long-shot to close-up in a few seconds, it seems to fulfil the Chorus' demand that we revive history 'now' by 'jumping o'er times, / Turning the accomplishment of many years, / Into an hour-glass' (1.1.30–1).

a) Olivier's Globe, *Henry V* (1944)

b) Selection from Merian's *View of London* c. (1638)

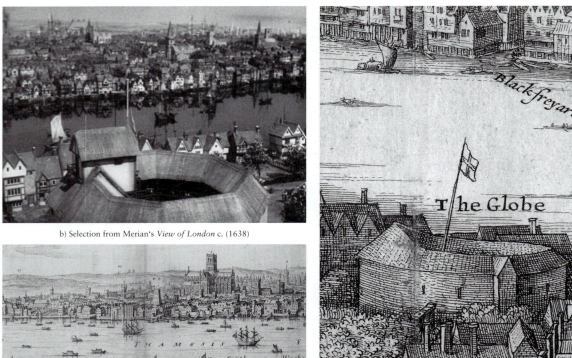

c) The Second Globe, from Hollar's *Long View of London* (1647)

7 Visual perspectives of time and space a) The Globe, Laurence Olivier, *Henry V*, 1944 b) *View of London* c. 1612, M. Merian, 1638 c) The Second Globe, Wenceslaus Hollar, detail from *Long View of London*, 1647.

The latest remediation of Shakespearian theatre, in the virtual world Second Life™, takes up this rivalry. In virtual reconstructions of the Globe, as in modern London, players and designers revive Shakespeare's plays, and tourists come to see them online. To claim these spaces as *authentic*, those who work and visit there need to confer on them the special qualities attributed to Shakespeare's Globe: access, the power of audience imagination and a shared experience of community. To do this they return to the cinematic vocabulary established by Olivier. Visual representations of virtual Globes (as of this writing there were several in Second Life™) borrow the signature 'thatch zoom' from Olivier's opening sequence, pulling the viewer from a panoramic long-shot into the centre of the circling roof (see Figure 8, top row). And they feature rotating pans of the Globe stalls that stress interaction and collectivity (see Figure 8, bottom row).

For the new media texts illustrated above, the thatch zoom and stall pan motifs rival as well as imitate cinema's popular, accessible realism. When Olivier's camera arrives at the Globe, the scene cuts before we descend into the open circle of roofs, for the camera is shooting a tiny model. A crane shot inside the full-sized film set is needed to record the descending stall pan. By contrast, the default director's camera in the sLiterary Globe (see Figure 8, top right) places us at just this moment of arrival and incipient immersion. What happens next may be given over to the director. Or it may be controlled through a playgoer's mouse view, or by flying his or her avatar down to the ground. Or it may alternate between these options, however he or she chooses. The rotational pan that represents the interior of the Globe has, since Olivier's time, become a signature of first-person video games, where it conveys autonomous player agency and choice.[16] For both actual and virtual Globe theatres, the motif embeds this first-person agency in the collective audition evoked by Olivier. Yet these online cameras present themselves not only as confirming, but also surpassing what cinema offers: moving around and shooting freely as each playgoer chooses, apparently without constraint.

As this example reminds us, in the late twentieth century the computer screen converged with and remediated a host of other formats, including film and television screens, the printed page, painting, recorded sound and graphic arts. This process further broke down the invidious binary between visual and verbal in Shakespeare studies. Digital facsimiles and online archives made a host of early texts more widely accessible. Literary scholars returned to the study of page layout and print history as 'complex viewers' as well as close readers.[17] Conversely, we now revisit movies and TV shows as aesthetically rich, historically and geographically situated texts, as we do literary texts. The republication of older film and television in

a) 'Renaissance Island Globe Grand Opening', Bernadette Swanson, (machinima movie)

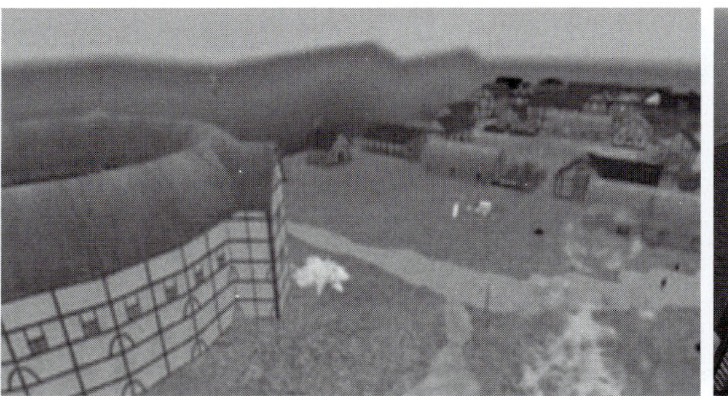

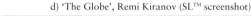

b) sLiterary Globe, Second Life®, default camera position before performance (SL™ screenshot)

c) 'Shakespeare_068', Cherie Daniels (SL™ screenshot)

d) 'The Globe', Remi Kiranov (SL™ screenshot)

8 Virtual Globes: thatch zoom and stall pan a) Machinima movie: 'Renaissance Island Globe Grand Opening' (outside), Second Life™, HVXSilverstar, 2008 b) Screenshot: sLiterary Globe default camera position, Second Life™, Katherine Rowe, 2008 c) Screenshot: playgoers at the sLiterary Globe. 'Shakespeare_068', Second Life™, Cherie Daniels, 2008 d) Screenshot: 'The Globe', Second Life™, Remi Kiranov, 2008.

digital formats fosters such extended close reading for a host of newly accessible materials. For decades, the only televisual Shakespeare widely available after broadcast was the ambitious BBC Television Shakespeare project (1978–85). These made-for-TV versions of the full canon of Shakespeare plays were issued on VHS. The DVD release of an earlier BBC mini-series, *An Age of Kings* (1960; 2009), presenting the two history cycles, gives us a longer view of the lively broadcast history for Shakespeare. It also illuminates a wider range of televisual modes for Shakespeare adaptation.

As digital reproduction and online archives make a century of adaptations increasingly accessible, and as new understandings of textuality expand what counts as Shakespearian, the question 'Is it Shakespeare?' returns in a different way. Labour, rather than shelf space, is the principal constraint on what can be collected and studied. Thus archivists have more leeway in their definitions of 'the Shakespearian', but also a more significant challenge in articulating the limits of that category. In the early development of the *International Database of Shakespeare on Film, Television and Radio* (2008), curators wrestled with principles of selection and coined new categories for indexing.

When taxonomies are re-examined, familiar categories expand. Thus the longstanding practice of adapting story and theme has come to include prequels, sequels and spin-offs, such as *Hamlet 2* (dir. Andrew Fleming, 2008) and *O* (dir. Tim Blake Nelson, 2001 – reworking *Othello* in a high-school setting). Other categories begin to show definable variations. In the catch-all term 'post-modern' adaptation we can discern diverse interests in collage, sampling, and whole-scale re-working. Some updatings, such as Eric Rohmer's *Conte d'hiver* (*A Tale of Winter*, 1992) and Gus Van Sant's *My Own Private Idaho* (1991), signal their connections to specific works (*The Winter's Tale*, the *Henry IV* plays) by passing through Shakespearian interludes. Others, like Levring's austere film *The King is Alive* (2000), redistribute different character functions from a play across multiple film characters.[18]

As new media archives grow, new adaptation categories are formally recognized. In this way, the video mash-up, melding multiple sound and video sources into a new work, has taken its place in a long history of Shakespearian pastiche and parody. Historical patterns of citation and quotation also become more visible when tracked across an archive. Certain lines float free from their source plays. Thus Malvolio's 'some are born great' and Iago's exhortations to protect one's 'good name' tend to lose their ironic moorings and become straightforward guidelines for success as they cycle through popular culture. Conversely, some lines and speeches carry thematic burdens with them, especially Hamlet's most famous soliloquy. In John Ford's seminal Western, *My Darling Clementine* (1946), Doc Holliday

(Victor Mature) recites that speech and falters when he comes to 'thus conscience does make cowards of us all', interrupted by a tubercular coughing fit. Breaking off at this line in this way, the film signals Holliday's struggle with his own lack of honour and interprets the soliloquy as his meditation on death.

The way that editing and dialogue work together in this example underscores one of the most important tenets of recent media scholarship, that we should 'resist notions of media purity'.[19] Even before the advent of synchronized sound, for example, movie-going involved both words and sound. The verbal experiences of audiences ranged from intertitles to *films racontés* (prose summaries of silent films), to lectures at film societies, live translations and narration. Moreover, ambient sound (noisily interactive audiences, traffic outside the Nickelodeon, the projector) and live music were regular presences in early cinema.

Keeping the interplay between different media in mind helps us see how, with the advent of synchronous sound, movies continued to use early verbal techniques. Thus, in a gripping scene from Kurosawa's *King Lear* adaptation, *Ran* (1985), the film invokes a Japanese art form that developed with silent film: the *benshi*, or live translator. Japanese theatre conventions converged with the role of the *benshi* in the early twentieth century, becoming a powerful mode of cross-cultural performance and interpretation.[20] At this pivotal moment in *Ran*, the character functioning as the Fool, Kyoami (Shinnosuke 'Peter' Ikehata), adopts *benshi* conventions, interpreting onscreen emotions the audience otherwise have little access to. The Lear figure, Lord Hidetora (Tatsuya Nakadai), sits in frozen silence in a sea of storm-tossed grass. Kyoami circles around him, chanting his story in terms that are broadly thematic and intimately psychological.

When new media adopt the functionality of earlier media, the meaning and role of the latter may change. This is particularly clear in the evolving use of words on screen. Before the advent of synchronous sound, movie intertitles had served to explain onscreen events and provide narrative continuity. Yet words on screen were also a staple of early non-narrative experiments, such as Dada and Surrealist film. When synchronous sound began to serve continuity functions in narrative film, intertitles migrated along several paths, sometimes converging with counter-continuity effects. The Lettrist artist Maurice Lemaître, a successor to the Surrealists, uses intertitles in this way. Flashing a title-card part way through his screening/performance event, *Le Film, est déjà commencé?* (1951), he seeks to rouse discomfort and discontent. The intertitle sums up this idea by quoting a passage from *Macbeth* (5.3.57): 'what rhubarb, cyme, or what purgative drug would scour' the diseased land and make it healthy again? The words on the intertitle are addressed not to Shakespeare's Doctor but to the audience, seen here as the only source of physic in corrupt times. But the imagined cure is the words themselves, used to break the lulling effects of realist continuity and call the audience to action.

Rethinking audiences

A principal player in the scenes of media transition sketched above is the audience member: playgoer, reader, moviegoer, television viewer, gamer, and so on. In exploring the ways audiences use and respond to screen adaptations, Shakespearians tend to follow the larger trends in media reception theory. (More precisely, we could say that the genealogy of reception studies crosses media and disciplines.) This section explores these trends in film, television and new media theories of reception. Yet two challenges are worth addressing at the outset. The first is ephemerality. How groups and individuals respond to performances of any kind is notoriously inaccessible to researchers, because responses to a performance event are transient and because the responses that matter are usually understood by scholars to be internal. Whatever records we have of reception (diaries, focus-group interviews, surveys, video tapes) are thus doubly displaced from the interior experience in which meaning is generated: externalized and re-coded by the very recording method that makes them accessible.

A second caution is important to students of Shakespeare who mine the field of reception studies. In this field earlier periods (especially original performances of Shakespeare) are often cited for comparison or contrast with present-day ones in ways that sometimes over-generalize about the former. For example, in an otherwise thoughtful discussion of the problems involved in decoding internal 'symbolic or cognitive engagement with performances', a sociologist concludes: 'undoubtedly, documented accounts of the "reception" of the first production of a Shakespeare play ... would feel free to assume what the audience thought from how they acted' because in those 'days' playgoers reacted vociferously and those reactions were understood to be transparent.[21] The preconception here is that public and private theatres in Renaissance London were spaces of unscripted response. In fact, like the modern Shakespeare classroom, they were venues with their own social codes for emotion display, emotion experiment and education.[22] Though it may seem counter-intuitive, audience responses in any period may be *both* authentic *and* socially scripted, in other words, *performative*. The performative nature of response – especially in communal contexts such as cinema and live theatre – complicates what we think we are studying when we approach questions of reception. For that reason, cross-period comparisons should be grounded in careful study of Renaissance reception practices: what we have learnt about reading in the period (see Chapter 2) and what we have learnt about playgoing (see Chapter 4).

Media historians emphasize two important ways in which the study of audience responses to audio-visual texts has changed over the past century. First, views of *audience agency* have shifted significantly: from early to mid-century conceptions of film and television viewers as passive and receptive consumers of mass-media; through a growing interest in the active uses to which viewers put their viewing experiences and the gratifications they found in them; to a late-century focus on audience selectivity, resistance, appropriation and re-making of the kind envisioned by Bellour. In keeping with this latest phase of scholarship, critics prefer the term *intertext* to describe the source materials for adaptation. Derived from literary theory, the concept of intertextuality locates the production of meaning in the reader or viewer, who generates that meaning in relation to a network of other texts he or she has viewed, read and heard.

To understand the pay-offs of attending to intertextual networks, consider a particularly playful and creepy mash-up, 'Me vs. You' (Joe Burgess, 2006). This short video mashes Dimitri Buchowetzki's silent *Othello* (1922) together with sound samples from a techno band and a well-known slasher film, *The Texas Chainsaw Massacre* (dir. Tobe Hooper, 1974). The video credits cite the film by referencing its central character, Leatherface, a cannibalistic serial killer who (characteristic of this sub-genre of horror film) wears a mask made of human skin. Recombining these images and sounds, the video relocates the play in a lineage of slasher films. At first glance this mash-up seems marginally funny, off-putting and slight. Looking more closely, we might begin to think about how *Othello* signifies differently in this disturbing new network of intertexts – prompting the kind of self-reflection that Taymor invites when she films a present-day audience in a coliseum, in *Titus*. Othello himself has a back-story involving cannibals. Should we connect that to Leatherface, and if so, how? Are we to understand adaptations as a kind of cannibalism, consuming earlier texts? Alternatively, might we view the history of *Othello* revivals as one long, repetitive serial-killer story? Perhaps we should view revival itself as a kind of serial violence.[23] By recycling a dehumanizing stereotype (an accomplished black man who devolves into a killer), are *we* the ones who make Leatherfaces – false masks – out of black skin?

The shifts from understanding audiences as passive, then active, then interactive may be attributed to technological changes that, over time, enable different modes of engagement. After all, interactivity is the hallmark of media such as hypertext and digital video. Yet arguably the technological changes that turn viewers into makers simply call our attention to modes of reception available in many media, though perhaps not always visible or well studied. Looking back to the example of the sLiterary Globe, we might observe that playgoers there attend performances in part to socialize, in part to show off elaborate self-creations (avatars) and in part as a place to capture imagery they can later weave into records of their online lives. Audiences have been going to the theatre for these reasons since Shakespeare's time. For both serious and satirical purposes, Renaissance playgoers sometimes brought their commonplace books to record speeches they liked and planned to quote or re-use at another time. In *The Gull's Hornbook* (1609), Thomas Dekker lampoons gallants at the theatre for such self-promoting behaviour.

The second fundamental shift in audience theory concerns *the way transmissions and messages are understood to work*. Early critics of mass communications saw radio, television and film (for better and worse) as powerful technical conduits delivering messages directly into listeners' and viewers' minds.[24] In this view, the meanings invested in specific texts are seen as fixed and stable. Mass audiences receive them and share the common understandings they create: whether about national identity in time of war, consumer tastes or human rights. By the late century, systematic studies of reception had made it clear that audiences understand, select and respond to media contextually and discursively, interpreting meaning actively and in socially conditioned ways. A ready example might be the different geo-cinematic contexts for interpreting Luhrmann's Mercutio (Harold Perrineau), in 1996. For audiences trained in contemporary Hollywood conventions, Mercutio's flamboyant dance sequence at the Capulet party seems to conform to a familiar stereotype: the gay, black, druggie side-kick whose tragic death will motivate the hero. In the context of Australian traditions such as Sydney Mardi Gras and *Priscilla, Queen of the Desert* (dir. Stephan Elliot, 1994), Mercutio's drag-queen turn reads very differently: as an exuberant moment that signals the suspension of restrictive social codes in Verona Beach, codes that keep Romeo and Juliet apart.[25] In this wild interlude, in other words, Romeo and Juliet are temporarily free to meet each other as themselves, not as Montague and Capulet.

Just as audience studies refocused attention on the daily practices and locations of listening and viewing, so too has Shakespeare studies. Recent work on adaptations of *Othello*, for example, rethinks the meaning of the play in specific settings and viewing contexts. The Nigerian-born novelist Ben Okri describes watching the play as 'practically the only black person in the audience'; a college professor explores the meanings of O in the classroom, after the Columbine High School shootings.[26]

Fruitful approaches

What are the best ways to navigate more than a century of media innovation and convergence? This wealth of adaptations can be challenging for a student of Shakespeare on screen. The four principles that follow may guide thoughtful exploration.

1. *Mine the scholarship specific to your medium, format or genre.* Learn the history and conventions of the adaptation mode you are studying. For example, when considering documentary adaptations, such as *Looking for Richard* (dir. Al Pacino, 1996), it is valuable to know the conventions of the genre. An awareness of the different modes of address that characterize documentary – offering viewers the chance to become the ones who know about 'things as they are' – clarifies how Pacino stages conflicts of authority over who really understands and really knows Shakespeare.

2. *Distinguish media from display technologies.* Separating these two concepts can help avoid false generalizations. For example, this essay occasionally uses 'screen' as shorthand for a range of display technologies: large, medium and small screens, made of white vinyl, or a cathode ray tube (CRT), or liquid crystal display (LCD), etc. These different screens display a variety of media: print, live broadcast, movies and videos, still images. Those media in turn have different functionalities and histories of exhibition. For all these reasons, shorthand terms like screen should be used with caution, since generalizing about media risks ignoring differences in format, and vice versa. For example, students and scholars alike may react negatively to the Hamlet played by Ethan Hawke (dir. Michael Almereyda, 2000). They often feel annoyed by his immersion in his media (cameras, televisions, computer workstation) and attribute Hamlet's alienation to this apparently over-mediated life. Yet like the media we use daily, some of these formats also redress his alienation.[27] His Pixelvision videos and editing of 'found footage' allow him private space to remember and grieve, escaping an environment in which he is constantly under surveillance. A large screen and the collective viewing provided by cinema is required, however, when Hamlet wants to use some of his footage to provoke a guilty reaction from Claudius. Certainly this Hamlet is alienated. Ambient modern anxiety about the socially alienating affects of new media (IM, Facebook, anonymous confession boards, online gaming) make a good twenty-first-century correlative for his separateness. But to generalize too much about the alienating effects of Hamlet's media risks missing the different needs – self-expression, family conflict, withdrawal – supplied by the very different screen formats he uses.

3. *Replay: take time to close read.* As the preceding discussion makes clear, movies, like all texts, generate conflicting interpretations. Careful interpretation means attending to patterns of story, image, editing, sound and other effects,

then analysing those patterns. To explain why the technologies in Almereyda's film generate conflicting responses, for example, we might dig more deeply into the film's formal patterns. We could begin by looking at story, scene and props. The technologies through which Hamlet communicates come from different historical moments: there are floppy disks and payphones here (belated technologies in 2000); a 1970s toy camera (Pixelvision, now reborn as an independent video art form); and a high-end, state-of-the-art video-editing station. This anachronistic mix evokes the idea of media change *as such*. In doing so, it activates a recurring set of anxieties that have attended media in transition from the advent of writing, through the printing press, to film, TV and computers.[28] In its darkest version, evoked by this noir film, media transition is associated with commercial exploitation, the disintegration of political discourse, and the loss of human connections with each other and the natural world.[29] At a moment when students' own mediated social lives are often the subject of public anxiety, a student discussing this scene in a classroom or paper may have something to gain socially by taking a critical stance. By rehearsing ambient anxieties about media addiction and alienation, he or she presents herself as a knowing, sceptical, discriminating user who can tell the difference between a virtual interface and real experience. By mounting this critique, in other words, he or she performs a social 'script' that affirms his or her media health against a backdrop of media anxiety.[30]

And yet a tenet of recent media history is that technological change is 'a fully social practice.'[31] The scenes of Hamlet at his desk working with his video materials make this case, contradicting the interpretations above. To see this, we need to look closely at patterns of shot selection, editing and the arrangement of images in the frame of the screen. A single soliloquy makes a good example. Hamlet meditates wearily on the 'uses of this world' (1.2.134) in voice-over. As his thoughts unfold, the scene alternates between three camera angles: home-movie footage of his parents and Ophelia on the monitor screen; his hand on the computer trackpad, playing and rewinding and replaying this footage; and his face as he watches the screen. Across these various cuts, a subtle human gesture transfers from Old Hamlet's image on screen to his son, mediated by the editing hand (see Figure 9). The gesture conveys authentic internal experience, passed from father to son, and confirms that these media serve both mourning and reconnection.

4. *Rewind: ask yourself how attention to remediation and convergence illuminate the Shakespearian material you are working with, and vice versa.* Close study of adaptations across different media helps provide a vocabulary for thinking about Shakespeare's texts themselves, not just the ways they have been adapted to audio-visual formats for more than a century. The reading above, for example, explores how Almereyda interprets Old

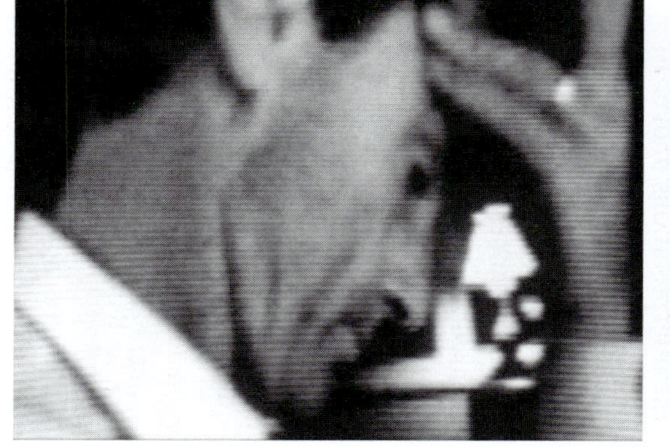

9 Replay as a vocabulary for intimacy. Three shots of Hamlet at his workstation, Michael Almereyda, *Hamlet*, 2000.

Hamlet's charge to his son, 'remember me', in a new technological context. The correlative that Almereyda offers here – playback as a mode of memory and expression, not just reception – helps us understand Shakespeare's Hamlet too, as engaged in replay. His replay progresses from imaginative reiteration (writing his father's injunction in 'the book and volume of my brain', 1.5.103), to dramatic repetition (revisiting a ghost who has appeared already), to creative reworking (adapting an old stage play, 'The Murder of Gonzago', to replay Old Hamlet's murder).

Reading actively and comparatively in this way enriches our understanding of both Renaissance and modern intertexts. It also expands our collective prospects for creative remakes in the future.

RESOURCES

Bardbox, ed. Luke McKernan (2008). YouTube Shakespeare collection: http://bardbox.wordpress.com/

BFI *Screen Online*. www.screenonline.org.uk

BUFVC International Database of Shakespeare on Film, Television, and Radio. www.bufvc.ac.uk/databases/shakespeare/index.html

Burt, Richard, ed. *Shakespeares after Shakespeare: An Encyclopedia of the Bard in Mass Media and Popular Culture*, 2 vols. London: Greenwood Press, 2007.

Corrigan, Tim. *A Short Guide to Writing About Film*. New York: HarperCollins, 1994.

Corrigan, Tim and Patty White. *The Film Experience: An Introduction*. Boston: Bedford/St Martin's, 2004.

International Shakespeare Editions Shakespeare in Performance Database. http://internetshakespeare.uvic.ca/Theater/sip/index.html

Film Indexes Online. A ProQuest subscription database combining the standards of the field, the British Film Institute's *Film Index International* and the American Film Institute's *AFI Catalogue*. Avoid IMDb as a reference source, as it is prone to errors.

McKernan, Luke, and Olwen Terris, eds. *Walking Shadows: Shakespeare in the National Film and Television Archive*. London: BFI, 1994.

Rothwell, Kenneth. *A History of Shakespeare on Screen: A Century of Film and Television*. Cambridge: Cambridge University Press, 2004, 2nd edn.

READING LIST

Burnett, Mark and Roberta Wray. *Screening Shakespeare in the Twenty-First Century*. Edinburgh: Edinburgh University Press, 2006.

Cartelli, Thomas and Katherine Rowe. *New Wave Shakespeare on Screen*. Cambridge, MA: Polity Press, 2007.

Donaldson, Peter. '"In fair Verona": Media, Spectacle and Performance in *William Shakespeare's Romeo+Juliet*', in *Shakespeare after Mass Media,* Richard Burt (ed.). New York: Palgrave, 2002, pp. 59–82.

Henderson, Diana, ed. *A Concise Companion to Shakespeare on Screen*. Oxford: Blackwell, 2006.

Jackson, Russell, ed. *The Cambridge Companion to Shakespeare on Film*. Cambridge: Cambridge University Press, 2007.

Lanier, Douglas. 'Shakescorp *Noir*', *Shakespeare Quarterly*, 53:2 (2002), 157–80.

Leitch, Thomas M. 'Twelve Fallacies in Contemporary Adaptation Theory', *Criticism*, 45:2 (Spring 2003), 149–71.

Naremore, James, ed. *Film Adaptation*. New Brunswick: Rutgers University Press, 2000.

Rothwell, Kenneth. 'How the Twentieth Century Saw the Shakespeare Film: Is it Shakespeare?', *Literature/Film Quarterly*, 29:2 (2001), 82–95.

Walker, Elsie. 'Authorship: Getting Back to Shakespeare: Whose Film is it Anyway?', in *A Concise Companion to Shakespeare on Screen*, Diana Henderson (ed.). Oxford: Blackwell, 2006, pp. 8–30.

MEDIA CITED

An Age of Kings (1960; 2009). UK, BBC Television. Snd., bw., 60/75 mins., 15 episodes.

Arden (2006–8). Online game project of the Synthetic Worlds Initiative. http://swi.indiana.edu/

Buchowetzki, Dimitri, dir. *Othello* (1922). Germany, Wörmer Film. Silent, bw., 93 mins.

Burgess, Joe Boyce, creator. 'Me vs. You' (2006). USA, Blind Hill Pictures. Snd., bw., 1 min. 26 secs. YouTube.com, posted 2 November 2008.

Dando, Walter and William Dickson, dir. *King John* (1899). Silent, bw., 2 mins.

Daniels, Cherie (historiana), creator. 'Shakespeare_068' (2008). USA, Second Life™ screenshot. posted Flickr.com, 22 June. Reproduced by permission of the artist. www.flickr.com/photos/historiana/2602472510/in/set-72157605756500850/

Fleming, Andrew, dir. *Hamlet 2* (2008). USA. Snd., col., 92 mins.

Ford, John, dir. *My Darling Clementine* (1946). USA, Twentieth Century Fox. Snd., bw., 97 mins.

Hollar, Wenceslaus. *London from Bankside* (Cornelium Danckers, 1647). By permission of the Folger Library.

Hooper, Tobe, dir. *The Texas Chainsaw Massacre* (1974). USA, Vortex. Snd., col., 83 mins.

Jarman, Derek, dir. *The Angelic Conversation* (1985). UK, BFI Production/Channel 4. 35mm, snd., col., 81 mins.

Kiranov, Remi, creator. 'The Globe' (2008). USA, Second Life™ screenshot, Flickr.com, posted 19 December 2008. Reproduced by permission of the artist. www.flickr.com/photos/remikiranov/3120461228/

Kurosawa, Akira, dir. *Ran* (1985). Japan, Greenwich Film. Snd., col., 160 mins.

Lemaître, Maurice, dir. *Le Film, est déjà commencé?* (1951). France. 35mm, snd., bw. 62 mins.

Levring, Kristian, dir. *The King is Alive* (2000). USA/Denmark, Good Machine/Zentropa Entertainments. Snd., col., 110 mins.

Madden, John, dir. *Shakespeare in Love* (1998). USA, Miramax. Snd., col., 122 mins.

Merrian, M. *View of London*, from Gottfried, Johann Ludwig *Neuwe archontologie cosmica* (Wolfang Hoffmans, 1638). By permission of the Folger Library.

Nelson, Tim Blake, dir. O (2001). USA, Miramax. Snd., col., 95 mins.

Pacino, Al, dir. *Looking for Richard* (1996). USA, Twentieth Century Fox. Snd., col., 109 mins.

Rohmer, Eric, dir. *Conte d'Hiver* (*A Tale of Winter*) (1992). France, C.E.R./Les Films du Losange/Sofiarp. Snd., col., 114 mins.

Swanson, Bernadette (HVX Silverstar, at the Machinima Institute in Second Life™), creator. 'Renaissance Island Globe Grand Opening' (2007). USA, Machinima movie. YouTube.com, posted 24 July. Reproduced by permission of the artist. www.youtube.com/watch?v=YIXaL4RncFw

Taymor, Julie, dir. *Titus* (1999). USA/UK, Clear Blue Sky Productions. Snd., col., 162 mins. DVD edn.

Van Sant, Gus, dir. *My Own Private Idaho* (1991). USA, New Line. Snd., col., 104 mins.

NOTES

General Acknowledgements. Andy Parker and Meredith Skura discuss 'literary history and/as media history' in 'The Future of the Literary Past,' *Modern Language Association*, December, 2008.

My gratitude to the members of English 324, Fall 2008, who helped test these ideas. For the good counsel of Claire Busse, Tom Cartelli, Alice Dailey, Jane Hedley, Matt Kozusko, Zack Lesser, Kristen Poole, Lauren Shohet, Garrett Sullivan, Jamie Taylor and Arlene Zimmerle: *I do return those talents, / Doubled with thanks and service.*

1 Raymond Bellour, 'The Unattainable Text' (1975), trans. Ben Brewster, in Constance Penley (ed.), *The Analysis of Film* (Bloomington, IN: Indiana University Press, 2000), pp. 21, 1.

2 Jerome J. McGann, *A Critique of Modern Textual Criticism* (Charlottesville: University of Chicago Press, 1983), p. 52.

3 Peter S. Donaldson, 'Shakespeare in the Electronic Age', ms, 2009. Previously published online, ArdenNet, 1998.

4 Kenneth Rothwell, 'How the Twentieth Century Saw the Shakespeare Film: Is it Shakespeare?' *Literature/Film Quarterly*, 29:2 (2001), 259.

5 Thomas M. Leitch, 'Twelve Fallacies in Contemporary Adaptation Theory', *Criticism*, 45:2, (Spring 2003), 161.

6 Elsie Walker, 'Authorship: Getting Back to Shakespeare: Whose Film is it Anyway?' in Diana Henderson (ed.), *A Concise Companion to Shakespeare on Screen* (Oxford: Blackwell, 2006), pp. 8, 9.

7 Julie Taymor, quoted in Richard Schechner, 'Julie Taymor: From Jacques Lecoq to *The Lion King*, an Interview', *The Drama Review*, 43:3 (1999), 46.

8 Thomas Cartelli and Katherine Rowe, *New Wave Shakespeare on Screen* (Cambridge: Polity Press, 2007), p. 34.

9 Walker, 'Authorship', p.14.

10 Mark Burnett, *Filming Shakespeare in the Global Marketplace* (New York: Palgrave Macmillan, 2007); Richard Burt (ed.), *Shakespeare after Mass Media* (New York: Palgrave, 2002); Barbara Hodgdon, *The Shakespeare Trade: Performances and Appropriations* (Philadelphia: University of Pennsylvania Press, 1998).

11 Robert Stam and Allesandra Raengo, 'Introduction', in *Literature and Film: A Guide to the Theory and Practice of Film Adaptation* (Oxford: Blackwell, 2005), pp. 5–6.

12 Robert Hamilton Ball, *Shakespeare on Silent Film: A Strange Eventful History* (New York: Theatre Arts Books, 1968), p. 15.

13 Henry Jenkins, *Convergence Culture: Where Old and New Media Collide* (New York: New York University Press, 2006).
14 Jay David Bolter and Richard Grusin (eds.), *Remediation: Understanding New Media* (Cambridge, MA: MIT, 1999).
15 Philip Auslander, *Liveness: Performance in a Mediatized Culture* (London: Routledge, 1999).
16 Zachary Lesser, *Renaissance Drama and the Politics of Publication: Readings in the English Book Trade* (Cambridge: Cambridge University Press, 2004), Chapters 2 and 4.
17 On the rotational pan as a signature of gaming, see Peter Donaldson, 'Game Space/Tragic Space: Julie Taymor's *Titus*', in Barbara Hodgdon and W. B. Worthen (eds.), *A Companion to Shakespeare and Performance* (Oxford: Blackwell, 2005), p. 457.
18 M. A. Caws, 'Taking Textual Time', in E. B. Loizeaux and N. Fraistat (eds.), *Reimagining Textuality: Textual Studies in the Late Age of Print* (London: University of Wisconsin Press, 2002), p. 149.
19 Cartelli and Rowe, *New Wave Shakespeare*, p. 143.
20 David Thorburn and Henry Jenkins, *Rethinking Media Change: The Aesthetics of Transition* (Cambridge, MA: MIT, 2003), p. 11.
21 Sarah Sheplock, 'Japanese Influences: Cultural Adaptation in Kurosawa's *Ran*', unpublished essay, 18 December 2008.
22 Sonia Livingstone, 'The Changing Nature of Audiences: From the Mass Audience to the Interactive Media User', in Angharad Valdivid (ed.), *A Companion to Media Studies* (Oxford: Blackwell 2006), p. 349.
23 Katherine Rowe, 'Humoral Knowledge and Liberal Cognition in Davenant's *Macbeth*', in Gail Kern Paster, Katherine Rowe and Mary Floyd-Wilson (eds.), *Reading the Early Modern Passions: Essays in the Cultural History of Emotion* (Philadelphia: Penn Press, 2004), pp. 169–91.
24 Theodore Adorno and Max Horkheimer, 'The Culture Industry: Enlightenment as Mass Deception', in *Dialectic of Enlightenment*, trans. John Cumming (New York: Continuum, 1972), pp. 120–67.
25 Peter S. Donaldson, '"In Fair Verona": Media, Spectacle and Performance in William Shakespeare's *Romeo and Juliet*', in Richard Burt (ed.), *Shakespeare after Mass Media* (Basingstoke: Palgrave, 2002), pp. 59–82.
26 Ben Okri, 'Meditations on *Othello*', *West Africa*, 23 March (562–4) and 30 March (618–19), 1987; analysed by Julie Hankey, 'Introduction', *Othello*, *Shakespeare in Production* (Cambridge: Cambridge University Press, 2005), 2nd edn, pp. 2–3; Gregory Semenza, 'Shakespeare after Columbine: Teen Violence in Tim Blake Nelson's O', *College Literature*, 32:4 (2005), 99–124.
27 Cartelli and Rowe, *New Wave Shakespeare*, p. 49.
28 See Plato, *Phaedrus* (274b–278e), for the critique of writing; see Thorburn and Jenkins, *Rethinking Media Change*, p. 1, for the rest of this summary.
29 Douglas Lanier, 'Shakescorp *Noir*', *Shakespeare Quarterly*, 53:2 (2002), 157–80.
30 Katherine Rowe, 'Medium-Specificity and Other Critical Scripts for Screen Shakespeare', in Diana Henderson (ed.), *Alternative Shakespeares 3* (New York: Routledge, 2007), p. 37.
31 Lisa Gitelman, 'How Users Define New Media: A History of the Amusement Phonograph', in Thorburn and Jenkins, *Rethinking Media Change*, p. 62.

21

ANDREW DICKSON

Shakespeare: reading on

Complete works

It sounds obvious, but the best first step – indeed, the best single Shakespearian investment it's possible to make – is to get hold of a reliable version of the words Shakespeare wrote. A collected edition of the plays and poems should not merely provide a reliable, helpfully annotated set of texts, it should also be honest about the decisions that went into editing. It should contain essential supplementary information as well: an account of Shakespeare's life, background on his linguistic and political contexts, stage history, suggestions about how to approach and interpret the works and tips on what to read next (this chapter has its own thoughts on each of those topics too).

That said, no complete works is perfect; editors argue too much for that. The safest choice remains *The Riverside Shakespeare*, edited most recently by G. Blakemore Evans (1997), which contains solid historical background, detail on documentary sources and criticism, light glossing on the page and some of the best short essays on the plays still in print. Yet Riverside's presentation of the texts is somewhat old-fashioned, and many prefer to use the more experimental *William Shakespeare: The Complete Works*, known as the 'Oxford Shakespeare', edited by Stanley Wells and Gary Taylor, which was originally published in 1986, then revised in 2005. The Oxford editors follow what they regard as the 'theatrical' versions of the plays and indulge in some outré decisions – such as offering two versions of *King Lear* – in the aim of exposing, rather than airbrushing, the realities behind Renaissance texts. Yet the result is not terribly user-friendly: Oxford lacks on-the-page notes, and textual analysis is relegated to a second volume, *William Shakespeare: A Textual Companion* (1987). A version of the Oxford text with abundant editorial matter is available, edited by Stephen Greenblatt and others, published by Norton (revised 2008), but its critical focus – heavily influenced by North American New Historicism – is somewhat narrow.

Another option is Macmillan's handsome *Complete Works*, edited by Jonathan Bate and Eric Rasmussen (2007), the first modernized edition of the 1623 Folio. The performance history is unapologetically Stratford-focused – the volume is marketed by the RSC – but it offers readable introductions to the works as well as an interesting, if sometimes eccentric, textual philosophy (and the glossing is more detailed than Riverside). A logical follow-on, less dusty than it sounds, is to use a facsimile of the First Folio, edited and printed by Shakespeare's theatrical colleagues in 1623. Cheap facsimiles are easy to find, but the standard reference is *The Norton Facsimile*, edited by Charlton Hinman (1968, revised 1996), a 'perfect' Folio assembled from multiple copies of the real thing.

Editions of single works

If you're concentrating on an individual play or poem, a collected works will soon prove frustrating: not only will it fail to answer many of your questions, it is also likely to damage your wrists. A single-volume text should offer more editorial assistance as well as detailed coverage of stage history, source material, critical reception and much more. Many individual series are available, varying in pocketability, price-point and scholarly seriousness. As with collected editions, no one brand is uniformly recommendable, though it's a good idea to leaf through several to see which suits – some texts will be perfect to slip into a bag or use in a rehearsal room, others overflow with scholarly apparatus.

At the top of the market are the editions published by three venerable publishers: Cambridge University Press, Oxford University Press and Arden (currently an imprint of Bloomsbury). All have the same essential aim, to provide a painstakingly vetted version of the text with detailed on-page notes, backed up by academic contextual material. Although not yet finished, the Arden third series volumes (general editors Richard Proudfoot, Ann Thompson and David Scott Kastan, 1995–) are generally the heftiest, encompassing stout critical introductions, extensive on-page notes and textual collations, plus such extras as facsimiles of early editions, doubling charts and excerpts from sources. Similar in scope, and nearly as full, are the editions published by Oxford (1982–), which are edited independently from the Oxford *Complete Works* but similarly under the stewardship of Stanley Wells. The New Cambridge Shakespeare (1984–, present editor Brian Gibbons) is printed in a larger format than Arden and Oxford and generally includes lighter editorial matter, but retains a strong focus on performance; the publishers have recently begun to issue updated versions to keep abreast of developments on stage.

Myriad alternatives are available if you want something less extensive. The Macmillan series (2008–), with texts drawn from the RSC *Complete Works*, offers attractively produced volumes with extended introductory essays and unstuffy textual notes, although only half the series are published at the time of writing. Students and teachers might try the Cambridge Schools Shakespeare, edited by Rex Gibson (1992–), which offers the complete New Cambridge text opposite straightforward notes and suggestions for study. Many American students and actors swear by the elegant and unfussy Pelican Shakespeare, edited by Stephen Orgel and A. R. Braunmuller (2000–), whose volumes are of excellent value – as are those published by the Folger Shakespeare Library, edited by Barbara A. Mowat and Paul Werstine (1992–) which contain slightly more editorial matter but again at a bargain-basement price. T. J. B. Spencer's New Penguin series, reissued with new introductions in 2005, is an old favourite, but now looks somewhat dated; the books' chief selling-point remains their petite size and uncluttered layout.

Several specialist editions are also available. The Cambridge Early Quartos series (1996–) is a set of modernized versions of influential first quartos, edited on the basis that these texts need to be understood in their own right. (*Shakespeare's Plays in Quarto* (1981), edited by M. J. B. Allen and Kenneth Muir, provides a set of unedited facsimiles in one volume.) Another Cambridge series, *Shakespeare in Performance*, offers individually edited volumes with footnotes referencing historical performances in detail.

Mention must also be made of the series that all but invented modern Shakespeare editing, the New Variorum, which began under the editorship of H. H. Furness in 1871 and has been gliding unhurriedly through the canon ever since; under the auspices of the Modern Language Association it is now in its third edition. Textual aficionados will learn much from its exhaustive collation of variant readings, many embellished with learned historical annotations, while extensive supplementary notes excerpt key criticism and sources. Texts are also now available digitally as part of the Electronic New Variorum Shakespeare project.

Companions, handbooks and general reference works

Anyone looking for a one-volume reference should reach immediately for Michael Dobson and Stanley Wells' *The Oxford Companion to Shakespeare* (2001), an A–Z encyclopaedia covering hundreds of Shakespearian topics and containing in-depth entries on each of the works – the best reference book of its kind, serious in scope yet terrific fun to read.

Other companions offer different approaches. The best narrative introduction is Stanley Wells' spirited and highly readable *Shakespeare: The Poet and his Plays* (1997), which examines Shakespeare's output chronologically. In collaboration with Lena Cowen Orlin, Wells has also edited *Shakespeare: An Oxford Guide* (2003), a chunky collection of essays on Shakespeare's life, genres and afterlives, with a particularly useful section on competing critical approaches. Two other excellent introductory anthologies are *William Shakespeare: His World, His Work, His Influence*, edited by John F. Andrews (three volumes, 1985), and *A Companion to Shakespeare* (1999), edited by David Scott Kastan. A-level and university students might also find the *Cambridge Introductions to Literature* series of value; so far there are volumes published on Shakespeare, the history plays, the tragedies and the comedies. My own *The Rough Guide to Shakespeare* (2005; revised 2009) is different in format, a play-by-play, poem-by-poem handbook that includes academic components such as critical essays, performance histories and recommended reading alongside reviews of productions on DVD, audio and the Web.

Shakespeare's life and context

It takes tact and persistence to make the dusty evidence of Shakespeare's time on earth speak of a life actually lived, so it is small wonder that myths and half-truths about his life abound. Given this, it is wise to begin with the facts. S. Schoenbaum's magnificent *William Shakespeare: A Compact Documentary Life* (1977; revised 1987), distilled from his earlier *Documentary Life* (1975), does just that, marshalling all the known information about Shakespeare into one slim volume, but is far less medicinal than it sounds. An excellent alternative is Park Honan's more recent *Shakespeare: A Life* (1998), which draws on wider social history but never mistakes fiction for fact.

Among other accounts, E. K. Chambers' *William Shakespeare: A Study of Facts and Problems* (two volumes, 1930), is a much-revered classic. Anthony Burgess' *Shakespeare* (1970) is quite literally novelistic, but valuable, while Stephen Greenblatt's *Will in the World* (2004) is readable and energetic, if perhaps too enthusiastically speculative for some. A stern rebuke to more sentimental portraits is offered by Katherine Duncan-Jones' *Ungentle Shakespeare* (2001), which is generous on the Warwickshire backdrop but not especially to Shakespeare himself. Something similar could be said for Germaine Greer's *Shakespeare's Wife* (2007), which uncovers some genuinely fascinating facts despite its hectoring tone. Jonathan Bate's *Soul of the Age* (2008) offers itself as a biography of Shakespeare's intellect as much as his life, but overflows with insight on both.

Two brilliant 'keyhole' accounts zoom in for the close-up. James Shapiro's *1599* (2005) spends time with Shakespeare during the year that the Globe opened for business, while Charles Nicholl's *The Lodger* (2007) forensically teases out the period the playwright spent living in the house of a Huguenot wigmaker and his wife. Both are indebted to E. A. J. Honigmann, whose *Shakespeare: The Lost Years* (1985) endeavours to fill in the blanks between the christening of Shakespeare's twins in 1585 and the day in 1592 when he surfaced in London.

It is also worth getting a feel for the broader historical sweep. E. M. W. Tillyard's *The Elizabethan World-Picture* (1943) was for many years the standard work, and remains useful if its larger generalizations are handled with care. Less cautiously recommended are Julia Briggs, *This Stage-Play World* (1983, revised 1997), a vivid introduction to the so-called 'High Renaissance'; and Keith Thomas' *Religion and the Decline of Magic* (1971), which throws light on early modern battles between witchcraft and Christianity.

Anyone interested in the perils as well as pleasures of biography should pick up Schoenbaum's wickedly readable *Shakespeare's Lives* (1970, revised 1991), an unflattering portrait of several writers whose own lives became swallowed up by Shakespeare's.

Shakespeare's reading and sources

Scholars have long sought to locate Shakespeare not simply in a biographical framework, but in a literary one too, scouring his reading matter for insights into the plays and poems. Good modern editions will examine the sources that influenced that particular text, so check there first.

Two short overall introductions are particularly excellent: Kenneth Muir's *The Sources of Shakespeare's Plays* (1977), a pragmatic work-by-work primer; and Robert S. Miola's slim but handy *Shakespeare's Reading* (2000), which divides the works by genre. Thus armed, you will be ready to confront the most comprehensive survey, Geoffrey Bullough's monumental eight-volume collection, *Narrative and Dramatic Sources of Shakespeare* (1957–73), which offers either complete texts of the source or a relevant chunk, plus some thoughts on how they were read. The remaining works – *Edward III*, *Sir Thomas More*, *Cardenio* and *The Two Noble Kinsmen* – are covered in G. Harold Metz's *Sources of Four Plays Ascribed to Shakespeare* (1989).

Forbidding, but still useful, is T. W. Baldwin's mammoth *Shakspere's Small Latine and Lesse Greeke* (two volumes, 1944, also available free online at http://durer.press.uiuc.edu/baldwin), whose title quotes Ben Jonson's sniffy assessment of his rival's limited language abilities. As Baldwin demonstrates, Jonson was wrong, and successive scholars have focused on Shakespeare's extensive debt to classical authors. T. J. B. Spencer's *Shakespeare's Plutarch* (1964) anthologizes sections of Sir Thomas North's translation that colour the Roman plays. *Shakespeare and Ovid* by Jonathan Bate (1993) offers a sophisticated analysis of a poet whose interest in fluxive identities clearly infused Shakespeare's own. Robert S. Miola covers the remaining classical debts in *Shakespeare and Classical Tragedy* (1992) and *Shakespeare and Classical Comedy* (1994). R. A. Brower's *Hero and Saint: Shakespeare and the Graeco-Roman Tradition* (1971) is broad in scope, but genuinely insightful. *Shakespeare and the Greek Romance* by Carol Gesner (1970) is useful on the ancient narrative forms that lie behind the late plays, though less good at isolating their differences. Emrys Jones argues in *The Origins of Shakespeare* (1977) that the playwright might well have had some contact with Greek tragedy and is especially suggestive on the cultural environment that nourished the first history cycle.

Of obvious importance to both sets of histories – and many later plays too – was Shakespeare's ransacking of Elizabethan historians. Peter Saccio's *Shakespeare's English Kings* (1977, revised 2000) is a good primer, profiling the Plantagenets that dominate the two tetralogies and comparing chronicles such as Halle and Holinshed with Shakespeare's rendering of events. John Julius Norwich's *Shakespeare's Kings* (1999) is also worth browsing, while Annabel Patterson draws interesting if contentious conclusions in *Reading Holinshed's Chronicles* (1994).

The influence of medieval mystery plays and seasonal entertainments has long intrigued scholars. The standard study is C. L. Barber's much-loved *Shakespeare's Festive Comedy* (1959, revised 1972), but it's worth testing some of its orthodoxies against François Laroque's spikier *Shakespeare's Festive World* (1991). Emrys Jones' *The Origins of Shakespeare* (see above) also includes useful detail on Shakespeare's debt to medieval drama and might be paired with Leo Salingar's *Shakespeare and the Traditions of Comedy* (1974), which traces comedic influences from classical times on. Andrew Hadfield and Paul Hammond deal with authors including Erasmus, Montaigne and Machiavelli in their collection *Shakespeare and Renaissance Europe* (2004). Another major source, often neglected, is covered in Stephen Marx's *Shakespeare and the Bible* (2000).

Shakespeare's stages

Any biography worth its salt should describe Shakespeare's working environment, and there are useful essays on Renaissance stagecraft in many editions of the complete works. For a more complete picture, however, it is worth doing some focused study.

Andrew Gurr has for many years dominated the field, and two of his works are must-reads. *The Shakespearean Stage, 1574–1642*, now in its fourth edition (2009), has kept pace with emerging research and provides a detailed, balanced – if sometimes slightly airless – analysis of companies, players, playhouses, staging and audiences. This last constituency is analysed in more depth in Gurr's *Playgoing in Shakespeare's London*, also in its third edition (2004). *Shakespeare's Theatre* by Peter Thomson (second edition, 1992) is a page-turning introduction, perhaps the best, while the hazards of working on the Renaissance stage are pungently narrated by Leeds Barroll in *Politics, Plague and Shakespeare's Theatre* (1991). Anne Righter's elegant, suggestive *Shakespeare and the Idea of the Play* (1962) reveals how deeply the mysteries of theatrical illusion seeped into Shakespeare's imagination.

Several works place Shakespeare in the wider theatrical frame. *The Elizabethan Stage* by E. K. Chambers (four volumes, 1923) is still a cornerstone, if rather difficult to assimilate. More digestible is Glynne Wickham's *Early English Stages 1300 to 1660*, abundantly illustrated, in which volumes two (1963) and three (1972) cover the period 1576 to 1660. Before reaching for these multi-volume works, it might be worth snacking Michael Hattaway's excellent *Elizabethan Popular Theatre* (1982), a single-volume introduction that tells you much of what you need to know; *A New History of Early English Drama*, edited by J. D. Cox and David Scott Kastan (1997), full of up-to-date scholarship; and *Shakespeare and Co.* by Stanley Wells (2006), which places Shakespeare as merely one hard-working writer among many.

Those after historical specifics might try two works by Irwin Smith, *Shakespeare's Globe Playhouse* (1956) and *Shakespeare's Blackfriars Playhouse* (1964), though some of Smith's findings have been challenged by more recent scholarship, some of which is touched on by Jean Wilson in *The Archaeology of Shakespeare* (1995). Another form of material evidence is analysed in *Staged Properties in Early Modern English Drama*, edited by Jonathan Gil Harris and Natasha Korda (2002), which draws fascinating conclusions from props both small and large. R. A. Foakes' elegantly produced catalogue *Illustrations of the English Stage, 1580–1642* (1985) presents facsimiles of crucial documents, while Jean E. Howard's *Theatre of a City* (2007) turns the mirror the other way, analysing how London stages represented the metropolis itself.

Scholars now have access to a full-size working model of an Elizabethan theatre, the new Globe on London's Bankside. John Orrell's *The Quest for Shakespeare's Globe* (1983) was influential in deciding the new building's form; Orrell's follow-up, *Rebuilding Shakespeare's Globe* (1989), written in collaboration with Andrew Gurr, narrates the project as it entered physical reality. Christie Carson and Farah Karim-Cooper (eds.), *Shakespeare's Globe: A Theatrical Experiment* (2008), a sumptuously produced set of essays, brings the story up to the present day. But it has to be said that a trip to the Globe itself will provide an infinitely more vivid sense of what things might have been like for Shakespeare than any number of books.

If a visit isn't workable, the pen-and-ink drawings of C. Walter Hodges, which reimagined the Jacobethan stage long before the new Globe became a reality, might be the next best thing. Hodges' work is collected in *The Globe Restored* (1953, second edition 1968) and *Enter the Whole Army* (1999), and also adorns the New Cambridge Shakespeare (see above, p. 326) – each image scrupulously scholarly but irrepressibly vivid.

Later stage history

Individual editions usually describe the route a particular script took from the Renaissance playhouse to the modern theatre, but the experiences of individual texts vary so widely that it is important to get a sense of the larger story. The most engaging and insightful overview is Jonathan Bate and Russell Jackson (eds.), *The Oxford Illustrated History of Shakespeare on Stage* (revised 2001), which places superb photographs alongside contributions on specific periods. Stanley Wells and Sarah Stanton marshal an equally good series of first-rate essays in *The Cambridge Companion to Shakespeare on Stage* (2002), and offer valuable global coverage. More conventional, but very readable, are Robert Speaight's delightful and lavishly illustrated *Shakespeare on the Stage* (1973) and the coffee-table-style *Shakespeare in Performance*, edited by Keith Parsons and Pamela Mason (1995). The essays in Robert Shaughnessy's compendium *Shakespeare in Performance* (2000) add literary theory to the mix, while my own *Rough Guide to Shakespeare* (see above) includes stage histories for every play, and reviews film and audio adaptations.

Specific periods in Shakespearian stage history are variously charted. Useful studies of the Restoration to the end of the eighteenth century include George C. Odell's *Shakespeare from Betterton to Irving* (two volumes, 1920), Tiffany Stern's *Rehearsal from Shakespeare to Sheridan* (2000), Michael Dobson's *The Making of the National Poet* (1992) and Cecil Price's *Theatre in the Age of Garrick* (1973). The Romantic, Victorian and Edwardian eras are handled by Richard Foulkes (ed.), *Shakespeare and the Victorian Stage* (1986), Gail Marshall and Adrian Poole (eds.), *Victorian Shakespeare, Vol. 1: Theatre, Drama and Performance* (2003), Joseph W. Donohue, *Theatre in the Age of Kean* (1975), Cary M. Mazer, *Shakespeare Refashioned: Elizabethan*

Plays on Edwardian Stages (1981) and Robert Speaight, *William Poel and the Elizabethan Revival* (1954). Students of the period will also learn much by dipping into one of the many biographies of star actor-directors such as Charles and Edmund Kean, Samuel Phelps, Sarah Siddons and Henry Irving.

Into the twentieth century, helpful general surveys are John Russell Brown's *Shakespeare's Plays in Performance* (1966), J. L. Styan's *The Shakespeare Revolution* (1977), Richard David's *Shakespeare in the Theatre* (1978) and Dennis Kennedy's *Looking at Shakespeare: A Visual History of Twentieth-Century Performance* (rev. 2001). Kenneth Tynan's *Theatre Writings*, edited by Dominic Shellard (2007), captures a master-critic at work, while Peter Holland's *English Shakespeares* (1997) homes in on 1990s productions. Stanley Wells' *Shakespeare in the Theatre* (1997) anthologizes delicious nuggets from contributors including Hazlitt and Evelyn Waugh.

On individual plays, Marvin Rosenberg's masterly quintet, *The Masks of Othello* (1961), *The Masks of King Lear* (1972), *The Masks of Macbeth* (1978), *The Masks of Hamlet* (1992) and *The Masks of Antony and Cleopatra* (2006), is unique: scene-by-scene, line-by-line rehearsals of the texts illuminated by insights gained from hundreds of productions. More prosaic, but also rooted in stage history, are Cambridge's *Shakespeare in Performance* series (mentioned above, p. 327).

For up-to-date reviews, the journal *Theatre Record* reprints clippings from the British press of professional UK productions. Those with a taste for data could try Michael Mullin's *Theatre at Stratford-upon-Avon* (two volumes, 1980); more recent production information is contained on the RSC website (www.rsc.org.uk). *Shakespeare Survey* (also available online, www.cambridge.org/online/shakespearesurvey) and *Shakespeare Quarterly* (see below, p. 340) both review productions in detail, although they are rather conservative in their coverage.

For North American performances, Charles H. Shattuck's *Shakespeare on the American Stage* (1976) is still the best primer, while Errol G. Hill's *Shakespeare in Sable* (1984) is fascinating on the subject of African American theatre. On non-English performances around the world – an area of study that has exploded in recent years – accounts are provided by Wilhelm Hortmann's *Shakespeare on the German Stage: The Twentieth Century* (1998), Zdeněk Stříbrný's *Shakespeare in Eastern Europe* (2000), Poonam Trivedi and Dennis Bartholomeusz's *India's Shakespeare* (2005), Li Ruru's, *Shashibiya: Staging Shakespeare in China* (2003), Tetsuo Kishi and Graham Bradshaw's, *Shakespeare in Japan* (2005) and many more. Sonia Massai's excellent *World-Wide Shakespeares* (2005) offers infinite worlds bounded in a nutshell.

The age-old hostility between academics and actors has finally begun to recede, and first-hand performance accounts should be essential reading for any student. One of the most thoughtful collections is Carol Rutter's *Clamorous Voices* (1983), a series of interviews with female actors on the major Shakespearian roles; compare straightforward diaristic accounts by Antony Sher's *The Year of the King* (1985), on Sher's performance as Richard III, and Oliver Ford Davies' *Playing Lear* (2003), which records Ford Davies' attempt on the pinnacle of the repertoire. Actor Michael Pennington's beautifully written *User's Guides* to *Hamlet* (1996), *Twelfth Night* (2000) and *A Midsummer Night's Dream* (2005) are full of insights on matters of interpretation as well as production. More RSC stars feature in the Cambridge University Press series *Players on Shakespeare* (1985–).

Among directors, it is hard to challenge the magisterial wisdom of the *Prefaces to Shakespeare* (two volumes, 1946–7) by Harley Granville-Barker, arguably the most radical Shakespearian of the early twentieth century. John Barton's *Playing Shakespeare* (1984) and Peter Hall's *Shakespeare's Advice to the Players* (2003) are both brilliantly practical and subtly informative.

Film and TV

Screened Shakespeare dates back to the dawn of cinema and continues through the age of popular cinema, mass television and into the digital era. Many stage productions have been shot for posterity, and, of course, film has produced plenty of bespoke adaptations, from silent shorts to big-budget Hollywood blockbusters.

The Cambridge Companion to Shakespeare on Film, edited by Russell Jackson (2000, revised 2007), is thought-provoking, though perhaps overemphasizes certain auteurs (chiefly Olivier, Kurosawa, Kozintsev and Branagh). Similar names crop up in Kenneth S. Rothwell's *A History of Shakespeare on Screen* (1999, revised 2004), which covers much of the same ground chronologically. Though older, Anthony Davies and Stanley Wells (eds.), *Shakespeare and the Moving Image* (1994) is worth looking at, particularly when it comes to small-screen adaptations. Mark Thornton Burnett and Ramona Wray bring things up to the present with their collection *Screening Shakespeare in the Twenty-First Century* (2006), which is interesting on more esoteric adaptations, as is *Shakespeare, The Movie II*, edited by Richard Burt and Lynda E. Boose (2003).

Though obviously not up to date, Rothwell's *Shakespeare on Screen: An International Filmography and Videography*, compiled with Annabelle Henkin Melzer (1990), is exceptionally detailed (try the Internet Movie Database (IMDb), http://imdb.com, for newer filmography). More basic in scope is *100 Shakespeare Films* by Daniel Rosenthal (2007), a redaction of his lavishly illustrated *Shakespeare on Screen* (2000). My *Rough Guide to Shakespeare* (see above, p. 328) reviews the most significant screen adaptations with tips on how to get hold of them.

Texts and editing

Most serious single-volume editions will offer some account of a particular text and its provenance. Few, however, will offer a glimpse of the journey all early printed books have taken, or of the questions and challenges that confront editors as they grapple to make Renaissance works comprehensible to the modern reader.

Shakespeare and the Book by David Scott Kastan (2001) is a brilliant exposition of the basics, from Renaissance printshops to digital texts via quartos, folios and foul papers, but also one that makes a strong case for the essential materiality of the book. It could be supplemented by Richard Proudfoot's short but immensely informative *Shakespeare: Text, Stage and Canon* (2001).

On matters editorial, F. P. Wilson, *Shakespeare and the New Bibliography* (1970), updated and revised by Helen Gardner, is a lucid account of the kind of editing that sought to wrest 'ideal' texts from the chaotic conditions of Renaissance publication. Fredson Bowers' slim *On Editing Shakespeare and the Elizabethan Dramatists* (1966) is more of a field guide, but still helpful. The most thoroughgoing exposition of on-the-page decision-making is Gary Taylor and Stanley Wells' *Textual Companion* to the Oxford Shakespeare (see above, p. 325), which includes discussion of canon, chronology and modernization both for specific texts and in general; Wells' *Re-Editing Shakespeare for the Modern Reader* (1984) lays out much of its philosophy. Charlton Hinman's magisterial *The Printing and Proof-Reading of the First Folio of Shakespeare* (two volumes, 1963) is the standard reference work, exhaustive on seventeenth-century bibliography as filtered through the Folio.

Revisionist trends in editing – including what has been called, a touch archly, the Newer Bibliography – are outlined by several key works, including Gary Taylor and Michael Warren (eds.), *The Division of the Kingdoms: Shakespeare's Two Versions of 'King Lear'* (1983), Leah Marcus' engaging *Unediting the Renaissance* (1996), and Ann Thompson and Gordon McMullan (eds.), *In Arden: Editing Shakespeare* (2003). A different view is put forward by Lukas Erne in *Shakespeare as Literary Dramatist* (2003), which argues that Shakespeare did not simply write as a man of the theatre, but with an eye to publication too. Erne has edited, with Margaret Jane Kidnie, an excellent collection, *Textual Performances: The Modern*

Reproduction of Shakespeare's Drama (2004), which examines the issues from many angles. A pugnacious account of collaboration and its impact on Shakespeare's texts is given by Brian Vickers in *Shakespeare: Co-Author* (2002).

The 2006 edition of *Shakespeare Survey* (volume LIX), edited by Peter Holland, provides a freeze-frame of the current state of Shakespearian editing; Andrew Murphy's *Shakespeare in Print: A History and Chronology of Shakespeare Publishing* (2003) supplies the historical background. And for anyone blinded by science, John Jones' commendably alert *Shakespeare at Work* (1995) provides a reminder that the purpose of editing – indeed, of writing – is literature.

Language and concordances

The best overview is Russ McDonald's pocketable *Shakespeare and the Arts of Language* (2001), which covers day-to-day linguistic issues but never loses sight of Shakespeare and is particularly good on Renaissance rhetoric. For a ground-breaking account of what rhetoric really meant to Elizabethans, try Richard A. Lanham's *The Motives of Eloquence: Literary Rhetoric in the Renaissance* (1976). Frank Kermode's *Shakespeare's Language* (2000) is grumpy, but good on the basics.

Among reference works, Ben and David Crystal's *Shakespeare's Words* (2002) is probably the most useful one-volume glossary – not least because it is filled with insightful mini-essays – but is indebted to C. T. Onions' *A Shakespeare Glossary*, updated by Robert D. Eagleson (1911, revised 1986). Gordon Williams' commendably unprudish *A Glossary of Shakespeare's Sexual Language* (1997), will open your eyes to what might be described as the fertility of Shakespeare's language. Also well worth consulting is the magisterial *Oxford English Dictionary*, which aims to chart every shift in every sense of every word in the language. Among individual studies, M. M. Mahood's *Shakespeare's Wordplay* (1957) gives a clear sense of how the meanings of words collide, while for a dazzling demonstration of what close linguistic study can achieve, William Empson's *Seven Types of Ambiguity* (1930) and *Some Versions of Pastoral* (1935) are rightly revered.

On the question of language spoken rather than read, Patsy Rodenburg's *Speaking Shakespeare* (2002) and Cicely Berry's *The Actor and the Text* (1992) are both distilled from many years' experience. George T. Wright's *Shakespeare's Metrical Art* (1988) is an insightful analysis of how rhythm works line by line, while Helge Kökeritz's *Shakespeare's Pronunciation* (1953) is the standard reference work on how Jacobethan English actually sounded; Fausto Cercignani's *Shakespeare's Works and Elizabethan*

Pronunciation (1981) provides substantial technical backup. Bruce Smith's suggestive *The Acoustic World of Early Modern England* (1999) broadens Shakespeare's soundworld beyond language to the noises that filled the city itself.

Among concordances, Marvin Spevack's *The Harvard Concordance to Shakespeare* (1973), boiled down from his eight-volume *A Complete and Systematic Concordance to the Works of Shakespeare* (1968–75), is the gold standard. Readers without access could either use an older concordance such as John Bartlett's (1894), readily available second-hand, or search a website such as Open Source Shakespeare (www.opensourceshakespeare.org).

Some critical trends

Shakespeare criticism comes in many shapes and sizes. Of the thousands of relevant books, this list isolates a tiny handful of historical trends; anthologies such as the *Critical Essays* series published by Garland (1984–) offer another way in, selecting keynote essays on individual plays and poems.

The most detailed guide through the first two centuries is Brian Vickers' anthology *Shakespeare: The Critical Heritage* (1974–81), six hefty tomes that cover from 1623 to 1801. Into the Enlightenment, excerpts from Shakespeare's greatest critic and editor are quoted at length in Bertrand H. Bronson and Jean O'Meara (eds.), *Johnson on Shakespeare* (1986), while Jonathan Bate's *The Romantics on Shakespeare* (1992) is another useful anthology, cherry-picking Coleridge, Goethe, Hazlitt, Hugo and others. Ann Thompson and Sasha Roberts' fascinating anthology *Women Reading Shakespeare, 1660–1900* (1997) somewhat redresses the gender imbalance.

Among Victorian critics, both Edward Dowden's *Shakespeare: A Critical Study of His Mind and Art* (1875) and A. C. Swinburne's *A Study of Shakespeare* (1880) are worth taking account of, especially when it comes to reading the works biographically. A. C. Bradley's *Shakespearian Tragedy* (1904) is arguably the most influential work of criticism ever printed, offering a novelistic account of *Macbeth*, *King Lear*, *Hamlet* and *Othello*. Anne Ridler's two handy volumes of *Shakespeare Criticism 1919–35* (1936) and *Shakespeare Criticism 1935–60* (1963) include some prime cuts, among them essays by Cleanth Brooks and L. C. Knights, who defined the so-called 'new criticism'. Russ McDonald's massive compendium *Shakespeare: An Anthology of Criticism and Theory, 1945–2000* (2004), moves through to the era of gender studies and post-colonialism; Michael Taylor's lean *Shakespeare Criticism in the Twentieth Century* (2001) does similar, but in far fewer pages.

Among individual critical movements of the last fifty years it is impossible to spotlight all but a few – and, of course, the very best critics resist pigeon-holing. Political readings of Shakespeare reached their first apogee in Lily B. Campbell's *Shakespeare's Histories* (1947) and *Shakespeare's History Plays* by E. M. W. Tillyard (1944), only to be upturned by Jan Kott's radical *Shakespeare Our Contemporary* (1964), which admitted the playwright into a world of secret police and covert surveillance. Surveillance and censorship also loom large in the work of the so-called 'new historicists', who offer a yet darker view of Jacobethan power politics; the totemic account is Stephen Greenblatt's *Renaissance Self-Fashioning* (1980).

Juliet Dusinberre's *Shakespeare and the Nature of Women* (1975) is a founding text of feminist criticism. An interesting cross-section of later feminist writing is contained in Dympna Callaghan (ed.), *A Feminist Companion to Shakespeare* (2000), while among individual studies influenced by gender studies two of the best are Janet Adelman's *Suffocating Mothers: Fantasies of Maternal Origin in Shakespeare's Plays, Hamlet to the Tempest* (1992) and Stephen Orgel's *Impersonations: The Performance of Gender in Shakespeare's England* (1996).

The utility of French-influenced literary theory is argued by Patricia Parker and Geoffrey Hartman (eds.) in *Shakespeare and the Question of Theory* (1985), while the three volumes of *Alternative Shakespeares*, edited by John Drakakis (1985, 2002) and Diana E. Henderson (2008), cull a selection of materialist and Marxist essays. Readings influenced by post-colonialism and globalization have opened many new horizons; particularly recommended are Ania Loomba's *Shakespeare, Race and Colonialism* (2002), James Shapiro's *Shakespeare and the Jews* (1996) and *'The Tempest' and its Travels*, edited by Peter Hulme and William H. Sherman (2000).

The history of Shakespeare criticism has become a study in its own right. Useful works here are Jonathan Bate's *The Genius of Shakespeare* (1997), a biography of Shakespeare's reputation, and Michael Dobson's *The Making of the National Poet* (see above, p. 332), which focuses on the Restoration and early eighteenth century. To bring things up to date it might be worth sampling *Shakespeare Among the Moderns* (1997) by Richard Halpern, which moves from high modernism to New Historicism, and Edward Pechter's *What Was Shakespeare?* (1995), a good-humoured guide to the fissiparous world(s) of post-structuralism.

Music, art, other literature

The best introduction to Jacobethan musical practice is David Lindley's superlative *Shakespeare and Music* (2006), which covers everything from

Renaissance theory to what kind of instruments the King's Men kept backstage. Though elderly, E. W. Naylor's *Shakespeare and Music* (1896, revised 1931) was a pioneering work of scholarship and is still worth consulting. On the stories behind the sundry ballads, songs and rounds found in the plays, see Peter J. Seng, *The Vocal Songs in the Plays of Shakespeare: A Critical History* (1967); less detailed, but perhaps more readable, is Ross W. Duffin, *Shakespeare's Songbook* (2004), which is handily packaged with a CD. Also excellent is Alan Brissenden, *Shakespeare and the Dance* (1981), a subtle and thoughtful book that finds rhythm in even the most unmusical of plays.

Anyone wanting to find out about Shakespeare's many musical afterlives is not so well served. Phyllis Hartnoll's historical survey *Shakespeare in Music* (1964) is excellent as far as it goes but sorely out of date, and never steps outside the opera house and concert hall. Julie Sanders' *Shakespeare and Music: Afterlives and Borrowings* (2007) is wider ranging but only fitfully illuminating. By contrast, Gary Schmidgall's *Shakespeare and Opera* (1990) is excellent and offers interesting theories on dramaturgy. Among catalogues, Bryan N. S. Gooch and David Thatcher's *A Shakespeare Music Catalogue* (five volumes, 1991) offers excellent reference coverage, while E. R. Hotaling, *Shakespeare and the Musical Stage: A Guide to Sources, Studies and First Performances* (1990) is useful, but not exactly user-friendly.

Anyone interested in the subject of Shakespeare and art will find things easier. The best book on the subject remains W. Moelwyn Merchant's classic *Shakespeare and the Artist* (1959), which begins in the visual world of Renaissance England and ends with epic Romantic paintings. Two catalogues are also recommended: Jane Martineau (ed.), *Shakespeare in Art* (2003) includes all the major post-eighteenth-century paintings and much interesting nineteenth-century work; while valuable essays and documents can be found within Tarnya Cooper's *Searching for Shakespeare* (2006).

The subject of Shakespeare's influence on later literature could make for an entire lifetime's reading. A pleasant taster is John Gross' *After Shakespeare* (2003), which collects snippets, observations and quips from authors as varied as Goethe, Proust, Dickinson and Ionesco.

Journals and bibliographies

Given the mind-numbing quantities of Shakespearian criticism, printed bibliographies might not be the best place to start, doomed (as indeed this one is) to go out of date almost as soon as they are printed. The best way to chase down reading tips is to use a decent edition, which will offer focused ideas for reading, while companions and reference books almost always include pointers for further research.

A good way to keep on top of what's current is to browse one of several journals devoted to Shakespeare. The American *Shakespeare Quarterly*, begun in 1950 and now based at the Folger Library, is known for high-quality articles, performance accounts and book reviews, and attracts contributions from scholars worldwide. Its British cousin, *Shakespeare Survey* (1948–), is composed mainly of essays on a particular theme, for instance 'The Poems and Music' (1962), 'Characterisation in Shakespeare' (1981) and 'Theatres for Shakespeare' (2007), all of which are still available in paperback, and subjects freshly published editions to unsparing textual scrutiny. *Shakespeare Studies* (1965–), founded by J. Leeds Barroll, includes original academic work and round-table debates. Another journal, *The Year's Work in English Studies*, also covers new Shakespearian criticism in detail.

Germany's long relationship with Shakespeare is attested to by *Shakespeare Jahrbuch*, the oldest journal of its kind (1864–). It features essays in both languages and welcome coverage of productions in continental Europe. Another nation with strong Shakespearian connections is Japan, where the Shakespeare Society of Japan publishes its own *Shakespeare Studies*, which attracts an excellent range of contributors and offers book (plus some Japanese stage) reviews.

The *Times Literary Supplement* is the UK academic community's weekly journal of record and from time to time features special Shakespeare issues (in 2003 it published a short collection of excerpts, *The TLS on Shakespeare*, featuring many of the *Supplement*'s more infamous reviews). The *London Review of Books* and, across the Atlantic, the *New York Review of Books* review many Shakespeare titles, usually taking a quirkier approach. All three maintain good subscriber websites.

No printed bibliography is complete, but *A Shakespeare Bibliography* (1975), the catalogue of the Birmingham Shakespeare Library, comes close. Its digital equivalent is the World Shakespeare Bibliography (www.worldshakesbib.org), an awesomely thorough record of everything published on Shakespeare from 1961 onwards – and many performances alongside – which is searchable online for a fee.

Online

Although technology may not have (yet) reached the stage where it's as pleasurable to use a screen as read a book, the Internet has revolutionized the way we grapple with raw information. Research tools such as online texts, dictionaries and bibliographies have unlocked the gates to vast quantities of specialized data, while even all-purpose search engines such as Google (google.com) can, if used correctly, point the way to assorted digital delights.

Among general jumping-off points, Mr William Shakespeare and the Internet (http://shakespeare.palomar.edu) lists plenty of reliable links. The University of Victoria's Internet Shakespeare Editions (http://ise.uvic.ca) offers much more than its title implies, being especially valuable for its in-depth pages on individual works, while the World Shakespeare Bibliography (see above) is superb, if only available to subscribers.

Online texts vary in their reliability (the best are linked to by the gateway sites listed above), but can be useful for searching. Bartleby has put the out-of-copyright 1914 Oxford Shakespeare up online for free (www.bartleby.com/70), while the best freebie concordance is Open Source Shakespeare (http://opensourceshakespeare.com). For facsimiles of Shakespearian and other early printed texts, try the British Library's Shakespeare in Quarto site (http://bl.uk/treasures/shakespearehomepage.html) and the Furness Collection (http://dewey.library.upenn.edu/sceti/furness). Google Books is a typically ambitious project to scan every book ever published; it already offers many complete digital texts alongside previews of copyrighted material, everything text-searchable (http://books.google.com).

Several good study and education sites exist. About Shakespeare (http://shakespeare.about.com) has plenty of useful information, as does Britannica's Guide to Shakespeare (www.britannica.com/shakespeare). Students might enjoy dipping into the US-based Shake Sphere (www.cummingsstudyguides.net/xShakeSph.html) or hanging out at Shakespeare High (www.shakespearehigh.com), both aimed at schools, while researchers can register for Shaksper (www.shaksper.net), an email-based discussion group that is home to fervent debate (though the so-called 'authorship controversy' is, thankfully, banned). Shakespeare Post (www.shakespearepost.com) does a decent job of aggregating Shakespearian news.

Specialist scholarly databases also have much to offer. The English Short-Title Catalogue (http://estc.bl.uk) is a full-spec database of every English title that appeared in print between 1475 and 1800, over 460,000 items. Early English Books Online (subscription-only; eebo.chadwyck.com) contains many of these titles in downloadable PDF format, while JSTOR does the same for a hundred-odd scholarly journals (subscription-only; http://www.jstor.org). Also capacious is Literature Online, which boasts over 350,000 full-text English works in poetry, drama and prose, plus 190-odd journals, reference works and video clips (subscription-only; http://lion.chadwyck.com). *The Oxford English Dictionary* now lives on the Web and boasts some supremely useful search tools (subscription-only, http://oed.com).

On UK performances, Designing Shakespeare (www.ahds.ac.uk/performingarts/collections/designing-shakespeare.htm) is a valuable audio-visual database covering British productions 1960–2000, while the British

Universities Film and Video Council maintains a database of Shakespeare on film, TV and radio (www.bufvc.ac.uk/shakespeare). For older stage history, Records of Early English Drama (www.reed.utoronto.ca) is a unique project reconstructing local drama up to the closure of the theatres in 1642. It's also worth dipping into YouTube, which offers plenty of Shakespearian snippets alongside the pratfalls and pet videos (http://youtube.com).

And, perhaps ironically, the Web is now the easiest way to get hold of books, especially second-hand or rare – which will include many of the titles in this bibliography. Major bookselling sites such as Amazon (www.amazon.com, .co.uk, .de, etc.) offer an extensive selection in print, or you could try a used-book specialist such as AbeBooks (www.abebooks.com).

Happy reading …

INDEX

Note: Page numbers for illustrations are given in italics. Works by Shakespeare appear under title; works by others under author's name.

Cambridge Companions To ...

AUTHORS

Edward Albee edited by Stephen J. Bottoms

Margaret Atwood edited by Coral Ann Howells

W. H. Auden edited by Stan Smith

Jane Austen edited by Edward Copeland and Juliet McMaster

Beckett edited by John Pilling

Aphra Behn edited by Derek Hughes and Janet Todd

Walter Benjamin edited by David S. Ferris

William Blake edited by Morris Eaves

Brecht edited by Peter Thomson and Glendyr Sacks (second edition)

The Brontës edited by Heather Glen

Frances Burney edited by Peter Sabor

Byron edited by Drummond Bone

Albert Camus edited by Edward J. Hughes

Willa Cather edited by Marilee Lindemann

Cervantes edited by Anthony J. Cascardi

Chaucer edited by Piero Boitani and Jill Mann (second edition)

Chekhov edited by Vera Gottlieb and Paul Allain

Kate Chopin edited by Janet Beer

Caryl Churchill edited by Elaine Aston and Elin Diamond

Coleridge edited by Lucy Newlyn

Wilkie Collins edited by Jenny Bourne Taylor

Joseph Conrad edited by J. H. Stape

Dante edited by Rachel Jacoff (second edition)

Daniel Defoe edited by John Richetti

Don DeLillo edited by John N. Duvall

Charles Dickens edited by John O. Jordan

Emily Dickinson edited by Wendy Martin

John Donne edited by Achsah Guibbory

Dostoevskii edited by W. J. Leatherbarrow

Theodore Dreiser edited by Leonard Cassuto and Claire Virginia Eby

John Dryden edited by Steven N. Zwicker

W. E. B. Du Bois edited by Shamoon Zamir

George Eliot edited by George Levine

T. S. Eliot edited by A. David Moody

Ralph Ellison edited by Ross Posnock

Ralph Waldo Emerson edited by Joel Porte and Saundra Morris

William Faulkner edited by Philip M. Weinstein

Henry Fielding edited by Claude Rawson

F. Scott Fitzgerald edited by Ruth Prigozy

Flaubert edited by Timothy Unwin

E. M. Forster edited by David Bradshaw

Benjamin Franklin edited by Carla Mulford

Brian Friel edited by Anthony Roche

Robert Frost edited by Robert Faggen

Elizabeth Gaskell edited by Jill L. Matus

Goethe edited by Lesley Sharpe

Günter Grass edited by Stuart Taberner

Thomas Hardy edited by Dale Kramer

David Hare edited by Richard Boon

Nathaniel Hawthorne edited by Richard Millington

Seamus Heaney edited by Bernard O'Donoghue

Ernest Hemingway edited by Scott Donaldson

Homer edited by Robert Fowler

Horace edited by Stephen Harrison

Ibsen edited by James McFarlane

Henry James edited by Jonathan Freedman

Samuel Johnson edited by Greg Clingham

Ben Jonson edited by Richard Harp and Stanley Stewart

James Joyce edited by Derek Attridge (second edition)

Kafka edited by Julian Preece

Keats edited by Susan J. Wolfson

Lacan edited by Jean-Michel Rabaté

D. H. Lawrence edited by Anne Fernihough

Primo Levi edited by Robert Gordon

Lucretius edited by Stuart Gillespie and Philip Hardie

David Mamet edited by Christopher Bigsby

Thomas Mann edited by Ritchie Robertson

Christopher Marlowe edited by Patrick Cheney

Herman Melville edited by Robert S. Levine

Arthur Miller edited by Christopher Bigsby (second edition)

Milton edited by Dennis Danielson (second edition)

Molière edited by David Bradby and Andrew Calder

Toni Morrison edited by Justine Tally

Nabokov edited by Julian W. Connolly

Eugene O'Neill edited by Michael Manheim

George Orwell edited by John Rodden

Ovid edited by Philip Hardie

Harold Pinter edited by Peter Raby (second edition)

Sylvia Plath edited by Jo Gill

Edgar Allan Poe edited by Kevin J. Hayes

Alexander Pope edited by Pat Rogers

Ezra Pound edited by Ira B. Nadel

Proust edited by Richard Bales

Pushkin edited by Andrew Kahn

Rilke edited by Karen Leeder and Robert Vilain

Philip Roth edited by Timothy Parrish

Salman Rushdie edited by Abdulrazak Gurnah

Shakespeare edited by Margreta de Grazia and Stanley Wells (second edition)

Shakespearean Comedy edited by Alexander Leggatt

Shakespeare on Film edited by Russell Jackson (second edition)

Shakespeare's History Plays edited by Michael Hattaway

Shakespeare's Last Plays edited by Catherine M. S. Alexander

Shakespeare's Poetry edited by Patrick Cheney

Shakespeare and Popular Culture edited by Robert Shaughnessy

Shakespeare on Stage edited by Stanley Wells and Sarah Stanton

Shakespearean Tragedy edited by Claire McEachern

George Bernard Shaw edited by Christopher Innes

Shelley edited by Timothy Morton

Mary Shelley edited by Esther Schor

Sam Shepard edited by Matthew C. Roudané

Spenser edited by Andrew Hadfield

Laurence Sterne edited by Thomas Keymer

Wallace Stevens edited by John N. Serio

Tom Stoppard edited by Katherine E. Kelly

Harriet Beecher Stowe edited by Cindy Weinstein

August Strindberg edited by Michael Robinson

Jonathan Swift edited by Christopher Fox

J. M. Synge edited by P. J. Mathews

Tacitus edited by A. J. Woodman

Henry David Thoreau edited by Joel Myerson

Tolstoy edited by Donna Tussing Orwin

Mark Twain edited by Forrest G. Robinson

Virgil edited by Charles Martindale

Voltaire edited by Nicholas Cronk

Edith Wharton edited by Millicent Bell

Walt Whitman edited by Ezra Greenspan

Oscar Wilde edited by Peter Raby

Tennessee Williams edited by Matthew C. Roudané

August Wilson edited by Christopher Bigsby

Mary Wollstonecraft edited by Claudia L. Johnson

Virginia Woolf edited by Susan Sellers (second edition)

Wordsworth edited by Stephen Gill

W. B. Yeats edited by Marjorie Howes and John Kelly

Zola edited by Brian Nelson

TOPICS

The Actress edited by Maggie B. Gale and John Stokes

The African American Novel edited by Maryemma Graham

The African American Slave Narrative edited by Audrey A. Fisch

Allegory edited by Rita Copeland and Peter Struck

American Modernism edited by Walter Kalaidjian

American Realism and Naturalism edited by Donald Pizer

American Travel Writing edited by Alfred Bendixen and Judith Hamera

American Women Playwrights edited by Brenda Murphy

Ancient Rhetoric edited by Erik Gunderson

Arthurian Legend edited by Elizabeth Archibald and Ad Putter

Australian Literature edited by Elizabeth Webby

British Romanticism edited by Stuart Curran

British Romantic Poetry edited by James Chandler and Maureen N. McLane

British Theatre, 1730–1830 edited by Jane Moody and Daniel O'Quinn

Canadian Literature edited by Eva-Marie Kröller

Children's Literature edited by M. O. Grenby and Andrea Immel

The Classic Russian Novel edited by Malcolm V. Jones and Robin Feuer Miller

Contemporary Irish Poetry edited by Matthew Campbell

Crime Fiction edited by Martin Priestman

Early Modern Women's Writing edited by Laura Lunger Knoppers

The Eighteenth-Century Novel edited by John Richetti

Eighteenth-Century Poetry edited by John Sitter

English Literature, 1500–1600 edited by Arthur F. Kinney

English Literature, 1650–1740 edited by Steven N. Zwicker

English Literature, 1740–1830 edited by Thomas Keymer and Jon Mee

English Literature, 1830–1914 edited by Joanne Shattock

English Novelists edited by Adrian Poole

English Poets edited by Claude Rawson

English Poetry, Donne to Marvell edited by Thomas N. Corns

English Renaissance Drama edited by A. R. Braunmuller and Michael Hattaway (second edition)

English Restoration Theatre edited by Deborah C. Payne Fisk

Feminist Literary Theory edited by Ellen Rooney

Fiction in the Romantic Period edited by Richard Maxwell and Katie Trumpener

The Fin de Siècle edited by Gail Marshall

The French Novel: From 1800 to the Present edited by Timothy Unwin

German Romanticism edited by Nicholas Saul

Gothic Fiction edited by Jerrold E. Hogle

The Greek and Roman Novel edited by Tim Whitmarsh

Greek and Roman Theatre edited by Marianne McDonald and J. Michael Walton

Greek Lyric edited by Felix Budelmann

Greek Mythology edited by Roger D. Woodard

Greek Tragedy edited by P. E. Easterling

The Harlem Renaissance edited by George Hutchinson

The Irish Novel edited by John Wilson Foster

The Italian Novel edited by Peter Bondanella and Andrea Ciccarelli

Jewish American Literature edited by Hana Wirth-Nesher and Michael P. Kramer

The Latin American Novel edited by Efraín Kristal

The Literature of Los Angeles edited by Kevin R. McNamara

The Literature of New York edited by Cyrus Patell and Bryan Waterman

The Literature of the First World War edited by Vincent Sherry

The Literature of World War II edited by Marina MacKay

Literature on Screen edited by Deborah Cartmell and Imelda Whelehan

Medieval English Literature edited by Larry Scanlon

Medieval English Theatre edited by Richard Beadle and Alan J. Fletcher (second edition)

Medieval French Literature edited by Simon Gaunt and Sarah Kay

Medieval Romance edited by Roberta L. Krueger

Medieval Women's Writing edited by Carolyn Dinshaw and David Wallace

Modern American Culture edited by Christopher Bigsby

Modern British Women Playwrights edited by Elaine Aston and Janelle Reinelt

Modern French Culture edited by Nicholas Hewitt

Modern German Culture edited by Eva Kolinsky and Wilfried van der Will

The Modern German Novel edited by Graham Bartram

Modern Irish Culture edited by Joe Cleary and Claire Connolly

Modernism edited by Michael Levenson

The Modernist Novel edited by Morag Shiach

Modernist Poetry edited by Alex Davis and Lee M. Jenkins

Modern Italian Culture edited by Zygmunt G. Baranski and Rebecca J. West

Modern Latin American Culture edited by John King

Modern Russian Culture edited by Nicholas Rzhevsky

Modern Spanish Culture edited by David T. Gies

Narrative edited by David Herman

Native American Literature edited by Joy Porter and Kenneth M. Roemer

Nineteenth-Century American Women's Writing edited by Dale M. Bauer and Philip Gould

Old English Literature edited by Malcolm Godden and Michael Lapidge

Performance Studies edited by Tracy C. Davis

Postcolonial Literary Studies edited by Neil Lazarus

Postmodernism edited by Steven Connor

Renaissance Humanism edited by Jill Kraye

Roman Satire edited by Kirk Freudenburg

The Roman Historians edited by Andrew Feldherr

Science Fiction edited by Edward James and Farah Mendlesohn

The Spanish Novel: From 1600 to the Present edited by Harriet Turner and Adelaida López de Martínez

Travel Writing edited by Peter Hulme and Tim Youngs

Twentieth-Century Irish Drama edited by Shaun Richards

The Twentieth-Century English Novel edited by Robert L. Caserio

Twentieth-Century English Poetry edited by Neil Corcoran

Victorian and Edwardian Theatre edited by Kerry Powell

The Victorian Novel edited by Deirdre David

Victorian Poetry edited by Joseph Bristow

War Writing edited by Kate McLoughlin

Writing of the English Revolution edited by N. H. Keeble